BEHAVIOR MANAGEMENT IN THE SCHOOLS.

Related Titles of Interest

Improving Social Competence: A Resource for Elementary School Teachers
Pam Campbell and Gary N. Siperstein
ISBN: 0-205-13757-1

Teaching Social Skills to Children and Youth: Innovative Approaches, Third Edition
Gwendolyn Cartledge and JoAnne Fellows Milburn (Editors)
ISBN: 0-205-16507-9 Paper   0-205-16073-5 Cloth

Cognitive and Behavioral Interventions: An Empirical Approach to Mental Health Problems
Linda W. Craighead, W. Edward Craighead, Alan E. Kazdin
and Michael J. Mahoney
ISBN 0-205-14586-8

School Refusal: Assessment and Treament
Neville J. King, Thomas H. Ollendick, and Bruce J. Tonge
ISBN: 0-205-16071-9

Solving Discipline Problems: Methods and Models for Today's Teachers, Third Edition
Charles H. Wolfgang
ISBN: 0-205-16569-9

The Three Faces of Discipline for Early Childhood: Empowering Teachers and Students
Charles H. Wolfgang and Mary E. Wolfgang
ISBN: 0-205-15649-5

BEHAVIOR MANAGEMENT IN THE SCHOOLS
Principles and Procedures

Second Edition

Richard M. Wielkiewicz
College of Saint Benedict

Allyn and Bacon
Boston   London   Toronto   Sydney   Tokyo   Singapore

To my parents, Michael and Mary Wielkiewicz

Copyright © 1995, 1987 by Allyn and Bacon
A Simon & Schuster Company
Needham Heights, Massachusetts 02194

Library of Congress Cataloging-in-Publication Data

Wielkiewicz, Richard M.
    Behavior management in the schools : principles and procedures /
Richard M. Wielkiewicz. — 2nd ed.
      p.   cm.
    Includes bibliographical refrences and index.
    ISBN 0-205-16458-7 (cloth). — ISBN 0-205-16459-5 (paper)
    1. Behavior modification. 2. School children—Discipline.
I. Title.
LB1060.2.W54 1995
371.1′024—dc20 —dc20
[371.1′024]   94-29668
                                    CIP

Printed in the United States of America
10 9 8 7 6 5 4 3 2 1   98 97 96 95 94

CONTENTS

PART ONE   PRINCIPLES

**1   Why Won't They Do What They're *Supposed* to Do? A Systematic
        Approach to Child Behavior Management**   **1**

An Introduction to Behavior Management   2
Basic Behavior Management Techniques   3
Assertive Behavior and Child Management   5
Child Rights, Parent Rights, and Teacher Rights   6
Plan of This Book   14
Review   14

2   Basic Principles of Child Management and Behavior Modification   **16**

Four Basic Techniques of Altering or Maintaining Behavior   16
Other Dimensions of Behavior Management Techniques   21
Review   28

**3   Step-by-Step Procedures for Assessment and Management
        of Behavior Problems**   **30**

A General Method for Assessment of Problem Behaviors   31
Steps in Conducting a Formal Behavior Management Program   39
Conclusion   51
Review   51

4   Issues in Designing an Appropriate Behavior Management Program   **52**

Primary Issues   52
Secondary Issues   55
Conclusion   69
Sources of Additional Information   70
Review   70

PART TWO   PROCEDURES

**5   Prevention of Behavior Management Problems in the School, Regular
Classroom, Special Classroom, and Home**   **72**

Prevention from the Administrative Perspective   73
Prevention in the Regular Classroom Setting   81
Prevention in Special Classrooms   89
Home–School Relationships and Prevention   92
Conclusion   93
Review   93

6   Selecting Appropriate Behavior Management Programs   **95**

Selecting a Behavior Management Program   97
Conclusion: Remain Flexible   100
Review   100

7   Management of Behavior Excesses in the Regular Classroom   **102**

Decreasing Undesirable Behavior   102
Designing Effective Extinction Programs   103
The "Coupon Program": An Effective School- or Home-Based Method of
    Using Response Cost to Reduce Behavior Excesses   107
Timeout in Regular Classroom Settings   111
The Good Behavior Game Plus Merit   115
Review   118

8   Management of Behavior Excesses in Special Classrooms   **120**

The Response Cost Lottery   120
Timeout in Special Classrooms   124
An Introduction to Cognitive-Behavioral Techniques for Remediating
    Inattentive and Impulsive Behavior   133
Review   138

9   Management of Behavior Excesses in the Home   **139**

Parent Training Programs   139
Ignoring and Extinction at Home   140
Response Cost Contingencies at Home   145
Timeout at Home   153
Conclusion   155
Review   155

10   Management of Behavior Deficits in the Regular Classroom   **156**

A Basic Regular Classroom Behavior Management Program   156
Behavior Management of School Refusal and School Phobia   160
A Remediation Plan for School Phobia   161

Other Ways of Remediating Anxiety   168
Use of Home Notes to Monitor School Performance   169
Monitoring and Rewarding Daily School Performance   174
Behavior Contracts   178
A Case Study: Jack   185
Conclusion   186
Review   186

11   Management of Behavior Deficits in Special Classrooms   **188**

A Basic Token Reward Program for Teaching Skills   188
A Token Reward Program for General Classroom Use   193
Behavior Management of Children's Social Skills   203
A Program for Improving Social Isolation   205
Other Research on Social Isolation as a Skill Deficit   209
Conclusion   211
Review   211

12   Management of Behavior Deficits in the Home   **212**

Helping Parents with Common Child-Rearing Problems   212
Behavior Contracts at Home: A Parent Handout   216
Token Programs at Home: A Parent Handout   220
Final Word   231
Review   231

Glossary   **232**

References   **240**

Index   **255**

Preface

The purpose of this edition of *Behavior Management in the Schools* is the same as that of the first edition: to provide a sound introduction to the principles of behavior management and describe the application of these principles in school environments. *Behavior Management in the Schools* will be a useful manual for school psychologists, special and regular education teachers, school social workers, child advocates, school administrators, and other individuals who provide care to children in a professional or volunteer capacity.

This book provides a sound, empirically based introduction to the principles of behavior modification and the practical, specific information needed to apply these principles successfully in a school environment. A large gap often exists between theoretical knowledge gained in college classes on behavior management and the practical issues involved in developing behavior management programs in school environments. *Behavior Management in the Schools* closes the gap between theory and practice by describing techniques for managing child behavior in a concrete, step-by-step manner. These step-by-step procedures guide the reader through the process of developing, modifying, and fading out behavior management programs. At the same time, the reader is encouraged to approach behavior management in a flexible manner, adjusting each program to meet the unique needs of each child.

The book also emphasizes that behavior exists in an ecological context consisting of the home, school, community, and cultural environments. Issues such as depression, suicide, or child abuse that should take precedence over behavior management programming are discussed. Two chapters on home-based behavior management procedures reinforce the ecological perspective and provide guidance in developing behavior management programs with greater consistency. In sum, *Behavior Management in the Schools* combines a practical and scholarly approach to behavior management of school-age children.

Behavior Management in the Schools has two parts. Part One describes the general principles of learning and behavior management, which are covered in Chapters 1, 2, 3, and 4. Chapter 5 addresses prevention of behavior management problems in regular classrooms, special classrooms, and the home. Part Two begins with a brief review of the basic issues involved in selecting behavior management programs in Chapter 6. Chapters 7 through 12 describe specific, step-by-step procedures for managing behavior problems encountered in schools. These six chapters are organized according to the general type of behavior problem (behavior excess or behavior deficit) and the environment in which the program will be conducted (regular classroom, special classroom, or home).

In the time I have been teaching courses in behavior management and related areas, I have developed discussion questions, case examples, and in-class exercises that should prove useful to instructors. Each chapter ends with a list of key terms, discussion questions, and at least one small group instructional activity. Several new behavior management programs, forms, and handouts will also make the book easier to use and more helpful. I have made every effort to update the references and include the latest in behavior management technology.

Practitioners will also find *Behavior Management in the Schools* user-friendly. For those already familiar with the general principles of behavior management, Chapter 5 provides a detailed discussion of the day-to-day application of these principles from the perspective of preventing behavior problems. It discusses issues such as organizing a regular classroom, managing school bus behavior, and developing a levels or privileges system of behavior management for a special classroom. Chapter 6 overviews the organization of Part Two and provides a summary of issues that will influence selection of a behavior management program. The remainder of Part Two describes behavior management programs for a variety of situations in a consistent, step-by-step manner that is easy to follow. Each description is accompanied by suggestions for adapting the program to particular situations. In sum, this book has been organized to provide practitioners with quick access to useful information.

I would like to gratefully acknowledge the editorial assistance of AnneMary Wielkiewicz and helpful reviews provided by Anthony J. M. Marcattilio, St. Cloud State University, St. Cloud, Minnesota, and Jane Harmon Jacobs, Valley Medical Dental Center, Renton, Washington.

R.M.W.

ABOUT THE AUTHOR

Richard M. Wielkiewicz is an associate professor of psychology at the College of Saint Benedict in St. Joseph, Minnesota. In addition to working for several years as a school psychologist, Dr. Wielkiewicz has been a regular and special education consultant, researcher, and coordinator of behavior management programs for children and adults at all levels of functioning. He holds a Ph.D. in psychology from the University of Hawaii and completed school psychology training at Moorhead State University, Moorhead, Minnesota. He is the senior author of *Training and Habilitating Developmentally Disabled People: An Introduction,* published by Sage Publications.

CHAPTER 1

WHY WON'T THEY DO WHAT THEY'RE *SUPPOSED* TO DO? A SYSTEMATIC APPROACH TO CHILD BEHAVIOR MANAGEMENT

Children of all ages and ability levels sometimes behave in ways that create problems for themselves and their caretakers. Instead of doing what they're "supposed" to do, they have problems ranging from minor annoyances to dangerous physical aggression. Too many children are exposed to abusive living situations, drugs, crime, and poor role models both in real life and on television. This makes it harder to provide them with productive learning experiences and exacerbates problems that occur in school. School-based professionals, parents, and consultants who have the knowledge and skills to keep schoolchildren engaged in learning tasks and doing what they're "supposed" to be doing are in the best position to help youngsters learn to be responsible adults. Behavior management techniques can provide a useful tool for accomplishing these goals. The purpose of *Behavior Management in the Schools* is to describe these techniques in a clear and concrete manner that will be useful and easily applicable to the problems of children who need help.

Children generally do what they're supposed to do because they are rewarded for good behavior or experience unpleasant consequences for misbehavior. The behavior of children with problems in school often needs to be managed with structured programs. Behavior management programs conducted in school, home, and community environments can be useful tools for improving

children's adjustment. Under some circumstances, however, even the most well designed behavior management program may fail. A *systematic* approach to behavior management can be helpful in developing effective programs.

The approach described in *Behavior Management in the Schools* is systematic in two senses. First, each description of a behavior program follows the same eight-step procedure, described in Chapter 3:

1. Identify the problem.
2. Refine the definition of the problem.
3. Assess the baseline rate.
4. Identify the reinforcer and contingency and write the program description.
5. Begin the program.
6. Observe the effects of the program.
7. Modify the program if necessary.
8. Fade out the program.

These eight steps are used as an outline to present each behavior management program described in this book. Consistently following this eight-step format helps communicate the general principles involved in successful behavior management.

The word *systematic* also refers to a way of looking

at the child's environment. Behavior management programs are most successful when the child's school, home, *and* community environments are considered along with the behavior management program itself. Frequently, a *combination* of school- and home-based interventions is needed because factors outside the school might interfere with a well-designed behavior management program. In this sense, intervention is *systematic* because it considers all the elements in the *system* within which the child functions.

The approach taken in *Behavior Management in the Schools* is that changing the behavior of children in a positive way requires an understanding of both how behavior is learned and the context or environment in which it occurs.

AN INTRODUCTION TO BEHAVIOR MANAGEMENT

The most successful model for producing behavior change is the behavioral or learning model. Its basic assumptions are that both desirable and undesirable behavior are *learned* and that the best strategy for remediating problem behavior is to structure the environment to reward desirable behavior. The model is known by a number of terms, including *behaviorism, behavior therapy, behavior modification, social learning theory,* and *behavior management.* A primary purpose of *Behavior Management in the Schools* is to describe the fundamental principles of learning and their application to changing children's behavior in school. Throughout this book, the generic term *behavior management* will be used to describe this process.

Successful behavior management does not depend solely on knowledge of the mechanisms of behavior change. It also requires understanding of the environmental context of behavior. The typical child spends most of his or her time in two environments: the home and the school. Neither environment is more important than the other. Each makes crucial contributions to the child's physical, behavioral, and cognitive growth. In the broadest sense, behavior problems observed in school really involve the entire system, including the child, the home, and the school. In order for a problem to be resolved successfully, the contribution of each component of the system needs to be assessed (e.g., Phares, Compas, & Howell, 1989). Usually, parents are eager to see their children succeed in school and will support the efforts of school personnel. However, problems in school may be an indirect result of a divorce, parental abuse, drug use, or other factors. In these cases, the child's parents may be unable to help the child with school problems because they are occupied with matters that are more important or more pressing for them. Resolving these complex problem situations may require a cooperative team effort involving teachers, parents, administrators, special education staff, social service representatives, and psychologists. Services such as family therapy, counseling, and even social service intervention may be needed to help the system focus on the best interests of the child.

Let's look at an example of this approach. Abused children, for example, are likely to show behavioral and academic problems in school. When school-based problems are brought to the attention of the abused child's parents, they may resist cooperating with the school. In such cases, focusing exclusively on the child's behavior may be successful only in remediating the academic and behavioral problems at school. If the child is truly to be helped, a lot of work would remain to be done. Parental training and involvement of social service agencies would also be important components of the intervention. A narrow focus on school behavior alone would be inadequate to meet the child's needs.

In the case of child abuse, school personnel need to be familiar with its indicators, which are reviewed in Chapter 4, and knowledgeable about their state's laws on reporting child abuse. Child abuse is not the only problem that may call for intervention beyond the school setting. Others will be discussed in subsequent chapters. The crucial point is that successful school-based behavior management often requires that school personnel look beyond the school environment for help in solving behavior problems.

The perspective taken in *Behavior Management in the Schools* is that child behavior occurs within a system consisting mainly of the school and home environments. Although this book is addressed to school personnel, its scope is not limited to management of behavior that occurs in school. Instead, the entire system in which the child functions is considered the potential focus of intervention. The reality of working within school systems is that many events relevant to the child's adjustment are outside the control of school personnel. Yet, this should not prevent personnel within the school system from trying to understand the entire system in which the child functions, because there are many opportunities for helpful and, in some cases, legally mandated interventions.

BASIC BEHAVIOR MANAGEMENT TECHNIQUES

When a behavior problem has been identified and it is agreed that it would be beneficial to modify the behavior, a working model of appropriate techniques is needed to guide the intervention plan. The model presented in this book, given the generic label *behavior management,* is based primarily on the principles of learning theory. Its roots are in the work of the great American psychologist Edward L. Thorndike. In a series of experiments with cats, Thorndike observed that responses followed by "satisfaction" (food, in this case) tended to be more likely to recur in the same situation. Responses followed by "discomfort" were less likely to recur in that situation. Thorndike summarized these observations in the well-known Law of Effect. Later, B. F. Skinner (e.g., 1938, 1953) extended these basic ideas in a more formal and comprehensive way.

The Law of Effect summarizes the observation that behavior is affected by its consequences in a predictable way. When behavior is followed by a desirable event, such as food or praise, the behavior is likely to be repeated. When behavior is followed by an undesirable event, such as pain or punishment, the behavior is less likely to be repeated. This fact forms the basis of modern principles of child behavior management. This law cannot be circumvented or repealed. Whether or not these principles are applied consciously, research demonstrates that they influence behavior.

For example, Brown and Elliott (1965) studied aggressive behavior in a nursery school class. Physical and verbal aggression were tallied separately. They found that the number of aggressive acts was cut in half when teachers were instructed to ignore aggression and pay attention only to cooperative behavior. Interestingly, it was very difficult for the teachers to ignore physical aggression, so the number of physically aggressive acts almost returned to the original level when compliance with the management plan was no longer monitored by the researchers. The number of verbally aggressive acts continued to decline.

Adult social attention directed at undesired behavior frequently rewards that behavior and therefore increases rather than decreases it. Negative social attention, such as scolding or telling a child to cease a behavior, can actually be rewarding from the child's perspective. Conversely, academic productivity can be increased when teacher attention is directed at students who are on task while off-task behavior is ignored (Becker, Madsen,

Arnold, & Thomas, 1967; Chadwick & Day, 1971; Hall, Lund, & Jackson, 1968; Kelly & Bushell, 1987; Madsen, Becker, & Thomas, 1968; Williams, Williams, & McLaughlin, 1991a; Zimmerman & Zimmerman, 1962) (see Ross, 1981, p. 211 ff.; and Ullman & Krasner, 1975, for further discussion).

The behavior of adults who unintentionally reward undesired behavior with negative attention can also be viewed as learned. In the typical classroom, when a child behaves in a disruptive manner the teacher is distracted from the job of teaching children. To eliminate the distraction, the teacher typically resorts to some sort of verbal admonishment, such as "Stop that!" or "Get to work!" Usually, the admonition is effective to the extent that the disruptive child immediately ceases the annoying behavior and the teacher is rewarded (or, more precisely, negatively reinforced) by the immediate removal of the annoying behavior. Unfortunately, although the teacher has obtained immediate relief, the overall frequency of disruptions, measured over days or weeks, does not necessarily decline. Instead, it may remain constant or even increase if adult attention is rewarding to the disruptive child or children. This is why objective counts of target behaviors play a central role in behavior management programs. Objectively counting how often a behavior occurs clearly shows what is happening to a particular behavior and how it is being influenced by events in the environment.

Dobson (1970) provides a humorous example of the same principle. He reported a classroom teacher who would yell and scream at her students when they were uncooperative. When this failed to bring order to the class, she resorted to climbing on her desk and blowing a whistle. The children enjoyed this so much that they would plot ways to annoy her. One can be fairly certain that such a production got the attention of the children to a sufficient degree that disruptive behavior ceased temporarily, but the overall effect on the classroom climate was to *increase* disruptions and off-task behavior.

Thus, child behavior is the product of a continuous and complex interaction between the child and the environment. Child behavior is influenced by events in the environment, such as adult attention, while adult behavior is simultaneously influenced by the child. Most of the time, the efforts of adults to influence behavior have the expected impact. However, the effects of reinforcement are not immediate and it is easy for adults to fall into a pattern in which their behavior has an unintended effect on the children they wish to teach and manage.

The best way to avoid this predicament is to measure carefully the frequency of both desirable and undesirable behavior so the effects of any intervention can be measured objectively.

At home, similar patterns of parent–child interaction may develop. Patterson, Cobb, and Ray (1973) described patterns of parenting observed in the course of research and intervention with families of aggressive boys. They labeled one of the parenting patterns the *diffusion* parent. According to their description, the diffusion parent ignores mild aggressive behaviors, such as teasing or yelling, that may lead to high-amplitude aggressive behavior such as hitting. Instead, the diffusion parent responds to high-amplitude aggressive behavior by nagging or yelling. The result is that aggressive behavior continues at a high rate because it is rewarded by adult attention. Diffusion parents are characterized by generally poor and inconsistent child management techniques that allow aggression to be rewarded and positive, prosocial behavior to go unrewarded. Thus, the parental reaction to aggressive behavior contributes to its persistence in this type of family. Such mothers also experience great difficulty in changing the way they interact with their children (Wahler, 1980).

Thus, parents and teachers may unintentionally increase undesirable behavior by rewarding it with negative attention. When adults scold, nag, or admonish children, the undesirable behavior may actually increase because adult attention, positive or negative, is rewarding to most children. In addition, the immediate effect of adult attention is that the annoying behavior temporarily ceases, and the long-term increase in the disruptive behavior is not immediately evident. On the other hand, the influence of positive adult attention on desirable behavior often is not immediately evident, either. Instead, the positive effects may be observed only over a long period of time as the child slowly acquires complex skills and disruptive behavior declines. The principles of child behavior management provide tools for ensuring that the directions taken by children's behavior are consistent with the goal determined by significant adults.

Thorndike's early research and observations are mainly of historical interest because much has been learned about human behavior since his time. However, the basis of behavior management remains the same as it was in 1898, when Thorndike first published his findings. Reward and punishment are still the primary techniques for controlling behavior. As observed by Thorndike, behavior is affected by its consequences— that is, the events that follow it. However, the effect is on the *future occurrence* of the behavior under the same or similar conditions. Consider a simple example.

A parent is shopping for groceries at the local supermarket. She has with her a somewhat tired four-year-old. About halfway through the shopping trip, the child begins to cry and whine—a sure signal to the mother that a tantrum will begin soon—but she decides to ignore the behavior and continues shopping. Minutes later, the crying is louder and the child is kicking and hitting at the grocery cart. In desperation, the mother gives the child some candy "to quiet him down." Not surprisingly, the child becomes quiet and the mother is relieved. Both mother and child are "satisfied." But what has been learned?

Although the immediate problem of the child's annoying behavior has been solved, this parent may be on the way toward creating a more difficult problem for the future. The next time the child is in the same or similar circumstances, the candy reinforcement has made it *more likely* that a tantrum will occur. Most children will learn to repeat behavior that is rewarded or reinforced with candy. *Reinforcement following a behavior increases the likelihood of future occurrences of that behavior under the same or similar circumstances.* The proof that an event is reinforcing lies in demonstrating that the behavior becomes more likely in the future, although it may require several reinforced instances of the behavior for an increase in its likelihood to become apparent. It is the gradual change in the frequency of the behavior that demonstrates the operation of reinforcement. Reinforcement is probably the most effective tool for changing the behavior of children, and it is an integral part of most of the behavior management programs described in this book.

Punishment operates in a manner similar to reinforcement, but its effect on behavior is the opposite. When a behavior is followed by a punishing event, the chances of the behavior recurring under the same or similar circumstances are decreased. Few examples of the operation of punishment in its "pure" form exist, but consider the curious child who touches and explores everything in sight. Imagine that the child is about to touch a hot dish when his mother says, "No! It's hot!" The child ignores the warning and touches the dish anyway, receiving a painful burn. The next time the parent gives a warning that something is "hot," the child will be less likely to touch it. This is how punishment operates on behavior.

Although punishment is frequently used to change child behavior, its use leads to several problems. As noted in earlier examples, a major problem is that events presumed to be punishing often turn out not to be. Another problem with the use of punishment is that the behavior problems of children are most often the result of both the *presence* of annoying behavior and the *absence* of desired behavior. Using punishment to eliminate the annoying behavior leaves the child still not knowing how to behave appropriately in the problem situation. Thus, the focus of behavior management should usually be on teaching and rewarding *new* skills. For instance, children who are physically aggressive will benefit from a program to reduce the aggressive behavior *and* to increase the positive social skills that they lack. Invariably, emphasizing positive reinforcement and rewarding appropriate behavior will lead to the best behavioral outcomes. At times, however, it is important to suppress behavior quickly and effectively (e.g., physical aggression). In these instances, a procedure called *timeout* is often used. This technique will be thoroughly described in subsequent chapters.

A third basic principle of behavior management is *extinction*. Extinction is the result of discontinuing reinforcement. Returning to the example of tantrums in the grocery store, consider what would happen over several months' time if the child received candy each time a temper tantrum occurred in the store. The principle of reinforcement predicts that tantrums would be increasingly likely. In fact, if the child received candy for tantrums at other locations, such as at home and at the baby sitter, they might occur at an intolerably high rate of several tantrums per day. Now, assuming that tantrums were being rewarded by candy, what might happen if the parent was instructed to withhold candy for tantrums? That is, the child could tantrum until exhausted, but no candy would be forthcoming. Most likely, the number of tantrums would decrease under these circumstances as long as there were no other sources of reinforcement for tantrums such as adult attention. When reinforcement is discontinued and a behavior slowly decreases in frequency, the process is called extinction. Extinction may also take place when behavior that formerly was rewarded by adult attention is ignored.

It is possible to combine the principles of reward, punishment, and extinction into a general rule on how to handle many situations involving children's behavior. This rule, which I call the Golden Rule of Behavior Management, is the best, most effective way to approach general classroom discipline. Following the rule will not only prevent many minor problems but can also alleviate existing problems. The Golden Rule of Behavior Management is this:

> Ignore, as much as possible, all minor annoyances and misbehavior, and spend as much time as possible giving positive attention to students who are behaving correctly.

The Golden Rule of Behavior Management encourages adults to direct their attention toward children who are behaving appropriately. A compliment ("Good job!"), smile, or thumbs-up sign directed at children who are performing as expected will reinforce desired behavior. This is a simple, effective, and empirically validated technique. At the same time, ignoring inappropriate behavior is an effective tool for prevention and remediation of behavior problems. Following the Golden Rule of Behavior Management will not guarantee a perfect classroom because there are many other variables that may influence a child's behavior. However, most children will respond positively to adult attention, and this will create a productive learning environment. Behavior management programs described in Part II can be used for those children who do not respond to the Golden Rule of Behavior Management.

Punishment, reinforcement, and extinction make up the core of child behavior management techniques. The details and terminology of these techniques will be reviewed in Chapters 2 and 3. Specific applications are described in Chapters 7 through 12. Before moving to the specifics of behavior management techniques, however, one often neglected aspect of child management will be considered: the way adults interact with children.

ASSERTIVE BEHAVIOR AND CHILD MANAGEMENT

Adults have great authority over children and are free to exercise this authority using virtually any style of interaction they choose. At one extreme, it is possible to be very timid; at the other extreme, it is possible to be very aggressive. Neither extreme is optimally effective. In the context of applying behavior management techniques with children, a style that represents the middle ground between these two extremes is necessary. This is known as behaving *assertively*.

Assertive behavior lies in the middle of a continuum of behavioral styles anchored at one end by nonassertion and at the other end by aggression. *Nonassertion* involves failing to express honest feelings, thoughts, and beliefs, or expressing one's thoughts and feelings in such a timid, apologetic, diffident, or self-effacing manner that they can easily be disregarded or ignored. Often, behaving nonassertively involves an underlying desire to avoid conflict, avoid hurting the feelings of others, or avoid losing the affection of others. By behaving in such a manner, however, one indirectly shows a lack of self- respect by allowing one's own rights to be violated. One also shows a lack of respect for the ability of others to handle disappointment, responsibility, or the consequences of their own behavior. Timidity and being taken advantage of are likely to characterize nonassertive people.

At the other end of the continuum is *aggression*. Aggression involves directly standing up for one's rights and expressing oneself in ways that are often dishonest, usually inappropriate, and always in violation of the rights of others. The usual goal of aggressive behavior is domination or winning, accomplished by humiliating, degrading, belittling, or overpowering other people so they become weaker and less able to express and defend their own rights and needs. Name calling, putdowns, and yelling often characterize aggressive behavior.

In the middle of this continuum of behavioral styles is *assertion*. Assertion involves standing up for one's personal rights and expressing thoughts, feelings, and beliefs in direct, honest, and appropriate ways that do not violate the rights of others. Messages are conveyed without dominating, humiliating, or degrading the other person. Assertive behavior is a positive approach to communication that involves respecting oneself and the adult or child with whom one is communicating. Directness and honesty tend to characterize the assertive individual's behavior.

Adults who behave assertively are at a distinct advantage over those who behave either nonassertively or aggressively. Those who behave nonassertively are likely to find that they are not really in control of their children or classrooms and that their sincere desire to create an effective, pleasant learning environment is not fulfilled. Those who behave aggressively may be in complete control, but it is at the expense of their pupils or children, who are likely to feel belittled, inferior, uninterested in learning, and unhappy. By contrast, an assertive style of child management allows for the honest and direct expression of the caretaker's wishes. Rules are clearly stated, and consequences of behavior are administered without belittling or insulting the child. In short, the caretaker is responsible for the rules, and the child is responsible for his or her behavior.

In order to apply the techniques discussed in this book successfully, an *assertive* style of behavior is essential. The techniques all involve administration of consequences (reward or punishment) for appropriate or inappropriate behavior. Success depends on clear, direct statement of the rules, followed by consistent and firm administration of consequences. If rules are stated apologetically or timidly, the likelihood of their being ignored or violated increases, and the likelihood of successful child management decreases. If one applies these principles in an aggressive manner, the rights and responsibilities of the children are sacrificed. Thus, a prerequisite for successful child management is the willingness and skill to take charge of the children assertively, clearly setting rules and limits for them.

Table 1.1 presents examples of assertive, nonassertive, and aggressive behavior. For those would like to pursue the topic further, the books by Alberti and Emmons (1978), Lange and Jakubowski (1976), and Silberman and Wheelan (1980) are recommended.

CHILD RIGHTS, PARENT RIGHTS, AND TEACHER RIGHTS

The word *rights* evokes those qualities of a behavior management program pertaining to its acceptability from a moral, ethical, or legal perspective. The use of behavior management procedures in the schools demands consideration of a number of issues relating to the rights of the child, the child's parents, and the child's teachers.

In the United States, the foundation on which human rights are based is the U.S. Constitution. Bersoff (1982) and Bersoff and Hofer (1990) have pointed out that the conduct of school administrators and practitioners often "directly and sharply" invokes constitutional principles. The constitutional principles most often invoked include the right to equal protection under the law, the right to due process, the right to privacy, and property rights.

The right to equal protection has been interpreted to mean that all children have the right to equal educational opportunity. It is contrary to established constitutional principles to discriminate against any group of children, such as those who are disabled, without "substantial and legitimate" reasons. According to Bersoff and Hofer (1990), the equal protection clause was used by many disabled children to argue successfully against exclusion

Table 1.1. Examples of Assertive, Nonassertive, and Aggressive Characteristics

ASSERTIVE	NONASSERTIVE	AGGRESSIVE
Persistent	Avasive	Nasty
Good listener	Flustered	Deprecating others
Politely refuses requests	Too nice	Makes accusations
Makes clear, direct requests	Is taken advantage of	Teases others
Empathic	Creates unclear expectations	Tricks, puts down others
Honest	Inhibited	Nags
Accepts others' feelings	Anxious	Gives harsh punishment
Fair	Self-blaming	Hurts others
Gives sincere compliments	Is treated unfairly	Discredits others
Accepts compliments	Begs, passive	Engages in power struggles
Active	Passive	Mean

from a free public education. The right to a free public education has also been defined as a property right guaranteed by the Constitution, which then invokes "due process" considerations.

The due process guarantees of the Constitution prohibit schools from denying access to educational privileges unless procedures are followed that are fundamentally fair and impartial. This includes the process of labeling individual students to provide them access to the rights granted to disabled students. To protect children from the stigma that could result from being labeled *disabled* or *handicapped,* schools are required to follow fair procedures and conduct impartial hearings, in which all interested parties have input into the decision. The need to conduct fair and impartial procedures is largely responsible for the flood of paperwork that accompanies the special education process. The purpose is to create a record documenting the need for special services and assuring that procedural requirements of fairness and impartiality have been followed.

Another basis for child rights is the United Nations Convention on the Rights of the Child. Melton and Erenreich (1992) suggest that the U.N. Convention provides an excellent framework for making decisions consistent with maintaining the dignity of the child. Although the Convention is not legally binding in the United States, Melton and Erenreich argue that it is likely to become an international standard for child mental health policy. The Convention consists of 54 articles (see U.N. Convention, 1991) covering the entire array of children's services and rights. For a detailed discussion, see Brassard, Hyman, and Dimmitt (1991) who offer many concrete suggestions for school professionals who wish to ensure children's rights as outlined in the U.N. Convention.

The remainder of this chapter will be devoted to ethical concerns that may be involved in the use of behavior management procedures with schoolchildren. My goal is to provide useful guidelines that are consistent with public law, the U.N. Convention, and the general principle that the best interests of the child should prevail in all interventions with children (see U.N. Convention, 1991, Article 3). However, school professionals must also be aware of any specific laws of their state that may affect the use of behavior management procedures. Timeout (see Chapter 7) is an intervention that is particularly likely to be regulated by state laws.

Rights of the Child

Children are generally not regarded as capable of protecting their own rights. Thus, school practitioners and parents are obligated to do their best to see that the child's rights are adequately protected. With respect to behavior management procedures, what are the important ethical concerns?

Assure that treatment is in the child's best interests. The primary ethical concern is to conduct behavior management programs that are in the best interests of children. This is a broad guideline incorporated into the U.N. Convention as Article 3. Its meaning is likely to change from situation to situation. It is clear, however, that many interests can come into play while developing a program for a child. In fact, the interests of parents, teachers, and the school can be in conflict with the child's interests. For example, a behavior management program might not be in a child's best interests when conditions outside of the school underlie problem behaviors observed in school. Although it is possible to apply behavior management principles without reference to other underlying problems, doing so could result in continuation of a harmful situation. For instance, hyperactivity and inattention are common behavior problems observed in the classroom. These problems can exist in isolation but have also been associated with childhood depression, sexual and physical abuse, parental divorce, and other family problems. Conducting a behavior management program while ignoring the possibility that more serious problems underlie the child's behavior would certainly not be in his or her best interest. To avoid this type of problem, a thorough assessment of the problem situation is needed. A procedure for conducting behavioral assessments is described in Chapter 3.

Another factor that can be opposed to a child's best interests is finances. In some cases, it could be to a child's advantage to remain in a regular classroom accompanied by a pupil support assistant or paraprofessional to assist in controlling behavior and helping the child to engage in academic tasks. If budgetary constraints make such a plan impossible, the interests of the school may reside in placing the child in an existing program rather than providing services specially tailored to meet his or her needs. In this case, it would be best if the child's interests were the overriding concern. One of the keys to developing programs in a child's best interest is to have a wide range of options available. Behavior management strategies are a particularly important component of child treatment because they can be conducted with little disruption and they have a proven, empirically based history of effectiveness.

Behavior management programs should be competently conducted and effective. Although the basic principles of behavior management are straightforward and easy to understand, the more advanced principles that play an important role in many behavior management programs are not as well understood. For instance, almost all those who teach children have had occasion to implement reward programs involving notes to parents, stickers, access to privileges, or other rewards available within the school. Many of these programs eventually fail because teachers to not know how to promote generalization of the program so that the desired behavior will occur after the program is discontinued. In addition, practitioners may not know how to modify a program if it does not succeed at first.

When a behavior management program is contemplated, the child has a right to competent treatment. That is, the practitioner should be familiar with all the principles that might influence the success of the program, including how to modify the program if it does not work and how to discontinue the program while maintaining the behavioral gains. In this book, each program is accompanied by suggested modifications that can be tried if it does not work at first. Also, each program description includes specific techniques for increasing the probability that behavioral gains will continue after the program is discontinued. It is the obligation of those who attempt to use these programs to develop a thorough understanding of both the mechanics of conducting the program and the principles that underlie it.

On a more concrete level, those who employ behavior management techniques should obtain training in both the general principles of learning and the specific techniques they wish to employ. Adequate course work and supervised experience in the application of these techniques to children is needed. Part I of this book provides a solid introduction to basic and advanced principles of behavior management, and those who go on to apply these principles will find more than adequate guidance in Part II. Yet, the practitioner is obligated to be sure that he or she has developed a solid understanding of the contents of these chapters before attempting to apply what has been learned. In addition, those in the schools should not attempt to conduct interventions that are beyond their competence. The practitioner who does not feel competent to conduct a particular behavior management program should obtain consultation and supervision, try a different approach, or refer the child to individuals who have the needed skills.

A child who is subjected to a behavior managment program also has a right to effective treatment. This does not mean that the practitioner must select a procedure that will work the first time it is applied. Rather, it is important that the effects of any behavior management program be monitored carefully. Programs that do not have the predicted effect should be modified. This means that all behavior management programs should begin by selecting a measurable target behavior that is carefully monitored throughout the program and beyond. Without the information gained from continuous measurement of the target behavior, the effectiveness of interventions remains a mystery. In the worst case, an intervention may actually exacerbate a problem. This situation need not be serious as long as those involved in the child's program are aware of the situation and make adjustments in the program. On the other hand, serious problems and even liability issues can arise if the effects of a particular program are not carefully monitored.

Children have a right to participate in decisions about their treatment as much as possible. Generally, children are assumed to be incapable of knowing what is in their best interests. Consequently, adults make most of the decisions regarding how they should behave and, when behavior goes beyond the limits set by adults, it is their responsibility, not the child's, to determine an appropriate course of action. However, there are several advantages to allowing children to participate in planning behavior management programs as much as their age and maturity allow.

One clear advantage is that the chances of success increase when the child participates. Even the youngest kindergarten child is capable of expressing preferences for various activities or rewards, which could be very useful if used in the context of behavior management programs. Furthermore, it is even possible that children can contribute to formulating a program's goals. As children become older, the success of a behavior management program may hinge upon the child's successful participation in the initial planning stages. When children reach adolescence, it may be next to impossible to conduct a successful behavior management program in the school without their input.

Another advantage of allowing children to participate in planning behavior management programs is that they can learn increased responsibility and independence. Furthermore, their input may lead to revisions in the way the child and his or her problems are viewed. This is consistent with the trend toward allowing children, particularly adolescents, more responsibility in making important decisions and acknowledging independence from their parents as they near the age of majority.

The right to treatment and a free and appropriate public education. A wide range of behavior problems may be targeted in a behavior management program. At one end of the continuum lie innocuous but slightly annoying behaviors that may disappear when adults begin to ignore them. At the other extreme are serious behavior problems that require detailed assessment, highly structured management programs, and considerable professional time to remediate. The more serious the problem, the greater the likelihood that a successful behavior management program will, at least temporarily, interfere with the child's regular classroom instruction. In general, practitioners must be careful that behavior management programs either do not interfere with regular classroom instruction or do so to the minimum extent necessary to remediate the behavior problem.

On the other hand, children who show a problem that prevents or interferes with their ability to benefit from regular classroom instruction also have a right to receive an "appropriate" education that meets their individual needs. This may include even the most structured behavior management programs conducted away from the child's regular classroom. The line that divides the "right" to appropriate treatment from the "right" to be left in the regular classroom free from interference is whether the child meets the criteria for one of several specific disabilities.

The word *disabled* often evokes images of children with physical challenges such as blindness, deafness, or the need to use a wheelchair for mobility. This image is only partially correct. Certainly, many children with easily observable physical disabilities receive special education services. This label, however, also applies to conditions that are not so easily observable, such as severe emotional or behavioral problems, learning problems that interfere with achievement in one or two academic areas, and difficulty in producing understandable speech. These challenges and several others have the potential to interfere with a child's ability to benefit from regular classroom instruction and could lead to the use of special education services.

Children labeled *disabled* simply have more rights than nondisabled children, although these rights are really the prerogatives of the child's parents until age eighteen. The precise nature and meaning of these rights will be discussed in the next section, "Parent Rights." In this section, the focus is on the issue of where and how behavior management programs are conducted without violating the child's rights. It seems that the best way to approach this issue is to proceed from the simplest to the most complex situations with regard to both the nature of the behavior problem and the behavior management program employed to remediate it. Typically, the simplest case that might require a behavior management program would involve the classroom teacher who identifies a behavior problem and takes steps, independent of other school personnel, to remediate it. Such steps could range from ignoring inappropriate behavior or revising classroom rules to employing a simple behavior management program targeted at the individual child. Teachers, acting independently within their own classrooms, are generally considered to have the freedom to plan and implement interventions to improve the academic performance and behavior of their students.

When a child is singled out for special attention, even while remaining within the regular classroom, the nature, severity, and resistance to change of the problem behavior become important considerations. Some problems, such as autism, severe childhood depression, cerebral palsy, retardation, and learning disabilities that interfere with educational progress, would make the child eligible for special education services. When such a child is found, a complete psychological and educational evaluation must be completed (with the consent of the child's parents) to determine the child's needs and how they can be met by the school district. The individual teacher's principal will be able to help make the appropriate referral and start the process of identification, if it is needed. Some problems do not, in themselves, create a need for special education services, and the initial attempt to remediate them should be made in a regular classroom. This would include many of the common discipline problems faced by the classroom teacher, such as being off task, not completing assignments, and engaging in minor disruptive behavior.

The severity of a behavior problem depends on its intensity, duration, frequency, and the degree to which it disrupts the class. Less severe problems are likely to be resolved within the classroom without a need for special services. The most severe problems may require immediate attention of those who provide special education services. This is especially true if the behavior interferes to a significant degree with the education of other children or is dangerous to the child or others. Within these extremes are behavior problems that are annoying, may interfere with normal classroom functioning, and occur fairly often, but do not clearly fall into either the "minor problem" or "disabled" categories.

Children in this last group often need formal behavior management programs conducted within the regular classroom. This can be very difficult for a busy teacher working with a classroom of twenty to thirty students.

To add to the complexity of this situation, it is unknown whether the student will eventually need services for students with disabilities. Consequently, it is important to be aware of the child's right to remain in a regular classroom, if possible, and the right to receive special education services, if they are needed. What this amounts to is a double bind, in which the best solution is to document what is done in attempting to solve the problem and to establish contact with the child's parents.

Regardless of the circumstances, behavior management programs that result in the child being treated differently than other children in the classroom should probably be conducted with the active cooperation of the child's parents. Procedures that employ home-based rewards (see Chapter 10) are a very effective method of involving parents actively. In addition, detailed records of attempts to remediate a problem should be kept. These records should describe the behavior management program and its effects on the problem behavior. This documentation is useful in establishing whether a need for special education services exists.

If a behavior management program has been implemented for a reasonable period of time, appropriate modifications have been attempted, and positive changes have not occurred, it would be prudent for the classroom teacher to obtain the consultation of the school's principal, a special education teacher, or a school psychologist. At this point, numerous options are available, some of which would invoke student rights as spelled out in Public Laws 94-142, 99-457, and 101-476. The cornerstone of rights for children with disabilities is Public Law 101-476, the Individuals with Disabilities Education Act (IDEA). It specifies parent rights, definitions of disabling conditions, and rules to ensure that fair and valid decisions about children are made. A related law is Section 504 of Public Law 923-112 (Rehabilitation Act, 1973) which is also meant to ensure that children receive appropriate services in school. These laws were passed by the U.S. Congress and were designed to protect the rights of disabled individuals. They are very specific in outlining the procedures that schools need to follow in determining whether a child is disabled and then providing needed services. These procedures begin with a thorough assessment of the problem behavior by special education personnel and require the informed written consent of the child's parents. Following assessment, the special education team, including the child's parents, determine whether a need for special education services exists. If such a need is found, a team consisting of school professionals and the child's parents would then determine the best way to meet that need.

Another option, prior to special education assessment, is for consultants to help the classroom teacher manage the behavior problem within the classroom. However, there is still the double bind of deciding whether it is more appropriate to maintain the child in a regular classroom versus providing special education services, if they are needed. There is no simple resolution to this situation. However, thoroughly documented efforts to resolve the problem within the regular education classroom are consistent with Public Law 94-142, which states that education for children with disabilities should take place in the "least restrictive environment" available to meet that child's needs.

What this means is that disabled children should be educated with nondisabled children to the maximum extent possible and that removal from the regular classroom should occur only when education in regular classes cannot be achieved satisfactorily because of the nature or severity of the disability. Documented attempts to resolve the problem within the regular classroom, which involve parents to the greatest extent possible, are probably the best way to ensure that this provision of the law has been satisfied. In rare instances, parents will refuse to cooperate with intervention efforts or allow school practitioners to intervene with a behavior problem. In such cases, consultation at the highest levels of school administration may be necessary to determine an acceptable course of action.

Section 504 of the Rehabilitation Act of 1973 is a broader piece of legislation than IDEA because it applies to many disabled children who do not qualify for services under IDEA. Section 504 is an antidiscrimination law that applies to any child who has a mental or physical condition that substantially limits one or more major life activities such as learning. Children with ADHD, graduates of special education, students with drug and alcohol dependency, students with special health needs, and other groups may qualify as handicapped under Section 504. When a student is identified as handicapped under this law, the school may develop an Individualized Education Plan (IEP) or an accommodation plan designed to meet the individual student's unique needs. Behavior management techniques are among the accommodations that have been suggested. For a more detailed discussion of Section 504 obligations and requirements, the article by Jacob-Timm and Hartshorne (1994) is recommended.

To summarize briefly, behavioral interventions can be considered to take place at three different levels within a classroom environment. At the first level are interventions conducted by the classroom teacher as part of normal discipline procedures. At the second level are interventions that focus on a particular child, who is treated at least somewhat differently than other children in the class. At the third level are interventions that are performed as part of a plan developed to meet the needs of a child who is in a regular classroom for at least part of the school day. Although a child's rights are important at all three levels of intervention, they become more clearly articulated at the second and third levels because of the actual or potential need for special education services or accommodations required under Section 504.

The next section, on parents' rights, provides a detailed review of the rights of children and their parents. This discussion will clarify many of the issues already introduced.

Parent Rights

For the most part, prior to age 18, children's educational rights are held by their parents or guardian. The clearest articulation of these rights is included in Public Law 94-142, the Individuals with Disabilities Education Act (IDEA) and Section 504 of the Rehabilitation Act. An abridged copy of the rules and regulations for the implementation of Public Law 94-142 is included as Appendix C of Reynolds and Gutkin (1982) and Gutkin and Reynolds (1990). What follows is a discussion of parent rights as described in Public Law 94-142. Although it is possible to conduct most behavior management programs without involving the child in special education services, a significant number will directly involve such services, and they will at least be considered in many other cases.

The right to a free and appropriate public education in the least restrictive environment. This right is the central feature of Public Law 94-142, which is essentially a grant-giving statute that contributes toward the cost of educating children with disabilities. A disabled child is one who has been evaluated in accordance with accepted procedures and found to be mentally retarded, hard of hearing, deaf, speech-impaired, visually handicapped, seriously emotionally disturbed, orthopedically impaired, other health impaired, deaf-blind, multihandicapped, or having specific learning disabilities, and who needs special education or related services. As noted in later chapters, almost any of these disabilities may be a causal factor when a child's behavior in school leads to contemplation of a behavior management program. Some of these conditions would contraindicate behavior management approaches until the precise nature of the child's disability is understood and other strategies have been implemented.

For instance, the academic performance of a child with an undiagnosed hearing deficit is not likely to improve when a behavior management program to improve academic performance is implemented. Instead, medical intervention should be given priority. It is always important to remember that a behavior management program is only one of several potential responses to problem behavior. Another way of responding is to conduct a more detailed assessment to determine whether a disability exists that is interfering with academic progress. This process is discussed in greater depth in Chapters 3 and 6. When a child experiences difficulty in school, however, one possibility is that the child is disabled. Public Law 94-142, related regulations, and court decisions have established that a child with a disability has a *right* to a free and appropriate public education. This right is balanced by procedural safeguards designed to prevent the mislabeling of a child if, in fact, no disability exists.

Although the appearance of problem behavior may be a signal that any of a number of problems may exist, the most likely category of disability for a child with behavioral problems is "seriously emotionally disturbed." The definition of *seriously emotionally disturbed* in the regulations of Public Law 94-142 covers a fairly broad range of conditions, which have existed "over a long period of time and to a marked degree." These conditions include an inability to learn not explainable by other factors, an inability to establish or maintain satisfactory interpersonal relationships with peers and teachers, inappropriate behavior or feelings, unhappiness or depression, and physical symptoms or fears associated with personal or school problems. This definition includes schizophrenic children but not those who are autistic. The latter are categorized as "other health impaired."

The definition of *seriously emotionally disturbed* includes a very broad range of childhood behaviors, many of which might be considered as potential targets of behavior management programs. Consequently, when a behavior management program is contemplated, it is possible that the child may be in need of special education services. The key to the process of serving children with disabilities is the Individualized Education Program, or IEP. Once a child has been evaluated and

identified, the education team writes a statement of how that child is functioning in school, a statement of goals for improving that level of functioning, and a statement of what special education services the child will be receiving. The resulting document is the IEP. The process of evaluating a child and writing the IEP must actively involve the child's parents in a number of ways that will be discussed in the next section. Of greater importance in the present context is to discuss the concept of least restrictive environment as it applies to special education.

Although it is true that Public Law 94-142 mandates that all children with disabilities be identified and served, this is balanced by a requirement that special education take place in the least restrictive environment. This means that children with disabilities must be educated with nondisabled children to the maximum extent possible. In addition, disabled children are to be removed from the regular education environment and placed in a special class only when the nature of severity of the disability is such that education in a regular classroom with supplementary aids and services cannot be achieved satisfactorily.

Behavior management programs can be very important techniques for educating children with disabilities in the least restrictive environment. This is especially true for children who may be labeled *seriously emotionally disturbed*. Their IEPs could be written to include behavioral goals to be accomplished using formal behavior management programs. Furthermore, by using a behavior management program prior to the formal assessment process, it may be possible to avoid labeling the child. Although the right to receive services, if needed, is important, the bias of placement should be toward the least restrictive environment, which would imply that placement is to be avoided if needs can be met in the regular education environment. A well-designed behavior management program may play a crucial role in keeping the child with behavior problems in a less restrictive environment.

Parental rights to participate in the entire process of identifying and placing disabled children. Basically, Public Law 94-142 and its associated regulations require that a child's parents be an integral part of the team that makes decisions about the child. Their participation begins when the child is initially identified as potentially needing special services. Before an evaluation can be carried out to determine whether the child is disabled in some way, the informed, voluntary, written consent of the child's parents is necessary. By *informed,* it is meant that the parents are made fully aware of the purposes of the evaluation. By *voluntary,* it is meant that no benefit to the child may be made conditional on the parents' consent. Finally, the consent must be *written* and must describe the evaluation activity that the school district intends to perform.

As the process of special education placement continues beyond the preplacement assessment, parental rights to have input into the process also continue. Briefly, these rights include the right to consent to or refuse special education placement for their child; the right to obtain an independent educational evaluation should they disagree with the results of the school's evaluation; the right to know where their child's records are kept and to know who has access to them; the right to be notified when a change in a special education program or placement is considered; the right to participate in an annual review of the IEP each year and to participate in future education planning for their child; the right to have their child's records maintained confidentially; and, finally, if the child's parents and the school district disagree with respect to actions that are proposed, the right to request a due process hearing conducted by an impartial officer with free or low-cost legal services made available.

The practice of behavior management in schools invokes numerous considerations of both parental and student rights. A mass of statutes, court decisions, and generally recognized principles can influence the practice of those who wish to conduct behavior management programs in the schools. As with many complicated endeavors, however, adherence to a few simple principles can help greatly in avoiding potential pitfalls. With respect to the use of behavior management programs in schools, I suggest that the following be kept firmly in mind and that, when some doubt arises, consultation with experts be sought before any program is begun:

1. Do not conduct procedures that have the potential to deny educational privileges to a child.
2. Use procedures that are effective. More specifically, keep track, via formal data collection or informal observations, of the results of any behavior management program that goes beyond normal classroom procedures.
3. Begin with the simplest behavior management procedures and proceed to more complex procedures only if they are needed. When initial programs fail, consider whether the child might be categorized as

seriously emotionally disturbed and therefore in need of special education services.
4. Seek the active cooperation of parents in behavior management programs. If parents balk at the implementation of a particular program, obtain consultation.
5. When detailed assessment of the child seems warranted, obtain parental permission, consult with special education staff, and assemble an assessment team before proceeding. At this stage, the child's parents should be actively involved.
6. Always remember that behavior management programs are to be conducted in the interest of serving a child with problems at school.
7. Allow the child to participate in the planning of the behavior management program to the maximum extent possible.

Rights of Teachers

Teachers, of course, are an integral part of the educational process. It is important that those supervising or directly implementing behavior management programs, including teachers themselves, be aware of the needs of classroom teachers. One of the basic rights of teachers is to have a classroom environment free from disruptions that consistently interfere with teaching. Even Public Law 94-142 states that when a child with a disability is so disruptive in a regular classroom that the education of other children is seriously impaired, placement in a regular classroom would not be considered appropriate. Thus, it should never be necessary for a teacher to sacrifice the educational progress of the majority of students in a classroom to the needs of a single student.

Behavior management programs should generally be simple but effective. Teachers are frequently the administrators of behavior management programs. When teachers are asked to fulfill this role, all involved should be aware that teachers cannot afford to be burdened with complicated record-keeping procedures or time-consuming programs that decrease instructional time for the remainder of the class. If a program is needed that requires detailed monitoring of the child's behavior, removal of the child from the classroom, or physical control to prevent injury to the child or others, it must be questioned whether a regular classroom is the appropriate setting for that child. Instead, referral to special education personnel, such as the school psychologist, or hiring of a classroom aide is needed.

Another right of teachers is to have their opinions and impressions respected. Both teachers themselves and those school practitioners who work outside the regular classroom should remember this. For those who work outside the classroom, it is important to remember that a child's classroom teacher has had more hours of contact with the student than any other person in the school. Therefore, the teacher is likely to be a very valuable source of information, whose participation should be actively sought in the process of planning behavioral interventions. For teachers themselves, it would be important to remember that the best interests of the child may not be served unless the time and effort are taken to add their input into the planning process. Even if a teacher is unfamiliar with the technical aspects of a particular behavior management program, his or her knowledge of the child can save time and effort and can greatly improve the team's chances of successfully remediating the problem.

In sum, the classroom teacher is an invaluable part of the team when behavior management programs are implemented. Both those who work in the classroom and those who come into the system from outside the classroom must cooperate to the greatest extent possible to ensure the maximum chances of successfully remediating problem behavior. Mastery of the basic principles and specific procedures of behavior management by all who work in school systems can contribute greatly to the overall academic and personal success of children in school.

PLAN OF THIS BOOK

The remainder of the book is divided into two parts. Part I consists of this chapter plus Chapters 2, 3, and 4. Chapter 2 presents an overview of the basic theoretical principles of behavior management. Chapter 3 presents general step-by-step procedures for assessing and managing problem behavior. Chapter 4 is concerned with important issues in selecting appropriate behavior management programs. These issues range from the goals of the behavior management program to diagnostic questions such as whether the child might be depressed, hyperactive, or a victim of abuse. Consideration of each of these issues is necessary to plan a behavior management program that is effective in meeting the needs of any child.

Part II begins with Chapter 5, on preventing behavior management problems in the school and home. Chapter 6 discusses selection of a particular behavior management program according to the needs of the child. The remaining six chapters discuss management of behavior deficits and behavior excesses in each of three environments: the regular classroom, special classrooms, and the home. Each chapter ends with several questions that can be used for discussion, for small-group exercises, or for testing your understanding of the key concepts in each chapter.

REVIEW

Terms to Remember and Review

reward	punishment
Law of Effect	diffusion parent
assertive	nonassertive
aggressive	handicapped
Public Law 94-142	IEP
seriously emotionally disturbed	disability

Study and Discussion Questions

1. In what two senses does *Behavior Management in the Schools* present a *systematic* approach to behavior management?
2. What are the basic assumptions of the behaviorist or learning model of behavior management?
3. Why is ignoring undesirable behavior often an effective intervention?
4. What is negative attention? What effect does negative attention often have on children's behavior?
5. Explain how it is possible for an adult to be rewarded by the immediate response of children to an admonition or scolding even though the long-term effect on the children's behavior is to increase disruptions.
6. Explain the effect of reinforcement on future behavior.
7. Give an example of the operation of reinforcement.
8. Explain the effect of punishment on future behavior.
9. Give an example of the operation of punishment.
10. What are the major problems with the use of punishment as a method of behavior management?
11. Explain in your own words the Golden Rule of Behavior Management.
12. Why is an assertive style of communication an

asset to the individual conducting a behavior management program?

13. Explain the concept of *least restrictive environment* as it applies to children with disabilities.

14. Discuss the advantages of allowing children to participate in decisions about their treatment.

15. Summarize the role of a student's classroom teacher in developing a behavior management program.

Group Project

In small groups, discuss each individual's responses to questions 5, 6, 7, and 8. Pick the best example and present it to the rest of the class. Be sure that each group member has a clear understanding of the workings of reinforcement and punishment.

CHAPTER 2

BASIC PRINCIPLES OF CHILD MANAGEMENT AND BEHAVIOR MODIFICATION

Behavior management is an *empirical* endeavor. This means, first, that there is a solid research base for behavior management techniques and, second, that the behavior management practitioner pays close attention to the outcome of a behavior management program and adjusts it as needed to produce the desired results. The beginnings of behavior management come from the work of Thorndike, Skinner, and Pavlov, who provided the foundation for understanding how behavior is influenced by the environment. Many others followed the paths they blazed. Hersen and Ammerman (1989) provide a nice overview of the historical development of behavior management with children, whereas Kazdin (1978) provides a thorough historical background on the general development of behavior management techniques. The usefulness of behavior management is supported by a vast empirical base of scientific studies showing the value of these techniques for remediating problem behaviors (e.g., Lipsey & Wilson, 1993). Scientific journals such as *Behavior Research and Therapy, Behavior Modification, Journal of Applied Behavior Analysis,* and the *Journal of Consulting and Clinical Psychology* continue to add to this data base providing the foundation for the procedures described in *Behavior Management in the Schools*.

A behavior management program can be as simple as praising a child for completing worksheets or as complex as punishing physical aggression with a period of brief social isolation (timeout). Regardless of complexity, all behavior management plans are based on one of four basic techniques for altering or maintaining behavior: positive reinforcement, punishment, negative reinforcement, or negative punishment. Understanding these four techniques is essential to designing and executing successful behavior management programs. They are described next.

FOUR BASIC TECHNIQUES OF ALTERING OR MAINTAINING BEHAVIOR

We all know that behavior is affected by the events that follow it. Children who are praised for cleaning their rooms are more likely to clean their rooms in the future. A child who is spanked for running into the street is less likely to run into the street again. These two examples illustrate *positive reinforcement* and *punishment*, the two methods that adults most frequently use to modify children's behavior. Another method of changing children's behavior is to take away something desirable, such as dessert. The child who misses out on dessert after throwing food at the dinner table is experiencing *negative punishment*. Finally, children whose behavior allows

16

them to terminate something unpleasant are experiencing *negative reinforcement*. For example, some children may feign illness in order to avoid school, especially on days when they are not prepared. Feigning illness is then negatively reinforced and more likely to reoccur when the child wishes to miss school.

These four basic techniques are the core of behavior management procedures. Any professional who is responsible for managing children's behavior needs to be familiar with them. Knowing these four techniques not only allows the professional to design sound programs but also enables him or her to understand the reasons behind the development of some behavior problems. The next step is to describe these four techniques in greater detail.

Two terms must be defined before this task is undertaken: *stimulus* and *contingency*. A stimulus refers to any perceivable event in a child's environment—a sound, movement, picture, verbal command, buzzing fly, itch, tap on the shoulder, word on a printed page, or anything else to which the child can respond in some observable way. Stimuli used in behavior management programs may be considered appetitive, aversive, or neutral. An appetitive stimulus is one that the child is likely to seek out, especially if a need for that stimulus is present. Food, especially sweets and snacks, are the best examples of appetitive stimuli; but under the right circumstances, positive attention from adults is also a powerful appetitive stimulus. An aversive stimulus is one that the child would usually avoid. Aversive stimuli are typically painful to experience—for example, a spanking or a burn from touching a hot stove. A neutral stimulus is neither aversive nor appetitive but may acquire such properties under the right circumstances.

A *contingency* is a rule describing the relationship between behavior and an event or consequence. For instance, if a child receives a painful burn after touching a hot stove, the burn is *contingent* on touching the stove. A contingency can be either positive or negative. A positive contingency means that a stimulus is *added* to the situation contingent on some behavior. For example, if a child receives a sticker for producing a perfect paper in school, the contingency is positive because the sticker is *added* to the situation contingent on the perfect paper. A negative contingency indicates that a stimulus is *subtracted* from the situation contingent on a behavior. For example, if a child loses dessert for misbehaving at the dinner table, the contingency is negative because the dessert is *subtracted* from the situation contingent on the child's misbehavior.

Table 2.1 shows how the two types of stimuli and the

Table 2.1. Contingencies for Changing Behavior

The four methods of modifying behavior can be summarized in a two-by-two table that specifies the stimulus type and contingency. The stimulus type is either appetitive (e.g., food, money, attention) or aversive (e.g., pain, a spanking), and the contingency is either positive (the stimulus is presented—that is, added to the situation) or negative (the stimulus is removed or subtracted from the situation).

	STIMULUS	
	APPETITIVE	AVERSIVE
POSITIVE (add)	POSITIVE REINFORCEMENT (increases behavior)	(POSITIVE) PUNISHMENT (decreases behavior)
NEGATIVE (take away)	NEGATIVE PUNISHMENT (decreases behavior)	NEGATIVE REINFORCEMENT (increases behavior)

CONTINGENCY

two types of contingencies can be combined into four methods of altering or maintaining the frequency of a behavior. These four techniques are the core of behavior management techniques. All the techniques of behavior management, no matter how complex, are related to these four methods and derive their effectiveness from one of these effects on behavior. Note that it is the *relationship* between a stimulus and behavior—that is, the contingency—which determines how behavior will be affected. The effect on behavior is indicated within each cell of the figure. These four core techniques, positive reinforcement, punishment, negative punishment, and negative reinforcement, are discussed next.

Positive Reinforcement

To provide positive reinforcement means to *present* or add an appetitive stimulus contingent on a child's behavior. This is the most useful of the four techniques and the one that should be used most often by anyone involved in planning or implementing behavior management programs for children (or anyone else). The effect on behavior is to *increase* the probability that the reinforced behavior will occur in the future under the same or similar circumstances. For example, if a child is given a piece of candy each time she raises her hand, it is likely that hand raising would occur with increasing frequency until the child was stuffed with candy. In this example, the appetitive stimulus is the candy, and the contingency is that the candy is presented each time the child raises her hand. Similarly, a child who receives praise from his parents after bringing home a good school paper is likely to continue to strive to bring home such papers. In this case, the stimulus is parental praise, and the contingency is that praise is given when the child brings home a good paper. In both cases, the expected result is that the behavior followed by reinforcement will occur more often.

Unfortunately, it is not possible to predict with absolute certainty that presentation of a particular appetitive stimulus will increase behavior. For this reason, it is necessary to observe the effects of a stimulus on behavior before stating that the stimulus is positively reinforcing. The problem is that the effects of a stimulus depend on the particular child's experiences with it. For instance, some children do not like certain types of candy; other children are shy or anxious and try to avoid adult attention. If the child does not like the stimulus, it will not be effective as a reinforcer. Thus, the question of

whether a particular stimulus is positively reinforcing can be answered with certainty only after its effects on behavior are known. The need to verify empirically the effects of a stimulus and contingency on behavior is true for all four behavior management techniques.

Punishment

To punish a behavior means to *present* an aversive stimulus when that behavior occurs. It would be appropriate to call this technique *positive punishment* because the contingency is positive: A stimulus is being *presented* when a particular behavior occurs. The predicted effect is that the behavior will *decrease* in frequency. Punishment and negative reinforcement, which also involves an aversive stimulus, are the two techniques that should be used *least* often in behavior management programs. A typical example would be spanking a child immediately after unacceptable misbehavior. If a spanking is effective, the punished behavior will be less likely to occur after the spanking. For reasons to be discussed later, however, I do not recommend spankings or any other painful method for reducing the frequency of behavior. There are effective nonpainful methods of decreasing behavior, and aversive or painful events do not always decrease behavior because other contingencies may be simultaneously influencing behavior. In fact, more serious problems can result from using a painful aversive stimulus.

Negative Punishment

If the contingency is negative, a stimulus is *removed* when a behavior occurs. The predicted effect of negative punishment is that the behavior will *decrease*. Examples of the operation of negative punishment include all the occasions when a privilege is lost because of misbehavior. For example, if parents withhold dessert because of misbehavior at the dinner table, they are using negative punishment to decrease the probability that the same behavior will occur in the future. Loss of dessert contingent on misbehavior causes the likelihood of future misbehavior at dinner to decrease. In school, the child who misses recess as a consequence of misbehavior in the classroom is being negatively punished. In this case, it is presumed that the child enjoys recess and that its temporary loss will serve to punish—that is, decrease—the misbehavior that occurred in the classroom.

Negative Reinforcement

Negative reinforcement occurs when an *aversive* stimulus is *removed* as a consequence of a particular behavior. The predicted effect is that the negatively reinforced behavior will *increase* in frequency under the same or similar circumstances. Consider, for example, a child who is receiving a spanking from his or her parents. If the spanking is terminated as a result of some behavior such as loud screaming or crying, that behavior is then negatively reinforced and is more likely to occur during future spankings. That is, the crying and screaming of the child can be negatively reinforced by the prompt termination of the spanking. The next time a spanking occurs, the child will be more likely to cry and scream.

Another term used to describe such a situation is *escape*. It is easy to understand how the term derives its meaning, since it is possible to view the child's behavior as a means of escaping an uncomfortable situation. Another term that is often associated with escape is *avoidance*. When an avoidance contingency is in effect, behavior *postpones* the occurrence of an aversive event. In other words, the child does something to cause the aversive event to be canceled, at least temporarily. In contrast, an escape contingency means that the child has contact with the aversive stimulus before the aversive stimulus is terminated. Consider the child who has been spanked for some misbehavior but has also learned to terminate the spankings with a good show of grief and discomfort. With each successive spanking, the child learns to cry and scream in pain just a bit earlier so as to terminate or escape the spanking promptly. Eventually, the mere threat of being spanked may be enough to elicit crying and screaming. If the parent responds by not spanking the child, then the child can be said to have *avoided* the spanking.

Escape contingencies, avoidance contingencies, and negative reinforcement are rarely used in child management, and none of the techniques discussed in this book employ these techniques. It is important to remember these terms, however, because the contingencies do occur in the natural environment and sometimes can explain the unexpected results of attempts to manage the behavior of children.

Summary and Discussion

Table 2.2 illustrates each of the four basic techniques with concrete examples. To review briefly, behavior can be managed or maintained using four core techniques:

positive reinforcement, (positive) punishment, negative punishment, and negative reinforcement. Both positive and negative reinforcement will cause the frequency of behavior to increase, positive reinforcement by adding a stimulus and negative reinforcement by subtracting or taking away a stimulus. Both (positive) punishment and negative punishment will cause the frequency of a behavior to decline. Positive punishment means to present a stimulus that has this effect, and negative punishment means to take away a stimulus.

Whether a particular procedure will have the predicted effect is an empirical question that can only be answered by observing the procedure's actual effects on behavior. The important variable is how the child views the particular stimulus. For instance, most children love to pet small animals, particularly dogs and cats. One would predict that being given the opportunity to pet an animal would be positively reinforcing for most children. Some children, however, have a great fear of certain animals. For these children, the opportunity to pet an animal may be a punishing event. Thus, unless one has some information about the likes and dislikes of a particular child, only the child's behavior reveals what technique is actually being programmed. *The only way to judge the effectiveness of a behavior management program is to observe the effects of the program on the child's behavior.* If the program does not have the desired effects, it should be modified.

The four techniques discussed here have been a source of frustration for students in psychology and education classes. Part of the problem of understanding how to differentiate the techniques is to recognize that, in some ways, the division is arbitrary and depends on what behavior is being observed and what contingency is in effect. Consider a program to reward children for completing arithmetic worksheets by allowing them to go out for recess after lunch with the rest of the class. The stated rule is that all arithmetic worksheets must be completed in order for the children to "earn" recess. If completion of worksheets increased after the rule was implemented, then it would appear that completing worksheets was positively reinforced by allowing access to recess.

Yet, this statement does not tell the whole story of what happened to the children's behavior. Indeed, completion of worksheets increased as predicted. However, if the children were busy completing worksheets, other less desirable behaviors would then be less likely to occur—behaviors that, had they been observed, might have appeared to be negatively punished by the loss of recess. Note, in addition, that an appetitive (desirable) stimu-

Table 2.2. Examples of the Four Basic Techniques for Altering or Maintaining Behavior

BEHAVIOR	STIMULUS/CONTINGENCY	EFFECT ON BEHAVIOR
Reinforcement Joe does a super job of cleaning his area after an art lesson.	Ms. Syverson praises Joe for having such a clean desk after art class. (Appetitive stimulus; positive contingency)	Joe is more likely to clean up thoroughly after art class in the future.
Bonnie is crying loudly in the supermarket.	Bonnie's mother gives Bonnie a piece of candy. (Appetitive stimulus; positive contingency)	Bonnie is more likely to cry next time she is in the supermarket.
Janet is working hard at completing her assigned worksheet	Mrs. Smith walks by Janet and says, "Nice job!" (Appetitive stimulus; positive contingency	Janet is likely to continue working hard.
(Positive) Punishment Sara plays with an electrical socket at home.	Sara's mother spanks her. (Aversive stimulus; positive contingency)	Sara is less likely to play with an electrical socket.
José touches the hot door of the oven.	José receivesd a painful burn. (Aversive stimulus; positive contingency)	José is less likely to touch the oven door again.
Justin takes a toy away from Jack.	Jack immediately hits Justin with his fist. (Aversive stimulus; positive contingency)	Justin is less likely to take a toy away from Jack.
Negative Punishment Joe throws his fork across the table.	Joe is not allowed to have his favorite dessert. (Appetitive stimulus; negative contingency)	Joe is less likely to throw his fork again.
Patty does not spend any of the available class time to complete an assigned worksheet.	Patty misses recess with the rest of her class while she completes the task. (Appetitive stimulus; negative contingency)	Patty is less likely to waste class time again.
Amanda does not finish her home chores on Saturday morning.	Amanda's weekly allowance is not given to her Saturday afternoon. (Appetitive stimulus; negative contingency)	Amanda completes all of her assigned chores on Saturday morning a week later.
Negative Reinforcement Alonzo has a bad headache.	Alonzo takes two acetaminophen tablets and his headache goes away. (Aversive stimulus; negative contingency)	Alonzo is more likely to take acetaminophen next time he has a headache.
George steps out into bright sunlight and can barely see because it is so bright.	George puts on his sunglasses and he is much more comfortable. (Aversive stimulus; negative contingency)	George is likely to continue wearing sunglasses in bright sunlight.
Bonnie's mother hears Bonnie crying loudly in the supermarket and gives her a piece of candy.	Bonnie stops crying. (Aversive stimulus; negative contingency)	Bonnie's mother is more likely to give Bonnie candy when she is crying.

Source: Adapted from Wielkiewicz and Calvert (1989).

lus may be used both to increase and to decrease the frequency of a behavior, depending on the particular contingency. If the contingency is negative, the stimulus is taken away, and the predicted effect is that the behavior will decrease. In other words, when a behavior causes someone to lose something desirable, the behavior will be less likely to occur. If the contingency is positive, the stimulus is presented, and the predicted effect is that the behavior will increase in frequency. That is, when a behavior leads to something valuable, the behavior is more likely to occur. Thus, the same stimulus may have different effects on behavior depending on the contingency that governs what will happen when the behavior occurs.

Finally, it is important to remember that the effect of a particular stimulus can be unique to a particular child. One child may find adult attention very rewarding, as demonstrated by steady increases in behaviors followed by adult attention or praise. Another child may react very differently to attention and praise from an adult. Thus, the actual effect that a particular stimulus and contingency will have on a particular child is always an empirical question. We do not really know whether a "reinforcer" is *really* reinforcing until its effect on behavior is known. This is a key principle in successful behavior management. If a program is not working after a reasonable amount of time, then it should be modified. Finding a more effective reinforcer is often a good strategy.

OTHER DIMENSIONS OF BEHAVIOR MANAGEMENT TECHNIQUES

Although most behavior management techniques fall into one of the four basic categories just discussed, there are several other dimensions of behavior management technology with which the competent behavior management professional must be familiar. The most common of these other dimensions that are frequently relevant in behavior management programs are discussed in this section. Some knowledge of these concepts is necessary for the well-rounded behavior manager because they are useful both in designing behavior management programs and in understanding how behavior is learned and modified. The topics covered in this chapter are discrimination, schedules of reward, modeling, shaping, behavior chains, secondary reinforcement and token reward, the Premack principle, and several methods of decreasing undesirable behavior.

Discrimination

Reinforcement or punishment does not *always* follow a behavior. Often, certain conditions must be met before reinforcement or punishment will occur. At school, for instance, behavior considered appropriate on the playground (e.g., playing football or running) may meet with disapproval if it occurs in the classroom. Likewise, the child who voluntarily studies and completes worksheets during recess is likely to be regarded as "different" by his or her peers. The typical child learns to discriminate recess from the classroom by being rewarded for the behaviors considered appropriate in each setting.

When a behavior is not rewarded (or punished) unless a particular stimulus or set of stimuli is present, that stimulus is known as a *discriminative stimulus,* one that sets the occasion for or signals the availability of reward or punishment. When a child responds appropriately to a discriminative stimulus, the child is said to have learned the discrimination or learned to discriminate the stimuli that signal the appropriateness of behavior. Discrimination is also the name of the process by which a child learns to respond appropriately to stimuli that are similar. Examples would be learning to name colors or recognize the letters of the alphabet. Discriminations are learned because the discriminative stimuli signal what behavior is appropriate and likely to be rewarded.

A classroom teacher is teaching children to discriminate when she or he designates certain times (e.g., work periods) when talking is not allowed, and other times (e.g., free time) when talking is all right. The labels are used as discriminative stimuli when they are announced at the beginning of a particular period of time, and the teacher responds appropriately to behavior during those periods. The teacher who makes the stimuli as obvious and different from each other as possible will be the most successful at maintaining the desired conditions. For example, a reversible sign with DON'T TALK in red letters on one side and FREE TIME in green letters on the other side would be more effective than just an announcement from the teacher at the beginning of one period or the other.

A child who behaves unacceptably at school as a result of conflict and inconsistent discipline at home will have a harder time discriminating the contingencies that operate in school because of interference from the learning that takes place at home. Ideally, the child's parents would become involved in a behavior management program with the dual goals of improving the child's behavior in school and helping the parents improve their own child management skills. But eliciting parental cooperation is not always possible. The result is an unfortunate, though not hopeless, situation. Such children tend to respond slowly to behavior management programs at school because of their need to discriminate between the characteristics of the home and school environments. However, with patient, consistent administration of the behavior management program, these children can learn to behave appropriately in school even if behavior at home remains a problem.

Most behavior management programs involve explicit or implicit discriminative stimuli. The individual planning a behavior management program needs to take note of such stimuli and design the program to enhance their effectiveness. This involves, first, making the discriminative stimuli as distinctively different as possible. The more obvious and different the stimuli are, the more likely the child is to attend to them and learn to behave appropriately in their presence. Second, the consequences for behavior (either appetitive or aversive) should be as consistent as possible with respect to the discriminative stimuli. If consequences for behavior occur inconsistently across the discriminative stimuli, the child will not acquire the discrimination. Another method that may promote the acquisition of the discrimination is to provide different rewards in the presence of each discriminative stimulus (e.g., Carlson & Wielkiewicz, 1976; Overmier, 1988).

Extinction and Schedules of Reinforcement

Extinction refers to the gradual decrease in the frequency of a behavior that occurs when reinforcement is discontinued. The fact that extinction occurs is the reason that the initial advice to a teacher seeking consultation about a disruptive pupil is often "ignore the behavior and maybe it will go away." Extinction is also one of the techniques that underlies the Golden Rule of Behavior Management, introduced in Chapter 1: Ignore, as much as possible, all minor annoyances and misbehavior. The success of this advice depends on whether all sources of reinforcement can be eliminated. If the child receives no other reinforcement for the behavior, then extinction is likely to take place.

An interesting relationship exists between extinction and the proportion of responses that are reinforced. If every single response (of a certain class or type) is reinforced, then reinforcement is said to be *continuous*.

When some responses are not reinforced, reinforcement is said to be partial or *intermittent*. It is possible to deliver intermittent reinforcement on four different schedules: fixed interval, fixed ratio, variable interval, and variable ratio. In a fixed ratio schedule of reinforcement, reinforcement follows every nth response, where n may be any number greater than 2. (If $n = 1$, reinforcement is continuous.) When a variable ratio schedule is in effect, reinforcement still depends on the *number* of responses, but the number of responses required between instances of reinforcement varies unpredictably around some average value. In fixed and variable *interval* schedules, reinforcement is delivered for the next response following passage of either a fixed or a variable amount of time.

It is not important to remember the definitions of the four schedules of reinforcement, but it is important to understand the effect of continuous versus partial or intermittent reinforcement. The effect is simple. When reinforcement is discontinued, it will take much longer for an intermittently reinforced response to disappear than for a continuously reinforced response. That is, intermittently reinforced responses are said to be more *resistant to extinction* than continuously reinforced responses.

This well-established fact is important in planning behavior management programs for two reasons. First, if an assessment reveals that an undesirable behavior is being reinforced on an intermittent schedule, it will be much more resistant to change than a continuously reinforced response. In such a case, the program will work best if it is extended beyond normal time limits and if an alternative, incompatible response is strengthened as part of the management program. Second, when a new or previously weak skill is being modified via a behavior management program, it is important to move from continuous to intermittent reinforcement before the program is terminated, so the new behavior will exist at a maximum strength. This is the goal of Step 8 of a formal behavior management program.

Shaping and Behavior Chains

Many of the skills that children need must be learned in a stepwise manner, either because they are complicated or because they involve a large number of steps. Long division, tying a shoe, getting dressed, walking, and printing letters of the alphabet are examples of such skills. If these skills were taught by rewarding only perfect performance, both trainer and trainee would be very frustrated. Instead, such complicated skills are usually taught in small steps. The methods typically used are shaping and treating the skill as a behavior chain.

Shaping. Shaping a behavior means rewarding successive approximations of the target behavior. At first, one rewards less accurate or expert responses than will be acceptable later in the learning process. The criterion for reward is raised in small steps until only a polished performance is rewarded. That is, a performance that was acceptable and rewarded early in the training is not rewarded at a later time, because the criterion has been raised so that the child must emit a performance that is closer to the goal.

A parent teaching a child to hit a ball with a bat is one example of the shaping process. The parent begins by prompting the child (giving verbal directions, guiding the child in correct motions, and modeling for the child) to assume a proper batting stance. The first few times the ball is thrown to the child, the parent rewards any swing at the ball no matter how close it comes to the ball. As the child gains skill, the criteria for reinforcement (attention and praise) are changed. Slowly but surely, the child is required to come closer and closer to hitting the ball in order to receive positive feedback. Eventually, only physical contact with the ball is rewarded. Later, only good contact that propels the ball a fair distance is rewarded. In this manner the parent shapes or sculpts the behavior by changing the criterion for a reward until the goal of firmly hitting the ball is reached.

A teacher might use a similar technique to teach a child to write a letter of the alphabet. The teacher would begin by rewarding an attempt that is shaped somewhat like the target letter. As the child practices the letter, the teacher would raise the criterion for reinforcement until only a near perfect attempt, which clearly has all the major features of the letter and does not look like any other letter, is rewarded. In point of fact, it would be unusual for a teacher to sit down with individual children and shape their letter writing and copying skills. Instead, the usual technique is to have each child trace letters to learn their basic shape, then slowly reduce the amount of the letter that is traced while increasing the amount to be formed by the child. However, as the children's skill increases, the teacher must still judge which copies are acceptable and which copies indicate a need for more practice. In this manner, the children's letter copying is shaped by the feedback from the teacher.

Shaping and rewarding successive approximations may be necessary in any behavior management program in which the child learns a new skill. It is most helpful if the steps in the shaping process can be stated as part of the behavior management program. For instance, a fourth grader who does not show appropriate work behaviors in the classroom could initially be rewarded for being on task for 2 minutes. Then, over the course of the behavior management program, the amount of time spent on task and the amount of work required in a time period could be raised in successive steps until the child's behavior resembled that of other students in the classroom. Unfortunately, it is not very often that a behavior to be shaped has such obvious steps toward acceptable performance. Typically, shaping a behavior more closely resembles an art than a technique of science.

The most troublesome aspect of shaping a behavior is deciding when to raise the criteria for reinforcement. In my own experience, more reinforced trials are necessary for a given level of performance at the beginning of the shaping process than in the middle or at the end. Also, the process seems to go most smoothly when a fairly constant rate of reinforcement can be maintained. Thus, it would be desirable to raise the criteria for reinforcement at a slow enough pace that the rate of reinforcement does not drop suddenly. Otherwise the child may become frustrated over the loss of reinforcement and become uncooperative.

Behavior chains. A *behavior chain* is a series of discrete behaviors learned in a particular sequence. The steps in making a bed or doing a long division problem are examples of behavior chains. Typically, behavior chains are taught by beginning with the first step and taking the child through the chain in sequence until the entire chain of behaviors is mastered. This is appropriate when the child has the ability to memorize the sequence and is able to prompt herself or himself verbally while performing the chain. However, there is an alternative method of teaching behavior chains, rooted in animal learning experiments, which also is effective.

In this method, the *last* behavior in the sequence is taught first and then behaviors are added to the chain in *reverse* order. Consider bed-making as an example. In order to teach this skill to a young child, the parent would first perform all the steps in the process except the last, leaving it to the child to complete. Successful completion of the last step would be followed by generous social reinforcement and praise. Then, after the child had mastered the last step in the process, the parent would begin to complete the task except for the last two steps and would reward the child only if these were completed. As the child continued to learn, the parent would perform less and less of the sequence while the child would be required to do more and more in order to receive praise. Technically, what is happening is that each step in the sequence becomes a signal or discriminative stimulus for the next step in the sequence.

It would be possible to teach a variety of academic and nonacademic behavior sequences in the manner just described, but in both the classroom and the home several different teaching and learning processes are likely to be taking place at once. Behavior is being modeled by adults, who may be both shaping behavior and rewarding partial or complete performance of behavior chains. The point to remember is that various methods are available for teaching complex behaviors to children. When remediation of a behavior problem requires teaching a complex new skill to the child, these methods should be used.

Classical versus Operant Conditioning

The majority of behavior management techniques, including those discussed up to this point, involve what is called *operant* or *instrumental* conditioning. What these techniques have in common is a reward or punishment that is delivered as a *consequence* of a predefined *response*. The criterion as to whether operant conditioning has occurred is whether or not the probability of the target response changes across time.

Classical conditioning involves the same stimuli as operant conditioning, but the relationship of the stimuli is different. In classical conditioning, an appetitive or aversive stimulus is presented after a *stimulus*. When classical conditioning is being conducted in a laboratory, behavior is measured but has no influence on whether an aversive or appetitive stimulus is delivered. Classical conditioning, then, involves *pairing* of stimuli, independent of behavior. The outcome of classical conditioning is that the stimulus presented first takes on characteristics of the aversive or appetitive stimulus, in terms of its ability to elicit certain responses from the organism. Classical conditioning is believed to play a role in the acquisition of fear, anxiety, and phobias. In addition, some of the ways of managing phobias, anxiety, and fears involve techniques derived from classical conditioning.

Observational Learning

It is not always necessary that children learn new skills through trial and error. In fact, this type of learning can be inefficient and even dangerous. The natural environment is full of lethal consequences that would strike any adult or child who chose an incorrect response. Crossing the street at the wrong time, failing to heed obvious signs of impending danger, learning to swim, and learning to drive a car are only a few examples of learning situations with hazardous consequences. Instead of learning by trial and error, it is also possible to acquire new behavior via vicarious processes. Vicarious processes involve observation as opposed to direct participation.

Observation of a model engaging in some behavior can, according to Bandura (1969), result in three different effects. First, it is possible for the observing child to acquire new behaviors that were not previously in his or her repertoire. This might include virtually any behavior that could be the target of a behavior management program. The second potential effect of observing a model is that already learned responses could become either inhibited or disinhibited. This effect results from observing the consequences of the others' behavior. For example, a child's disruptive behavior could be inhibited by seeing another child experience punishment for similar behavior. The third effect that observing a model can produce is to set the occasion for performing some previously learned behavior—for example, when a classroom teacher and a child go to a window to watch an event taking place outside, and the other students in the class follow suit.

In addition to the simple presentation of an observable stimulus, several variables have an impact on the effectiveness of observational learning. Primary among these variables are attentional factors, because a child who is not attending to the relevant aspects of the model's performance will not learn enough to reproduce the behavior. Variables that influence attention include the attractiveness and rewarding qualities of the model, the vividness and novelty of the modeling stimuli, and motivational conditions. If a child is going to acquire behavior via observation at one point in time for performance at some later time, the information gained during the observation must be retained in memory. Repetition of the behavior sequence to be acquired and rehearsal of the material by the observer would be two variables generally conceded to have the greatest influence on retention. Although the first is under the control of adults, the second is not, except by indirect means. Again, motivational factors in the observational learning situation may greatly influence retention. Another factor, largely beyond the control of adults, is whether the child's motor skills are sufficient to allow the child to reproduce the observed behavior. If remediation of behavior via observational learning is attempted and either motor or memory processes appear to prevent acquisition of the new behavior, then additional assessment may be needed. Either a complete assessment of academic skills or assessment by an occupational or physical therapist may be in order.

Incentive and motivational processes also play a key role in observational learning. That is, a behavior management program can be designed to reward a child for copying the behavior of another. Beginning such a program is likely to have a positive effect on attention, motor performance, and retention as well. A behavior management program that does not directly involve observational learning can be enhanced by employing some of its principles. For instance, if one child in a class is exhibiting excessive disruptive behavior, rewarding another child in the class for appropriate behavior may enhance the probability that the first child's behavior will improve and may speed the progress of a behavior management program. In cases where a child lacks important skills, observational learning using a peer model could prove more efficient than shaping the behavior. In sum, observational learning can either serve as a useful adjunct to a behavior management program or be its central feature.

Secondary Reinforcement and Token Reward

A reinforcer has been described as an event or object, presentation of which leads to an increased probability of behavior in the future. For example, if a child receives candy from her mother when she is crying, the candy is likely to reinforce crying and make the behavior more likely in the future. Edible reinforcers such as candy or other food are regarded as *primary* reinforcers because they directly satisfy a biological need. Even the most cursory observation of human behavior, however, reveals that humans work to obtain many reinforcers that do not directly satisfy any biological need. Money, attention, good grades in school, the first spot in line, points, gift certificates, verbal praise, smile faces, and sports cards are just a few examples of effective reinforcers that do not directly satisfy a biological need. These kinds of reinforcers are called *secondary reinforcers.*

Secondary reinforcers gain their reinforcing power through *association* with primary reinforcers. For example, for most children, getting good grades in school is reinforcing, although the precise associations that make good grades reinforcing may vary from child to child. For some children, good grades may be reinforcing because they result in parental praise, which has been previously associated with having their parents meet important needs. For other children, good grades may be reinforcing because the children are paid for each "A," which gives them the means to buy food, clothing, and other material reinforcers. Secondary reinforcers play an extremely important role in understanding human behavior as well as in the development of behavior management programs. An excellent example of the structured use of secondary reinforcers is in token reinforcement programs.

Token reward programs are among the most useful procedures available for behavior management programs. The earliest descriptions of the structured use of token reinforcement were by Allyon and Azrin (1965, 1968). These authors constructed a structured *token economy* in a ward of a state mental hospital. Target behaviors consisted of responses that were necessary or useful to patients, such as washing dishes, mopping floors, learning job skills or self-care, or serving meals. These behaviors were rewarded with metal tokens that could be exchanged for opportunities to engage in behaviors that had a high probability of occurring when patients were free to choose their own activities. Attending movies and other special events, having opportunities to talk to hospital staff, and taking walks on the hospital grounds are examples of effective reinforcers. The results of the program were that hospital patients functioned more independently and effectively, and some were even discharged to a halfway house after long stays in the hospital.

Token rewards have been used countless times to improve the behavior of children (Kazdin, 1977, 1983; O'Leary & Drabman, 1971). For example, Ryback and Staats (1970) studied the efficacy of a home-based token reward program for children with reading deficits. First, the children were presented with new words to be learned until they could be read without error. Then the children were rewarded for reading paragraphs containing the new words. Finally, the children read a whole story silently and answered questions about it. During this training, correct responses were rewarded with tokens that could be exchanged for cash. More difficult responses were rewarded with more valuable tokens. As a result of the training, these children showed significant improvement in reading skill. Bushell, Wrobel, and Michaelis (1968) demonstrated that a token system increased on-task study behavior of a group of young children attending summer school as long as the backup reward was made contingent on having sufficient tokens. When the backup reward (access to a half-hour special event) was available without tokens, on-task behavior declined even though tokens (now worthless) were still distributed contingently.

The main advantages of behavior management programs based on token rewards are that tokens can be delivered without interfering with ongoing projects or behavior, and their effectiveness is not tied to a single reward. Because implementing a token reward program is very similar to paying people for their work, the concept is easy to communicate to consultees and parents, who are likely to view such programs positively. Almost anything of little or no value that children can exchange for something desirable can be used as a token. Gold stars, points, marbles, specially marked pieces of paper, various chips (e.g., poker chips), or anything else that children can conveniently receive and save by can be used as a token. Concrete objects that can be handled are best for younger children; points usually work well with older children. The simplest token reward programs can be implemented by telling the child, "If you can earn five of these, then you can trade them in for anything in this box!" The success of the program will depend on the child's understanding of the instructions and the value of the rewards contained in the box. Several examples of formal behavior management programs involving token reward are described in Part II.

The Premack Principle

David Premack (cited in Ross, 1981) observed that a response of higher probability can be used to reinforce a response of lower probability. Teachers and parents who say, "Before you can go outside, you must finish your work," are applying this principle. More than anything else, this principle serves as a reminder that by watching children one can learn what they like to do. Then, if one has or can gain control over the preferred activity, it can be used to reward less likely but desirable behavior. Furthermore, even the child who is most resistant to a behavior management program must be gaining some reinforcement from some source. By watching and learning what activities a child prefers, it can be possible to construct an effective behavior management program.

Timeout and Other Methods of Decreasing Undesirable Behavior

Almost all children engage in undesirable behavior at some time in their development. What is considered unacceptable behavior varies from parent to parent, teacher to teacher, situation to situation, and time to time. All school personnel are faced with deciding what constitutes acceptable boundaries for children's behavior. Once boundaries have been established, how to deal with unacceptable behavior becomes the important issue. Because spanking and other forms of corporal punishment are not given consideration in this book, other methods of decreasing or eliminating undesirable behavior are needed. Fortunately, several effective methods exist.

Ignoring behavior. The least troublesome method of eliminating behavior is to ignore it. This is particularly true for the classroom teacher, whose primary means of behavior control is verbal reprimand. Frequently, verbal reprimands have been found to have reinforcing rather than punishing properties; that is, reprimands often increase or maintain the strength of the behavior they follow. Similarly, embarrassed or exasperated parents who allow a child's temper tantrum to be followed by some desirable event are increasing the likelihood of a future tantrum in similar situations. By ignoring such behavior, the positive consequences that might follow it can be eliminated, thereby decreasing the chances that the child will behave unacceptably in the future.

There are two potential difficulties in attempting to eliminate behavior by ignoring it. First, it may be a relatively long time before the behavior is finally extinguished, especially if the behavior has been followed by positive consequences under similar circumstances in the past. A behavior that has appeared recently will be easier to eliminate. The second difficulty is that ignoring a behavior may lead to a temporary increase in its frequency before it begins to decline. This increase is typically attributed to the frustration that results from the unfulfilled expectation of reward. Furthermore, if the behavior is attended to (i.e., rewarded) after it has been ignored on several previous occasions, it will be even more difficult to eliminate the behavior because of the effects of intermittent reinforcement. Thus, the key to eliminating a behavior by ignoring it is to be patient and consistent.

Timeout. Timeout has already been mentioned several

times as a technique of nonviolent punishment. The essence of timeout is that a child is placed in a boring location, where nothing of interest is available, immediately after some undesirable behavior occurs. The timeout location should not be frightening or lacking in light or air (i.e., it should not be a closet). In school, an isolated chair, the hallway, an office, a coatroom, or a specially constructed area might be used for timeout. Some schools use a portable timeout area consisting of a U-shaped wall about 5 feet tall, which can be placed around a desk located in the rear of the classroom. Timeout is a simple procedure that can also be used at home, where the kitchen, a guest room, a stairwell, a laundry room, or a chair could become a timeout area.

The length of a timeout period can vary considerably. Some authors suggest 1 minute of timeout for each year of age. Thus, a typical range might be between 5 and 10 minutes. Timeout should be administered *immediately* after the undesirable behavior occurs. The person administering the timeout should be calm but firm. The timeout may be accompanied by some brief explanation, such as, "You can't stay here if you [hit the teacher]." If the child continues to display undesirable behavior, such as a tantrum, during the timeout period, the timeout should be extended until the child is behaving appropriately. The purpose of such an extension is to avoid rewarding undesirable behavior by releasing the child from the timeout. Some states and school districts have guidelines regarding the length and location of timeout periods, and these should be consulted to be sure they are not violated. Once the child has been released from timeout, it may be useful to discuss briefly why timeout was administered and have the child think of alternative ways that the situation leading to timeout could have been handled.

Wherry (1983) cautions that the use of timeout involves the potential for violation of the individual rights of the student. He advises that informed consent be obtained from the child's parents prior to the use of timeout, response cost, and overcorrection (a method used to suppress undesirable behavior). In addition, Wherry suggests the following guidelines for the use of timeout based on judicial proceedings:

1. Timeout should be employed only in situations where the student's behavior creates "substantive" disruption.

2. The length of timeout should not exceed 50 minutes to 1 hour.
3. The child should be provided with books or lesson materials during timeout.
4. The student should be closely and directly supervised.

In general, it seems that practitioners can avoid problems if timeout is employed only to decrease very disruptive behavior and if concurrent programs to increase desirable behavior are implemented.

It is also important to monitor the effect of timeout on the target behavior. Solnick, Rincover, and Peterson (1977) cite two attempts to use timeout that failed. In one instance, timeout was actually reinforcing to a girl who engaged in self-stimulating behavior during the timeout period. The opportunity to engage in such behavior during the timeout actually caused the target behavior to increase. Thus, in applying timeout, it is important to establish that it actually causes the target behavior to decrease. Within a classroom, this might fail to occur if the timeout allowed the child to escape from an unpleasant situation, such as doing seatwork, or if the child managed to obtain social reinforcement from peers during the timeout period. Observation of the child's behavior during the timeout period can provide some information about how the timeout period is functioning.

Solnick et al. also studied the effectiveness of timeout with a sixteen-year-old retarded boy. It was found that timeout was ineffective in reducing undesirable behavior until the nontimeout environment was enriched so that it included more reinforcing stimuli. Similarly, timeout administered in a school environment should result in the loss of at least some reinforcement, such as the opportunity to reveive positive attention from the teacher. If the timeout and nontimeout environments are not distinctively different, timeout can not be expected to be effective.

Foxx and Shapiro (1978) described a unique form of timeout that may be appropriate under some circumstances. For their procedure, each child is required to wear an object such as a ribbon that could be established as a discriminative stimulus for positive reinforcement. Whenever a student misbehaved, the ribbon was removed and the child was excluded from all forms of teacher-dispensed reinforcement and participation in rewarding activities. In this procedure, the child is in timeout but remains in the classroom. Foxx and Shapiro demonstrated that a three-minute timeout (extended if

misbehavior continued) was effective in reducing misbehavior. They suggested that the procedure would be
effective and convenient with lower functioning special education classes. An advantage of the procedure
was that classroom visitors knew with which students
they could interact and which students were to be ignored.

In order to implement such a procedure effectively, it
is necessary to establish the ribbons as discriminative
stimuli for positive reinforcement. Foxx and Shapiro
accomplished this by providing teacher praise and edibles to the students for good behavior and wearing their
ribbon. The procedure could also be faded out by substituting a less obvious discriminative stimulus such as
a wristband.

Removing a privilege. Another method of decreasing
undesirable behavior is to remove a privilege, reward, or
access to a desirable activity when a child behaves in an
unacceptable manner. This would represent an application of negative punishment, because an appetitive
stimulus is removed (subtracted) from the situation. For
instance, the child who misbehaves in class or fails to
complete work (assuming this is a reasonable expectation), could be forbidden from going outside for recess. Parents and teachers typically control numerous
rewarding activities that can be withdrawn when a
child's behavior is unacceptable. However, this method
will not work well if the child ends up losing all or most
privileges, because the child then has nothing further to
lose by misbehaving. In such cases, a concurrent program to reward appropriate behavior will be necessary.

Logical consequences. When the consequence for an
undesirable behavior is logically related to the behavior
itself, one is employing a behavior change technique
known as *logical consequences.* This technique involves
letting the natural and logical consequences of behavior
affect the child (Dreikurs & Grey, 1970). For example,
if a child has spent the morning in off-task behavior and
fails to complete seatwork, then a logical consequence
might be that the child must miss a desired activity (e.g.,
recess) in order to complete the unfinished work. In the
home, the parents of a child who refuses to pick up his
or her dirty clothes might respond by refusing to pick up
or wash the clothes. Dirty, unwashed clothes are made
the logical consequence of not picking clothes up. A
child who carelessly or purposefully breaks an object
could be required to pay for replacing the item. When
logical consequences for misbehavior can be identified,
they can be very effective in reducing the problem
behavior.

Saying "No!" One universal method of eliminating undesirable behavior is simply to say "No!" in a strong,
firm voice when undesirable behavior occurs. For some
teachers and parents, this technique is very effective,
whereas for others it is almost totally useless. Why? The
difference lies in the consistency with which a repeat
occurrence of the undesired behavior after the word
"No!" has been followed by some action, such as timeout
or loss of a privilege. If the child "knows" that the word
"No!" carries some weight and that repetition of the
undesired behavior will consistently lead to timeout or
loss of a privilege, then the child is likely to heed the
warning. On the other hand, if "No!" is an empty threat
only occasionally backed up by action, then the child is
not likely to respond.

Rewarding other behavior. Probably the most important aspect of decreasing undesirable behavior is to
provide fewer opportunities for such behavior to occur
by rewarding the behavior that is desirable in the same
situation. When desirable behavior occurs at a high rate,
undesirable behavior is less likely in that situation.
For example, if a child frequently behaves aggressively, the amount of aggression will decrease as the
amount of cooperative play increases. In all cases where
one is trying to decrease the frequency of an undesirable behavior, a concurrent program to increase
preferable behavior in that situation should be in
effect.

REVIEW

Terms to Remember and Review

positive reinforcement	negative reinforcement
(positive) punishment	negative punishment
stimulus	contingency
positive contingency	negative contingency
avoidance	escape
aversive stimulus	appetitive stimulus
secondary reinforcement	token economy
discrimination	primary reinforcer
extinction	shaping
schedules of reinforcement	behavior chain
classical conditioning	operant conditioning
secondary reinforcer	token reward

Study and Discussion Questions

1. Explain what is meant by a positive contingency.
2. Explain what is meant by a negative contingency.
3. What must be demonstrated before it can be stated that a stimulus is positively reinforcing?
4. What is the difference between avoidance and escape?
5. Why is it possible for the same stimulus to have opposite effects on behavior?

Group Project

Make up two additional examples of each of the four methods of increasing or decreasing behavior. Specify the stimulus, the contingency, the name of the procedure, and the predicted effect on behavior. What procedure—positive reinforcement, negative reinforcement, (positive) punishment, or negative punishment—was hardest to illustrate with an original example? Why?

CHAPTER 3

STEP-BY-STEP PROCEDURES FOR ASSESSMENT AND MANAGEMENT OF BEHAVIOR PROBLEMS

Assessment is the information-gathering process that leads to decisions about how a problem situation will be approached. Assessment of young children is challenging because they are not likely to provide much of the essential information needed for decision making. Young children are the least able to express their feelings accurately and discuss events that may be contributing to behavior problems in school. To conduct a reasonably complete assessment, information is needed from at least three sources: the child, the child's parents, and school personnel. A systematic approach to child behavior management must also examine the context out of which the problem behavior arises, including the child's developmental status and the systems in which the child functions (Lucco, 1991; Mash & Terdal, 1988).

Consider the plight of a six-year-old boy whose teacher has observed a precipitous decline in academic performance and the appearance of uncharacteristic disruptive behavior that disturbs the rest of the class. The most direct approach to this situation is to measure the baseline (preintervention) rate of occurrence for the key behaviors and develop a behavior management program to change them. One strategy might be to reward academic performance and negatively punish disruptive behavior with loss of a privilege. However, if assessment reveals that the child's parents are in the midst of marital

conflict surrounding a divorce, a broader approach is likely to be more helpful because learning and general behavior will almost certainly be adversely affected by the emotional conflict and turmoil surrounding the divorce.

In cases where environmental stresses underlie behavior problems in school, even the best behavior management program may fail to solve the problem. The child really needs additional services, such as counseling or family therapy, that address the entire context of the behavior. Often, the more severe the behavior problem shown by a child in school, the more likely it is that the problem does not exist in isolation but, instead, is part of a system of problems involving both the school and the child's home. Although problems within the family are sometimes beyond the reach of school personnel, it is a disservice to the child to ignore the possibility that interventions going beyond the school setting might be needed. Ideally, a menu of services should be available so the child can function at his or her best in school. For example, the child's long-term needs may be best served with a combination of individual counseling, a behavior management program, and family therapy.

One purpose of this chapter is to outline a general method for assessment of problem behaviors. By answering the assessment questions discussed in this chapter, a picture of the problem behavior and its context can be developed. The second purpose of the chapter is to describe the general process of managing behavior problems.

A GENERAL METHOD FOR ASSESSMENT OF PROBLEM BEHAVIORS

The assessment and management of children's behavior can be approached either formally or informally. An informal assessment or management approach is most helpful when it is believed that the problem behavior is not very serious and is restricted in scope. For example, a kindergarten child who frequently calls out in class and interrupts other students may present a minor problem, limited in scope, that can be resolved without resorting to detailed assessment or complicated behavior management procedures . Preventing more serious problems and avoiding disruption of the child's academic progress are the main goals of informal assessment and behavior management. Because time is limited in any educator's day and prevention is often the most cost-effective approach to solving problems, the behavior management efforts of school personnel are often informal. The characteristics of informal assessment and behavior management are (1) documentation is minimal; (2) assessment is limited; (3) parental involvement is minimal; (4) such programs are typically conducted by the classroom teacher, perhaps with some consultative assistance; (5) the success of the program is often judged subjectively; and (6) the program typically involves a relatively small time commitment.

A formal assessment or a formal behavior management program involves more attention to detail and addresses all the steps outlined in this chapter. The division between formal and informal procedures is arbitrary. Many times, an informal effort to resolve a behavior problem may evolve into a formal behavior management program. Most behavior management efforts, which are subject to the very real restrictions imposed by the limited resources available in a school, are likely to represent a compromise between the formal and informal approaches. The problem with informal methods is that something important may be overlooked. For example, one possibility that all educators must consider is that a child is the victim of some form of abuse. Educators are legally mandated to report such suspicions to appropriate child protection agencies.

It is also possible that an exclusive focus on *problem* behaviors could cause the real problem to be overlooked. For example, a child may occasionally show violently aggressive behavior in the classroom. However, a thorough assessment may reveal that the child lacks social skills, such as making requests and engaging in cooperative play, and consequently behaves aggressively to gain attention. Furthermore, it may turn out that the child is socially isolated and neglected at home, and thus has no opportunity to learn appropriate behavior. The child's best interests would not be served by implementing a behavior management program focused exclusively on the aggressive outbursts. Other services, such as family intervention and social skills training, would also be needed.

Regardless of whether an informal or formal assessment has been done, there is always the possibility that some important fact has not been obtained or that a hypothesis about the child was not tested. Any analysis of a problem situation, including the management program proposed to remediate it, is like a hypothesis subject to verification via an empirical test. That is, both the conclusions supported by the assessment results and the resulting behavior management program are subject to change as new facts become available. For instance, after many weeks of a moderately successful formal behavior management program, a child's mother could reveal to the assessment team that the child's father is an active alcoholic and that she has just filed for divorce. Such a revelation would shed new light on the problem. Although the behavior management program may be continued with only minor modifications, supplementary services, such as counseling or family therapy, may be needed to help the child cope with the family situation. The advantage of conducting a formal assessment is that a complete picture of the child's needs is more likely to be developed. Flexibility at all stages of the assessment and behavior management processes is an extremely valuable asset for all school personnel who conduct behavior management programs.

The following description of the formal assessment process has been adapted from Kanfer and Phillips (1970), with modifications to make it more applicable to the school environment and school-related problems. The ten steps involved in the assessment process are listed here, followed by a detailed explanation of each step.

Step 1: General analysis of the problem and its impact on academic learning and performance

Step 2: Clarification of the problem

Step 3: Motivational and reinforcement analysis

Step 4: Developmental analysis of the problem

Step 5: Analysis of the child's self-control

Step 6: Analysis of the child's social relationships in school

Step 7: Analysis of the child's sensory capacity

Step 8: Analysis of the child's home environment

Step 9: Analysis of interpersonal relationships at home

Step 10: Initial identification of the problem and targets for the behavior management program

Step 1: General analysis of the problem and its impact upon academic learning and performance. What is the thing to do when a behavior problem appears? The first step is to state the problem in general terms and reconstruct its history. Documentation of any informal attempts to correct the problem will prove very helpful if a formal behavior management program is necessary. The earliest attempts to remediate a problem may include strategies such as ignoring a behavior, placing the child in a different location, having a conference with the child, communicating with the child's parents, conferring with a colleague, or using "assertive discipline." When these initial informal efforts fail, a more structured approach can prove helpful.

If informal interventions have proved unsuccessful, a number of different personnel may become involved along with the classroom teacher who initially identified the problem. For instance, the child's parent may give permission for a school psychologist or special education teacher to assess the child. In some school systems, the teacher may consult formally with colleagues, a child study team, the school principal, or any other person with expertise in the problem area. Finally, the classroom teacher may find that help is unavailable or unnecessary and proceed to deal with the problem alone. Regardless of who is involved, the basic structure of the assessment process remains the same.

Once a problem has been tentatively identified, some initial questions about it should be answered. The most obvious question is: What is the problem? The answer should be stated in whatever terms seem appropriate at the time. It is also helpful to classify the problem as either a *skill deficit* (the child fails to emit a desired behavior) or a *behavior excess* (the child is doing too much of something undesirable). This distinction has a profound influence on the direction of the behavior management program. Skill deficits may include problems such as failure to complete assigned tasks, absence of social

interactions, poor grooming, or any other desirable behavior that occurs at a low rate. In contrast, behavior excesses are undesirable behaviors that occur too often, such as physical aggression, yelling at teachers, talking during work periods, or other undesirable but frequent behaviors. Generally, it is in the child's best interests to focus behavior management programs on skill deficits whenever possible because substituting appropriate behavior for problem behavior is likely to provide the best long-term solution. Reducing inappropriate behavior may leave the child still lacking in the skills needed for success in the problem situation.

Once the problem has been tentatively identified, its relation to academic performance can be assessed. This should be one of the primary questions because the main purpose of being in school is to learn. A cumulative file review will help in establishing a history of academic accomplishment that can be compared to the child's current performance. Eventually, a complete assessment of the child's academic skills (ability, achievement, and motivation) may be needed. The assessment may reveal that the child apparently has the academic skills to succeed in school but that the behavior problem is interfering with classroom performance. On the other hand, the assessment could suggest that the child has a learning problem that needs to be addressed. In such a case, behavior management procedures may be needed to supplement services directed at remediating the academic problem.

Shapiro and Lentz (1985) describe a behavioral approach to academic assessment that begins with a determination of the child's expected level of achievement and contrasts this with the child's current achievement. The method focuses on the curriculum the child is expected to master rather than on standardized achievement tests. Assessments of student progress are taken directly from the material the child is expected to learn. It may not be necessary to design specific tests for this purpose; regular classroom work may be sufficient to provide the needed information. As pointed out by Shapiro and Lentz, it is important to determine whether or not the child has actually mastered the skills being taught. A child who fails to complete an arithmetic worksheet independently, but who is known to be able to do the work when closely supervised, has a very different problem from the child who has not learned the skills needed to complete the worksheet. The distinction is important because a behavior management program may not be appropriate for the child who has a learning problem interfering with skill acquisition. When a learning problem is suspected, a thorough academic assessment may be recommended by the child study team.

It is also appropriate to analyze the problem behavior, as initially defined, in terms of its frequency, intensity, and duration. How often does it occur? How intense is it? How long does it last? At the early stages of assessment, these questions are probably best answered by keeping a running log that notes each significant incident in narrative form. Later, this record can be used to help develop a more detailed and concrete definition of the target behavior. It is also important to gain information regarding stimulus conditions that tend to surround occurrences of the problem behavior. This includes both conditions that precede the behavior and those that follow it—that is, when and where the behavior occurs; what, if anything, seems to set it off; and how adults and the child's peers react to it. A running log can be a valuable source of information for answering these questions.

Finally, it can be important to obtain a historical view of the problem situation. This means asking previous teachers if they encountered similar problems with the child and ascertaining what interventions have already been attempted. It may also be helpful to learn when and where the problem behavior was first observed, information that may provide a direction for planning an appropriate intervention. For example, considered the case of a first-grade child who exhibits severe temper tantrums. If an interview with the child's kindergarten teacher reveals that the first tantrum occurred when he encountered a nurse who was about to administer a hearing test, it may suggest a hypothesis that tantrums are a device for escaping feared situations. This, in turn, may lead to a more detailed assessment of the child's fears, resulting in a more effective behavior management program focused on the child's fearfulness and social skills deficits.

When Step 1 is complete, the assessor should have a general impression of the problem behavior, including a tentative definition, a brief history of the problem and previous intervention efforts, and a list of stimulus conditions that tend to surround the problem's occurrence. Interestingly, the activity of looking closely at problem behavior sometimes resolves the problem without any overt attempts at remediation. This can occur for different reasons, such as subtle shifts in patterns of attending to the child's behavior. Or the "problem" might simply be a temporary occurrence that does not require any intervention, or responds immediately to the standard management techniques used in the classroom.

Should this happen, it can be documented for future reference.

Step 2: Clarification of the problem. Step 2 is an extension of the first step. The goal is to define the problem behavior in more detail and learn more about it. In the early stages of analyzing the problem behavior, one individual in the school may take a leadership role in focusing attention on the situation. In Step 2, the child's behavior needs to be evaluated in several different environments, such as classrooms, the playground, the lunch room, and transition times. This may require that the child be observed unobtrusively and should answer the important question of whether the problem behavior occurs in a wide range of situations or is restricted to a single situation. If the problem behavior is restricted to a particular situation, class, subject, or time, further observation may suggest some reasons for the problem. For example, if behavior problems are restricted to arithmetic lessons, the child may have an academic problem that needs attention rather than a behavioral problem. In some cases, conflict with a particular peer may be the source of the problem. The circumstances surrounding occurrences of a behavior need to be considered in assessing it.

It is also useful to determine the impact of the problem behavior on others in the school—the child's peers, the classroom teacher, administrators, playground monitors, and anyone else who comes in contact with the child. Another important question is whether the child gains anything from the behavior that tends to maintain it over a long period of time. Peer or adult attention, escape from a problem situation, or other potential causes of the problem behavior need to be evaluated.

For problems defined as the absence of appropriate behavior, the approach is similar. For example, if the problem is defined as absence of friends and social relationships, it is important to assess whether similar behavior patterns are seen in varying situations. Does the problem occur across settings, or is it limited to a particular situation? Regardless of the nature of the problem, when Step 2 is complete, it is expected that a reasonably complete definition of the problem behavior has been developed. This definition, however, is not final. Mainly, it should serve to focus attention on issues as the assessment progresses. Information obtained in later steps may radically change this focus.

Step 3: Motivational and reinforcement analysis. Although behavior assessment and management focus on problem behavior, it is also crucial to learn about the child's strengths. This information can be used in planning rewards and incentives to offer the child in the behavior management program. Two questions should be answered: First, what does the child do well? Second, what does the child like in terms of activities, toys, or whatever else might be relevant to a behavior management program? Developing a picture of the child's strengths will also assist in maintaining a balanced perspective, which is particularly important in interactions with the child's parents. Also, as a child's educational program evolves, vocational success will depend on identifying what the child does well rather than on remediating weaknesses. A child who has a learning disability that makes learning arithmetic very difficult usually will not desire to pursue a career such as accounting that emphasizes this weakness. Instead, such children will opt for careers that emphasize their strengths.

Identifying the child's strengths will also begin the task of identifying reinforcers that might be useful in a behavior management program. This is an important process that continues throughout a behavior management program because effective reinforcers vary not only from individual to individual, but within the individual as well. A reinforcer that is effective for one child may not be effective for another child, and children may lose interest in reinforcers they once worked hard to obtain. Many variables, such as age, gender, family background, and experience, contribute to the reinforcement preferences. Although some reinforcers seem to have almost universal appeal, that appeal can be very short lived. To complicate matters, a reinforcer that is effective for a child may not continue to be effective indefinitely. This is the nature of reinforcement. Planning for a behavior management program needs to take this into account with a flexible approach to reinforcer selection. It is essential to be ready to change reinforcers when the results of the behavior management program indicate that a reward is losing effectiveness.

There are many ways to learn what might be rewarding for a child. Simply observing what children do when they are free to choose an activity should indicate what is reinforcing for them. The materials or equipment needed to perform a preferred activity may also serve as effective reinforcers. For example, if a child spends a lot of her free time playing computer games, ten minutes of computer time may be an effective reinforcer. A new computer game for a home system could also function as a reward. Other methods of learning what a child might find reinforcing include asking the child, asking parents or teachers, and administering a reinforcement survey that lists available activities and material rewards and asks the child to rate their attractiveness.

Step 4: Developmental analysis of the problem. Several questions related to the problem behavior can be pursued from a developmental perspective. The most important question concerns the child's developmental status relative to age. It is desirable to know whether the child's social, academic, self-help, and physical skills are age-appropriate. This can be ascertained most easily by formally or informally ranking the child with respect to his or her classroom peers in each of these areas. This analysis should establish expectations about the child's behavior and indicate at least to some extent whether the problem behavior really represents a deviation from behavior expected of a child at that stage of development. In addition, the assessor should be aware of the possibility that a more in-depth assessment of intellectual, physical, social, and adaptive skills may be necessary.

In addition to ascertaining the child's developmental status, it can be helpful to obtain a detailed history of the behavior problem. This may require interviewing both the child's parents and previous teachers, but it can prove extremely helpful. Although it may reveal that the problem is long-standing and becoming worse, it may also indicate that the problem has developed recently or that someone in the child's past has already devised an effective means of coping with it. Another interesting possibility is that adults who previously had contact with the child may not have regarded the behavior as a problem.

Finally, a brief medical history of the child and a detailed look at his or her school attendance record, along with any other pertinent data that may be in the child's cumulative file, can add to one's understanding of a problem behavior. The presence of a major medical problem or a history of frequent absences from school may both be important in planning a formal behavior management program.

Step 5: Analysis of the child's self-control. This analysis is directed at determining both the methods and the degree of self-control shown by the child in daily life. Self-control refers to the ability of the child to evaluate alternative responses to a situation, inhibit undesirable responses, and engage in an appropriate action (Kendall & Braswell, 1985). It includes an evaluation of both deficits and excesses in self-control. A deficit in self-control would be associated with behaviors such as impulsiveness, inability to follow rules, or unresponsiveness to normal classroom consequences. An excess of self-control would be characterized by failure to participate in activities, excessive fear, lack of friends, or extreme sadness. Either an excess or a deficit in self-control may indicate a need for a behavior management program, but absence of self-control is most likely to be associated with behaviors that are disruptive and attract attention from school staff.

The question of whether the child seems capable of exerting some self-control of the problem behavior provides an important clue to the nature of the needed intervention. If indications exist that the problem behavior is apparently within the control of the child, the problem can be viewed as a failure to perform a known skill. If the child is unable to exert any control over the problem behavior, there may be a need to learn how to inhibit problem behavior and how to behave appropriately in the problem situation. Behavior management programs for teaching new skills are naturally somewhat more complicated than programs to increase the frequency of a previously mastered skill.

To determine whether the problem behavior is under the control of the child, it is necessary to observe the child in different environments. If the child is able to control a behavior excess (such as aggressive behavior) or perform a skill that appears to be a deficit at other times, then one has evidence that the problem behavior is at least partially under the control of the child.

Kendall and Wilcox (1979) developed a scale for rating self-control in children. This scale is completed by a teacher, who rates the child's tendency to perform various behaviors related to self-control, such as production of work of consistent quality, ability to work for long-range goals, ability to follow instructions, accident proneness, distractibility, cooperation, and problem-solving skills. The scale provides useful information about the child's general level of self-control as well as suggesting other areas of inquiry.

Step 6: Analysis of the child's social relationships in school. For most of us, the social part of school was at least as important as the academics. We tend to remember who was popular and who was unpopular, and both our enjoyable and painful memories of school days are likely to involve social situations. Thus, social success in school is no doubt important to each child. Hughes and Hall (1987) suggested that social competence could be assessed as a function of the child's perception of social situations and the cognitive and behavioral skills used in various situation. This leads to three questions that could be asked in the assessment of social skills: First, does the child correctly interpret social situations? Second, can the child generate strategies for resolving social dilemmas? Finally, can the child *apply* problem-solving strategies to the social situation? In addition to asking these questions, it may be useful to observe whether the child has friends and how many. Note, also, whether the child is welcomed into group activities or rejected.

The child's social interactions with adults should also be observed. Some children prefer to socialize with adults in place of socialization with peers. Also, observers should be alert to the situation where encouragement to engage in interaction with peers actually serves as a reinforcement for not interacting with peers. Again, behavior in several environments should be observed so a clear picture of the child's behavior emerges.

Step 7: Analysis of the child's sensory capacity. Hearing and vision are crucial to any child's survival in school, and deficits in either of these senses can lead to both academic and behavioral problems. When a behavior management program is being contemplated, it is important to assess at least informally the child's hearing and vision. A child could appear to be ignoring or defying adult requests when, in fact, the requests are not being heard. A child who is disruptive when lessons are being presented on the board may be unable to see clearly what is being presented or may be asking neighbors for clarification. In any case, it is important to consider the possibility that sensory deficits are related to the child's problem. If any such deficits are suspected, a thorough assessment should be undertaken immediately.

Whenever a child's academic accomplishment is not meeting expectations, it is possible that his or her sensory capacity has fallen below optimal levels. This can occur even in a child who has previously passed a hearing or vision test. Because vision and hearing are essential to academic performance, it is absolutely imperative that a problem in these areas be ruled out when a child experiences academic difficulties. Tables 3.1 and 3.2 list behaviors associated with hearing and vision problems, respectively. A screening test for vision or hearing problems takes so little time and effort that the presence of any of these signs should be cause to contact the appropriate specialist. Obviously, if the screening indicates a potential problem, medical consultation should be sought as soon as possible.

Table 3.1. Behavioral Indicators of Hearing Difficulty

1. A history of frequent middle ear infections
2. Difficulty in comprehending directions or understanding conversation
3. Frequently requests repetitions of things said
4. Confusion of similar sounding words
5. Difficulty gaining the child's attention unless visual contact is made with the child

Step 8: Analysis of the child's home environment. A criticism sometimes leveled at the child assessment process is that it focuses almost exclusively on a symptomatic description of the child, ignoring family and systems factors (Kendall, 1987). As pointed out in Chapter 1, a child's maladaptive behavior may be a response to an unhealthy environment at home. For this reason, it is important for school personnel to obtain as much information as practical about the home environment of children who have behavior problems in school.

An analysis of any child's behavior at home depends on the willingness of the child's parents to share information with school personnel. Skill and diplomacy are needed to elicit information from parents who may feel somewhat threatened by any contact with their child's school. By contrast, other parents are willing to talk in great detail about their home life and how they see the

Table 3.2. Behavioral Indicators of Visual Difficulty

1. Irritated, watery, reddish, encrusted eyes or eyelids
2. Recurring sties
3. Complaints of not seeing well
4. Dizziness, headaches, or nausea following close work
5. Blurred or double vision
6. Excessive rubbing of eyes
7. Difficulty while doing close work (child tilts head, shuts one eye, thrusts head forward, is irritable, or blinks frequently while doing close work)
8. Difficulty in judging distances
9. Avoidance of close work
10. Loss of place
11. Reversal or confusion of letters

behavior of their child. It is important to avoid negative or judgmental comments about either the child or the child's parents when seeking information from them. In meetings with parents, the primary goals should be communicating accurately and maintaining a positive relationship. It may take several meetings before school personnel have an accurate picture of the relationship between the home environment and behavior in school. Unfortunately, some parents are blatantly uncooperative, and it is necessary to work around them as much as possible.

Assessing the family system consists of posing questions, forming hypotheses, and seeking confirmatory data, just as in conducting the school-based portion of the assessment. Techniques of assessment include administering standardized assessment instruments to the parents, asking questions of the parents, and observing the reactions and interaction of the parents during conferences and other times as opportunities are available. Some school districts employ school social workers who may be able to interview the parent(s) and the child at home.

Three areas are of interest in gathering information about the family: (1) the child's behavior at home, (2) how the parents cope with the child's behavior at home, and, (3) the marital relationship. The child's behavior at home is an important area of inquiry because it is useful to know whether problems seen at school also occur at home. Whether behavior at home and at school is similar or contrasting leads to ideas about the nature of the problem and how it can be remediated. For example, if the problem behavior occurs in the home with about the same frequency that it occurs in school, this suggests that the child has little self-control over the behavior and that the child may need to learn new skills for coping with the problem situation.

Learning how skillfully the parents' cope with their child's behavior can also assist in planning interventions. Parents sometimes need help in developing strategies for managing their child's behavior. Chapters 9 and 12 describe specific home-based behavior management programs that may prove helpful and effective. In the most extreme cases, families may need the assistance of social service agencies to prevent abuse or neglect. In contrast, discussion with the child's parent(s) may reveal that they are consistent and skillful in managing their child's behavior. They may be familiar with popular books on child management and may describe parenting classes or workshops they have attended. They may also suggest good ideas for managing the child's behavior in school and suggest other appropriate services for the child.

Assessment of the marital relationship is valuable because the existence of conflict is almost certain to be reflected in the behavior of the child. Conflict may be revealed in a number of ways. First, if only one parent is able to attend the conference, despite the best efforts of the school to invite both parents, this may suggest conflict. Typical parent conferences involve only the mother, but this does not provide the school with a picture of how the parents interact. If only one parent attends because the marriage has dissolved in a divorce, it may be helpful to inquire about the nature of the relationship prior to the divorce. Single parents are often quite candid about the behavior of the former spouse, and much can be learned by just listening.

When parents have undergone a divorce, the impact on the child is likely to be long-standing, particularly if the marriage was full of conflict, if one or both parents is or was alcoholic, or if the child was or is physically abused. A line of inquiry can be begun by asking the parent how the child was affected by the divorce and whether the child remains in regular contact with the noncustodial parent. Sometimes the conflict that led to the divorce is continued after the divorce by involving the child. Visits to the home of the noncustodial parent can be particularly difficult for children under these circumstances and may be associated with misbehavior at home or in school.

Obtaining information about the child's family system can be difficult. One way to simplify this task is to use a structured interview such as the Clinical Interview Form for Child and Adolescent ADHD Clients (Barkley, 1991) or the more general Structured Developmental History (Reynolds & Kamphaus, 1992). Using one of these instruments will ensure that a thorough history is obtained and will allow the practitioner to assess the role of family, developmental, and health issues in the school-based problem.

As the school staff and parents become more comfortable with each other, the place of the child in the family system should become more apparent. This process may extend over several meetings and is likely to involve special education staff, the principal, and/or the school's psychologist. In addition to discussing the practical issues of child management with the parents, those who participate should be aware of other issues. Fine and Holt (1983b) suggest that an assessment of the family system should seek answers to a variety of questions, including the following:

1. Who holds the power at home and school?
2. What roles does the child play in each setting?
3. What triangulation of relationships exists in each setting?
4. How rigid are the home and school systems?
5. How are different family members affected by the child's behavior?
6. How is the family system maintained?
7. What is lost and gained by family members if the child changes?

As any assessment progresses, it may be necessary to communicate with parents about various problems. Bowman and Goldberg (1983) have suggested "reframing" as a technique that can be valuable in communications with parents. The essence of reframing is that an attempt is made to alter the current behavior patterns by dealing with them in an indirect manner that avoids eliciting defensive behavior. LaClave and Brack (1989) describe reframing as finding a "more adaptive, and less painful, means of viewing the world" (p. 69). The idea of reframing is to attach new, less negative, even positive connotations on events so as to provide motivation for change and adaptation. For instance, suggesting that child misbehavior reflects a need to gain parental attention can help parents to see their child's behavior in a different light leading to beneficial change when they begin attending to desirable behavior. A reframe for presenting behavior management techniques to parents is to suggest that what the parents are doing would work for most children, but the child's uniqueness suggests that a different approach is needed. LeClave and Brack suggest the word *unique* has much better connotations than the word *abnormal*.

Coyne and Biglan (1984) describe reframing strategy as focusing not so much on the problem behavior itself as on altering patterns of coping with the problem. Reframing, then, is a technique of helping others to see the problem in a way that leads to more effective coping behavior. This approach can be especially helpful in breaking patterns of attending to undesirable behavior. By reframing the goal of the misbehavior from an attempt to annoy and irritate adults to an attempt to gain needed attention, it may be possible to modify patterns of attending to the child. The result is that the child receives attention for positive behavior and undesirable behavior disappears.

Reframing allows school personnel to communicate with parents without implying that they are responsible for their child's misbehavior. This approach encourages a collaborative relationship between parents and school staff. Most parents are motivated to maintain a positive self-image of their parenting skills and will respond defensively to suggestions that they are at fault or need to change in order to improve the child's behavior. The mechanism of change in the reframing technique lies in placing the behavior in a frame that emphasizes the positive motivations of all concerned. The goal is to reveal previously unrecognized positive and caring feelings, which are frequently masked by angry and apparently uncaring ones. Reframing the problem in this manner opens up new options for change for the family.

As in all behavioral assessments, the results are *hypotheses*, subject to revision as more data are obtained. The action taken by the school will depend, of course, on the nature and severity of the problem. In some cases, legal action may be mandated. In other cases, the school, with the assistance of appropriately trained personnel such as a school psychologist or social worker, can attempt to remediate the problem behavior of the child with the assistance of the family. The possibility that family systems problems will require referral to either private or public assistance agencies or professional therapists should always remain an option for those who work within the school system.

An issue that complements the assessment process concerns "taking credit" for improvement in the child's behavior problems or general adjustment. Although parents are likely to respond defensively to any attempts to blame them or have them take direct responsibility for their child's misbehavior or failure to perform, they would like to be able to take credit for improvements or the positive accomplishments of their children. Dunst and Trivette (1987) and Dunst, Johanson, Rounds, Trivette, and Hamby (1992) describe a way of thinking about helping relationships that emphasizes giving power to the client as opposed to taking credit for improvement that occurs. Their model states that parents need to attribute behavior change to their own actions in order to acquire a sense of control or competency. The idea is to "empower" parents so they are able to deal effectively with problems. In this way, not only is the short-term referral problem solved, but future problems may be avoided.

Step 9: Analysis of interpersonal relationships at home. At this stage of assessment, it is desirable to know the composition of the family living with the child, whether the child is living with natural or stepparents, how many siblings live at home, and whether any other people are living in the household such as stepsisters or -brothers. Once the composition of the child's household is understood, information about the relationships among the people living at home should be obtained. It is particularly important to learn how each person living in the household gets along with the child. Of equal interest is whether conflict exists in the family, particularly between the mother and father. It is also important to ascertain whether the parents and/or other significant adults in the family see the child's behavior in the same way and whether parents and other responsible family members respond consistently to the child's behavior. A divorce, either accomplished or impending, would also be a significant factor. If the parents are divorced, determining the degree of involvement of the noncustodial parent in the child's upbringing may also prove to be helpful.

Step 10: Initial identification of the problem behavior and potential targets for a behavior management program. Once an initial assessment has been completed, it is necessary to integrate the information and decide whether intervention is necessary. If intervention is needed, then the target of intervention must be determined. A frequent outcome of a thorough assessment is that the original problem behavior is discovered to be secondary to another problem identified by the assessment. Furthermore, the primary identified problem may not be the initial target of intervention for a variety of reasons. For example, intervening with aggressive behavior may need to take precedence over social skills training for safety reasons.

How does one get from the mass of data generated by the assessment process to a consistent, integrated view of the child that points to an intervention plan? First, it helps to realize that the process leading up to the intervention can be as simple or as complicated as one makes it. The complexity of an intervention plan is determined largely by two variables. The first is the level of the intervention—that is, whether it is an initial intervention conducted by a classroom teacher working independently or an intervention that involves a special education staffing team. As one proceeds to higher and higher levels of intervention (i.e., from teacher to administrator to school psychologist consultation to special education staff), the assessment is likely to be more detailed, because higher levels imply that the problem is of a more serious nature and that earlier intervention efforts have failed.

The complexity of an assessment is also influenced

by the nature of the initial data, which may indicate an immediate need for more information. As soon as a behavior is observed, it may be immediately apparent that the problem is serious and requires immediate attention. High-magnitude aggressive behavior resulting in injury to other children or threats of self-harm would fall into this category. Signs of physical or sexual abuse, or a variety of problems in several different environments, can also indicate the need for additional, more detailed assessment.

As one struggles to integrate the data obtained from a problem assessment, it also helps to realize that assessment is a continuous process and that conclusions implied by an assessment should not be regarded as final. Instead, they are best regarded as hypotheses, subject to revision at any time. One can never eliminate the possibility that some new bit of data will completely change one's view of a problem behavior, and the intervention that once seemed completely reasonable may suddenly appear inadequate or incomplete.

Finally, in my experience, the more one knows about a child, the more contradictions are generated. For example, the child's behavior may be inconsistent across environments, or different individuals may provide contradictory pictures of the child's behavior. The result is a confusing and unclear picture of the child's behavior. When this occurs, it is helpful to remember that the data may be confusing, but the child is behaving consistently with respect to his or her perception of the environment. The assessor's task is to identify that consistency and determine what, if any, interventions are implicated. With respect to resolving the contradictions, remember that only *one* child is being assessed and the contradictions exist from *your* perspective, not from the child's. I have often found that resolving the contradictions that an assessment inevitably produces makes the greatest contribution to my understanding of a child's behavior.

Table 3.3 provides a summary of the general assessment procedure just presented. This table can serve as a guide during the assessment process. Once the assessment team is certain that they have developed a good picture of the problem behavior and the child's needs, it may be appropriate to develop a behavior management program to remediate it. This decision is left up to the members of the assessment team. If a behavior to be increased or decreased that might have a significant impact on the child's adjustment in school can be identified, a behavior management program may be an effective component of an intervention strategy. In the sections that follow, the steps involved in actually conducting a behavior management program are described.

STEPS IN CONDUCTING A FORMAL BEHAVIOR MANAGEMENT PROGRAM

A formal behavior management program continues the assessment process. In a formal assessment, the goal is to gain an understanding of the system within which the child functions so it is possible to select an intervention that will have the most benefit for the child. Not only does the intervention follow from the assessment, but the intervention itself continues the assessment process. The effectiveness of the intervention provides feedback about the accuracy and focus of the assessment. When an intervention is unsuccessful, other hypotheses should be considered. The process resembles a continuous feedback loop in which each successive attempt to intervene generates additional information that improves the effectiveness of the next intervention.

The central characteristic of behavior management programs is that they should be sensitive to the information they generate. That is, the behavior targeted for intervention is carefully observed throughout the program, and the program itself is changed to accommodate the feedback that is generated. Unsuccessful programs are modified. Some successful modifications will be very simple—for example, using a reinforcer that the child finds more attractive. Other modifications may be more complex, such as adding social services or family therapy to a behavior management program. Viewed in this manner, behavior management techniques are powerful tools for changing behavior when they are applied flexibly.

A formal behavior management program consists of eight steps:

Step 1: Identify the problem.
Step 2: Refine the definition of the problem.
Step 3: Assess the baseline rate.
Step 4: Design the behavioral contingencies and write the program description.
Step 5: Begin the program.
Step 6: Observe the effects of the program and initiate steps to strengthen generalization beyond the training environment.
Step 7: Modify the program if necessary.
Step 8: Fade out the program.

Table 3.3. Summary of the General Assessment Procedure

Step 1: General Analysis of the Problem and Its Impact on Academic Learning and Performance
A. State the problem in general terms, including its history.
B. Is it a behavior excess or a skill deficit?
C. What is the impact of the problem behavior on academic performance?
    1. Is the child learning what is expected?
    2. Does the child either lack needed skills or fail to perform skills that are mastered?
    3. Is additional academic assessment needed?
D. Describe the problem's frequency, intensity, and duration.
    1. A narrative log of each relevant incident can be a helpful tool.
E. What conditions precede and follow the behavior?

Step 2: Clarification of the Problem
A. Consider causal relations that might exist among observations.
B. Define the problem behavior in more detail.
C. What evidence suggests that the problem behavior is maintained by circumstances in the environment?
D. Determine the impact of the problem behavior on others.
E. Does the behavior occur in a number of different situations, or is it generally restricted to a single situation?
F. What does the child gain from the behavior that tends to maintain it over a long period of time?

Step 3: Motivational and Reinforcement Analysis
A. What are the child's strengths?
B. What does the child like in terms of activities, toys, or whatever else might be relevant to a behavior management program?

Step 4: Developmental Analysis of the Problem
A. Are the child's skills age-appropriate?
B. What is the history of the problem behavior's development?
C. Obtain a brief medical history of the child.
D. Obtain a detailed school attendance history and review the childs cumulative file.

Step 5: Analysis of the Child's Self-Control
A. Evaluate the child deficits and excesses in self-control.
B. Does appropriate behavior appear in other environments?

Step 6: Analysis of the Child's Social Relationships in School
A. What role does attention play in maintaining the problem behavior?
B. Does the child have friends?

Step 7: Analysis of the Child's Sensory Capacity
A. Are the child's hearing and vision O.K.?

Step 8: Analysis of the Child's Home Environment
A. Does the behavior problem appear at home?
B. How are behavior problems handled at home?
C. What other problems are seen at home?

Step 9: Analysis of Interpersonal Relationships at Home
A. What is the composition of the child's household?
B. How do others in the family get along with the child?
C. Do responsible adults respond consistently to the child's behavior?
D. Is family conflict present?
E. Are the child's biological parents divorced? Is the noncustodial parent involved with the child? To what extent?

Step 10: Initial Identification of the Problem Behavior and Potential Targets for a Behavior Management Program
A. Integrate the information. Is intervention necessary?
B. What will be the target of intervention?
C. Will the target behavior contribute to the ultimate performance goals for the child, such as improved academic performance or improved social interaction on the playground?

D. Are additional data needed?
E. Reminders:
   1. Assessment is a continuous process.
   2. All conclusions remain subject to revision.
   3. Children behave consistently with respect to their perception of the environment.
   4. Resolving contradictions can help in understanding the child.

These eight steps are designed to stand alone and could be used without additional assessment to develop a behavior management program. The decision as to what approach is best must be left to the team or individual. There are also other approaches to this process that can be effective. For example, Kratochwill, Elliott, and Rotto (1990) describe the process of behavioral consultation as consisting of four steps: (1) identify the problem, (2) analyze the problem, (3) implement a plan, and (4) evaluate the plan. Those who consult with school personnel regarding behavior problems may find this article helpful. It is crucial to remember that behavior assessment and management are *continuous* processes. Intervention strategies can even be considered part of the assessment process because a child's responses to them may provide key information about the severity and persistence of the problem behavior (Christenson, Abery, & Weinberg, 1986; Wielkiewicz, 1986). Each step in a formal behavior management program will be described.

Step 1: Identify the problem. Many situations may suggest a behavior management program is needed. A child may appear to be a poor student, hostile, aggressive, hyperactive, lazy, disobedient, disruptive, anxious, or unhappy, or may engage in other behaviors that motivate school personnel to intervene. Once a problem has been identified in general terms, it is necessary to determine the nature of the assessment that will be undertaken prior to beginning a behavior management program. In some cases the next step would be to conduct the ten-step assessment discussed in the previous section. However, this may not be practical or necessary in many cases. The severity and pervasiveness of the problem behavior will determine the thoroughness of the initial assessment.

For example, if a child appears unmotivated to participate in music class but behaves appropriately in other classes, a thorough assessment may not be necessary. The usefulness of a more informal approach would be confirmed if the child maintained good academic performance in other classes. In this case, the child's teachers might develop a behavior management program for use only in music class as a first step toward resolving the problem. On the other hand, if the child was disruptive in music class, unmotivated in other classes, and performing below expectations academically, the severity and pervasiveness of the problems would suggest that a thorough assessment was needed.

Numerous paths may lead to a behavior management program. For this reason, the essential steps leading to a satisfactory definition of a problem behavior are included in the steps for both the assessment and intervention processes. Even in the absence of a formal and detailed assessment, it would be possible to follow the steps in a formal behavior management program and successfully resolve the problem. However, important factors that could influence intervention strategies might be overlooked. Another strategy is to begin a formal behavior management and a formal assessment at the same time. Indeed, some behavior problems require an immediate response. It is also possible that a formal behavior management program could be the next logical step in a long series of attempts to resolve a problem behavior. Regardless of the path that leads to a formal behavior management program, the process begins with a simple statement describing the nature of the problem.

Step 2: Refine the definition of the problem. The main goal of Step 2 is to develop an *operational definition* of the behavior that will be the target of intervention. The target behavior may be very different from the original statement of the problem behavior. For example, if the initial statement of the problem behavior states that the child is failing to perform academic work, "failure to perform academic work" would not be a good target behavior. It would make more sense to develop a behavior management program to *improve* specific areas of academic productivity. The resulting behavior management program may, for example, reward the student for each completed homework assignment. Thus, the program would be designed to reinforce productivity instead of punishing academic failure.

To refine the definition of the problem behavior, one

must state the problem in a manner appropriate for a behavior management program. Because the primary feature of all behavior management programs is the delivery of rewards, the event that determines when a reward will be delivered must be clearly recognizable. If it is not, the person conducting the behavior management program will not know precisely when to administer the prescribed contingency. The likely result is that responses to the child's behavior will be inconsistent and the behavior management program will be in danger of failing. The child will also be faced with unpredictable reward, and this will make it difficult to develop an idea of what is expected of him or her.

Personality traits and global behavioral labels (e.g., aggressive, disruptive, depressed, hyperactive, anxious) are not appropriate targets for a behavior management program because they do not specify *what* behavior occurring under *what* circumstances will be rewarded or punished. Instead, the problem behavior needs to be specified in concrete, measurable terms. A good definition of a behavior to be managed or modified has three basic characteristics. First, the target behavior should not require any interpretation on the part of the observer. In other words, it should be possible to determine easily when the target behavior has occurred without reference to whether the behavior was provoked by someone else or was intentional. Second, the behavior must be countable or measurable; that is, it must occur in discrete units that can be counted or it must be possible to determine what percentage of a particular time interval the child was performing the target behavior.

The third characteristic of a good definition of a behavior is that one should be able to explain the definition to another person. Once the definition of the behavior has been agreed on by two people, they should be able to observe the child for a period of time and independently (i.e., without consulting with each other) arrive at nearly identical results when recording their observations of the child's behavior. Psychologists who study the behavior of children employ several different techniques to ensure that their observational methods are reliable—that is, that they can be repeated across time and with different observers without changing the outcome. Although such stringent tests would be beyond the needs of an applied behavior management program conducted in school, it is helpful to consider whether a particular behavior management program has a reliable measure of the target behavior. Involvement of a second observer is one method to increase reliability of the observations.

In addition to defining behavior in terms that are concrete, countable or measurable, and reliable, it is important to specify the problem in terms of a behavior to be increased. This should almost always be possible. The exceptions are those few cases where the child's behavior presents a danger to self or others. For instance, if the initial definition of the problem behavior was disruptive classroom behavior, the problem could be redefined as a deficit in work behaviors. Then, instead of the child receiving punishment for disruptive behavior (e.g., timeout or being kept in at recess), the child could be earning rewards for completing assigned classroom work. A good general principle to remember is that the child who is engaged in desirable behavior does not have time to cause trouble.

Consider an example. School staff may be concerned about a child seen as disruptive by a classroom teacher. "Disruptive" is the initial definition of the problem. Further observation and discussion reveal that disruptive behavior is characterized by talking with classmates during periods when there is assigned work to be done, with the result that classroom assignments are not completed. Although it would be possible to make "talking to neighbor" the target behavior, it is likely to be more helpful to develop a program around the target behavior "completing assignments." If the child is engaged in completing work, talking and other disruptive behavior will be much less likely. Completing assignments is a behavior that is concrete and easily observable, and thus is a good target for intervention. Of course, other issues would need to be addressed, such as acceptable level of accuracy on assignments, but "completion of classroom work" would be an acceptable target behavior.

Weist, Ollendick, and Finney (1991) have suggested that an *empirical* approach to selecting target behaviors is needed. In their review they point out how difficult it is to select a valid target behavior, one that will bring about maximum benefit to the child if the behavior is changed. It is difficult to establish beforehand whether a target behavior is empirically valid, although review of the relevant literature and observation of successful peers can greatly increase the likelihood that an empirically valid target behavior will be selected. There are, however, methods that can be applied easily in a school setting. The most important is to keep in mind ultimate performance goals for the child. In school, this usually means that the child's academic performance should correspond to ability. For example, if an intervention designed to improve on-task behavior does not lead to improved academic performance, it may not have been a valid intervention target. Perhaps the child lacks basic study skills and has only learned to appear to be on task.

An approach for identifying target behaviors recommended by Weist et al. (1991) is to use "template matching." This approach involves identifying one of the child's successful peers and determining the skills and performance levels of this student. When target behaviors and performance goals for the "target" child are matched to those of the "template" child, empirical validity of the target behaviors is more likely. For example, if the target child is emitting an unacceptable frequency of aggressive behavior on the playground, school staff could identify a "template" child with similar ability who experiences success on the playground. Careful observation of the template child could be used to establish an acceptable level of aggressive behavior and to identify the social or other skills that seem most strongly related to success on the playground. This kind of assessment may reveal that the target child needs to be less aggressive, learn how to play softball, and learn how to socialize appropriately when waiting to bat. These behaviors could then become the intervention targets. Later, the intervention team would also need to assess whether the target child's overall adjustment on the playground had improved to desired levels.

Selecting the target behavior is a crucial step in developing a behavior management program. In Part II, numerous illustrations will be provided.

Step 3: Assess the baseline rate. The baseline rate of a behavior refers to its frequency or rate of occurrence during a period of time when a behavior management program is *not* in effect. In applied behavior management programs conducted in school, baseline data are obtained prior to the beginning of a program. Once the program is begun, observational data continue to be collected using the *same* technique. Collection of baseline data provides the standard against which the success of the behavior management program is judged. If the frequency or rate of the target behavior changes sufficiently in the desired direction, the program is successful.

It is extremely important to collect data throughout a behavior management program because there is always the possibility that the program will not work as expected. For example, Jensen (1988) reported a case study in which a developmentally disabled student was required to pick up classroom items that he threw. This is a technique called *restitution,* in which the individual restores the environment to its original condition after

misbehavior. Parents are using a mild form of restitution when they tell their children to clean up a mess they have made. What Jensen discovered was that restitution was completely ineffective in reducing object throwing. In fact, object throwing did not decline until restitution was no longer required and the behavior was ignored. Data collection allows the practitioner to identify quickly when a program is not successful and to make the necessary changes.

Baseline observations may be collected in several different ways. The simplest technique is to count each occurrence of the target behavior. Counting can be used with almost any discrete behavior, although behaviors that occur very frequently may be difficult to count when the observer is busy with other tasks. When this technique is used, observations must be totaled over some time interval, such as an hour, day, week, or month, depending on how often the behavior occurs. For example, the number of times per week that a child cries, the number of times per day that a child hits another student in class, or the number of times per week that a child completes arithmetic worksheets could constitute the baseline data for a behavior management program.

Sometimes the absolute number of times a behavior occurs is not an appropriate baseline measure because the number of *opportunities* for the behavior either is limited or varies from week to week. In such cases, it is a good idea to determine a *percentage* for the behavior. For example, if the number of arithmetic worksheets assigned per week varies between 5 and 15, the baseline measure could be the percentage of assigned worksheets completed each week. The goal of the behavior management program would be to increase this percentage to near 100. Similarly, if the goal of a behavior management program was to encourage a child to arrive at school on time, a suitable baseline measure might be the percentage of days per week that the child arrives on time. Using a percentage gives the flexibility of dropping from the baseline data holidays and days when the child is legitimately absent or late.

Baseline observations can be recorded in a variety of ways. One of the simpler techniques is to make a mark on a piece of paper, on a card, or in a gradebook each time the target behavior occurs. The advantage of simply counting a behavior is that recording observations should not take too much of the observer's time, an important consideration for most classroom teachers. For some behaviors, it would be desirable to record each instance of the behavior along with a few comments about the situation, such as what led to the incident, what happened during the incident, and how others responded to it.

Some of the behaviors that become the subject of behavior management programs are so pervasive in the school that it is impractical to count each occurrence, either because the behavior occurs too often or because it is typically an ongoing behavior that cannot be accurately divided into discrete units for counting. Time on task, being out of seat, inattention, and tics or strange mannerisms are examples of such behaviors. Time-sampling procedures are the usual way of handling such situations.

When a time-sampling procedure is used, observations are recorded during a particular period of time, which occurs at a regular interval such as every day or once a week. Observations may be recorded during art period, for example, when another teacher takes over the class and the regular classroom teacher is free to observe. Alternatively, observations could be conducted during a certain hour each week when the school psychologist is available. An important consideration in using time sampling is to specify carefully when observations will be recorded. The goal should be to keep the conditions as constant as possible from one observation period to the next. As much as possible, observations should be recorded at the same time each day and under the same relative conditions, such as right after lunch, during an afternoon reading lesson, or during an independent work period.

Once a suitable time period has been designated, a number of recording techniques can be used. If the target behavior occurs in discrete units, then the behavior need only be counted during the observation period. Some behaviors do not occur in discrete units—for example, time on task or being out of one's seat. These behaviors do not occur in countable units, but it is possible to determine what percentage of time a student is engaged in either of these behaviors. This is accomplished by dividing the observation period into discrete intervals and employing some rule to determine whether the child will be counted as being engaged in the target behavior during the time period or some portion of it. A number of different methods for determining a baseline rate under these conditions can be used. At the end of the observation period, the number of intervals during which the student was engaged in the target behavior is divided by the total number of intervals in the observation period. The result is a decimal value, which can be multiplied by 100 to give the percentage of time that the child was engaged in the target behavior.

Consider some examples of observation methods. The most precise method of determining a baseline rate is to determine the total amount of time the child was engaged in the target behavior during a particular period of time. This can be determined using the classroom clock and a stopwatch. To begin the procedure, the observer determines the amount of time that the child will be observed after formulating an operational definition of the target behavior (e.g., "on task"). A ten- or twenty-minute interval should be sufficient. When the time interval begins, the observer uses the stopwatch to keep a cumulative record of the amount of time the child was engaged in the target behavior. That is, the stopwatch is allowed to run only when the child is engaged in the target behavior, so that the total amount of time engaged in the target behavior is obtained at the end of the observation period. The percentage of time engaged in the target behavior can be calculated on a daily basis along with data from a control child observed under the same conditions. To keep the conditions as equal as possible for the control and target childen, they could be observed on alternate days or during alternate five-minute periods.

Another, less precise, method is to estimate the rate of the target behavior by making observations at designated intervals during the observation period. At each designated point in the observation period, the child is observed and scored for the presence or absence of the target behavior. The advantages of this method are that it is easier to use and that accurate observations of a control child can be obtained by alternating observations of the target child and a control child. The method begins with the selection of an appropriate observation period and recording method. A prepared sheet divided into squares and having separate areas for recording data from the target child and control child would work well. An observation is made at designated intervals ranging from ten to sixty seconds, depending on the complexity of the coding system and the number of children being observed. The child's behavior during the interval is ignored. The observer records only what is occurring at the end of each interval.

For instance, using ten-second intervals, the observer looks at one of the children being observed every ten seconds, recording that child's activity on the record sheet. If three children (one target, two controls) were observed every ten seconds, each child would be observed three times per minute. A thirty-minute observation period would result in 90 observations per child. A percentage could be determined by dividing the number of times a particular behavior was observed by 90 and multiplying by 100.

Another method of observing on-task versus off-task behavior is to observe each student in a classroom for a short interval, such as four seconds each. A plus is recorded if the child is on task during the four-second interval and a minus recorded if the child is off task for any part of the four-second interval. Then the percentage of intervals on task can be computed for the target child and for the remainder of the class. It takes a little practice to coordinate recording and observation, but the technique avoids the biases that could result from choosing a particular control child to observe. I have found this method very useful because it focuses on the target child while providing interesting data regarding the general classroom climate.

The sophistication of any observation technique can be increased by comparing data from two observers. If the definition of the target behaviors is sufficiently concrete, substantial agreement should be found. If agreement is not substantial (80–100 percent), the definition of the target behavior probably needs clarification and revision.

By using one of these procedures, it should be possible to obtain baseline data for just about any behavior. There are a few additional points to keep in mind while obtaining the baseline data. First, it is important to specify clearly what procedures were used to gather the baseline data so these procedures can be continued *without change* when the behavior management program begins. If the conditions of baseline observation are not held constant, changes that occur in the target behavior may not be caused by the behavior management program.

Another point to remember is that baseline observations need not be restricted to a single behavior. By making up a simple coding system, it is possible to obtain information about several behaviors. This can be handy when the problem is an undesirable behavior, such as being out of seat, but it has been decided that the management program will focus on rewarding time on task. By observing both behaviors, it is possible to obtain a clear picture of the impact of the behavior management program.

Finally, it may be helpful to point out an interesting phenomenon that may occur when baseline observations are begun. It is possible that the act of obtaining the baseline data may, in itself, cause the observed behavior to change. The change may or may not be in the desired direction. For instance, if a teacher stops what he or she is doing, walks over to his or her desk, and makes a mark

in the gradebook every time a child emits or fails to emit a problem behavior, the child's attention may be drawn to the problem behavior and it may improve spontaneously. Another example of this phenomenon can occur when a disruptive behavior is rewarded by adult attention. If a teacher pauses to record each disruptive incident instead of asking the child to stop the behavior, the result may be a steady decline in the frequency of disruptive behavior as a result of extinction. When this occurs, it may be possible to avoid the need for a behavior management program. However, I recommend documenting the change in behavior because this record could be helpful in the future.

Step 4: Design the behavioral contingencies and write a description of the program. Precisely what is a *behavior management program*? A behavior management program is a conscious attempt to change or maintain behavior by using generally accepted principles of learning and behavior change. Chapter 2 described four basic techniques for altering or maintaining behavior: positive reinforcement, negative reinforcement, positive punishment, and negative punishment. Although many other components may enter into a behavior management program, these four basic techniques form the core of behavior management procedures. In most situations encountered in school settings, positive reinforcement is the most effective technique because strengthening desired behavior is the most direct route to resolving most behavior problems. Even if a child is dangerously aggressive, the ultimate goal should be to replace aggressive behavior with more socially and academically appropriate behavior, not merely to suppress aggressive behavior.

A typical behavior management program consists of three essential elements: a target behavior, a rewarding or punishing stimulus, and a rule or contingency that describes when and how the stimulus will be delivered to the child. For example, imagine that a child study team is concerned about a child's disruptive off-task behavior. The team might then decide that the best route to improving the situation is to increase the child's academic productivity by rewarding each seatwork assignment completed with 80 percent accuracy by giving the child five minutes of access to a computer game. In this case the target behavior is completion of assignments with 80 percent accuracy. The rewarding stimulus is access to the computer game, and the contingency or rule is that five minutes of computer time are earned for each worksheet completed with 80 percent accuracy.

Once a behavior management program has been designed, the best way to ensure that everybody involved clearly understands it is to write a description of the program. This also creates a written record of attempts to resolve the problem that can be helpful in the future should other services be needed by the child. A written program also helps to keep everybody current on changes and modifications of the program.

Selecting reinforcers. One source of resistance to the use of behavior management techniques in school is that it is sometimes felt that children should not be "bribed" to perform schoolwork. This often creates difficulties in developing behavior management programs. Christian (1983) has suggested a perspective that can be helpful in designing programs. He suggests that rewards used in school-based behavior management programs be placed on a hierarchy ranging from the most concrete rewards to the most abstract. The categories or levels of consequences, along with a few examples of each, include the following:

Infantile physical contact: hugs, pats, physical closeness
Food: milk, cookies, raisins, banana chips, candy, gum
Toys: marble, kite, clay, car, truck, doll
School implements: eraser, ruler, pencil, notepad
Privileges: free time, computer access, errands, collecting/distributing papers
Praise: verbal comments, grades, certificate, attention of special adult (e.g., principal)
Internal self-reinforcement: "I did well!" "I got all the problems right!," "My work is done!"

Christian points out that most children in regular elementary school classrooms are operating at the two highest levels of reinforcement, praise and internal self-reinforcement, most of the time. Thus, when dealing with a child's problem behavior, the goal should be to start at the highest level possible on the hierarchy and advance toward the even higher levels. Making the advance to higher levels of reinforcement and to complete independence from the behavior management program is the goal in Step 6.

As children grow into adolescents, selecting reinforcers becomes more challenging. Reynolds, Salend, and Beahan (1989) described five categories of reinforcers appropriate for secondary students. These five categories, along with a few examples of each, are listed here:

Edible reinforcers: ice cream, gum, candy, soda pop, pizza, fast foods, popcorn, raisins, fruit
Tangible reinforcers: stickers, T-shirts, magazines, comic books, bumper stickers
Activity reinforcers: free time, visit to weight room, time to watch a video, trips to vocationally relevant places
Social reinforcers: social attention from the teacher, notes from teachers or administrators, permission to make choices regarding learning activities, waiver of an upcoming assignment or quiz, public display of outstanding work
Group reinforcement: a party for the whole class, a class trip, recreational activities

Reynolds et al. also make several useful suggestions regarding selection of effective rewards for this age group. They note that the nutritional value of many food reinforcers is poor and that some caution in their selection is needed. Health factors, such as diabetes, may render some food reinforcers dangerous. Thus, it is important to consider several factors before using a food reinforcer. With respect to tangible reinforcers such as T-shirts, it is important to know what is popular at the time. Fads come and go so quickly that keeping current with adolescent culture is essential for professionals designing behavior management programs for this group.

Reynolds, Salend, and Beahan (1992) surveyed 110 secondary students with disabilities to determine their preferences for reinforcers. They identified four categories of reinforcers: activity, school-related, tangible, and edible. The most preferred reinforcers in the activity category included activities allowed by parents (special trip, privilege, or party), school field trip, free time, or seeing a VCR movie in class. Preferred activities in the school-related category related to improving grades (extra credit, dropping the lowest grade, etc.) and being excused from a punishment. The only item in the tangible reinforcer category was a coupon good toward a record (substitute a compact disc) or cassette tape, and the only preferred reinforcer in the edible category was pizza. In this study, students were asked to rate their preferences from a list of 90 reinforcers judged practical and acceptable by a group of teachers and students who were interviewed. As noted previously, effective reinforcers can vary from individual to individual as well as from week to week as fads come and go and student tastes change. Therefore, the task of choosing appropriate reinforcers for students is a never ending one.

Another important principle in reinforcer selection is the Premack principle. David Premack (1959) observed that a response of higher probability can be used to reinforce a response of lower probability. Teachers and parents who say, "Before you can go outside, you must finish your work," are applying this principle. More than anything else, this principle serves as a reminder that by watching children, one can learn what they like to do. Then, if one has or can gain control over a preferred activity, it can be used to reward less likely but desirable behavior. Even the child who is most resistant to a behavior management program must be gaining some reinforcement from some source. By watching and learning what activities a child prefers, it can be possible to find an effective reinforcer and contingency. Homme, DeBaca, Devine, Steinhorst, and Rickert (1963) applied the Premack principle to control behaviors of three preschool children. They found that low-probability behavior such as sitting quietly and looking at the blackboard could be rewarded by allowing the students to run around and scream, kick a wastebasket, or push an adult around the room in a caster-equipped chair.

Stating the contingency. Once a reward has been selected, it is necessary to state the contingency or rule for administering that reward. As explained in Chapter 2, the contingency defines the relationship between behavior and the reward (or punishment). A contingency can specify that a stimulus is either presented or removed when a behavior occurs or fails to occur. A contingency can be very simple, specifying that a simple reward such as food or positive attention be delivered when the child engages in a particular behavior. On the other hand, contingencies can be complicated, specifying relationships among a variety of behaviors, a point system, and rewards to be delivered by the child's parents at home. A variety of ways of designing effective contingencies are described in Part II.

The written program description. Once the reinforcer and the contingency have been selected, the final behavior management program needs to be described in writing. This is a major addition to the eight-step procedure described in the previous edition of this book (Wielkiewicz, 1986). There are several reasons for putting the program in writing. The most important is that reference to a written program helps to maintain consistency across environments and individuals. For example, if a substitute teacher takes over a classroom, following a written behavior management program is much easier than trying to learn the details over the phone. The written program also helps maintain consistency across time. If the behavior management program is part of an Individual Education Plan (IEP), especially if it involves a restrictive procedure such as timeout, state rules and regulations often require a written behavior management program. Finally, I believe that having a written program simply leads to superior behavior management programs. When all the key individuals have an opportunity to read a draft of the program and have input into the final product, the final draft tends to be a realistic program that has the enthusiastic support of those who will be responsible for administering the contingencies.

The content of the behavior management program can range from a couple of sentences to several pages depending on the complexity of the situation. The program should be very concrete in describing who will be responsible for various aspects of the program and when the tasks will be performed. If the program is developed on a word processor, this will make editing convenient. In order to avoid confusion, each draft should be dated. There are many formats for describing behavior management programs. One way of organizing a written description of a behavior management program follows:

Introduction
A. Background information and a brief history of the problem situation
B. Summary of key assessment information
C. Previous interventions

Procedure
A. Brief overview and summary of the procedure
B. Operational definitions of all target behaviors
C. Summary of baseline data
D. Clear statement of the reinforcer and the contingency
E. Parent contacts and permissions
F. Ethical considerations

Program Rules
A. Specific rules for running the program
B. Include names and responsibilities of individuals involved with the program
C. Date that the program is scheduled to begin
D. How to deal with specific situations such as absence or illness
E. How data will be collected and summarized

Goals and Objectives

A. Goals are the endpoints toward which a program is aimed and objectives are the steps to get there
B. If the student is in special education, goals and objectives will already be a component of the IEP

Notes

A. A place to note small changes to the program
B. A place to note major changes that require rewriting the program so that a running history of the program is available

Once a written program has been approved by the child study team, special education team, regular education teachers, parents, and others involved, the program is ready to begin.

Step 5: Begin the program. Beginning a behavior management program consists of simply announcing the rules of the program to the child. Children should not be given more details regarding the program than they are capable of understanding. For preschoolers and kindergarteners, it is probably best merely to tell them that they have an opportunity to earn something if they pay attention or get their work done. Older children are usually capable of understanding a more detailed explanation. Adolescents may be most responsive to a "behavior contract" (see Chapter 10), a document signed by the adolescent and others stating the rules of the program.

Once the program is begun, it is very important that it be administered objectively. The rules of the program should provide most of the necessary guidance as to when rewards are delivered or taken away. If the administrator of the program finds himself or herself in the position of making subjective judgments about what should be done, the program should be revised to eliminate the subjectivity. Keep in mind, however, that this is not an uncommon occurrence, because children tend to be curious about the limits of a program and will attempt to establish limits that are in their favor.

It is also important to avoid lengthy discussions with children as to whether a particular behavior meets the criteria for a reward. Such discussions could lead to inadvertently rewarding the child for ingenuity in explaining why he or she hit someone, failed to turn in an assignment, or otherwise met or failed to meet a rule of the behavior management program. However, when the child behaves in such a way as to merit a timeout period or loss of a reward, a brief explanation is in order. The explanation should focus on the child's behavior and not

contain any aggressive comments about the child. When a reward is delivered, it should always be accompanied by a positive comment.

Finally, it is important to be patient and remember that the behavior management program, and not the child, is subject to evaluation if things do not work out as expected.

Step 6: Observe the effects of the program and initiate steps to strengthen generalization beyond the training environment. This step is a continuation of what was begun in Steps 4 and 5. The baseline observations are continued throughout the program and, once the program is begun, become the indicator of the program's success or need for modification. If the target behavior changes in the desired direction, the program should be continued without modification until the appropriate behaviors are well established. At the point where desirable behavior is strong, steps to strengthen generalization beyond the training environment may be begun. The purpose of these steps is to bring the child's behavior under the control of the natural environment, without the structure and rules of the behavior management program. Strengthening generalization beyond the training environment becomes an issue when the child is in a special education class or the initial steps in the behavior management program have been conducted outside the regular classroom. In either case, it is desirable that behaviors learned in one setting also occur in others, including the regular classroom.

Strengthening generalization from a training setting to the classroom can be accomplished by either bringing elements of the classroom into the training environment or taking elements from the training environment into the classroom. For instance, having the child's regular classroom teacher visit a program that takes place away from the classroom can give the teacher a chance to evaluate elements that could be employed in the classroom. Then, by fading out those elements with which the teacher is not comfortable or cannot implement for practical reasons (see Step 8), it is possible to construct a program that is similar to the classroom.

Stokes and Baer (1977) and Rutherford and Nelson (1988) have reviewed the literature on the technology of promoting generalization. *Generalization* is defined as the occurrence of a trained behavior across different, nontraining conditions. Stokes and Baer described several methods of promoting generalization. The first category of methods for promoting generalization is "train and hope"—design a behavior change program without any explicit attention to promoting generalization and then note any generalization that happens. The second category of techniques, "sequential modification," means to assess generalization of a newly learned behavior and then, if generalization has failed to occur, initiate modifications designed to accomplish it. "Sequential" modifications consist of instituting the successful environmental manipulations in other settings. The third category of techniques introduces natural contingencies for maintaining the behavior. This is the most reliable method of promoting generalization and means to transfer control of behavior from the original behavior management program to stable, natural contingencies within the environment to which the child returns. One of the requirements of promoting generalization via this route is that behaviors must be carefully selected so that their occurrence will be rewarded by natural contingencies outside the training environment. This type of generalization is particularly important in training social skills, because the acceptance of the child's peers and significant adults determines success of the training.

A fourth category is the training of sufficient examples to obtain generalization across a number of untrained conditions. Stokes and Baer cited an example of their own work, in which developmentally disabled children were trained to greet adults. When a child was trained to greet one experimenter, generalization to other adults did not occur. However, when training was conducted with just two experimenters, the greeting response generalized to over 20 members of the institution staff, and to newcomers as well. Thus, although generalization to numerous settings may be desirable, it may not be necessary to conduct explicit training within each of these settings to obtain generalization.

Another category of technique is to "train loosely"—to be somewhat irregular in the conditions of training and in the definition of acceptable responses. Variations in the setting and in the exact stimuli presented to the child would also fall in this category. The more liberal the training conditions, the less likely behavior change is to be restricted to the exact training conditions.

Stokes and Baer also discuss the use of "indiscriminable contingencies," which means that, to some extent, contingencies (i.e., the rules for delivery of rewards) that are at least somewhat unpredictable are most likely to lead to generalization. This includes both the schedule of reinforcement and the conditions under which it is delivered. An essential component of many behavior management programs is to change gradually from continuous reinforcement (reinforcing each exam-

ple of a correct response) to intermittent reinforcement (allowing some responses to go unreinforced). This concept is explained more thoroughly in Chapter 4.

"Programming of common stimuli" means the inclusion of elements from environments targeted for generalization in the original training. For instance, if training in some academic skill is given in a particular setting, generalization to other settings is most likely to occur when elements from these settings are included in the original training. This could be done, for example, by including regular classroom worksheets in training that takes place in a psychologist's office or a resource room. Another technique would be to have the child's classroom teacher participate in training once behavior change has occurred in the original training environment. A related technique is to promote "mediated" generalization by training verbal labels to appropriate behavior in both the original environment and settings to which the behavior is to be generalized.

Finally, Stokes and Baer suggest that generalization, itself, may be a trainable response that should be reinforced, at least intermittently, when it occurs.

After an extensive review of the behavior management literature, Rutherford and Nelson (1988) concluded that there is still a lot to be learned about techniques of promoting generalization of newly learned behaviors. It is clear, however, that a key element is to design programs so that natural contingencies eventually maintain the target behavior. This means that natural reinforcers such as teacher praise, peer attention, and positive feedback at home should take the place of the structured behavior management program. Another important way of promoting generalization is to train students to self-monitor, self-evaluate, and self-reinforce the target behaviors (Hinshaw & Erhardt, 1991; Kendall & Braswell, 1993; Lam, Cole, Shapiro, & Bambara, 1994). However, Nelson, Smith, Young, and Dodd (1991) found evidence that self-monitoring procedures, themselves, will not necessarily generalize spontaneously to other settings unless specific training is conducted in those settings. Each of the behavior management programs discussed in Part II includes specific recommendations for promoting appropriate generalization of behavior to other environments.

Step 7: Modify the program, if necessary.   Depending on a number of factors, behavior management programs may be unsuccessful the first time they are implemented. The best thing to do when this occurs is take a look at the child and at the situation at home and school, and modify the program in a reasonable way. Several aspects of a behavior management program can be examined when it is ineffective.

First, the program may simply need more time to take effect. There are no concrete guidelines regarding the length of time required for a program to "take hold," but the frequency of the target behavior and the frequency of the reward or punishment should be determining factors. For a behavior management program involving a behavior occurring several times per day and punished by timeout, one would expect to see effects of the program within several days to a couple of weeks. For a program involving an infrequent behavior, such as completing homework, which is rewarded by points that can be used to "buy" other rewards each Saturday, improvement may not be noted for two to four weeks. Visual displays such as graphs of the frequency of a target behavior are very helpful because they can signal when the trend is up or down. Any sign that the behavior is changing in the expected direction suggests that the program should be extended without any modification.

A second reason for the apparent ineffectiveness of a behavior management program is that something important may have been overlooked when the original assessment was performed. My own experience has been that behavior management programs can sometimes be frustratingly ineffective when the child's home is unstable. An impending divorce, disagreement between the parents regarding rules and discipline, and alcoholism are examples of situations at home that can spill over into the school and complicate management of the child's behavior. When such situations arise, there is sometimes little that can be accomplished at school. However, a behavior management program that uses highly desirable rewards and involves the parents in any positive way may be successful. Alternatively, the school psychologist or social worker could become involved in assessing and working with the family and making a referral to other professionals, if appropriate.

Another potential reason for the ineffectiveness of a program is that it is either too simple or too complicated. A program could be too simple when a behavior targeted for change does not really capture the essence of the child's problem. For instance, an older child could be regularly failing examinations and in-class assignments. A reasonable strategy for dealing with such a problem might be to place the child on a behavioral contract that rewards academic success with privileges at home. However, this approach might not work if the child's problem was debilitating test anxiety. A program em-

phasizing relaxation and imagery techniques, study skills, and academic success might be more effective.

On the other hand, a program could be too complicated. Too many behaviors may be specified at once, the child may not have sufficient understanding of the program, or too many adults may be involved. In such cases, the solution is to simplify the program.

Perhaps the program design is sound, but the reward is insufficient to promote behavior change. Observation of and negotiation with the child are probably the best ways of determining more desirable consequences for behavior. Even timeout can be ineffective if the child finds it rewarding in some way. For example, the child might gain reinforcing peer attention by making faces while in timeout. Alternatively, the timeout may be more attractive than the activity the child leaves. A trip to the principal's office can be appealing if the child receives attention from adults while there. Any of these circumstances could decrease the effectiveness of timeout. In such cases, a response cost procedure or improved isolation of the child (within reasonable limits) may have the desired effects.

Other problems that could interfere with the success of a program include inconsistent administration of contingencies, an ambiguous definition of the target behavior, or too rapidly fading out the program. If these problems are noted, the behavior management program should be adjusted accordingly.

Step 8: Fade out the program. The truly successful behavior management program eventually puts itself out of business, so to speak. That is, elements of the program are slowly faded out so the target behavior occurs at a normal rate without the need for a formal management program. Fading a program is accomplished by reducing the amount and frequency of reward. At the same time, praise and other rewards from significant adults (e.g., good grades from the teacher, positive attention from parents) take the place of the structure of the behavior management program.

In order to fade out a program, two things are necessary. First, the amount of behavior between rewards must be *slowly* increased; second, abstract rewards must be *slowly* substituted for the concrete, material rewards with which most programs begin. The most likely problem to be encountered while fading out the program is that behavior deteriorates from previous levels. When this occurs, merely go back to an earlier step in the fading process and try again at a later time. Numerous examples of this process are provided in Part II.

CONCLUSION

Both assessment and management of child behavior are dynamic processes. Although each process has been presented as a series of steps, neither is strictly linear. Both are driven by the information that they generate. Thus, at any time the logical next step could be to return to an earlier step in the process in order to try something else or gather more information about the child. An important characteristic that administrators of behavior management programs must possess is flexibility. Children are always communicating with adults, and the wise adult listens and acts on the messages. This means being willing to revise hypotheses and change intervention strategies as necessary.

REVIEW

Terms to Remember and Review

assessment	baseline data
reinforcement	Premack principle
stimulus	contingency
generalization	"train and hope"
natural contingencies	train sufficient examples
train loosely	program common stimuli
indiscriminable contingencies	flexibility

Study and Discussion Questions

1. What are the main differences between formal and informal assessment and behavior management procedures?

2. What role does assessment play in helping to clarify the nature of the problem behavior?

3. Describe the circular nature of developing and running a behavior management program.

4. Redefine each of the following behaviors in terms that would be appropriate for a behavior management program: depressed, anxious, disruptive, aggressive, dumb, lazy, socially awkward. Use the criteria from Step 2 ("Refine the definition of the problem") of the steps in conducting a formal behavior management program.

5. Why is it necessary to collect baseline data before beginning a behavior management program? What is the purpose of baseline data?

6. Discuss ways that behaviors learned in one environment can be programmed to occur in other environments.

7. What are some reasons that a behavior management program might be ineffective?

8. What does it mean to fade out a program? Why is this an important step in a behavior management program?

9. Why is it important for administrators of behavior management programs to be flexible?

Group Project

Develop a set of criteria for determining whether a behavior management program should be conducted as an informal versus a formal intervention.

CHAPTER 4

ISSUES IN DESIGNING AN APPROPRIATE BEHAVIOR MANAGEMENT PROGRAM

Successful behavior management programs are designed by professionals who know how to apply the basic principles of behavior management and know the individual child whose behavior is to be changed. In many cases, a *team* is involved in the design and implementation of a behavior management program. The team could be a teacher and a consultant, a formal child study team, or a special education team serving a handicapped child. A team approach is helpful because each individual on the team can contribute his or her special expertise to developing a program that is in the child's best interests.

A typical sequence in the development of a behavior management program may begin with a classroom teacher who develops a strategy for remediating a behavior problem. If the program does not work, he or she then might seek consultation and, together, teacher and consultant would develop another plan for remediating the problem. If this effort fails, more individuals may become involved until a team encompassing several individuals and the child's parents has been formed. As the number of individuals involved in the team increases, the process takes on a more formal structure. Increasing amounts of documentation are required, and the decisions made by the team have a more profound impact on the child. This is the nature of the educational process. Ultimately, a special education team may decide that the child is in need of special education services for handicapped children.

As intervention strategies are developed, there are several issues of which the team must be aware. Some issues have such a profound impact on programs that they must be considered each time a behavior management program is designed. These are *primary issues*. Other issues appear less frequently but may still have a strong impact on the development of interventions. These are *secondary issues*. The distinction between primary issues and secondary issues is based on how often they appear. Primary issues must be addressed for each behavior management program, whereas secondary issues may or may not be considered each time a behavior management program is implemented. When a secondary issue needs to be addressed, however, it may be crucial to understanding the child and developing a successful behavior management program.

PRIMARY ISSUES

Four primary issues must be considered each time a behavior management program is implemented:

1. What is the goal to be accomplished?
2. In what environment is the goal to be accomplished?

3. What is the developmental status of the child?
4. What is the least restrictive behavior management program?

A discussion of each of these primary issues follows.

What is the goal to be accomplished?   The phrase *behavior management* implies a concrete, goal-oriented activity. Every behavior management program needs to have an endpoint or goal. The three main goals of behavior management are prevention, reduction of behavior excesses, and improvement of behavior deficits.

For the teacher meeting a class on the first day of school, the main goal should be to manage learning tasks effectively and *prevent* behavior problems requiring individual attention. This goal requires close attention to the general principles of sound behavior management, particularly the Golden Rule of Behavior Management, a reminder to ignore, as much as possible, all minor annoyances and misbehavior and spend as much time as possible giving positive attention to students who are behaving correctly. A more complete discussion of guidelines for general classroom management is presented in Chapter 5.

Even in the most skillfully managed classrooms, the need to develop an individual or group behavior management program will occasionally arise. When this happens, an important issue is whether the identified problem is a *behavior excess* or a *behavior deficit*. A parallel way to view this question is whether the problem is an externalizing or internalizing problem (Kendall, 1991). Most behavior problems should be defined as behavior deficits, implying that the child needs to learn new skills or make use of already learned skills more consistently. Even in cases where the child is disrupting a classroom, there is usually a task that the child is expected to be doing when the disruption occurs. Increasing the amount of time engaged in this task is an effective way to decrease the disruptive behavior. Thus, before it is concluded that a problem represents a behavior excess, the situation should be observed closely to determine whether there is some other skill that the child could learn to take the place of the disruptive behavior.

A behavior excess is characterized by behavior that is dangerous or interferes unacceptably with the structure and activities of the regular classroom. Physical aggression is the most common example of a behavior excess. Programs to decrease behavior excesses, especially the use of timeout, require skill, careful planning, and careful attention to the child's rights because instructional

time in the regular classroom is sometimes lost. Chapter 7 describes a coupon program for reducing behavior excesses that can be conducted in a regular classroom with no assistance from support personnel. This program has proved effective in reducing behavior excesses in many cases without interfering with regular classroom instruction.

Preventing problems, remediating behavior deficits, and reducing behavior excesses are the three main goals of behavior management. Part II describes concrete programs for reaching each of these goals.

In what environment is the goal to be accomplished? The environment in which a behavior management program is conducted places definite restrictions on the design of the program. As I began my career as a school psychologist, this was one of the first lessons I encountered in designing behavior management programs. Programs *must* be compatible with the environment in which they are implemented. If the program is too complex, requires time that is not available, or needs a level of supervision that cannot be supplied, it is unlikely to succeed. A classroom teacher cannot be expected to implement successfully a behavior management program that targets several behaviors that occur frequently throughout the day, uses a complex reward based on points, and requires an hour of record keeping at the end of the school day. This type of program would demand too much from a person whose primary task, teaching thirty students or several classes each day, is very demanding to begin with. A behavior management program needs to be compatible with the environment in which it will be conducted.

Although many variations and hybrids are possible, there are three main environments with which school personnel must be concerned: regular classrooms, special classrooms, and the home. Regular classrooms are typically structured around a lead teacher who may have a variety of assistants available. Assistants may be paid pupil support assistants or teaching interns nearing the end of their academic training. Consultants from outside the classroom may also be available on a part-time basis to assist in administration of behavior management programs. For the most part, regular classrooms demand the simplest effective behavior management alternative.

Special classrooms are environments in which much more individual attention is provided. Classes are much smaller than the typical regular classroom, and more contact with instructional and pupil support personnel is available. Pupils in special classrooms are usually receiving special education services as a consequence of their educational needs and the presence of a handicapping condition such as a learning disability, emotional or behavioral disorder, developmental disability, or other condition that interferes with their ability to benefit from instruction in regular classrooms. The staffing available in such programs means that more complex programs are possible in special classrooms.

The home environment can play a key role in remediating many behavior problems manifested in school. Parents can provide backup rewards for programs conducted in school, or they can conduct behavior management programs at home. Having similar programs in the home and the school can provide an element of consistency that makes for faster learning. Another important consideration is that many parents' only access to professional services for their child is through the school. For these reasons, it is important for school personnel both to enlist the support of parents and to provide them with support whenever possible.

What is the developmental status of the child? Child behavior management should be viewed in a developmental context for two reasons. First, one's view of problem behavior needs to be tempered with knowledge of what is appropriate at each age level. For example, a high rate of activity and short attention span are typical of preschool children but might be considered a problem in a fourth-grade child. Second, a child's ability to understand the relationship between behavior and rewards will be different at the various developmental stages. An awareness of developmental issues will enable the practitioner to interpret behavior more accurately and design more effective programs. For more detailed treatments of child development, see Berger (1994), P. M. Miller (1983), Newman and Newman (1979), Simeonsson and Rosenthal (1992), Thomas (1979), Turner and Helms (1990), Wimbarti and Self (1992), or any recent general psychology textbook (e.g., Weiten, 1992).

Keeping a developmental perspective will enable the practitioner to match techniques to the cognitive skills of the child. If one indiscriminately applies techniques without considering the age of the child, some unnecessary failures are likely to result. Complex procedures with long delays between behavior and its consequences are generally most appropriate for older children. Simple procedures with concrete, immediate consequences are generally most appropriate when managing the behavior of younger children. For convenience, childhood can be

considered to consist of three overlapping stages: early childhood, middle childhood, and adolescence. A brief discussion of programs for each age group follows.

Early childhood runs from about age one to age six or seven. The types of behavior management programs likely to be successful with children in early childhood emphasize concrete goals, immediate consequences, and material rewards. Children in early childhood would not respond well to programs with long delays or complicated relationships between behavior and rewards. Subtle distinctions, such as the difference between "accidental" actions and "purposeful" actions, are not likely to be understood. Immediate consequences, such as praise, a brief period in a "thinking" (timeout) chair, or a sticker are most likely to work with this age group. A token program that has a very concrete method of illustrating progress toward the backup reward, such as covering a page with stickers or filling a jar with marbles, may also be effective.

Middle childhood can be loosely defined as the ages from seven to twelve. More complex behavior management procedures can be employed with children in middle childhood. These would include fairly complex token reward programs in which the child earns points for good behavior that can be exchanged for various material rewards. Home note programs, in which the child's teacher rates classroom behavior on a daily or weekly basis and the child's parents provide rewards contingent on the quality of the ratings, are also likely to be effective. During middle childhood, the entire range of common behavior management procedures is likely to be effective if appropriate individual adjustments are made. The coupon program described in Chapter 7 is likely to work especially well during middle childhood, although it may be successful with adolescents as well.

Adolescence has often been characterized as a period of *Sturm und Drang*—great "storm and stress." The period runs from about age 13 to young adulthood or whenever the child leaves home to work, attend college, or marry. Adolescents, whether or not they have developed internal standards of conduct congruent with societal expectations, will normally have developed advanced cognitive skills. Along with advanced cognitive skills comes a desire for independence from adults. Consequently, adolescents are likely to respond best to programs in which they have a major say. Probably the most common approach with adolescents is behavioral contracting. The key element in such contracts is that they allow the adolescent input into the process. In fact, good behavioral contracts specify that parties signing the contract are to both receive and grant privileges to the other party. With this technique, the adolescent has the opportunity to change his or her own behavior as well as significant others. Other programs can succeed as well with adolescents, when adults have control of potent reinforcers. An important key to success is to ensure that any program for any child is developmentally appropriate.

What is the least restrictive, developmentally appropriate program? The last primary issue is to select the least restrictive, developmentally appropriate behavior management program that will meet the child's needs. The *least restrictive alternative* refers to meeting a child's needs with techniques and in environments that are as similar to the child's normal environment as possible. The *most restrictive* alternative is to use a timeout that isolates the child from instructional activity. The least restrictive alternative is to employ the rules and consequences that apply to all children in the classroom or school. As a rough guideline, a list of behavior management procedures in approximate order of restrictiveness from least to most restrictive is shown below. Nelson and Rutherford (1983) described a similar hierarchy exclusively for timeout and related procedures.

Least Restrictive

Praise and natural contingencies
Consequences described in classroom rules
Consequences described in schoolwide rules
Reinforcing notes to parents
Reinforcement of specific behaviors
Ignoring of inappropriate behavior
Token programs
Monitoring of school performance with checklist
Response cost programs
Brief chair timeout in classroom
Removal of normal privileges
Timeout that isolates the child

Most Restrictive

Behavior management programming should begin with the least restrictive option that will meet the child's needs. As a general rule, isolation timeout, although it can be a very effective contingency, should always be planned by a team of individuals including all the educational staff who contact the child, a representative administrator, and the child's parents. Restrictions on the use of timeout vary from state to state. At least one state (Minnesota) requires a written program, a timeout room that meets specific safety standards, and the opportunity to request a review of the program by an outside committee, prior to implementing timeout with a handicapped child. Other restrictions on using timeout will be discussed in Chapter 7.

Part II of *Behavior Management in the Schools* is organized around these three primary issues. Chapter 5 discuss prevention of behavior problems. Chapters 7, 8, and 9 discuss management of behavior excesses in the regular classroom, special classroom, and home, respectively. Chapters 10, 11, and 12 discuss management of behavior deficits in these three settings. Chapter 6 provides a more detailed guide to selecting specific behavior management programs to meet specific needs. Programs that vary in their suitability for the three age groups are presented within each chapter.

SECONDARY ISSUES

Secondary issues in selecting behavior management programs are secondary only in the sense that they are not considered *each* time a behavior management program is planned. These issues are not only crucial to designing good programs but may indicate a need for additional services without which success may be very difficult to attain. Three secondary issues will be discussed:

1. What is the status of the child's family system?
2. What are the child's cultural roots, and how should they influence school programming?
3. What diagnostic issues are raised by the child's behavior?

What is the status of the child's family system?   A child's family system plays a key role in the success of any behavior management program. All behavior management programs will be more successful if cooperation and active participation of the child's parents are elicited. However, if the target behavior is part of that child's role in the family, is related to family stresses, is directly supported by parenting practices, or is somehow reinforcing to family members, a behavior management program may be unsuccessful unless the entire system is changed (Fine & Holt, 1983b; Wielkiewicz, 1992; Zimmerman & Sims, 1983).

Strong evidence indicates that parental practices are related to behavior problems in school (Patterson, 1986; Patterson & Stouthamer-Loeber, 1984; Ramsey, Walker, Shinn, O'Neill, & Stieber, 1989). Ramsey et al. found that children with the most severe behavior problems were subjected to ineffective, unfair, and inconsistent parent management practices. Parents of this group were also significantly less skilled at solving family problems such as conflict, unemployment, and financial emergencies. Although the types of research that can be performed to study the relationships between parenting practices and school adjustment do not allow inferences of causal relationships, it seems reasonable to assert that these studies indicate that parenting practices can play a definite role in maintaining maladjusted behavior in school. The conclusion is unavoidable: Behavior management programs in school are likely to have the greatest success when the family becomes actively involved in assisting in problem remediation.

In order to develop effective programs for children, it is important to communicate effectively with parents. One of the most important components of good communication is *listening*. The child's parents know more than anyone else about the child. Acknowledging the parents' expertise and giving them the opportunity to share information about the child should be one of the goals of a parent conference. Listening to parents (or anyone else) is not just a matter of being polite and quiet. It also means that the listener must truly gain some understanding of the ideas and feelings being communicated. One useful technique is to rephrase what has been said and repeat it back to the parents while acknowledging the feelings that were expressed. By saying things back to the parents in different words, one is able to check on the accuracy of one's own interpretation of what has been said while validating the value of the parents' contribution.

In the process of communicating with parents, team members need to be alert to family systems issues that may have an impact on the child's behavior. Signs of marital distress, an impending divorce or separation, physical abuse, parental alcoholism, or other serious family problems may indicate a need for intervention beyond a behavior management program. Although it may not be possible to involve parents in additional services, it should be possible to offer additional services to the child. Individual counseling, support groups, self-esteem enhancing activities, and support from significant adults in the school may increase the effectiveness of behavior management programs. The school can also have a significant impact on the family system by involving parents in positive ways with school-based behavior management programs. If signs of family distress are evident, conducting a formal assessment, as described in Chapter 3, may provide important information that can be influential in developing the best program for the child.

What are the child's cultural roots, and how should they influence school programming? A complete view of any child must also consider the community and culture in which the child lives. Some children live in violent and dangerous environments with profound poverty and homelessness that certainly interferes with their ability to benefit fully from learning experiences (e.g., Rafferty & Shinn, 1991; "The Most Innocent Victims," 1990; Youngstrom, 1992). There is no doubt that both overt and subtle racism in our society also have profound effects on schoolchildren with minority backgrounds. Minority children can develop a sense that they are not really in control of the events that affect them. This can lead to feelings of unhappiness and frustration and to the appearance of being uninterested in learning. Students may turn to involvement in gang activities, which can provide a sense of belonging and accomplishment unavailable in school activities (Cantrell & Cantrell, 1993; McEvoy, 1990). Dealing effectively with minority pupils requires sensitivity to other cultures and an ability to acknowledge the existence of racist elements in ourselves and our society.

Behavior management techniques are based on universal principles that can work regardless of the cultural background of the child. However, behavior management programs for minority pupils must be designed by individuals who are familiar with the child's cultural background. It would be unfair to demand that a child change behaviors that are rooted in cultural traditions. For example, among many Native American groups, children who make eye contact with adults are considered to be showing lack of respect. In contrast most teachers regard lack of eye contact as an indicator that the child is not paying attention. A clash of these values could lead a teacher to identify lack of eye contact as a problem behavior when, in reality, it is not. It is also important to avoid overgeneralizing from what is known about a particular culture to individuals within that culture; each culture has its own subgroups, and individuals within a culture will vary considerably with respect to their identification with both the majority and the minority culture (Marsella, 1993).

Space prohibits a complete discussion of characteristics of cultural groups here; it would take an entire book to do the topic justice (e.g., Sue & Sue, 1990). However, a few guidelines for fair treatment of minority students can be abstracted from sources on this topic (Frisby, 1992; Jones & Herndon, 1992; Marsella, 1993; Nuttall, De Leon, & Valle, 1992; Sattler, 1988; Sue & Sue, 1990; Williams, 1989). First, all school-based professionals must strive to deal with their own negative biases and racism. In order to treat all students fairly, it is important to be able to appreciate both the individual and his or her cultural heritage. This may mean that school-based professionals must actively seek opportunities to educate themselves about the cultures they contact.

A second guideline is to stay focused on the child's best interests. Identifying each child's strengths and developing them can improve both academic and behavioral functioning in school by increasing motivation. Third, it is crucial to maintain a systems view of behavior. One must evaluate not only the behavior of the individual child, but also the familial and cultural context of the behavior, especially its nonverbal aspects (Miranda, 1993). Furthermore, the source of conflict between the child's behavior and the school system may lie not in the child's behavior, but in conflict between the *systems*. That is, school and cultural values, such as their relative emphasis on competition, may be in conflict. The solution is for the systems to come together and determine cooperatively what is in the child's best interests. Focusing exclusively on changing the child's behavior may intensify conflict between the child and the child's own culture unless the target behavior is compatible with family values, cultural values, and the school system. Finally, as in all aspects of behavior management, a data-based, active, flexible, and problem-solving approach is needed in dealing with minority children and their families. For those desiring to pursue this topic further, Alladin (1993) has prepared an annotated bibliography.

What diagnostic issues are raised by the child's behavior? Behavior management is a powerful tool for helping children adapt to their school and home environments. However, it is not the only tool available for assisting children with their problems. Counseling, hospitalization, special education, social services, family therapy, and medical intervention may also benefit a child, either alone or in conjunction with a behavior management program. Sometimes, behavior management alone is incapable of meeting a child's needs. For example, a child may be acting out in a physically aggressive way toward classmates. After appropriate consultation with parents, a successful program to increase adaptive behaviors could make it appear that the problem has been resolved. But what if the underlying reason for the child's aggressive behavior was physical maltreatment from parents or a sibling? In this case, a successful behavior management program really leaves the most critical issue, helping the child avoid physical abuse, unresolved.

Alternatively, imagine an adolescent girl whose academic performance declines drastically. The behavior management perspective suggests that a program to reward academic accomplishment is needed. But what if her poor academic performance is a symptom of alcohol abuse. A behavior management program may succeed only if it is combined with treatment for the alcohol problem. Often, information gained by assessing a child and developing a behavior management program can also suggest that other critical interventions should be considered. The signs and symptoms that point toward such interventions can occur in clusters that suggest one or more of the common diagnostic categories, such as ADHD (Attention-Deficit Hyperactivity Disorder), depression, anxiety, school phobia, a specific learning disability, or mental retardation. Alternatively, behavioral observations may suggest problems such as physical abuse, sexual abuse, family conflict, or parental divorce, that are not diagnostic categories but do suggest a need for intervention.

Regardless of whether behavior management strategies are being used to remediate a problem situation, school personnel need to be alert to situations that demand additional action (e.g., signs of a potential suicide attempt) or suggest a need for additional services (e.g., teenage alcoholism). The more commonly occurring examples of these situations are reviewed in this section. The purpose of this review is to help the reader learn to recognize signs and symptoms that suggest additional investigation so that a complete intervention program can be developed. Remaining alert for these possibilities will prevent needless frustration for both school personnel and children while enabling schools to intervene in each child's best interests.

Hyperactivity. Hyper is a prefix meaning "excessive." To say that a hyperactive child exhibits too much activity is really an understatement. In the regular class-room, a hyperactive child is likely to be noticed, first, because he or she (most likely he) is typically engaged in activities other than assigned classroom work. The child's time is occupied by a variety of irrelevant activi-ties, such as running around the classroom, annoying other students, playing with objects in or around his desk, fidgeting, talking, and other behaviors in opposi-tion to the goals of the classroom. Such students are likely to experience great difficulty in properly organiz-ing a task and are also likely to switch from an assigned task to some irrelevant, off-task activity, even when they are closely supervised. From the classroom teacher's point of view, these children are also likely to be noted for their inability to pay attention or follow directions. Essex and Schifani (1992) suggested that failure to identify and provide appropriate education for hyperac-tive children may even result in legal liability for the school system. It is critical that school personnel be familiar with the symptoms of hyperactivity and develop appropriate educational plans for these children when they are identified (Wielkiewicz, 1993).

Hyperactivity is one of the most commonly identified behavioral problems of children, with estimates of its incidence ranging from about 3 percent to as high as 20 percent. Boys are three to ten times more likely to be labeled hyperactive than girls. Studies that follow chil-dren diagnosed as hyperactive into later life indicate that hyperactivity declines somewhat but associated prob-lems may be present even in adulthood (Barkley, 1990; Weiss & Hechtman, 1993).

DSM-IV, the *Diagnostic and Statistical Manual of Mental Disorders,* published by the American Psychiat-ric Association (1994), contains diagnostic criteria for all recognized mental disorders. It refers to hyperactivity as Attention-Deficit/Hyperactivity Disorder defining three related disorders: ADHD, Combined Type; ADHD, Predominantly Inattentive Type; and ADHD, Predominantly Hyperative-Impulsive Type. To meet the criteria for ADHD, Combined Type, six out of nine symptoms reflecting inattention *and* six out of nine symptoms reflecting hyperactivity-impulsivity "must have persisted for at least 6 months to a degree that is maladaptive and inconsistent with developmental level." To meet the criteria for ADHD, Predominantly Inattentive Type, only six out of the nine symptoms reflecting inattention need to persist and to meet the criteria for ADHD, Predominantly Hyperative-Impul-sive Type, six out of nine symptoms reflecting hyperac-tivity-impulsivity need to be present. In addition, some

symptoms causing impairment must have been present before age seven years, impairment must be present in two or more settings, impairment must be "clinically significant," and symptoms should be independent of several other possible disorders. This represents a sig-nificant change from the *DSM-III-R* (American Psychi-atric Association, 1987) criteria, which did not recognize subtypes of ADHD (see Barkley, June 1993, for further discussion.

Table 4.1 shows characteristics of hyperactive chil-dren as seen from parents' points of view. This table has been used as a handout to assist parents in learning about their hyperactive children. Its purpose is both to educate parents and to give them a description of the hyperactive child that they could give to relatives, friends, teachers, babysitters, or others who come in contact with their child.

ADHD is usually identified when the child is between four and seven years old. The transition into a first-grade classroom is particularly crucial for children with ADHD because the amount of time spent doing seatwork and other structured activities places a great strain on their attentional capacity and ability to inhibit impulsive behavior. Problems associated with hyperactivity tend to continue into adolescence, and studies indicate that adolescents with a history of ADHD are at risk to de-velop symptoms of conduct disorder, low self-esteem, substance abuse, and other maladjustments, although motor hyperactivity, impulse control, and attention span tend to improve (Barkley, 1990; Cantwell, 1986). For more thorough discussions of ADHD, the books by Barkley (1990) and Goldstein and Goldstein (1990) are highly recommended.

Behavior management programs are often needed with ADHD children of all ages. Timeout, the "coupon" program, home notes, token programs, and daily/weekly report cards can all be useful. Consistent, immediate, frequent, and obvious consequences are helpful in deal-ing with ADHD children. It is also particularly important to focus on rewarding appropriate behavior with these children (Barkley, 1993, April). However, additional services are often needed. When a potentially ADHD child is identified, the school may need to consider a special education assessment, referral to professionals qualified to diagnose ADHD, and other support services to ensure that an appropriate program is developed.

Childhood depression. Children who are hyperac-tive, aggressive, or disruptive tend to attract the most attention. Children who are quiet, withdrawn, and sad

Table 4.1. Characteristics of Hyperactive Children

Parents of hyperactive children typically observe that their children show some or all of the following characteristics:

Hyperactive children do not respond to typical discipline techniques. When hyperactive children are sent to their rooms as punishment, they will quickly find something else to do and completely forget why they are being punished. Instead, timeout chairs and other structured discipline techniques are needed. Parents of hyperactive children often attend workshops or read books to improve their child management skills.

Hyperactive children tend to learn rules because they have consequences, not because the rule has any merit or moral value. Consistent consequences will help the hyperactive child learn important rules. When a rule is broken, it is usually ineffective to explain its purpose.

Hyperactive children are impulsive. They do many things so quickly they obviously did not take time to consider the consequences. Hyperactive children may learn to be less impulsive if they clean up, repair, or engage in other forms of restitution for their impulsive behavior.

Hyperactive children may move from one uncompleted activity to another but are capable of spending hours concentrating on an activity that attracts their interest. Parents frequently wonder why the child can watch TV for hours but cannot concentrate on their homework for more than a few minutes at a time.

School problems, both academic and behavioral, are common among hyperactive children. Structured classes, a minimum of distractions, behavior management programs, and special education services may sometimes be needed to help these children succeed in school.

Medication can be a great help in the management of hyperactivity, but it can be used only part time and does not teach needed skills. Parents must remain conscientious in their approach to child management even when medication has been prescribed.

Hyperactive children must learn to slow down, stop, and think about consequences before they do something. Parents can teach their children by using cues like STOP!, FREEZE!, or THINK!, when they see the child is headed for trouble. Parents can also teach the child how to analyze problems systematically and evaluate possible solutions.

Although the problems caused by hyperactivity seem to require endless attention, the child's success as an adult will depend on developing a good self-concept and finding a vocation that uses his or her strengths and talents. Jobs that allow freedom to move around and do not require a lot of time at a desk may be preferred by adults who were hyperactive as children.

Expectations about hyperactive children can occasionally lead to false accusations and attempts to blame them for things they really did not do. Make sure the facts and evidence are clear before demanding restitution or administering punishment. Also, it takes two children to fight, so either punish both or let them settle it themselves.

but do not disrupt the education of others are not as likely to attract attention. In some children, however, ordinary sadness crosses the border into depression, which is a serious problem for a significant number of school-age children.

Schwartz and Johnson (1985) estimated that depression occurs in about 28 percent of children referred to clinics and in about 2 percent of the general population. Milling and Martin (1992) concluded that depression occurs in 2 percent to 5 percent of children depending on their age. Signs of depression include poor appetite or loss of weight, increased appetite or significant weight gain, loss of energy, fatigue, tiredness, difficulty in concentration or thinking, and sleep irregularities. Sleep irregularities are characterized by difficulty getting to sleep or staying asleep, too much sleep, or awakening

unusually early. Other signs of depression include, first and most important, a distinctively depressed mood characterized as sad, blue, hopeless, down in the dumps, low, or irritable. In children, a persistently sad facial expression can be used to infer a depressed mood. Other signs of depression include apathy, indecisiveness, lack of interest in activities formerly regarded as fun or enjoyable, excessive or frequent crying, statements indicating lack of self-worth, self-reproach, apprehension, poor school performance, excessive or inappropriate guilt, low self-esteem, statements about death or suicide, a suicide attempt, social isolation, nonreactivity, and psychomotor disturbance (Cantor, 1983; DSM-III; DSM-III-R; *DSM-IV;* Milling & Martin, 1992).

The DSM-IV presently recognizes Major Depression, Single Episode, and Major Depression, Recurrent (with or without seasonal pattern), and Dysthymic Disorder (or Depressive Neurosis). Dysthymia differs from Major Depression in being less severe and of longer (more chronic) duration. Depression can also occur in conjunction with a diagnosis of Bipolar Disorder, which would include episodes of both depression and mania at different times. It is rare for a child to receive a diagnosis of Bipolar Disorder. Major Depression and Dysthymic Disorder are more common in children. Barkley (1990) notes that Dysthymia may be common in children with ADHD. Milling and Martin (1992) found that co-occurrence of depression with anxiety or conduct disorder is a common finding in the childhood depression literature.

Within the school environment, several circumstances might bring behaviors associated with depression to the attention of school practitioners. Academic problems, manifested in poor work habits, and an inability to concentrate are likely to initiate concern, especially if there is a change from previous levels of performance. Another cause of concern is that a child may show signs of a low self-concept, manifested in frequent self-directed negative statements. Finally, a child may be performing at or near the average level academically but nevertheless attract attention because of persistent sadness, social isolation, crying, expression of suicidal intent, or other signs of depressed mood. Kazdin (1988) noted that there are many nonspecific signs of school problems suggesting depression, such as poor peer relations, poor or reduced academic performance, acting out in the classroom, difficulty in concentration, or problems with cognitive tasks. Judging whether these symptoms suggest childhood depression depends on whether the behavior reflects a *change* in behavior, whether depressed mood persists for a long period (e.g., longer than a week or two), absence of a clear cause of the behavior, whether the symptoms are associated with impaired daily functioning, and whether the child is noticeably different from his or her peers.

Numerous measures for the assessment of depression are available, such as the Piers-Harris Children's Self-Concept Scale (Piers, 1984), the Behavior Evaluation Scale (McCarney, Leigh, & Cornbleet, 1983), or the Children's Depression Inventory (Kovacs, 1980/1981; Finch, Saylor, & Edwards, 1985). Asarnow and Carlson (1985) describe an instrument called the Depression Self-Rating Scale (DSRS), which could be quickly administered and allows the administrator to classify children as depressed or not depressed, according to DSM-III criteria, with an accuracy of about 75 percent. However, an interesting finding is the identification of subgroups of children who tended to deny depressive symptoms. Thus, multiple sources of data are needed when it is believed that a child may be depressed.

Sheras (1992) reviewed a number of studies of adolescent depression. He found that symptoms of depression as expressed by adolescents included grief, shyness, episodes of aggressiveness, suicidal behavior, apathy, insecurity, difficulty in learning, mutism, unmotivated weeping, withdrawal from friends, bleak outlook on life, changes in eating and sleeping habits, loss of joy in life, risk taking or reckless behavior, preoccupation with death, increased somatic complaints, problems concentrating on schoolwork, frequent mood changes, low self esteem, and decreased attention to physical appearance. Sheras also cited data indicating that adolescents may also tend to mask or hide depressive feelings via denial, acting out, delinquency, and other behaviors. Sheras concluded that research on adolescent depression has not progressed to the point where it is clearly differentiated from either adult or childhood depression.

Environmental events, such as abuse (Kazdin, Moser, Colbus, & Bell, 1985), parental alcoholism (Tharinger & Koranek, 1988), or divorce (Drake, 1981; King, 1992), are often associated with depression in children. A focus on remediating the behavioral or cognitive signs of depression may be unsuccessful if the child lives in an abusive or neglectful home. In some cases, a resolution of the child's problems in school may require far-reaching environmental changes at home. Family counseling or a referral to social service agencies may prove superior to behavior management programs conducted at the school. Depression can be a serious, debilitating disorder that interferes with both academic and social functioning. Referral to a school psychologist, private practitioner, or mental health center would be a prudent course of action if depression is suspected. Depression is often treated with medication and behavior management programs designed to improve the associated behavior deficits.

Depression can also be associated with suicidal behavior. I believe it is so critical to recognize and react appropriately to signs of suicide that it is discussed separately in the next section.

Child or adolescent suicidal behavior. Behavior management is an enterprise based almost entirely on assessment. The consequence of emphasizing assessment is that those who practice behavior management are likely to learn a lot of important things about the children they manage and teach. One of these things concerns signs that a child or adolescent may be considering suicide. Recognizing these signs is critical and may even prevent a tragedy.

Depression is often associated with plans or thoughts about suicide, but any behaviors suggesting suicidal intent must be responded to regardless of whether depression is suspected. Even children as young as or younger than age five can behave in ways that would purposefully lead to death (Cantor, 1983; Rosenthal & Rosenthal, 1984). Guetzloe (1989) cites statistics indicating that suicide is the second leading cause of death among people ages fifteen to twenty-four and the sixth leading cause of death among children ages five to fourteen. Thus, it is important for educators to be aware of the signs predicting a possible suicide and to know how to react to those signs. Any statements regarding thoughts or plans of suicide *must* be taken seriously and professional consultation immediately sought. Most cities will have a crisis line, hotline, or similar telephone counseling service that can help in identifying the seriousness of a suicidal threat and provide access to additional sources of help.

The main role for educators reading this book is to understand that suicide is a serious problem among young people or young children and that it is often accompanied by overt signs. Many schools or school districts have suicide policies to which school personnel can refer for guidance on actions to take when a suicidal student is encountered. Detailed assessment and treatment of the suicidal individual should be left to qualified professionals. The educator's job is to recognize the critical signs and safely deliver the child to the appropriate sources of help.

Many sources discuss signs of suicidal intent among children and youth. The most common signs are listed next with a brief explanation of each. Educators who encounter these signs should seek consultation immediately, making sure that the child will be in a supervised environment in the meantime.

- *Any verbal threat of suicide.* Individuals who threaten or talk about suicide as an option often follow through. Therefore, any such threat must be taken seriously. When such threats include specific plans that could be lethal, risk of an actual attempt should be regarded as extremely high. Teachers may hear such talk directly from a student or receive reports of it from others. The statements may be direct and unambiguous or vague, such as references to "not being around anymore" or hopelessness about the future.

- *A past history of suicide attempt(s).* A past history of suicide attempts places the individual at high risk for another attempt.

- *Signs of depression.* Depression is discussed in the previous section. It should be noted that many suicides occur in depressed individuals.

- *Hopelessness.* Research indicates that hopelessness is probably a more accurate predictor of suicidal intent than depression alone (e.g., Asarnow & Guthrie, 1989). Hopelessness is the belief that nothing can or will improve the current situation.

- *Extreme changes in behavior.* Abrupt changes in mood or behavior fall in this category. In dealing with depressed students, it is particularly important to realize that an abrupt improvement in a depressed individual may reflect a decision to commit suicide.

- *Occurrence of a situational crisis.* A situational crisis, particularly one that results in a loss of a valued relationship, embarrassment, humiliation, feelings of hopelessness, or any other blow to self-esteem, could lead to suicidal behavior. A crisis could be the death of a loved one or friend, an arrest or appearance in juvenile court, argument with a significant other, academic failure, or any other event that could have an impact on self-esteem or generate hopelessness.

- *Making final arrangements.* This includes behavior such as saying goodbye to friends, giving away valued possessions, and other signs of settling affairs.

- *Reckless behavior.* Alcohol abuse, reckless driving, fighting, acts of delinquency, defiance, poor school performance, and other reckless and impulsive acts have been associated with depression and suicide.

- *Familial dysfunction.* Family dysfunction and conflict such as abuse, neglect, and familial alcoholism have been associated with suicidal behavior.

- *Exposure to suicide.* The occurrence of a suicide in a school is likely to place others at increased risk for suicidal behavior. Friends and relatives of the victim and those not knowing the victim who have a history of risk factors may need to be screened for current suicide risk (Garland & Zigler, 1993).

Assessments needed to plan behavior management programs occasionally produce information suggesting a suicide attempt is a possibility. Also, all teachers, but especially those teaching in special education classrooms, are likely to develop the kinds of relationships with children and adolescents that may result in a student revealing suicidal intent. When behavior suggests that a suicide attempt is a possibility, school personnel must react decisively and without delay. If the threat is regarded as serious, the school psychologist, the school principal, an emergency room, a suicide hotline, or a local mental health center should be contacted for advice. Ideally, reference to a districtwide suicide policy will provide concrete and helpful information. Meanwhile, the student must remain under supervision until a course of action is taken. For those wishing to pursue this topic further, see Garland and Zigler (1993), Guetzloe (1989), Milling and Martin (1992), Sheras (1992), or Whitaker and Slimak (1990). The Guetzloe (1989) book is particularly recommended for its thoroughness and relevance to educators.

School phobia. It is normal for a child to have some fears. Most childhood fears are outgrown without becoming the focus of adult attention. Such fears might include loud noises, strangers, and separation in the first year of life; various imaginary creatures or dogs in the second and third years; the dark in the fourth year; or school and social situations when the child reaches school age (cf. Ollendick, Matson, & Helsel, 1985). What divides a common age-appropriate fear from an unreasonable fear or phobia, which might be a target for behavior management, is its appropriateness and the extent to which it interferes with normal activity. For instance, it is normal for an adolescent to be somewhat anxious about an upcoming test. It is not reasonable if the anxiety is so great that the student is unable to concentrate and answer questions for which he or she is completely prepared. For present purposes, two specific examples of significant childhood problems related to anxiety will be discussed: school phobia and test anxiety.

School phobia is the childhood fear that most often receives attention in the research literature. Its main characteristic is avoidance of school. Because frequent or continuous absence from school creates problems for the school, the parents, and the child, it is not surprising that this is one of the most common phobias treated by clinical and school psychologists. Durlak (1992) discusses two kinds of school phobia, Type I (acute) and Type II (chronic). Acute school phobia develops in grades 1 to 3, responds well to intervention (70 percent to 90 percent success rate), and has a low incidence of long-term negative effects. Chronic school phobia, on the other hand, appears in grade 6 or later, does not respond as well to intervention (50 percent success rate), and is accompanied by other psychological and academic problems.

The school-phobic child's responses to parents' attempts to get the child to go to school may include complaints, on school days, of physical symptoms, such as headaches, nausea, vomiting, and stomach aches. It is also likely that the child will show unrealistic fear revolving around an attachment theme, such as fear that harm will befall the parents or that the child will become lost and permanently separated from home and family. School phobia often evolves into a very difficult situation for parents, which begins when parents reinforce the child's early efforts to avoid school with their attention and sympathy. Then, as the situation escalates, with absences reaching an unacceptably high frequency, the child may show *extreme* resistance to attempts at forcing school attendance. The resistance may greatly exceed the parents' ability to cope, even to the extent that their best and most persistent efforts to get the child to school may fail because of the intensity of the child's resistance. It is at the point where the situation has gotten out of control that school personnel are often requested to intervene.

When absence from school becomes the focus of intervention, school personnel need to consider whether the underlying cause is fear of the school environment. Fear is a strong motivator because avoidance or escape from the fear-evoking situation is negatively reinforcing. Thus, programs for treating school phobia are more complex than simply reinforcing school attendance. In addition, a team approach involving the child's parents, classroom teachers, school psychologist, and school administrators is almost always needed to manage school phobia. Family therapy can also become an essential component of intervention. When absence from school appears to be the result of school phobia, it is recommended that a team approach to intervention and assessment needs to be implemented.

Test anxiety. Poor academic performance is one of the most common school problems. Four basic areas must be assessed when a behavior management program is considered for a child experiencing academic difficulties: ability, achievement, motivation, and sensory capacity. The importance of such an assessment is twofold.

First, a behavior management program may be unnecessary, or even harmful, under some circumstances, such as when the child has a hearing problem. In such a case, rewards for academic achievement will not be nearly as helpful as a trip to the doctor. Second, academic programming must take place at a level that is appropriate to the child's academic skills. For instance, a child of average ability who shows a large deficit in reading achievement may need individual tutoring or special education in order to be successful. Behavior management strategies that ignore the need for additional help may cause great frustration for the child.

Low to moderate amounts of anxiety would be expected in most test situations and, in fact, are typically associated with optimum performance. Highly motivated pupils are likely to experience some anxiety when faced with an evaluation of their accomplishments. How does one differentiate normal anxiety, which boosts performance, from excessive anxiety, which interferes with test performance? In addition to reports of physical discomfort during and preceding the test situation, one would also seek evidence that test performance was lowered. A typical report under such circumstances would describe inability to recall information that they felt they knew very well. It would be especially noteworthy if the information were recalled immediately or soon after the individual left the test. This, and general reports of being preoccupied with anxiety and worry rather than coping with the task of taking the test (i.e., studying appropriately), would indicate that test anxiety was interfering with performance to the extent that some behavior management programs may prove beneficial. If test anxiety is suspected, referral to an expert is recommended.

Developmental disabilities. A developmental disability refers to a cognitive or physical impairment that manifests before the age of 22 and results in a lifelong need for supportive services (Patton, Payne, & Beirne-Smith, 1986). Mental retardation is the most common example of a developmental disability. Mental retardation is defined by deficits in general intellectual functioning and adaptive behavior, which adversely affect a child's educational performance. General intellectual functioning is measured with an individually administered test of intelligence. These tests are constructed so that a test score (IQ) represents that individual's relative standing within a standardization group representative of the U.S. population. An average score is 100. IQ scores that place an individual in the lowest 2 percent of

the population are generally considered to represent mental retardation. This would be an IQ score of 70–75 or below on most intelligence tests. However, the exact score used to define mental retardation (and thus make the child eligible for special services) may vary from school district to school district. Different terms are also used around the country to indicate mental retardation.

In addition to impaired intellectual ability, a child must also show concurrent deficits in adaptive behavior to be considered developmentally disabled. Adaptive behavior refers to the effectiveness of individuals in meeting the standards for personal independence and social responsibility expected for their age and cultural group. Standards of adaptive behavior vary with the age of the child. At age 5 or 6, the focus of assessment would be on skills such as tying shoes and dressing, whereas at the adult level the focus would be on vocational skills and social behavior. Adaptive behavior is usually assessed using a standardized instrument such as the Vineland Social Maturity Scale, the newer Vineland Adaptive Behavior Scales, or the American Association on Mental Deficiency's Adaptive Behavior Scale, School Edition. The items on these scales are answered using data from interviews with adults who have significant amounts of contact with the child, typically teachers and parents. For a more detailed discussion of issues in the assessment of adaptive behavior, see Witt and Martens (1984), Reschly (1990), or Wielkiewicz and Calvert (1989).

Recently the American Association on Mental Retardation (AAMR) revised its definition of mental retardation to place more emphasis on adaptive behavior and the amount of support needed by the individual (Turkington, 1993). The old terms (*mild, moderate, severe,* and *profound*) used to describe the degree of retardation have been replaced with descriptors for the levels of support needed by the individual (*intermittent, limited, extensive,* and *pervasive*). The definition also states that, in addition to significantly subaverage intellectual functioning, the individual should show concurrent limitations in two or more of these adaptive skill areas: communication, self-care, home living, social skills, community use, self-direction, health and safety, functional academics, leisure, and work. The advantage of the revised definition is that it places the emphasis on the services needed by the individual rather than on test scores.

A child who shows deficits in both adaptive behavior and general intellectual ability is likely to find much of the regular classroom work too difficult. Consistent failure in the regular classroom is likely, depending, of course, on the degree of the deficit. Special educational help would probably be necessary to supplement regular classroom work. Any formal or informal behavior management program must be designed to take into account the child's current level of performance. Children who are developmentally disabled are likely to respond very well to such programs because of their concrete and structured nature. It should also be noted that these children may show other behavior problems discussed in this chapter and that they are often mainstreamed into regular classrooms. Any behavior management programs developed for a developmentally disabled child will be planned by a special education team and are never the exclusive responsibility of a single person.

Giftedness. Giftedness is not a mental handicap, but it can create problems for the gifted child, parents, and other school staff members (Gridley, 1990). Giftedness is commonly defined by an IQ score above 130 (that is, in the uppermost 2 percent of the population) or special talents in academic areas, creativity, leadership, or the arts. Unidentified gifted youngsters can be very troublesome. Sometimes they do poorly in typical classroom work because, from their perspective, the work may be boring and repetitive. They are also likely to give strange, creative, or funny answers to questions. These children are not a behavior problem, but special efforts must be made to foster and not smother their talents. Behavior management programs that reward performance in regular classroom work with opportunities to engage in more challenging activities may be beneficial (e.g., Ehrlich, 1982; Whitmore, 1980).

Learning disabilities. A specific learning disability exists when there is a deficit in one of the *basic psychological processes* involved in using written or spoken language. It may be manifested by problems in listening, reasoning, speaking, reading, writing, spelling, or arithmetic. Handicaps that result from mental retardation, sensory or motor handicaps, or environmental handicaps are excluded from the category of learning disabilities. This is the definition embodied in Public Law 94-142 (see Appendix C of *The Handbook of School Psychology,* Reynolds & Gutkin, 1982, or Gutkin & Reynolds, 1990; Hammill, 1990; or Kirk & Chalfant, 1984). Unfortunately, this definition depends greatly on undefined terms and does not provide concrete guidance for identifying a learning-disabled child.

Current educational practice and state laws tend to focus on the concept of a discrepancy between achievement and ability in classifying children as learning disabled. That is, when achievement is unexpectedly lower than what would be predicted from an assessment of intellectual ability, a learning disability is presumed to exist. The method of conducting such an assessment is to compare the results of an individually administered ability assessment with performance on individually administered tests of achievement. When achievement in a subject area is significantly lower than what one would expect given knowledge of intellectual ability, a learning disability is said to exist.

The most common type of learning disability usually involves low achievement in reading. A typical child with a learning disability is likely to have an average IQ score, which is at or near the 50th percentile. Yet, achievement in reading is far below the average for the child's age and grade, around the 10th percentile or lower. The actual magnitude and even the method for determining whether there is an ability–achievement discrepancy varies across school districts and states. However, the general principle remains the same: A learning disability is defined by performance in an area of school achievement that is much lower than expected achievement as predicted by individual tests of intelligence.

Children of average or above-average intelligence who show evidence of a learning disability are likely to be somewhat frustrated by their inability to achieve in a specific subject area. Some care must be exercised that any behavior management programs to improve academic performance are compatible with the child's current functioning level in that area of achievement. If the child is presented with goals beyond his or her capabilities, such as answering questions about a passage of reading when it is not known whether the child has the skill to read the passage, great frustration may result and the child's achievement could worsen. Thus, in planning for the academically disabled child, it is important that behavior management programs be compatible with the educational goals for the child. However, when a child is identified as potentially having a learning disability, an assessment of motivation for performing academic work should not be neglected, since poor motivation may account for low achievement.

Serious emotional/behavioral disturbance. The category of serious emotional/behavioral disturbance is defined by special education law and elaborated by state and district guidelines. Generally, it includes behavior problems that adversely affect educational performance. Problems named in the rules for implementing Public Law 94-142 include an inability to build or maintain satisfactory interpersonal relationships, inappropriate behavior or feelings, depression, and a tendency to develop fears or physical symptoms associated with school or personal problems. Also included are children who have an inability to learn not explained by intellectual, sensory, or health factors. The need for a behavior management program could also signal that special education services should be considered. Although state educational agencies have been slowest in developing programs for emotionally disturbed children, special education services may be needed by children who show these characteristics.

Formal behavior management programs for such children are usually appropriate and effective. The behaviors targeted in behavior management programs will usually include academic performance as well as other behavior deficits or inappropriate behavior. On the other hand, an effective behavior management program can also be an important element in either preventing behavior problems that might result in a special education label or helping children with severe emotional or behavioral problems reintegrate into regular classroom settings (Axelrod, 1992).

Teenage and preteenage alcoholism. Numerous television specials, newspaper and magazine articles, and school officials have voiced concern over the prevalence of alcoholism among children and youth. Prevalence rates aside, from the school and family perspective, even a single alcoholic child is one too many. Because drinking alcoholic beverages is such a dominant activity in our society, it is sometimes difficult to recognize problem drinkers, whether adults or children. Yet, any formal or informal behavior management program targeted at a drinking youngster is unlikely to be successful unless drinking behavior is also changed. For a more complete discussion, see *Young Alcoholics,* by Tom Alibrandi (1978) or Lawson and Lawson (1992).

Professional intervention is almost always necessary for the teenage or preteen alcoholic. The entire family is likely to be involved in a system of which the teen alcoholic is only one part. A major impediment to obtaining help is failure to recognize that a problem exists in the first place. Furthermore, many of the problems discussed in this book may either be signs of alcoholism (i.e., academic failure) or the direct result of alcoholism. In either case, behavior management programs are likely

to fail unless the drinking is also changed. Thus, the success of some behavior management programs will depend on the ability of responsible adults to recognize the possibility that the youth may have a drinking problem.

Parents or teachers may be seeing the effects of alcoholism if any of the following behaviors are observed: personality changes and/or mood swings, irresponsibility, association with a drinking crowd, consistent reports from others about the child's drinking problems, an arrest for driving while intoxicated, fights with others, general dishonesty, bottles in bedroom or car, dwindling liquor supply at home, smell of alcohol on breath, deteriorating relationship with family, drunk behavior, or irresponsible driving. If a drinking problem is suspected, professional consultation is probably needed and behavior management is not likely to succeed in improving the child's adjustment. However, behavior contracts specifying that the child attend school, not engage in drinking behavior, and come home on time can be useful in illustrating the powerful influence that alcohol plays in a child's life because alcoholic children will not be able to keep such a contract. This can help both the child and the parents realize that a problem exists.

Family system disturbances: Parental divorce. Many family problems can affect the behavior of a child in school. Instead of attempting to list such problems, two problems that affect a large number of children will be examined: divorce and alcohol abuse.

Parental divorce is likely to affect about 30 percent to 75 percent of school-age children (Bane, 1979; Conoley & Bahns, 1992; Drake, 1981; Hetherington, 1979), and children from divorced families are more likely than their counterparts from intact families to be referred to a school psychologist, to be in programs for reading difficulties, and to have repeated a grade in school (Guidubaldi, Cleminshaw, Perry, & Mcloughlin, 1983). Beattie and Maniscalo (1985) found that children in special education classes were significantly less likely to be living with both biological parents than were students in regular education classes.

There are many reasons for expecting parental divorce to have negative effects on children. Conflict and disequilibrium before and during the divorce are likely to cause significant family stress. The availability of important adults, discipline styles, economic circumstances, and support systems are all likely to be changed by divorce. Parenting skills are also likely to deteriorate (Hetherington, 1979; King, 1992) and the ability of the parents to cooperate is likely to decline (Camara & Resnick, 1989). If dissolution of the marriage involves open conflict between the parents, one might expect numerous negative sequelae, such as inconsistency in discipline practices, exposure to poor models of social behavior, feelings of abandonment, emotional neglect, and self-blame (Pfeffer, 1981).

Emery (1982) and King (1992) reviewed much of the literature on the effects of divorce on children. Both reviewers concluded that parental conflict was more important than whether or not a divorce was obtained. Children living in homes characterized by interparental conflict had the greatest risk of showing behavioral problems, and their risk was greater than that of children from either broken or intact homes that were relatively harmonious. Such conflict in both broken and intact families appears to lead to problems characterized by "undercontrol" (e.g., aggression, acting out, etc.). Boys are more likely than girls to exhibit "obviously maladaptive" behavior, and girls are likely to respond to marital turmoil in more subtle ways such as by becoming anxious or withdrawn or experiencing problems in relationships with the opposite sex. Slater and Haber (1984) found that conflict in the families of adolescents was associated with higher levels of anxiety, lower self-esteem, lower self-concept, and a tendency to view events as being outside their control. Adjustment was not related to whether their parents were divorced or separated.

Parental divorce has also been shown to have different effects as a function of the age of the child. Preschool children have been observed to exhibit diffuse anger and grief, aggression, regression, self-blame, rejection of strangers, anxiety, moodiness, and irritability. Preadolescent children apparently exhibit a somewhat better understanding of the divorce process, responding with grieving, fear, fantasies of responsibility and reconciliation, depression, displaced aggression, anger toward parents, and loyalty conflicts. Adolescents reportedly show sadness, shame, embarrassment, anxiety about the future and marriage, premature or promiscuous sexual behavior, deidealization of their parents, and withdrawal (Drake, 1981; Guidubaldi et al., 1983; King, 1992; King & Kleemeier, 1983).

Guidubaldi and Perry (1984) studied the entire entering kindergarten class in a suburban school district. They found that children living in single-parent families entered kindergarten with significantly less social and academic competence than children from intact families. This finding persisted across a wide variety of measures of social and academic competence and when the analysis controlled for the impact of socioeconomic status. In general, there is little doubt that parental divorce influences a child's adjustment in school.

Drake (1981) pointed out that a child's school can be an important source of stability and support at a time when the home is unstable. Any adult in the school may become a source of support, and teachers can ease the transition to a single-parent family by showing sensitivity to the child. For example, the teacher can include examples of working mothers and single-parent families in examples used in class. In addition, a school staff member can provide support and positive feedback at a time when the parents are too preoccupied by other issues to fulfill this role.

Guidubaldi et al. (1983) suggested that school personnel can advise divorcing and divorced parents of the need to maintain contact with their children. This is particularly important in the case of boys from households where the mother has custody. The school can be particularly important in providing opportunities and encouragement to the noncustodial parent to remain involved with the child's school by including them in conferences and providing them with copies of the child's progress reports. These authors also state that individual and group counseling for children of divorced families should be given priority in schools. The rationale and outline for such an intervention is described by Kalter, Pickar, and Lesowitz (1984).

With respect to specific issues surrounding behavior management programs in cases where marital conflict has an impact on the child's behavior, several suggestions can be made. First, school staff members must be alert to the possibility that marital conflict underlies a child's behavior or academic problems. Frequently, this is not difficult to determine because marital partners in conflict often volunteer negative information about their spouses. Such information may include reports that the other partner is often absent, has a drinking problem, is unemployed, or "doesn't care." Family therapy, participation in group therapy, parenting skill classes, support groups for children of divorced parents, and other locally available community services may be helpful to all involved in the situation. Behavior management programs can also assist in remediating problems in the school and home, but some cautions are necessary.

Parents experiencing the emotional turmoil surrounding separation and divorce may not be capable of administering or conducting behavior management programs involving their children. They may experience difficulty setting limits, enforcing rules, administering contingencies, and following through with promised rewards or punishments. In the worst cases, undesirable behavior may be rewarded by one parent as a way of "getting" the other parent, making behavior management efforts extremely difficult. It is important for school personnel to avoid being drawn into the conflict between divorced or divorcing parents; they should focus instead on the needs of the child. Programs that involve the child's parents in key roles may be difficult. The optimal strategy may be to centralize behavior management programs within the school environment and keep parental involvement to a minimum until it is clear that a parent is ready to assist.

Parental divorce is an event that will be experienced by a large portion of school-aged children. In many cases, parental divorce will be associated with problems in school that will require referral to professionals outside the school and/or behavior management programs based in school. Sad as it may be, divorce is a fact of life for many children and, regardless of the negative impact, it is possible for school personnel to manage the resulting behavioral problems. However, conducting behavior management programs with this group may require paying special attention to their unique needs and making available other support services for them.

Family system disturbances: Parental alcoholism. The basic symptom of alcoholism is continued use of alcohol despite negative effects on the individual's social, familial, and occupational life. Overt behaviors associated with alcoholism include drinking excessive amounts of alcohol and tolerance for increasing amounts, frequent drunkenness, inability to fulfill obligations, arrests for driving while intoxicated, drinking to avoid withdrawal symptoms, and inability to cut down or stop drinking despite repeated attempts (DSM-IV). As a result of continued drinking and the problems it brings, alcoholics tend to deny the problem, blame others for their problem, spend unreasonable amounts of money on alcohol, show unpredictable and impulsive behavior, resort to physical and verbal abuse, lose the trust of family and friends, develop feelings of despair and hopelessness that may lead to a suicide attempt, and show a decline in physical health (Ackerman, 1983).

School personnel may be seeing the effects of alcoholism when parents arrive at school meetings drunk or with alcohol on their breath or when they receive reports of drinking from children or a nondrinking spouse. Signs that a child may live in an alcoholic family may include frequent tardiness, especially on Monday mornings;

consistent concern with arriving home on time; avoidance of argument and conflict; social isolation; inability to concentrate; an exaggerated concern with achievement; and emotional lability (Tharinger & Koranek, 1988). Alcoholism is far too complex to be treated or even diagnosed by school personnel, but school personnel can often recognize when a drinking parent is at risk. The children of alcoholics are at high risk for becoming adult alcoholics themselves. They also are likely to manifest serious social, emotional, and behavioral problems as children. Tharinger and Koranek (1988) describe parental alcoholism as a form of child maltreatment.

Behavior management programs for children of alcoholic parents may have a low rate of success because alcoholism is a family system problem that involves all family members in a complex web of conflict, denial of the importance of the parents' drinking, and poor communication. The roles that nondrinking family members play in the family system are often rigid and supportive of continued drinking by the alcoholic family member. One commonly described role is that of the Scapegoat. The Scapegoat is the focus of the family's anger and resentment, sometimes even being blamed for the alcoholic's problems. The Scapegoat plays the role by acting out in a very overt manner. The behavior is likely to be maintained by negative attention from family members. The role that this child plays within the family system is likely to be more powerful than the most well designed school-based behavior management program. Other roles with the alcoholic family system are equally unhealthy but less noticeable to individuals outside the family system.

Instead of behavior management alone, a menu of services is likely to best meet the needs of children of alcoholics. Services that schools can provide include advocacy and referral, discussion groups, individual and group counseling, and access to self-help groups such as Alateen and Al-Anon.

Child abuse. Child abuse has attracted a great deal of attention in recent years. It is a social problem with profound and far-reaching effects (Bonner, Kaufman, Harbeck, & Brassard, 1992). It is a rare week that goes by without some mention of either specific cases of abuse being processed in the courts or some general article about child abuse appearing in the news media.

The school's role in helping abused children begins with knowledge of what constitutes abuse, what behavioral indicators accompany it, and what are the obligations of school personnel under state laws governing reporting of child abuse (Guyer, 1982). The main role of school personnel is to recognize abusive situations and take appropriate action to end them. However, school personnel are not child abuse investigators. When indicators of abuse are observed, the role of school personnel is to document carefully what was observed, what was said, or what happened, and to provide appropriate social service agencies with an objective report. Investigation of whether abuse actually occurred is the responsibility of social services and legal authorities.

Many of the problem behaviors seen in school may be indicators of abuse, and further consideration of a child's behavior may lead to a suspicion that abuse is occurring. When this happens, it is imperative that grounds for suspicion be accurately documented and required procedures for reporting these suspicions be followed. The child-focused nature of a behavior management program can sometimes lead to such a report. Ending abuse is so clearly in a child's best interest that educators who are contemplating a behavior management program must always be alert to signs of abuse. In cases where child abuse has already been substantiated, successful behavior management programs begun in the school may be valuable tools for helping the parents improve their own skills.

Many parents who abuse their children have a history of abuse in their own childhood. They are also likely to be ignorant of the basic facts of child development, which leads to unrealistic expectations and attribution of impossible motives to their children. Wolfe (1985) reviewed studies comparing abusive and nonabusive parents. He found that abusive parents generally display symptoms of depression and health problems and are likely to be involved in stressful family situations that impair their competence as parents. Their children come to reflect the qualities of this environment, behaving in ways that present the parent with many problem situations, which in turn helps maintain a relatively high level of conflict. The general pattern within an abusive family is one of disharmony, conflict, frustration, stress, and the relatively infrequent use of positive rewards. Generally, abusive parents are impaired in the skills needed to function as competent parents; they become involved in a continuing cycle of reciprocal coercive interactions with their children. Thus, any view of the origins of abusive parenting must consider the entire context of the family system (cf. Belsky, 1980).

Child abuse can be divided into several categories: physical abuse, sexual abuse, emotional abuse/neglect, and physical neglect. These categories would include the majority of neglectful or uncaring parents who fail to cooperate with the school in the resolution of their child's problem behavior. To balance the perspective somewhat, such parental behavior also may result from a lack of motivation, lack of parenting skills, a parent's own history as an abuse victim, or a host of other causes. It would be unfair, then, to condemn the parents: The entire family is the logical focus of intervention.

Physical abuse is the easiest type to detect because many of the indicators are visible marks and bruises. Such signs of possible abuse include bruises in different stages of healing or in unusual places, unusually shaped bruises suggesting contact with an object, "stocking" or "glove" burns suggesting the limb may have been dipped in a hot liquid, or inappropriate treatment of the child's injuries in terms of bandages and medication. The child's behavior may also be an indicator of abuse if any of these signs are present: The child expresses fear of the parents, the child cries frequently, the child seems "different," the child is withdrawn or shy, the child appears depressed, the child inappropriately accepts strangers, the child seems hesitant or afraid to go home, the child is hyperalert to the social cues of the parent, the child behaves very differently when the parents are present than when they are absent, or the child is frequently absent from or late to school. Characteristics of abused children themselves, such as premature birth, difficult temperament, and handicapping conditions, are also associated with a high probability of abuse.

Williams (1983) and Bonner, Kaufman, Harbeck, and Brassard (1992) noted that a consistent finding in research on the effects of child abuse is that abused children are significantly more aggressive than nonabused children. Other behaviors that she found to be associated with physical or sexual abuse included hyperactivity, withdrawal, passivity, sexual malfunctioning, guilt, shame, anxiety, running away from home, and suicide attempts. The "belt theory" of delinquency, discussed further in Chapter 5, attributes delinquent behavior to overly harsh parental punishment. Finally, moderate to severe physical injury and even death are possible outcomes of the most severe parental abuse of children.

Barahal, Waterman, and Martin (1981) studied the social/cognitive development of a sample of abused children who were not showing signs of behavioral problems. They found IQs of the abused children to be about 10 points lower than those of a well-matched group of control children. In addition, the abused children showed less confidence in their ability to influence events in their environment than the nonabused children. This difference was strongest for negative events. In addition, the abused children were lowest in sensitivity to socioemotional contexts and highest in egocentricity. Barahal et al. concluded that remediating the social skill deficits of abused youngsters may be necessary if the generation-to-generation cycle of child abuse is to be broken.

A common characteristic of abusive parents is that they tend to show ignorance of the developmental sequence in children. Teachers and others who contact the parents directly are likely to find such parents have unrealistic expectations for their children. In addition, they typically lack support systems such as relatives and friends, may be socially isolated from other parents, may offer absurd or inconsistent explanations for their child's injuries, may be uncooperative or passive in encounters with school personnel, may show signs of a drinking problem, may describe the child as "different" or "bad," or may appear "different" or "strange" themselves.

Another possibility is that parents may reveal abusive tendencies by misattributing negative motivation to the behavior of their child. Bauer and Twentyman (1985) found that physically abusive mothers tended to agree that their children were attempting to annoy them, even when the available information was insufficient to justify such a conclusion. Thus, it may be useful to determine the attributional style of parents with respect to the behavior of their children. A tendency to attribute negative motivation to their children's behavior may suggest a potential for abusive behavior.

Physical neglect is accompanied by a cluster of indicators that generally center around the quality of parental care. Obvious indicators include signs of malnourishment, inappropriate clothing given the weather conditions, torn or dirty clothing, dirty appearance, lack of needed medical attention, and extreme fatigue. Neglected children may also be avoided by their peers for various reasons, for example because they smell bad. However, children from impoverished backgrounds may also appear this way. Parents who are doing their best given their economic circumstances would not be considered neglectful.

Sexual abuse is more difficult to detect but might be indicated if the child manifests complaints of genital or abdominal pain, sexual behavior or language unusual for the child's age, excessive fear of being touched, severe nightmares, acting out, running away from home, signs of depression or anxiety, chemical abuse, a dramatic change in school behavior, evidence of a sudden change in relationships with parents, or evidence that the child assumes the role of "parent" at home. Victims of sexual abuse are about ten times more likely to be girls than boys. One of the most reliable indicators of sexual abuse is a direct report by the victim. Of course, this is much more likely to occur with older than with younger children.

Emotional abuse and neglect are difficult to prove or detect and are unlikely to elicit responses from social or legal agencies that are overburdened by cases of physical and sexual abuse. However, any programs that deal directly with the children of such parents are likely to be made more difficult if parental support and cooperation, beyond signing necessary documents, are not obtained. In such cases, it may be helpful to remember that most children are capable of learning to behave appropriately in school, regardless of the home situation. Also, one healthy response to a neglectful home situation is for the child to become attached to a trustworthy adult outside of the home.

Abuse and neglect of children are difficult problems with which to cope. The various indicators just listed provide a reasonably complete listing, but the individual needs also to rely on judgment and subjective feelings in entertaining the hypothesis that abuse or neglect underlies the problem behavior of the child. If either the subjective impression or the objective evidence is strong, then additional consultation should be obtained.

Children of abusive parents are likely to be depressed, act out, and have less than a normal belief in their ability to control significant events in their lives. Social skills training and other formal programs may be beneficial and could be successful in changing behavior without any change in the parents.

CONCLUSION

This chapter was designed to provide an overview of issues relevant to planning a behavior management program. Primary issues discussed were deciding on the goal to be accomplished, the environment in which it is to be accomplished, and the developmental status of the child. These three issues need to be addressed in planning any behavior management program. Secondary issues can be just as important as the primary issues, but they are not as likely to arise. The three secondary issues discussed were the cultural background of the child, the status of the child's family system, and the diagnostic issues raised by the child's behavior. The discussion of diagnostic issues was not exhaustive, but it did cover the common problems likely to have the greatest impact on planning a behavior management program. Among these issues are two that educators need to consider regularly, abuse and suicide, because their impact on the child is so profound.

SOURCES OF ADDITIONAL INFORMATION

Chapters 1 through 4 have been designed to provide a thorough introduction to the techniques of behavior management. For readers who wish to pursue the topics that have been discussed in more detail, numerous sources are available. A few will be mentioned here.

The most basic principles of learning and behavior modification may be found in any introductory psychology textbook such as Morris (1988), Huffman, Vernoy, and Vernoy (1994), Darley, Glucksberg, Kamin, and Kinchla (1981), or Weiten (1992; 1994). More advanced books on basic learning and the theories built up around it would include Bolles (1975), Bower and Hilgard (1981), Maser and Seligman (1977), and, for a historical perspective, Hearst (1979) or Dollard and Miller (1950). Books that describe the application of learning principles to human behavior include Staats (1963, 1975), Sulzer-Azaroff and Mayer (1991), Bandura (1969, 1977), Martin and Pear (1988), and Turner, Calhoun, and Adams (1981). Books devoted to the topic of managing the behavior of children include Le Croy (1994), Alberto and Troutman (1986), Kerr and Nelson (1989), Morris and Kratochwill (1983a), Ollendick and Cerny (1981), and Ross (1981). The latter three books are compared by Prout (1984). Benson (1979), Millman, Schaefer, and Cohen (1980), and Bellack and Hersen (1985) briefly describe therapies for a wide variety of behavior problems. The handbook edited by Walker and Roberts (1983, 1992) provides a more general overview of childhood problems and their treatment. These works would provide a fairly current knowledge base for the school practitioner.

To maintain currency with the most recent developments in learning theory and behavior management, professional journals provide the best source of information. Among those I have found valuable are *Journal of Consulting and Clinical Psychology, School Psychology Review, Psychological Bulletin, Child and Youth Services, Annual Review of Psychology, Journal of Applied Behavior Analysis, Behavior Research and Therapy,* *Child Development, Psychology in the Schools,* and the *Journal of School Psychology.* Every practitioner must develop his or her own library and journal reading preferences. The books and journals just cited represent only a sample of what is available to the professional.

REVIEW

Terms to Remember and Review

primary issue	secondary issue
behavior excess	behavior deficit
early childhood	middle childhood
adolescence	hyperactivity
ADHD	childhood depression
school phobia	test anxiety
mental retardation	adaptive behavior
giftedness	learning disability
alcoholism	physical abuse
serious emotional/	sexual abuse
behavioral disturbance	

Study and Discussion Questions

1. What is the most important distinction between primary and secondary issues as defined in this textbook?

2. What are the advantages of a team approach over working individually in developing a behavior management program?

3. Why is it better to define a target behavior in terms of a behavior deficit rather than a behavior excess?

4. Explain the Golden Rule of Behavior Management in your own words. Why is this rule such an important element of good classroom management?

5. Describe what characteristics a behavior management program should have to succeed in a regular classroom? Special classroom? The home?

6. Explain how a child's developmental status can influence behavior management programming.

7. In what ways can a family influence a child's behavior in school?

8. How can a conflict between cultural values and school values be resolved?

9. What was the author's purpose in discussing selected diagnostic categories and issues?

10. What characteristics of the typical regular class-

room would conflict with the behavior and characteristics of a hyperactive child?

11. What are the key indicators that a child or adolescent may be suicidal?

12. What are the most important indicators of physical and sexual abuse? Why should all educators be familiar with these indicators?

Group Projects

1. You and your fellow group members have been assigned to the governor's task force on the year 2000. The mission of the task force is to decide how the public and private resources of your state will be used to improve the quality of life for its residents. Your group has been assigned the job of writing a report addressing the needs of children in the year 2000 and beyond. Your report should be written in two sections. In the first section, your group should reach a consensus on the three most important environmental stressors that have a negative impact on children. In the second section, you are to write three goals for each of the three stressors. These goals must be concrete, realistic programs for improvement of children's lives. For example, if "inadequate education system" was one of the group's identified stressors, your group would write three goals for improving the educational system. A goal such as "improve the educational system" would not be adequate because it is too vague and everyone would agree with it. A better goal would be to say "hire more teachers until the typical elementary class has no more than 17 students." This goal represents a concrete action that has a clear criterion for completion.

2. If there are any unique cultural groups within the community, it would be helpful to learn about their culture and how it might influence school performance and school programming.

CHAPTER 5

PREVENTION OF BEHAVIOR MANAGEMENT PROBLEMS IN THE SCHOOL, REGULAR CLASSROOM, SPECIAL CLASSROOM, AND HOME

Any school visitor can sense the climate of the school building. Some schools seem dynamic and alive with evidence of enthusiastic learning in every hallway. Recent student projects are displayed, the building is neat and clean, and the sounds from classrooms are joyous and full of life and love of learning. Other school buildings project a sense of dullness and lack of enthusiasm for learning. Sullen students are waiting outside the vice principal's office, and the voices coming from classrooms are dull, frustrated, or angry. Displays of student projects are nonexistent or yellowed with age; a piece of student work has fallen to the floor, where it waits to be taped up for the hundredth time. What makes these schools so different?

Obviously, school climate is determined by many factors—the school board, budget, physical plant, strategic planning, unions, and a host of other elements. The key element is maintaining the focus of the school on successful learning in a context where order and discipline are maintained (U.S. Department of Education, 1987, p. 58). Emphasis on positive reinforcement and fair, effective, and consistently enforced rules, with reasonable consequences for rule violations, can make a major contribution to a positive school climate. Good behavior management practices on a schoolwide basis can prevent many of the problems that might require formal behavior management programs or referral to other programs.

This chapter looks at school administration, regular classrooms, special classrooms, and children's home environments from a behavior management perspective. The goal is to discuss how behavior management principles can be integrated into the broader school environment and become an important tool in encouraging a positive school climate. Behavior management principles work *all the time* whether they are applied in a structured program to maintain order and discipline or in a disorganized, haphazard manner with no plan. The difference is that in the latter case the outcome will be much less predictable because the individuals controlling the reinforcements are not aware of the behaviors actually being rewarded. This chapter will provide some guidelines for developing an integrated, schoolwide program to maintain order and discipline and keep students focused on learning. For a broader view of school effectiveness, see Bickel (1990), and for a discussion of adopting formal prevention programs in schools see Hightower, Johnson, and Haffey (1990).

This chapter has four major sections, each concerned with prevention of behavior problems from a particular perspective. The first section discusses prevention from the perspective of the school administrator. The second section discusses prevention from the perspective of the regular classroom teacher, and the third section from the perspective of special classroom teachers. The last section discusses how the school can promote better behavior management practices at home.

PREVENTION FROM THE ADMINISTRATIVE PERSPECTIVE

School administration is a challenging and rewarding profession. Principals are responsible for the educational progress of hundreds of children, and their decisions can have a lifetime impact on those children. Knowledge of behavior management principles is one of the vital components of the school administrator's skill because sound application of these principles can make a tremendous contribution to maintaining a positive school climate. When children are treated fairly, know the rules, and are confident that fair consequences will follow violations of the rules, they will be able to focus their efforts on the main task of learning.

The remainder of this section describes major issues encountered by school administrators from the perspective of behavior management. The first sections cover schoolwide behavior management policies; suicide, abuse, and crisis policies; support services and special programs; and dealing with chronic problem situations. The last section focuses on an area that can often be highly problematic but receives little formal attention: behavior on the school bus.

Schoolwide Behavior Management Policies

School administrators have two critical behavior management responsibilities: (1) to facilitate development of, administer, and enforce general school policies and rules, and (2) to provide backup for the discipline referrals of classroom teachers.

The most crucial elements of school rules are that they are clearly communicated to all students and that they are enforced with clear and consistent consequences. A brochure explaining the rules to students and/or parents should be made available at the very beginning of the school year. This handout should be written in clear and understandable language and should probably omit many details and qualifications. In other words, it should have the tone of an informative summary, not that of a legal contract. A more detailed policy manual should be available to all teachers, staff, students, and parents. If the student/parent brochure is too long or complicated, many important aspects of school policies and procedures will not be communicated clearly to those who most need to know.

The brochure probably needs to contain more information than just the school rules and discipline policies.

It should be an introduction to all important school policies, such as attendance, being excused for appointments, contacting children during school hours, medication procedures, and other day-to-day issues. Above all, however, the brochure must establish that the primary mission of the school is to promote and enhance student learning. A clear mission statement that emphasizes this point would make an excellent opening paragraph in any handbook.

According to *What Works* (U.S. Department of Education, 1987) the discipline policies of successful schools share five traits:

1. Discipline policies are aimed at actual problems, not rumors of problems.
2. Each policy is a joint effort of the school community and reflects community values.
3. Misbehavior is clearly defined so that students know what is acceptable and what is not acceptable.
4. Consequences spelled out in discipline policies are consistently administered.
5. A readable and well-designed handbook is often used to inform parents and students about the school's discipline policy.

School policies should be reviewed and revised regularly to be sure they are current with the needs of the children and the school. Finally, it must always be remembered that the main purpose of school policies is to promote student learning. Behaviors that interfere with the ability of students to learn or make an environment unsafe should be the primary targets of the discipline policy. Anything administrators do to provide a better learning environment and protect teachers from unnecessary disruptions will improve the climate and overall success of the school.

Communicating the school discipline policy is a critical administrative task, but what about the content of the policy? As discussed, the policy must contain school rules that are clear, enforceable, and owned by the students and community, and that have effective, consistently enforced consequences. At the same time, a good policy needs some flexibility built into it so that students who occasionally slip are not penalized in an overly harsh manner that takes them away from instructional time and creates a negative attitude toward school.

Silberman and Wheelan (1980) have suggested a few guidelines for good rules that are consistent with the general principles of behavior management. First, they suggest that rules must be clear both to children and to the adults who set them. Conflict may easily arise when children and adults have different ideas concerning whether the requirements of a rule have been met. For instance, if a school rule states that "students may not be late for class," there is a lot of room for ambiguity and misunderstanding. Must they be in the classroom when the second bell rings? Must they be within ten feet of the classroom door? Must they be in the classroom and seated when the bell rings? Must they be in the school building when the bell rings? Both students and adults should know the exact requirements of any rule. For example, a school rule could state that "students must be seated at their desks when the second bell rings." This rule provides explicit instructions to the student concerning appropriate behavior.

The second guideline suggested by Silberman and Wheelan is that rules should be enforceable. To be enforceable, they suggest, a rule should represent a realistic value that the child is capable of obeying, and responsible adults should be able to monitor whether it is obeyed. For example, a school rule stating that swearing and foul language are forbidden may be consistent with school and community standards. On the other hand, how much of the things that students say can be monitored by an adult? A more realistic version of this rule might state that swearing and foul language are forbidden in classrooms.

Silberman and Wheelan also suggest that holding a discussion about a rule before enforcement begins can be helpful to both the children and the adults involved. A discussion provides an opportunity to clear up ambiguities and misunderstandings and allows the adults to present the rationale for the rule. Children also may have ideas about how the rule can be improved and made less aversive from their perspective.

The final guideline for good rules is that adults should have some plan for dealing with violations of the rule. If a contingency plan is devised beforehand, responsible adults can avoid reacting unfairly or angrily. When the consequence is specified as part of the rule, it becomes the students' job to behave appropriately and the job of the adults to administer rules fairly and consistently. Generally, if the limits on their behavior are stated clearly, students will occupy their time with the task of learning and few students will require formal behavior management programs to remediate unacceptable behavior.

School policies will necessarily differ according to the age of the children. For children in primary grades, rules and policies need to be as simple as possible and directed mainly at parents, who need to help the child arrive at school with materials needed for the school day. Elementary school children are closely supervised by their teachers throughout the school day, so classroom rules (discussed in the next section) carry the primary weight for maintaining order in the school environment. As students spend more time moving between classrooms on individualized schedules and come in contact with a number of different teachers and supervisors, school-wide rules and policies become more prominent.

Dealing effectively with rule violations and misbehavior is only one aspect of managing behavior. The other side is rewarding appropriate behavior. A school's policies should include opportunities for *all* children to be recognized for their positive accomplishments. Special certificates, displays of academic or artistic work, notes to parents, and other awards for both ordinary and extraordinary accomplishments should be available to all students. Punishment merely suppresses undesired behavior. Reward is what strengthens desired behavior. Letting all children know that their accomplishments are recognized is the best way to increase desired behavior. When desirable behavior is occurring, there is no opportunity for undesired behavior.

Natural and logical consequences can effectively deter some undesirable behavior. Using logical consequences consists of allowing natural consequences to affect behavior or designing consequences that match or fit the misbehavior. For example, school rules often state that running inside the school building is forbidden. An immediate, effective consequence for running within the building is to have the child return to the beginning of the route and walk it at a normal pace. This consequence will be adequate to suppress most running and is cost-effective in terms of both student and staff time. Furthermore, the student is given an opportunity to practice correct behavior. The student may also receive another logical consequence for being late to class or missing out on time to socialize with peers. Similarly, misbehavior in the lunch room can result in eating at a "quiet table" where no talking is allowed. Finally, if a child misbehaves during recess, the privilege can be lost for a day or two. Simple, logical consequences, administered immediately after the misbehavior, that do not take away from instructional time are the best response to violations of most school rules.

School administrators also need to be prepared to deal with classroom discipline referrals. In most schools, a classroom discipline referral occurs when a child is "sent to the office" as a result of consistent and/or intolerable rule violations. Administrators should see this as a relatively rare experience at the elementary school level, but it is crucial that advance preparation for handling these situations be made.

First, a uniform method for referring children to the office should exist. A discipline slip, phone call, intercom communication, or some other form of memo that tells office staff why a student is being referred needs to start the process. The discipline slip can be used to begin the critical written log for that student. It is vastly preferable that students be escorted to the office because all kinds of risks are inherent in allowing a child who is under stress to make the trip alone. Once the child arrives at the office, every effort must be made to make the experience boring. Too many times the student arrives at the office, remains seated while the administrator conducts business, and receives the attention of anyone who enters the office. At the same time, the child may be able to watch all the interesting activities that occur—parent visits, health emergencies, phone calls, deliveries, and so forth. To a child having difficulty in class, these activities may be much more interesting than learning multiplication tables. If this is the case, the child may find the trip to the office reinforcing, which means that he or she will be more likely to "earn" a trip to the office in the future. This situation must be avoided.

Instead, the child should be seated in a designated chair or area, away from interesting activity. Furthermore, office staff must be instructed not to interact with the child. Teachers and others who enter the office should be aware of a policy stating that students seated in a particular place are to be ignored. Essentially, students referred to the office for disciplinary purposes should be socially isolated as they await their conference. A disciplinary conference should not be a time when the administrator gets to know the child on a social basis. The conference should focus on the issue at hand, dealing with misbehavior. Learning more about the child should be reserved for a later time. A significant delay between the misbehavior and the conference decreases the likelihood that the conference will be followed by improved behavior unless the time gap is bridged so the child clearly understands why he or she was sent to the office. The written discipline slip can be an invaluable source of information at this time.

Three basic issues should become the focus of the discipline conference. First, it must be made clear what behavior violated the classroom rules and, therefore, why the child has been sent to the office. Second, the conference should focus on the *appropriate* behaviors that should occur in the same or a similar situation in the future. Third, an effective consequence should be administered. Developing effective consequences is not an easy task because the child has already demonstrated at least partial immunity to the consequences employed in the regular classroom. However, there are many options available. One option is to issue a warning that a particular consequence will occur if another referral to the office is made. This can be very effective with those children who are intimidated by the office referral in the first place. These children generally respect adult authority and are not too likely to become repeat offenders.

Other students, who have not developed respect for adult authority, may need an effective aversive consequence. What options are available to the school administrator? Removal of school privileges can be an effective consequence. Spending recess time in the office for a couple of days, losing bus privileges, missing a lyceum or other entertaining presentation, being detained after school, or having to attend a parent conference are options available to the administrator. For older students, in-school suspension or after-school detention can be very effective. Out-of-school suspension should be an option of last resort because instructional time is lost and it may actually negatively reinforce misbehavior. Suspension or expulsion may also invoke due process requirements (Overcast, Sales, & Sacken, 1990) that need to be followed. For the first offense, a warning along with a review of future consequences may be effective. For the second offense, loss of a privilege such as recess or lyceum can be used with younger children. For the third offense of younger children or second offense of older children, a parent conference or a phone call to parents and after-school detention or in-school suspension can be effective. The possibility of these consequences should be spelled out in the school's policies so they can be administered in a timely manner. Otherwise, their effectiveness will decline.

In-school suspension has become an increasingly popular method of creating consequences for inappropriate behavior, particularly among junior and senior high schools. In-school suspension consists of assigning a student to a special classroom in which freedom is severely restricted. Social contacts and breaks are eliminated, trips to the bathroom and lunch are supervised, and the student is required to complete class assignments. In-school suspension is an effective alternative to suspension from school because the social and enjoyable aspects of school attendance are eliminated while academic work is completed in a highly restrictive and work-oriented atmosphere.

Sullivan (1989) has suggested that the elements of a successful in-school suspension program include taking a rehabilitative rather than a punitive approach, evaluating the program effectively, making the program part of an overall schoolwide discipline program, avoiding the use of in-school suspension for minor offenses, providing effective counseling for students, having adequate financial support with full-time professional staffing, keeping excellent records with individual student files, and maintaining consistency and fairness by having written guidelines for use of in-school suspension. Sullivan also suggests that establishing good communication between each student's regular classroom teachers and the suspension supervisor is crucial to ensure that current assignments are available. Clear communication of rules in effect during in-school suspension, consequences for rule violations, and requirements for completing in-school suspension and being readmitted to regular classes are also essential. The keys to successful in-school suspension programs are identical to those for other behavior management techniques. The program needs to be carefully monitored to ensure that it accomplishes what is expected.

Some administrators may consider using corporal punishment, hitting a pupil with a hand or paddle. Research evidence is heavily against the use of corporal punishment in schools. One problem is that corporal punishment may seriously hurt a child. Another problem is that it is often administered under circumstances that almost guarantee it will not suppress the target behavior. In many cases, the time between the misbehavior and the punishment is so great that the connection between the misbehavior and the punishment is lost from the child's perspective. In addition, the misbehavior may be rewarded by peers, which may counteract the effects of the punishment. Another serious problem is that each occurrence of the misbehavior may not be punished. If this occurs, the punishment is also likely to lose effectiveness. Finally, children who are punished in school may not be receiving much positive feedback at school or home. If the child is not given ample opportunity to earn rewards with appropriate behavior, punishment will not lead to improved behavior (see Azrin & Holz, 1966).

One researcher has found such a strong relationship between what he calls "severe parental punishment" and delinquency that he has proposed the "belt theory of delinquency." The theory proposes that one cause of delinquency is the experience of severe parental punishment (Welsh, 1976). Research has indicated that corporal punishment administered in school or at home can also lead to violence as an adult (Strauss, 1991; Townsend, 1984).

In my opinion, the use of corporal punishment in schools is not justified. The child whose annoying and aggressive behavior tempts even the most caring and thoughtful educator to consider corporal punishment is probably the least likely to benefit from it. Instead, such a child needs a caring adult to take an interest in him or her and make an appropriate referral to a school psychologist, social worker, or counselor. Most likely, the resulting assessment will reveal that the child has needs that go far beyond the school environment. For additional discussion of punishment in schools, see Bongiovanni and Hyman (1978), the Council for Children with Behavioral Disorders (1990), Hyman and Wise (1979), or Kazdin (1982).

Erickson (1988) described a successful schoolwide discipline program based on the concept of a discipline "ticket." A "ticket," completed by the teacher, playground supervisor, or other responsible adult, was issued to children who violated school rules. It gave the student's name, the date, and the nature of the offense. Using physical aggression, throwing objects, refusing to obey a teacher's command, using disrespectful or abusive language, stealing, and engaging in "continuous disruptive behavior" were the major offenses that could result in a ticket. With a first ticket, the child's parents were contacted and the offense and penalty explained to them. The penalty was cleaning lunch tables during recess. A second ticket also resulted in parent notification, and the student was required to assist the school custodian after school for two days chosen by the parents. A third ticket meant a visit to the principal, who assigned after-school work, called the parents, and visited with teachers to determine whether follow-up such as assessment by the school counselor or psychologist was indicated.

Another key component of the program was a monthly assembly to honor students for notable accomplishments in areas such as sports, scholarship, art, music, and citizenship. Awards given at such programs could consist of certificates; school supplies; small prizes; or coupons good for food, video games, movie rentals, or any other suitable reward. The assembly itself was highlighted by an enjoyable, interesting program of entertainment. Students who received discipline tickets during the month were not allowed to attend the assembly. Instead, they reported to a detention room to do schoolwork.

This discipline program need not be followed rigidly. I believe that, when possible, first offenses should be handled without parent notification. This allows the student to self-correct behavior with less stress. Also, some parents are not mature enough to handle such a situation properly and could make things worse by using overly harsh punishment or becoming defensive and uncommunicative with the school. I would recommend that the student engage in schoolwork during after-school or lost recess time because the misbehavior has probably resulted in lost instructional time, and the student may need the extra work. Finally, I would recommend conducting a face-to-face parent conference, perhaps after the second offense, rather than a phone conference. This provides an opportunity to reassure parents that effective consequences have been planned and that further steps are possible if the problem is not resolved. It also gives the administrator an opportunity to assess the home climate informally.

Developing a schoolwide discipline policy is an administrative task that requires flexibility, careful planning, and continuous monitoring. Like a behavior management program for an individual child, schoolwide policies need to be monitored continuously to determine whether they are functioning as expected. Regular review by administrators, teachers, parents, and community members is essential to keep the program functioning effectively.

Suicide Prevention, Abuse Prevention, and Crisis Policies

The behavior problems seen by administrators are often indicators of more serious underlying issues faced by the pupil, among them unhappiness and depression, suicidal crises, and abusive home environments. Administrators or teachers who learn enough about an individual student to contemplate serious disciplinary action or a behavior management program may find themselves facing one of these situations. Admittedly, these situations are not behavior management issues, but I believe they are so important that they need to be reviewed here.

Suicide prevention. Guetzloe (1989) cites studies indicating that around 12 to 15 percent of children ages six to nineteen have either reported making serious attempts to take their own lives or had serious thoughts of doing so. Suicide is considered by most researchers to be the second leading cause of death among adolescents (Sheras,

1992). Davis (1985) used suicide statistics to project that out of a high school population of 2,000 students, suicidal thoughts could be expected in about 27 percent of the students, attempted suicides in 50 students, and a completed suicide about every four years. These figures provide convincing evidence that suicide, attempted suicide, or serious thoughts of suicide occur at virtually any age and in schools of any size. A district suicide prevention policy with which all teachers from kindergarten through high school are familiar can be an important component of a school-based suicide prevention program.

The main purpose of a district suicide prevention policy is to communicate to teachers that suicide is an issue that the district takes seriously and strives to prevent. The policy can also familiarize teachers and staff with signs that precede suicide and provide a concrete set of guidelines regarding how to react to a student who is or may be threatening suicide. The policy needs to provide names of contact persons who can help assess suicide potential, emergency numbers to call, and procedures for obtaining immediate help in an emergency. Development of a suicide prevention policy should be a joint effort of school district personnel, parents, and representatives of community services where emergency help can be obtained. Knowing how to mobilize the district's and community's emergency resources may contribute to saving a life.

For more information and resources on developing a suicide prevention program, see Davis (1985), Garland and Zigler (1993), Guetzloe (1989), Poland and Pitcher (1990), Rogers-Wiese (1990), or Whitaker and Slimak (1990).

Abuse prevention policies. Recognizing signs of child abuse and responding appropriately are important responsibilities of all educators. However, teachers and staff members who suspect a child is being physically or sexually abused need to know precisely how to discharge their legally mandated reporting responsibilities. A written child abuse prevention policy, similar to the suicide prevention policy, is an excellent way to provide guidance and support. Basically, a child abuse prevention policy needs to establish the importance of preventing or ending child abuse, explain the important signs and characteristics that accompany abuse, and explain how to discharge the responsibility for making the mandated report. Names of individuals who can assist in obtaining forms or composing a letter will be helpful, as will a summary of state laws pertaining to reporting suspected child abuse.

Cosentino (1989) provides a broad description of school-based programs for prevention and detection of child sexual abuse, including ways that schools can provide support for victims. The article also includes a valuable appendix describing useful materials, along with guidelines for developing preventive programming.

Support Services and Special Programs

Chapter 4 discussed several conditions, such as depression, parental divorce, hyperactivity, parental alcoholism, student alcoholism, and child abuse, that can cause or exacerbate child behavior problems. The resulting behaviors often require intervention such as a formal behavior management program. A formal behavior management program can be very cost-effective in that it can obviate the need for more expensive and restrictive programming at a later date. However, an alternative approach is to identify students at risk for behavioral and academic problems and intervene to prevent development of these problems (e.g., Peterson, Zink, & Farmer, 1992). Examples of the kinds of support services and special programs that can prevent serious behavior problems will be discussed in the remainder of this section.

One level of preventive services for pupils is any one of a variety of specific support groups that could be made available to children according to their needs and developmental level (Gazda, 1976). One example is support groups for children of divorced or separated parents (Hodges, 1991). Transition services for adolescents returning from chemical dependency or other residential treatment programs, eating disorder groups, groups for those with obesity, groups for children or adolescents with alcoholic parents, and groups for children who have been physically or sexually abused are examples of other prevention programs that can be offered within a school. A school psychologist, counselor, or social worker would be qualified to develop these kinds of services according to the needs expressed by parents and teachers.

Dealing with Chronic Problem Situations

A student with a chronic problem is one who does not respond as expected to the usual discipline methods used in a classroom or school. Erickson (1988) called them "ticket syndrome" children, which meant that they received an unusually high number of discipline tickets. These situations can be very frustrating for administra-

tors and teachers alike, because consequences that work well most of the time are ineffective. What are some steps that can be taken to help resolve these situations favorably?

One of the first steps in dealing with a chronic discipline problem is to recognize the usefulness of complete documentation. Developing a complete history enables the team to see clearly the nature of a problem, see what interventions have been tried, and to provide the best programming for the child more efficiently. School administrators should maintain a file on each child who comes to their attention for disciplinary reasons. The file need not be complex or highly structured. Dropping a brief note into a folder each time an incident occurs is sufficient in the early stages. Alternatively, a standardized form that includes the child's name, the date, description of the problem, initial reactions of the involved staff or teacher, actions taken by the responsible administrator, and responses of the student could be completed and placed in one file. This file is then available when it becomes apparent that a particular child has been seen frequently for disciplinary purposes. A trail of documentation that begins as early as possible can assist greatly in determining how serious a problem is, what assessment needs to be done, and what interventions are worth considering. Because a disciplinary contact with a principal or other administrator represents a serious step in the disciplinary hierarchy, it is prudent for administrators to document all disciplinary contacts with children.

Classroom teachers, on the other hand, need more flexible criteria for deciding when to begin documenting a child's behavior. Documenting each and every minor incident is impractical, but what makes an incident major enough to justify beginning a running log or file? First, certain behaviors should be documented regardless of the outcome of any consequence. Physical or verbal aggression, blatant defiance of adult authority, consistent failure to complete assigned work, and other impulsive or destructive acts are serious enough that future intervention may be needed, so easily accessible notes about these types of incidents could be very useful. Other unusual behaviors should also be documented. The goal is not to anticipate future problems, which might bias the way the student is treated, but to keep a record of current concerns. The crucial element in this type of documentation is that the *behaviors* eliciting concern are concretely and objectively defined.

The transition from a documented concern to a serious problem needing immediate attention can occur in a few seconds or over the course of a school year. When the transition occurs in a few seconds, it is most likely the result of a dramatic, often aggressive, and intolerable behavior. Striking another student with an object having the potential to cause serious harm or making a threat toward a teacher are probably the two most common behaviors that fall in this category. The most helpful reaction to these behaviors is to schedule a team meeting that includes all the student's teachers, key administrators, the school psychologist, the parent(s), and others who may be able to contribute. The goal of the meeting is to develop a plan for dealing with the immediate crisis, monitoring future behavior, and develop a plan for any future incidents. Table 5.1 presents a sample referral form that has proved useful in these and similar situations.

Table 5.1. Student Performance Checklist

Student's Name: _____ Grade: _____

Teacher's Name: _____ Subject; _____

Date: _____

This student hasd been referred to the child study team. Please complete the rating scale below by assigning a number from 1 to 5 to each of the behavior catgegories. Please be as frank and objective as possible and rate the student's ehavior as you have observed it during the past two weeks. Also, please comment regarding any rating below 3.

Key
5 = Outstanding performance
4 = Good performance
3 = Acceptable performance
2 = Improvement needed
1 = Unacceptable

Behavior	Rating	Comments
General classroom behavior		
Homework assignments completed		
Brings needed materials to class		
On-task behavior		
Quality of completed work		
Social relationships with peers		

Approximately what grade (A–F)
has this student earned up to now? _____

Additional Comments:

Please return completed form to: _____

Sometimes school rules or policies will specify how the situation should be handled. In other cases, the team must develop a unique approach. Suspension from school is a common response to some behaviors. It has the advantage of removing the child from the school and providing a "cool down" period for those involved. It also gives the team a chance to develop a plan of intervention or supervision. The disadvantage of suspension is that the pupil may be negatively reinforced by leaving school. That is, being able to escape the demands of school may be rewarding from the student's perspective. If the student's parents are unable to provide close supervision during the suspension period, the student is likely to find opportunities to engage in a number of rewarding activities, such as watching TV or playing video games. The unsupervised time could also give the student opportunity to engage in illegal behavior. For these reasons, a tightly supervised in-school suspension is often a more effective response to student misbehavior.

When a student steadily accumulates discipline referrals across a school year, the problem may not be obvious until a file is started, the student's first report card comes out, or it becomes evident in some other way that a problem exists. The referral form in Table 5.1 can contribute to clarifying the picture of the student's performance. In these cases, documentation can prove invaluable by providing information regarding problems that are escalating or declining. If the student has accumulated ten discipline slips in the first month of school, eight in the second month, and three in the third month, the administrator has strong evidence that standard consequences have been effective. On the other hand, monthly increases in discipline slips signal that the problem is escalating and that another intervention strategy is needed.

Regardless of whether problem behaviors requiring discipline referrals to the office are increasing or decreasing, a team meeting can help to clarify how the student is doing and confirm whether subjective impressions are congruent with the objective data. Although discipline referrals may have declined, it is possible that the teachers have noted escalating misbehavior but have declined to refer because it causes an even greater classroom disruption. Also, the team meeting can address academic performance, which may parallel behavior problems. In some cases, a referral for an academic evaluation may take priority over other interventions.

Referral to support programs, an alcohol treatment program, family therapy, or any number of other inter-

ventions could be recommended by the team. A behavior management program is just one of many alternatives that could be tried, alone or in conjunction with other interventions. The task of the team is to make recommendations that are in the child's best interests.

Behavior on School Buses

A ride on a school bus can be a chaotic experience full of screaming, poking, tripping, throwing objects, and other dangerous behavior that distracts even the best driver. In the worst cases, verbal and physical harassment can make the bus ride a nightmare for less assertive children. To complicate matters, most school bus drivers are trained to drive a vehicle, not manage children's behavior. Farmer (1985) noted that increased disciplinary problems on board school buses were an important issue for managers of school transportation systems. How does a school administrator ensure that schoolchildren behave in an acceptable manner while they are on the bus? A search of the behavior management literature related to school buses produced very thin results. However, if the established principles of behavior management are applied in a reasonable manner, programs that will keep problem behaviors on the school buses to a minimum can be designed.

One approach to reducing behavior problem on the school bus was documented by Wells (1991) in an article describing a school bus equipped with television monitors and a videotape player used to show educational videos during the bus ride. Although an expensive solution, the article reported that disciplinary problems were significantly reduced as children focused their attention on the programs, which made them less likely to misbehave.

A complementary approach to school bus discipline has lately appeared in several reports around the country (Leff, 1992). Instead of showing videos to the students, the students become the stars of a video. The technique works like this: Buses are equipped with "black boxes" with a flashing red light on the front. The boxes *may* or *may not* contain a real video camera aimed at the student riders. A smaller number of video cameras are rotated randomly among the boxes. Thus, any student who misbehaves has a very real chance of being videotaped in the act. Leff reported that the Orange County Florida schools used this system and virtually eliminated the need for bus drivers to write up students for discipline problems. When a behavior record is recorded on videotape, it is hard to deny having violated a rule. The advantages of the system are that school districts are able to save money by not purchasing a video camera for every school bus, and there is a "monitor" on the bus to record rule violations. The disadvantage is that most of the time, no videotaping is actually being done. Thus, some rule violations can go unrecorded and receive no consequence.

Using a more traditional behavior management approach, Schantl (1991) developed a motivational program that rewarded students in grades K–5 for positive bus behavior on a monthly basis. The core of the program was a school safety patrol formed to help safeguard students using the bus. It consisted of two fifth-grade students seated in the front and rear seats on each bus. Patrol members could report dangerous situations to the bus driver, monitor students as they entered and exited the bus, and hand out "ticket citations" to students who violated rules. Referral to the student's teacher was made for these tickets except that severe discipline infractions, safety violations, or excessive trash were written on a "Bus Conduct Report" which was sent to the school office for administrative handling. Bus rules required that riders remain seated, talk only "when the lights were off" (apparently required for safety at railroad crossings and stops), keep hands and feet away from windows and aisles, place all objects on the floor of the bus, and be facing forward at all times. Two faculty members patrolled the bus ramp at the school to enforce rules and ensure orderly loading and unloading.

The contingency worked like this: Each bus received 100 points per week. Then points were deducted for rule violations, 10 points for a major violation and 5 points for a minor infraction. Buses with about equal frequencies of discipline problems were placed in groups of four or five, and the bus from each group with the most points remaining at the end of a month received the "Bus of the Month" award. Students riding the Bus of the Month received rewards that varied from pizza parties to snow cones.

The school bus discipline plan was presented throughout the school in all classrooms, banners were made promoting school bus safety, and bus drivers were consulted about the plan. There was also a bus newsletter reporting on how the discipline plan was going, buses still in contention for "Bus of the Month," and other news and features. A quiz covering bus-riding rules was administered in each student's classroom.

Although the project lacked the controls necessary to be considered a scientific study, it reduced discipline referrals by more than 50 percent. Thus, basic behavior management techniques can be applied to school bus behavior. In my opinion, the key to any successful program for school bus behavior is that there must be a responsible individual or a video camera on the bus to observe behavior objectively. If this is not possible, the bus driver is left with this responsibility, which means he or she must divide attention between the behavior of riders and the hazards of the road. Asking the bus driver to do this may be creating an additional hazard. Of course, having adult monitors ride each school bus would work best, but limited funding for ancillary personnel may make this solution impractical. My suggestion is that the first step in gaining control of school bus behavior is to monitor behavior in an effective manner using older children, adult volunteers, school staff members, or videotaping. Then, an appropriate incentive program linked to the school's total discipline plan can be designed.

PREVENTION IN THE REGULAR CLASSROOM SETTING

Regular school classrooms are the primary vehicle for educating our young people. The more smoothly and efficiently regular classrooms function, the better will be each child's education. Behavior management principles can make a substantial contribution to a teacher's ability to stay focused on academics and spend a minimal amount of time dealing with misbehavior. The core principle is the Golden Rule of Behavior Management. The rule states that the most effective method of classroom control is to give praise and positive attention to students who are behaving according to expectations and to ignore as much as possible minor annoyances and misbehavior. If this rule is combined with a fair set of classroom rules, with fair consequences, consistently enforced, the majority of classroom behavior problems at all grade levels can be prevented.

To provide the broadest coverage, the present topic is divided in four sections. The first section discusses the most general principles of successful classroom management and discipline. The remaining three sections deal specifically with the three major grade divisions, elementary school, middle school, and high school.

General Principles of Successful Classroom Management

I once served as the school psychologist in a school with two fourth-grade classes. One was rigidly structured, with each student sitting perfectly straight, both feet on the floor, intently engaged in completing assigned work. There were no disruptions for pencil sharpening, getting forgotten materials, bathroom breaks, or trips to the drinking fountain. Each student was expected to have materials ready and homework completed. During seatwork time, the students were on task an amazing 90 percent of the time. The classroom was so quiet, one could hear a pin drop. In fact, if a pin did drop, I am sure it would have melted from the gaze of the teacher before hitting the floor.

The other fourth-grade class provided an incredible contrast. Students were everywhere, in small groups, intently engaged in different activities. To the uninitiated observer, the classroom was chaotic. Students were moving in every direction, engaged in so many different tasks that it was difficult to do any formal observation. The students were at different work stations engaged in a variety of exciting learning projects—working on the computer, writing a play, and designing the sets to go with it. The teacher was able to direct each project simultaneously. It took several sessions of observation until I was able to realize that this class was just as highly organized as the first class and that the amount of learning was almost certainly equal in both classes. In fact, both fourth-grade classes were wonderful places to learn. The main difference between these two classes was in the style and personality of the two teachers. Both were very competent and deeply concerned about their students. However, each approached classroom organization in a different way, one that was suited to his or her unique personality.

The first thing beginning (and sometimes the advanced) teachers must think about before planning a classroom structure is their own personality and needs. If a teacher needs organization and structure, classroom rules, consequences, and procedures need to be congruent with these needs. For a teacher who thrives in a loosely structured environment and would like to see students who are free to structure their own time and have opportunities to engage in a number of varied and interesting activities, classroom rules, consequences, and procedures will need to be congruent with these needs. Behavior management principles are adaptable to a number of different teaching strategies and classroom goals, but the teacher needs to have something in mind before setting these principles in motion.

Almost all classroom teachers are concerned with the problem of maintaining "discipline" in their classrooms. Discipline, in this context, means their freedom to teach and interact with students without interruption from misbehaving students. No single system of classroom management has gained wide popularity and acceptance. The main reason for differences across classrooms is that teachers, themselves, are different from each other. The management style of any individual teacher is likely to be the result of a combination of factors—personality, knowledge imparted by coursework, and personal experience.

Despite the wide range of possible classroom management styles, a few guidelines can be specified for general classroom management that are consistent with the principles of behavior management:

Guideline 1: Specify a clear and concrete set of classroom rules. Rules are one of the most basic elements of classroom discipline. A few simple rules, fairly and consistently enforced, can be the basis for a productive and happy classroom. When rules are unnecessarily complicated, unfair, or inconsistently enforced, much of the teacher's time will be spent in nonteaching tasks, productivity may be low, and some students may suffer from the insecurity that can result from an unpredictable environment.

Silberman and Wheelan (1980) concretely describe characteristics of good rules. First, they suggest that rules must be clear to both children and the adults who set them. Conflict may arise when children and adults have different ideas concerning whether the requirements of a rule have been met. For instance, if a classroom rule states that students should prepare for their reading lesson right after lunch, what does this mean? Should all books and materials be out before the bell rings? Or should the students be discussing the story they read most recently? Both students and adults should know the requirements of any particular rule. Usually, a clear rule is stated in a positive manner that lets everyone know what is appropriate behavior in the situation. For example, "When the WORK sign is up, students will remain in their seats and complete assigned work," is more informative and than "Be quiet when the WORK sign is up."

Silberman and Wheelan also advise that rules should be enforceable. To be enforceable, a rule should represent a realistic value that the child is capable of obeying, and a responsible adult should be able to determine easily whether it is obeyed. If a rule covers a specific behavior, the teacher needs to be able to monitor the behavior consistently. Thus, rules should not cover behavior that occurs under the supervision of other adults.

These situations should have their own rules and consequences. Also, rules should be realistic. For example, a rule that required students to be on task all the time would be unenforceable. A more reasonable version of the rule needs to be developed, perhaps with the help of the students affected by the rule.

Holding a discussion about a rule before enforcement begins can be helpful to both the children and the adults involved. A discussion provides an opportunity to clear up ambiguities and misunderstandings and allows the adults to present the rationale for the rule. Children also may have ideas about how rules can be improved and made less aversive from their perspective. The discussion also gives the students some "ownership" of the rule so that they are more likely to internalize it. Teaching classroom rules needs to be an explicit part of a teacher's lesson plans at the beginning of each school year. Rosenberg (1986) demonstrated that a brief daily review of classroom rules prior to instructional activities improved the behavioral and academic performance of five disruptive boys. In a regular classroom setting, regular rule review early in the school year may improve compliance, whereas more frequent or extended review could be used with disruptive or distractible children who have greater difficulty complying with classroom rules.

Guideline 2: Specify a clear set of consequences for rule violations and be consistent in the application of these consequences. Silberman and Wheelan (1980) suggest a "three-chance plan" for handling rule violations. The first time a rule is broken, a warning is given, which can be as simple as stating the rule. The second time a rule is broken, the warning is repeated and the consequence (e.g., extra work, a logical consequence, or detention) is stated. The third time a rule is broken, the stated consequence is administered. The three-chance plan can be modified into a two-chance plan for those who feel that giving two warnings is excessive. In a two-chance plan, the first time a rule violation occurs, both the rule and the consequence are stated. If the behavior recurs, the consequence is administered. Effective verbal reprimands need to be a warning to the student that a consequence will be administered if the behavior recurs or continues. This is one of the critical elements of using verbal reprimands effectively.

One problem with the three-chance plan is that a teacher may not be able to remember how many warnings and for what rule violation have been given to a particular student. In the Assertive Discipline technique (Canter & Canter, 1992), it is suggested that the teacher use a clipboard or notebook to record each student's name when a warning is given. This could be supplemented with a brief note (even just the number of the rule broken would suffice) about the particular behavior. This has the advantage of being a memory aid plus providing a detailed written record of minor disruptions. Handing the student a yellow ticket with the word WARNING printed on it could serve as a concrete reminder to correct his or her behavior.

It is crucial that a teacher plan consequences ahead of time. Having a concrete plan makes it easy to follow through and gives the teacher a feeling of confidence. It also takes away the arbitrary and unfair nature of some discipline techniques because students are well aware of the consequences that will result from violations of classroom rules. Canter and Canter (1992) suggest a hierarchy of consequences based on the number of rule violations. The first rule violation results in a warning. The second or third rule violation results in an easy-to-administer consequence. The fourth violation results in contacting the child's parents, and the consequence for a fifth violation or a *severely* disruptive behavior is an immediate trip to the principal's office.

Not all teachers are comfortable with this type of hierarchy. One alternative is to reverse the consequences for the fourth and fifth rule violations. That is, a fourth violation results in an immediate trip to the principal's office, and a fifth violation leads to contact with parents, which is also conducted by a school administrator. As noted earlier, not all parents are concerned or mature enough to respond appropriately to contact from the school. Thus, contact between school administrators and parents should not necessarily be seen as a punishing event for the child. Instead, it should be an opportunity to set up an intervention that will remediate the current problem.

Specific consequences for rule violations can cover a wide range and will need to vary with the age and grade of the student. One particularly effective consequence suggested by Canter and Canter (1992) is to delay the child's transition to the next activity (recess, lunch, home, next class) for one minute. They report this consequence is effective with children of all ages. Other consequences are discussed next according to grade level.

When the consequences are specified and rules are clearly understood, it becomes the student's job to behave appropriately and the teacher's job to administer rules fairly and consistently. Generally, if limits on behavior are stated clearly, students will occupy their time with the task of learning and few students will require formal behavior management programs to remediate unacceptable behavior.

Guideline 3: Usually, the most effective way to deal with a behavior that is annoying but falls outside the classroom rules is to ignore it. Verbal reprimands frequently *increase* the occurrence of misbehavior because attention from an adult is reinforcing. The effectiveness of a verbal reprimand can be increased by making the reprimand privately to the student, being near the student when the reprimand is delivered, and using an assertive style with good eye contact. This allows the student to save face and eliminates the possibility that peers will laugh or otherwise reinforce the reprimanded student (Kerr & Nelson, 1989; Williams, Williams, & McLaughlin, 1991a). In general, reprimands should be avoided. Instead, use the three-chance plan just discussed. This will ensure that verbal threats are backed up with a consequence, thereby increasing their effectiveness.

Guideline 4: Remember to use frequent verbal praise directed at students who are behaving appropriately. Praise and positive attention for appropriate behavior are the most critical elements in maintaining a smoothly running classroom (e.g., Hall, Lund, & Jackson, 1968; Madsen, Becker, & Thomas, 1968; Mathews, McLaughlin, & Hunsaker, 1980; Williams et al., 1991a). Thomas (1991) developed a list of 110 different phrases for praising students. Table 5.2 shows some examples from Thomas (1991) and Barkley (1987a, 1987b). Barkley (1987a, 1987b) also gives three excellent suggestions for providing the most effective positive feedback. First, give immediate approval as much as possible. Second, be specific with the praise that is given. "I like it when everybody works so hard" is better than "That's good." Third, never use backhanded praise, such as "It's about time you learned to stay in your seats" or "Why can't we have more days like this?"

Giving genuine, warm, and spontaneous praise should be a habit of every teacher. It both reinforces and cues correct behavior and will make any other classroom management technique more effective. Frequent praise is effective at all levels of instruction, from kindergarten to senior high school.

Guideline 5: Keep in mind the advantages of employing an assertive style of interacting with children, and avoid aggressive and nonassertive behavior. Managing all the activities that transpire in a typical classroom requires that the teacher set clear, attainable goals for students. Recall from the discussion in Chapter 1 that assertive behavior lies in the middle of a continuum of

Table 5.2. Examples of Positive Feedback and Approval

Physical

Hand on shoulder	"O.K. " sign
"Thumbs up sign	Smile
Wink	Nodding of head
Sticker on paper	A note to student
A note to parent(s)	Arm pump
"Touchdown" dance	Raised arm

Sports figures, TV characters, cartoons, TV commercials, and comic books may model other gestures and signs of approval that may become popular with students.

Verbal

"You're on the right track."	"You did a lot of work today."
"Great!"	"Fantastic!"
"Thanks for _____."	"Way to go!"
"Tremendous!"	"Awesome!"
"That's it."	"You're really working hard."
"You're really improving"	"Good job!"
"Wow!"	"How did you think of that?"
"You've been practicing."	"Nice going!"
"Great effort."	"It's nice when you _____."
"Terrific!"	"Beautiful."

behavioral styles, anchored at one end by nonassertion and at the other end by aggression. Timidity and being taken advantage of characterize nonassertive people. Name calling, putdowns, and yelling characterize the behavior of aggressive individuals. Directness and honesty tend to characterize the assertive individual's behavior.

An assertive style of classroom management means that rules and expectations are stated honestly and directly and consequences of behavior are administered without belittling or insulting students. The assertive teacher is fair to all students and makes guidelines for behavior so clear and distinct that students have little difficulty defining the limits of classroom behavior. Clearly communicating expectations to students is one of the most crucial elements of effective classroom discipline. All students need to know the expectations for their behavior in order to comply. Students with the most potential for developing serious behavior problems are the least likely to be familiar with the structure of a classroom and will benefit the most from a thorough introduction to classroom rules.

Guideline 6: Use clear signals to separate "work" from "free" time. Transitions from one activity to another are often the most difficult periods for both students and teachers. Teachers will find their classrooms run most smoothly when they plan transition times carefully and provide students with clear signals that indicate what is expected. Making the stimuli that signal each period as obvious and different from each other as possible will help both students and teachers identify what behavior is appropriate. For example, a reversible sign with NO TALKING in red letters on one side and FREE TIME in green letters on the other side would be more effective than an announcement at the beginning of the period, especially for younger or distractible students.

Guideline 7: Classroom management is likely to be most successful when the focus is to keep students actively engaged in useful learning tasks. Research indicates that a major factor in student learning is the amount of time students spend actively engaged in learning tasks (Shapiro, 1987). Furthermore, a student who is engaged in a learning task can not simultaneously engage in misbehavior. Thus, the major goal for classroom teaching is to keep students engaged in learning tasks using well-planned lessons and a variety of presentation methods.

Guideline 8: When a behavior management problem becomes overwhelming or a child exhibits signs of a serious behavior problem, seek help and consultation. It would be unrealistic for a teacher to expect to manage a classroom without ever seeking help or consultation. Assuming a typical class size of about thirty students, even low-incidence disorders or handicaps are likely to appear in a class every couple of years or so. As I have tried to point out throughout this book, many behavior problems are related to environmental factors outside the school, such as parental divorce, abuse, or alcoholism. Even the best behavior management program may not meet a pupil's needs. Thus, a need for help and/or consultation means that the teacher is acknowledging the complexities of the real world, where a team approach to problem solving is often needed.

Most of the time a teacher should be following the Golden Rule of Behavior Management, ignoring minor misbehavior that falls outside classroom rules and providing frequent praise for appropriate student behavior. At some point a student may attract the teacher's attention because he or she violates rules significantly more often than other students, misbehaves in ways that are unusual or strange, engages in high-magnitude behaviors, or causes significant disruption of teaching. Other signs of serious underlying problems are discussed in Chapter 4. As soon as a pupil reaches this point, it would be a good idea to begin maintaining documentation on this child. Any special behavior management programs that are attempted should be noted, along with as much data on their impact as is practical. Good documentation will assist greatly in helping the child study team, principal, school psychologist, lead teacher, school counselor, social worker, colleague, or consultant gain a clear understanding of your concerns. Completing the form shown in Table 5.1 may also help clarify issues.

These eight guidelines are meant to help the teacher develop a plan for classroom management. They are meant only as guidelines, not as hard and fast rules. Each teacher will need to develop his or her own approach to classroom management and discipline. This approach will need to be compatible with the teacher's personality, the developmental level of the students, and schoolwide discipline policies. Table 5.3 summarizes the eight guidelines for easy reference.

The sections that follow discuss specific applications of these eight guidelines to elementary, middle, and high school classes.

Table 5.3 Guidelines for Classroom Managment

Guideline 1: Specify a clear and concrete set of classroom rules.
- Rules should be
  1. Clear
  2. Enforceable
  3. Discussed with students
- Regular rule review early in the school year may improve compliance
- More frequent review should be used with children having greater difficulty complying with classroom rules.

Guideline 2: Specify a clear set of consequences for rule violations and be consistent in the application of these consequences
- Consider using the "three-chance plan" for handling rule violations.
  1. First violation: Give warning.
  2. Second violation: Repeat the warning and state the consequence.
  3. Third violation: Administer the stated consequence.
- A two-chance plan may also be effective.
  1. First violation: Give warning and state the consequence
  2. S econd violation: Administer the stated consequence
- Effective verbal reprimands need to be a warning to the student that a consequence will be administered if the behavior recurs or continues.
- A clipboard or notebook may be used to record each student's name when a warning or consequence is given. This provides a valuable permanent record. An example of the sequence:
  1. Student violates "no swearing" rule.
  2. Student receives warning ("Remember, the rule is: No swearing. If it happens again, you will stay in class an extra minute.").
  3. Teacher records student's name, and nature of rule violation in notebook.
  4. Student swears again—consequence is administered.
- It is aboslutely crucial that a teacher plan consequences ahead of time.
- If the student continues to violate classroom rules, the teacher's options are:
  1. Send the student to the principal's office.
  2. Contact the child's parents.
  3. Develop an individualized behavior management program.
- The consequence for *severely* disruptive behavior is an immediate trip to the principal's office.
- Contact between school administrators and parents should be seen as an opportunity to set up an intervention that will remediate the current problem.

Guideline 3: Most of the time the most effective way to deal with a behavior that is annoying but falls outside the classroom rules is to ignore it.
- Remember that verbal reprimands frequently *increase* the occurrence of misbehavior because attention from an adult is reinforcing.
- The effectiveness of a verbal reprimand can be increased by making the reprimand privately to the student.

Guideline 4: Remember to use frequent verbal praise directed at students who are behaving appropriately.
- The most effective positive feedback is:
  1. Immediate
  2. Specific
  3. Not "backhanded" (e.g., "It's about time you learned to stay in your seats" or "Why don't we have more days like this?")
- Make praise genuine, warm, and spontaneous.
- Praise is effective at all levels of instruction, from kindergarten to senior high school.
- Notes to students and/or their parent(s), free time, and being first in line are examples of higher magnitude privileges that can be awarded for appropriate behavior.

Guideline 5: Keep in mind the advantages of employing an assertive style of interacting with children, and avoid both aggressive and nonassertive behavior.
- Directness and honesty characterize the assertive individual's behavior.
- State rules and expectations honestly and directly.
- Administer consequences without belittling or insulting students.
- Make fairness a priority.
- Make rules so clear and distinct that students have little difficulty defining the limits of behavior.

- Clearly communicating expectations is one of the most critical elements of effective classroom discipline.

Guideline 6: Use clear signals to separate "work" from "free" time.
- Plan transition times carefully and provide students with clear signals that indicate what is expected.
- A reversible sign with NO TALKING in red letters on one side and FREE TIME in green letters on the other side may help younger children with transitions.

Guideline 7: Classroom management is likely to be most successful when the focus is to keep students actively engaged in useful learning tasks.
- A student who is working will not be a discipline problem.

Guideline 8: *When a behavior management problem becomes overwhelming or a child exhibits signs of a serious behavior problem, seek help and consultation.*
- A team approach to problem solving is often needed.
- Maintain good documentation on difficult children.
- Sources of help include a child study team, principal, school psychologist, lead teacher, school counselor, social worker, colleagues, or consultant.

Elementary Classes

Children just beginning their school careers have a lot to learn about classroom structure, and this makes the tasks of the kindergarten teacher among the most difficult in education. Rules, structure, and learning activities may be new concepts to some kindergarten children. Therefore, the kindergarten teacher needs to make things as simple as possible—to minimize the number of rules and keep consequences simple. Three rules—for example, "Listen and follow directions," "Stay in your seat when the WORK sign is up," and "Keep hands and feet to yourself"—would be appropriate for most kindergarten classes. Daily review of the rules will probably speed learning. When the rules have been learned to the satisfaction of the teacher, they could be reviewed less frequently.

The transition to first grade is particularly problematic for some children because the change from a half day to a whole day of school and the increased academic expectations mean that the child must exhibit better self-control. Durlak (1992) points out that attention problems, learning problems, and disruptive/aggressive behavior are typically identified in the third grade, although severe cases may be identified earlier.

When a classroom rule is violated, young children should be given one warning (e.g., "If you leave your chair again, you will sit over there for five minutes"). Severe behavior disruptions can result in an immediate consequence. Many teachers in the early elementary grades use a "thinking chair" that is off to the side but still allows the student to see and hear classroom activity. Students are sent to the thinking chair for a short period when they violate a classroom rule or significantly disrupt the class. This has the double advantage of allowing the student to receive instruction while observing the fun other students are enjoying. Another effective consequence is to have the student wait one minute before joining the next activity. Waiting a minute to catch a bus, eat a snack, or join in free time would be especially effective.

Most children are sensitive to adult praise, and this seems especially true of younger children. Therefore, frequent praise for correct behavior will help make the classroom a manageable environment. Specific praise can also serve as a cue to other children, who will copy the child who was praised. For example, a teacher could say, "I like the way Amy has her scissors and worksheet out." Several children will then look at Amy and copy her behavior. The teacher should follow up by praising other children as they also find their scissors and worksheet.

In some cases, a teacher may find it difficult to manage a class for various reasons. A token program that employs a concrete progression to the backup reward may be helpful. Filling a jar, with marbles or other tokens, filling a sheet with stickers, or using another method that clearly shows progression toward the backup reward would be effective token systems for young children. Backup rewards could consist of free time, a popcorn party, or some other desirable activity. Young children are not likely to tolerate long delays between behavior and its consequences, so the classroom teacher needs to be immediate and frequent with praise or token rewards.

Another alternative is to reward students for academic success. Salzberg, Wheeler, Devar, and Hopkins (1971) showed that kindergarten children who were allowed to participate in a fifteen-minute play period when they printed letters with acceptable accuracy demonstrated increased accuracy compared to baseline conditions or when they received feedback only for their performance. Only half the children received the contingency on any given day, but the children were unaware of whose papers would be graded until they had completed their work. Children who were not graded went straight to the play area, and those whose graded papers did not reach a criterion of acceptable performance continued practicing their printing. This is just one example of many different contingencies that could be programmed for accurate academic performance and appropriate behavior in a regular classroom setting. Generally, the types of behavior management programs likely to be successful with children in the elementary grades would emphasize concrete goals, immediate consequences, and material rewards.

In contrast, one would predict that most elementary school children would not respond well to programs with long delays or complicated relationships between behavior and rewards. Subtle moral arguments, such as the difference between "accidental" and "purposeful" actions, are not likely to be understood. Only the physical consequences that result from actions are obvious. Thus, in planning a behavior management program for a child showing frequent aggressive behavior, one would not be likely to find success if an attempt was made to discriminate among the various circumstances that lead to aggression. Basically, all aggressive acts should meet with the same consequences. As the child's cognitive skills grow, more complicated social skills can be learned. The young child is dealing with social issues on a much more basic and concrete level than adults.

As children progress into the middle and late elementary school grades, an issue that gains increasing importance is homework. A recent review of the empirical literature on improving homework performance (Miller & Kelley, 1991) suggested that both homework completion and accuracy contribute to academic success. Reinforcing parental involvement also enhances the accuracy and productivity of homework. When homework begins to be assigned on a regular basis, expectations need to be communicated to parents so they can provide the proper support. Teachers may need to be very concrete in communicating their expectations about homework to parents. The information provided should include the amount and frequency of homework and the kinds of assistance that parents can offer. School–home notes that

provide feedback on the completion and accuracy of homework (see Chapter 10) may be helpful for students who have difficulty with homework completion. Chapter 12 discusses homework from the parental perspective.

Middle School Classes

The theme in the middle years of childhood is the growing cognitive ability of the child and how it interacts with the increasingly complex environment to which the child is exposed. Yet, a great dependence on external experience still exists, so the child is greatly influenced by environmental events rather than internal rules, standards, and reasoning. What are the implications for development of behavior management programs?

First, more complex behavior management procedures can be employed. This would include fairly complex token reward programs in which the child earns points for good behavior that can be exchanged for various material rewards. Home note programs, in which the child's teacher rates classroom behavior on a daily or weekly basis and the child's parents provide rewards contingent on the quality of the ratings, are also likely to be effective. Second, it has been my experience that it is important to reach troubled children at this stage to help them control their behavior within the bounds set by society. Many adolescents referred for severe behavior problems have histories extending back to middle childhood. Unfortunately, at adolescence, it is very difficult from a practical and legal standpoint for schools to exercise behavioral control. For children of middle school age, the entire range of common behavior management procedures is likely to be effective if appropriate individual adjustments are made.

School systems are structured in various alignments but middle school typically begins in the fifth, sixth, or seventh grade and continues until the eighth or ninth grade. Although students may be required to change teachers in any grade level, the transition to a daily schedule with different teachers and classrooms for each period can be difficult for many students. Classroom and school rules need to be adjusted to account for this. Typically, a rule that governs the transition period needs to be a part of classroom rules. The simplest one states, "Be in your seat when the second bell rings." It may be necessary for some teachers to elaborate on the rule by specifying what materials should be out and ready at the beginning of class. It is helpful if such a rule is consistently enforced by all teachers. As students mature, they will be able to internalize a greater number of rules, although five or six is probably the maximum that would be reasonable. Each teacher needs to find rules that create the type of learning environment he or she desires.

Unfortunately, some children begin becoming involved with alcohol and drugs during their middle school years. Though relatively rare within this age group, involvement with drugs at this age is likely to predict severe behavior problems by the time the child reaches adolescence. If there is suspicion of alcohol or drug use, some follow-up is needed despite the impression that the child is too young for such problems. Other issues that may arise in this age group include depression, self-destructive behavior, and test or performance anxiety (Durlak, 1992).

High School Students

By the time students arrive at high school, they should be well acclimated to the demands of school and able to adapt to a variety of classroom structures. They should be able to adapt easily to several classroom rules. Their problems, however, can be much more severe, with depression, addictions, and poor parental supervision complicating the picture. Students should be able to respond to classroom rules after one or two reviews, although extensive review may help more troublesome or distractible students. The social aspect of school is likely to be primary, and structuring a class so that students regularly work in small groups is likely to meet with some success while also functioning as an activity that can be used to reward other behavior. An effective consequence for rule violations is to keep the student after class for a minute or two, because walking and talking with friends is an important activity that students will not want to miss.

Adolescents, whether or not they have developed internal standards of conduct congruent with societal expectations, will normally have developed advanced cognitive skills. Along with advanced cognitive skills comes a desire for independence from adults. Consequently, adolescents are likely to respond best to programs in which they have a major say. Probably the most common approach with adolescents is behavioral contracting. The key element in such contracts from the adolescent's perspective is that it allows them input into the process. In fact, good behavioral contracts specify that both parties signing the contract are to both receive and grant privileges to the other party. With this technique, the adolescent as well as significant others has the opportunity to effect changes in his or her own behavior. Behavioral contracts, then, are appropriate to the advanced skills of this age group.

Despite demands for independence, however, it is still appropriate to employ more restrictive and concrete behavior management programs with this age group. Several useful programs for monitoring and rewarding school performance on a daily or weekly basis are discussed in Chapter 10. If a student objects to such programs because they attract the negative attention of peers, the student has the option of improving behavior sufficiently to make the program unnecessary. Throughout adult life, individuals who fail to meet their social and legal obligations come under intense monitoring and scrutiny. A compromise is to allow a student a week to improve behavior without the structure of a daily monitoring form. This gives the student a chance to improve while avoiding negative attention from peers. Failure to improve, however, leads directly to strict daily monitoring.

In dealing with adolescents, it is easy to become focused on attempting to correct the student's misbehavior. However, a key issue for all adolescents is to develop vocational goals and become productive members of society. In dealing with complex behavior problems, it is crucial that team members examine the student's vocational needs and develop programs that will lead to vocational success later in life. This means that the team needs to focus carefully on identifying the child's strengths because it is these qualities that will most likely become the basis for success in later life.

PREVENTION IN SPECIAL CLASSROOMS

Special classrooms have a limited number of students, usually fewer than six or seven, and are intended to give special instruction for students with academic or behavioral problems. In some instances, the classes are for meeting special education needs: in other cases the classes may be part of tutoring, dropout prevention, or other regular education programs. These classes are usually staffed by one lead teacher with additional support staff according to class size. The small size of the classes allow for more individualized instruction and behavior management programs than in regular classrooms. However, problem behaviors can be more severe and/or persistent than in the mainstream setting.

Prevention of behavior management problems in special classes depends on many of the same principles that apply to mainstream classes. In special classrooms, however, students are more likely to show behavior deficits. That is, they will not know how to behave appropriately and will need to be cued and shaped to learn appropriate behavior. Rules may need to be more explicit and reviewed daily with some students, and it may be necessary to define in greater detail just what students *should* be doing.

Effective intervention also includes constructing a classroom climate that is conducive to behavior change. McClannahan and Krantz (1985) discuss some components of effective learning environments for developmentally disabled children, which are relevant to any child with behavioral problems. First, the activities of both children and instructors need to be scheduled appropriately so that instructional time is maximized. Second, the responsible teacher needs to be present in the instructional area as much as possible. Third, teachers should be selected or trained to have low tolerance for deviant behavior. Instead, when deviant behavior is observed, appropriate instruction to eliminate deviant behavior should be conducted. Fourth, learning environments should be pleasant, in that a high rate of specific, rewarding praise is delivered. Finally, McClannahan and Krantz point out that instructors must be masters of the basic principles of rewarding and shaping behavior.

Students who have behavioral problems present a significant challenge to the teacher. Most such students will be receiving special education. This means that the bulk of their program will be specified in an Individual Education Plan or IEP. The IEP states long-term goals and short-term objectives for the student and guides both academic and behavioral programming. However, most teachers of special education classes also structure their classrooms in a general way that is compatible with the IEPs of most students.

Selinske, Greer, and Lodhi (1991) described a model called CABAS (Comprehensive Application of Behavior Analysis to Schooling). The core of the CABAS model is that each instructional trial is planned, presented, and recorded along with the student's response. For example, if the child was being taught to discriminate among shapes, he or she would be given an object and prompted to name its shape. The teacher would then record whether the student's response was correct or incorrect and provide the correct answer if it was incorrect. A correct response would result in praise and other reinforcers. Once the objective was attained, such as

three consecutive sessions (20 trials each) of identifying four shapes with 90 percent accuracy, the next objective in the curriculum sequence was begun. Application of this method requires finding appropriate curricula and careful planning to develop easy methods of recording and tracking student progress. Selinske et al. found increases in trials taught, correct responses, and achieved objectives applying this method across a two-year period for a school of visually impaired children with multiple handicaps. See the description of token programs (Chapter 11) for a more detailed description of this general approach.

Another general approach to managing behavior in a special classroom setting is to use a system of levels or privileges. In this kind of system there are several different levels of supervision and structure available that enable individualizing of programs within an overall organizational framework (Bauer, Shea, & Keppler, 1986; Hewett, 1968; Kazdin, 1977; Mastropieri, Jenne, & Scruggs, 1988). At the lowest level, students in the program are restricted and closely supervised; at higher levels, students are not so closely supervised. For example, at the highest level in the program, a student may be allowed an unsupervised visit to the school library. At the middle level, the student may be allowed a library visit only if accompanied by an adult; at the lowest level, the student might not be allowed to leave the classroom. Students begin at the lowest level, and their behavior determines whether they earn their way up or down the levels.

Barbetta (1990) described such a system called GOALS (Group-Oriented Adapted Levels System). This system is based on group contingencies in that the entire group earns a particular level rather than individual students being on different levels. Although the group approach has several advantages over the individualized approach, it may not be compatible with students' IEPs. In the GOALS system, students develop classroom rules and expectations with guidance from the teacher, making the rules less authoritarian and giving students more ownership. Then daily points are awarded to each individual student on the basis of how well they follow classroom rules. The entire group must then earn a predetermined percentage of points, which determines the level that the entire group is assigned for the next day. Other aspects of the GOALS program included provisions for cuing, correcting, and reinforcing behavior by students, in contrast to the usual teacher-centered model.

A primary advantage of level systems in special classrooms is that they provide a tight structure for those students who need it while being flexible enough to give more advanced students an opportunity to show that they are ready for greater freedom and responsibility. Here is another example of a typical hierarchy of levels that might be useful in a special classroom with students who have behavior problems.

Level 1. The student is on a token program that provides points for following classroom rules, staying on task, and working on IEP goals. Points or tokens should be awarded at least every half hour or even more frequently if staffing allows. The primary task of each student is to complete academic goals, but some students may have social or behavioral goals on their IEPs. Therefore, the system should be flexible enough to accommodate varied needs of individual students. The student is closely supervised at all times, and points or tokens are awarded only by the lead teacher and support personnel in the classroom. Although teachers must structure their individual classrooms according to their own needs and those of their students, a typical set of rules for a Level 1 program might consist of the following:

1. Students shall remain on task when work is assigned. Student receives 10 points for each half hour of on-task behavior. Student receives 5 bonus points for each assignment completed with 80 percent accuracy or better.
2. No putdowns, name calling, yelling, screaming, swearing, threats, or other verbally aggressive behavior. Student loses 5 points for each incident.
3. No physical aggression. Student loses 20 points for each incident.
4. Students must comply with all teacher directions within ten seconds. Student loses 10 points each time student does not follow a direction within ten seconds.
5. Students must remain in their seats unless given permission to leave.
6. No out-of-class privileges (assemblies, library, lunch, etc.)
7. On any necessary out-of-class trips (office, bathroom, etc.), student is accompanied by a staff person.
8. No "free" time, except that a student may select reading material from the class library to read quietly.
9. During group discussion periods, students are expected to (a) wait until they have been recognized

by the group leader before speaking, (b) be fair to other students, and (c) be good listeners. Student receives 20 points for following the rules. Student can receive 5 bonus points for making a "helpful" comment. *Fair* and *helpful* are concepts that will need to be defined by the group.

Level 2. Under most circumstances, students assigned to a special classroom have been exhibiting relatively severe behavior problems and are likely to need a fairly extensive period of time at Level 1 before graduating to the next level. The criteria for moving to Level 2 would be up to the teacher and the IEP team. One or two weeks earning 85 percent or more of the available points would be a good starting point for graduating a student to the next level. This could be adjusted to meet the needs and expectations of the lead teacher and the IEP team. At Level 2, the core rules for classroom behavior would still apply, but the student would have more flexibility and options available. Students at Level 2 may be allowed to leave their seats without permission to get materials, sharpen pencils, and, when appropriate, use the bathroom. They are allowed to "buy" free time with their points and can choose a wider range of activities in which to participate. A menu of free-time options should be developed in conjunction with students. Out-of-class privileges are permitted, but only when a supervisor is available.

Level 3. At this level, the student has earned the privilege of leaving the classroom on unsupervised trips (with a prior agreement on the amount of time the trip should take). A special privilege such as being able to purchase a soft drink, have lunch with a teacher or staff person, leave class early to go to lunch, or some other highly attractive option requested by students and agreeable to staff should be available for purchase with points earned. At this level, the team should be considering limited placement in mainstream classes with appropriate programming supports and supervision.

Level 4. This level is identical to Level 3 except that the student takes over the clerical and monitoring tasks of the token program. Initially, this will require frequent student–teacher conferences to review the self-monitoring aspect of the program (e.g., Drabman, Spitalink, & O'Leary, 1973). As the student progresses, student–teacher conferences can be less frequent and focused on more general issues.

Level 5. At this level, the student has demonstrated mastery of most behavioral goals and a good deal of independence. Ideally, these students should be subject to rules and consequences identical to those that apply to mainstream students. The only difference is that each incident is carefully documented. The rule for earning privileges is that the student must have completed assigned academic work. Once work is completed, the student may engage in activities without needing to purchase them with points. When a student graduates to this level, substantial time in mainstream classes is likely to be programmed.

One of the most important keys to success in development of successful special classrooms is the availability of a highly structured approach that gives students prompt feedback regarding appropriate and inappropriate behavior. Many students are assigned to special classrooms on the basis of behavior excesses that disrupt the flow of teaching in the mainstream. However, the needs of these students are mainly in the area of remediating behavior deficits. They need to learn more appropriate ways of dealing with conflict (see Deutsch, 1993; Feindler & Guttman, 1994) and they need to learn *how* to learn. Teachers in special classrooms may find that developing a levels program that meets their own and their students' needs is a good way to structure a positive learning environment. Other behavior management tools that will assist in meeting specific student needs are discussed in subsequent chapters.

HOME–SCHOOL RELATIONSHIPS AND PREVENTION

Prevention of childhood behavior problems begins at home. From birth, a child needs to be properly nourished, protected from environmental dangers (e.g., lead paint, accidents), and stimulated in a way that promotes intellectual growth. The most important way that parents can stimulate their children intellectually is to read to them frequently even when they are very young, and ask questions about the stories that require thinking and relating them to everyday events (U.S. Department of Education, 1987). Experience at communicating "stories" through drawing, scribbling, dictating, or conversation also is related to higher achievement in school, as is learning to count everyday objects at an early age. Parents can prime the intellectual pump and prepare their children for school by reading to them, helping them

count objects, and providing materials for drawing and scribbling. Schools can play a key role in educating parents, making materials available, and ensuring that each kindergarten class has received the full advantage of parental stimulation. Many schools accomplish these goals by offering early education programs for parents and children of preschool age.

Meyerhoff and White (1986) summarized a careful program of research into the kinds of parenting skills that promote intellectual growth of children. Their findings indicated that reviewing flash cards and providing expensive educational toys did not consistently give children an intellectual advantage. Instead, providing a stimulating environment, allowing children to roam and explore on their own, reacting enthusiastically to their discoveries, and providing learning experiences based on everyday events such as baking cookies or going to the supermarket give the greatest advantage to children. Schools that can communicate these basic principles to parents will be making great strides toward preventing later behavioral problems because children who are well prepared for success in school will be the least likely to develop behavior problems. As in sports, the best defense is a good offense. That is, productive time spent teaching children new skills is the best way to prevent behavior problems. Unfortunately, schools also have a role in protecting children from neglectful, incompetent, or abusive parents.

What are some of the specific things that schools can do to ensure that home environments contribute positively to the school success of children? One of the first is to communicate frequently and positively with parents. Sending notes home, phoning parents, providing meeting and recreational facilities on evenings and weekends, and sponsoring workshops are just some of the things a school can do to promote a positive community image. The goal is to communicate positively and frequently with parents and the community so that parents come to expect support from the school. Promoting this kind of image puts the school staff in a better position to communicate with parents when a problem develops. Instead of an adversarial relationship, parents and school staff will be members of a team with a common goal of doing what is in each child's best interests.

If this kind of relationship with parents is developed, parents are likely to seek advice from the school when they have problems with their children. Having social workers, nurses, teachers, and school psychologists available for consultation will also enhance team spirit and promote better home–school relationships. It is also helpful to develop a library of resources for parents. Excellent books on a variety of child-rearing subjects are available, and some of them could be checked out to parents . Books about child management skills include *Taking a Look at Discipline* by Garman (1983), *How to Help Children with Common Problems* by Schaefer and Millman (1981), *Sign Here: A Contracting Book for Children and Their Parents* by Dardig and Heward (1981), *Toilet Training in Less Than a Day* by Azrin and Foxx (1974), and *Effective Parents/Responsible Children* by Eimers and Aitchison (1977). One of the most popular programs is S.T.E.P. (Systematic Training for Effective Parenting). Most communities will have such programs regularly available. Parents can be referred to these programs, or they can be offered through the school.[1]

Within the school, it is possible to involve parents in behavior management programs and to provide instruction in the theory of behavior management via workshops. This not only contributes to remediating the problem behavior but can also give the parents supervised training in the use of behavior management principles. See Chapters 9 and 12 for specific descriptions of behavior management programs to be administered by parents.

For example, one excellent way to encourage parental involvement in behavior management programs is by using a home note system. The details of home note programs are described in Chapter 10. Their essence is that the teacher provides written feedback to parents regarding the acceptability of the child's behavior and academic performance in school. The parents then award points for good or improved behavior. The points can be used by the child to "purchase" rewards previously agreed on together by parents and child. Research suggests that training in behavior management skills accompanied by instruction in the principles of behavior management is an effective technique for helping parents cope effectively with the problem behavior of their children and that the instruction in general principles enhances the effect of the training in behavior techniques (McMahon, Forehand, & Griest, 1981). Home note programs provide one method of helping parents learn behavior management principles.

Any of these techniques may, in the right circumstances, allow parents to become involved in a positive way with the management of their child's behavior. This could begin the process of replacing previously unhealthy patterns of interaction with healthier ones. For a more detailed and thorough resource on enhancing home–school relationships, see the edited volume by Christenson and Conoley (1992).

CONCLUSION

The basic principles of behavior management are universal. Reinforced behavior will tend to reoccur in the future without regard to the intention behind any particular contingency. This is why it is important for school professionals to design school environments so behavior problems can be prevented. It is much more cost-effective to prevent a problem than it is to design a special program and hire people to administer behavior management programs. The key to prevention is to have a clearly articulated set of school rules, policies, and procedures, and to communicate them to parents, students, and school staff members. Regular review is also needed to ensure that the policies are effective and consistent with community standards. Although day-to-day problems can sometimes dominate the time of the most organized professional, a preventive approach to behavior management problems can provide an effective route to establishing a positive school climate.

REVIEW

Terms to Remember and Review

reinforcement	school climate
mandatory reporting	punishment
discipline slip	CABAS
GOALS	natural consequences
suicide	in-school suspension

Study and Discussion Questions

1. What are the signs that school climate is good and is contributing to successful learning?
2. What are some signs of an unhealthy school climate?

---

[1]The Center for Applied Psychology, Inc., P.O. Box 1586, King of Prussia, PA 19406, offers a catalog of such resources called Childswork/Childsplay.

3. What characteristics would make an in-school suspension or after-school detention effective in reducing target behaviors?

4. Using the criteria discussed at the beginning of the chapter, evaluate whether each of the following school or classroom rules would be effective:
   a. Students will be quiet at all times.
   b. No fighting is allowed.
   c. Students seen running in the school building will stop, return to where they started, and walk at a normal pace.
   d. Students must be dressed appropriately.
   e. Students may not have pierced ears.
   f. Students must have a parking permit and park in the designated parking lot. All cars without a permit will be towed at owner's expense.
   g. Students must be quiet in the lunch room.
   h. Students must have a pass to be in the hallways during class times.

5. Explain why in-school suspension may be a better consequence for misbehavior than suspension or expulsion from school.

6. Explain the three-chance plan. Cite both its advantages and its disadvantages.

7. Why are both consequences for rule violations and praise for appropriate behavior important components of a classroom management plan?

8. What adjustments need to be made in designing classroom management programs at the various grade levels?

Group Projects

1. Develop a brochure addressed to students or parents describing policies and procedures for an elementary school, a junior high school, or a senior high school. At a minimum, the brochure should have a mission statement, a list of rules and policies, and a description of consequences for violations of rules and policies. Students should assume that a more detailed policy manual backs up the brochure, so the brochure should be readable and not overly detailed.

2. Question 4 from the Study and Discussion questions can be difficult for some students. Small group discussion of individual answers may help students clarify the principles underlying development of good rules.

Individual Project

Students who intend to become either regular or special education teachers may find it helpful to write a Classroom Organization Essay describing how their individual classrooms would be organized. Students who have done this project generally agree that it is hard to do but very important because all teachers need to have planned their method of organizing the classroom before they begin their first day of teaching. Many students had not really thought about what they would do on that first day and were pleased to develop a written plan that could be used as a guide for the first several weeks. Of course, organizational styles will change with experience, but having a plan is the best way to go confidently about the business of teaching.

A Classroom Organizational Essay should address the following issues:

1. Describe the environment in which you hope to be teaching. Include the approximate grade, type of students (regular or special education), community (rural versus urban), and other pertinent information.

2. Briefly describe your own personality and how it might influence your approach to teaching and classroom management.

3. Describe your general approach to classroom organization. Include both the physical arrangement of the classroom and the way that activities will be organized during the typical school day.

4. List the rules you will expect students to follow and how you intend to enforce them.

Instructors who assign the essay may wish to add other questions.

CHAPTER 6

SELECTING APPROPRIATE BEHAVIOR MANAGEMENT PROGRAMS

Imagine it is the second week of a new school year and a fourth-grade student named Karly has thrown a book at another student, barely missing her. This is the third time in a week you have seen such behavior, but this time it is impossible to ignore. You tell Karly that she will be missing recess today. Karly responds by yelling that she didn't do anything, but she then becomes quiet (thankfully). During recess, Karly works quietly on a math worksheet she failed to complete earlier. When the other children return from recess, Karly hands in her paper, and you notice that only a few additional problems have been completed. However, there is no time to give this any thought so you begin the scheduled reading lesson.

Surprisingly, no behavior problems occur for about ten days, and it appears that the situation may have been resolved. On the eleventh day, however, Karly gets up in the middle of doing a worksheet, throws her books to the floor, walks to the back of the room, and begins playing a game in a learning center. Your class rules say that Karly should miss recess again, but your instincts tell you to back off and give the situation some more thought, so you walk around the room being as reinforcing as possible to those students who remain on task. At the end of the lesson, you prompt Karly to return to her desk and get ready for today's spelling test. She complies

without incident and there is no problem for the rest of the day. That evening, however, you sit down and begin a log of events since the beginning of the school year. You continue to take daily notes, and during the next two weeks five more disruptive outbursts occur. Obviously, a behavior management program might be needed, but how do you go about selecting the best possible intervention strategy?

The best place to begin is with the eight-step procedure for conducting a behavior management program discussed in Chapter 3. Step 1, "Identify the problem," and Step 2, "Refine the definition of the problem," are the first two issues that need to be addressed. In Karly's case, the main problems are disruptive behavior and aggressive outbursts, both behavioral excesses. Daily notes indicate that seven incidents have occurred in a six-week period, and weekly totals indicate an upward trend in number of incidents, with three in the sixth week. With one exception, Karly has missed recess each time she had an outburst. Your notes do not provide any hint that anything in particular sets off the outbursts, which seem to occur at just about any time during the day. At this point, all that can be said is that loss of recess has not been effective in reducing outbursts and that the problem seems to be getting worse.

At this point in the process, after the initial identification of the problem, more information is needed. The severity of the problem in this example suggests that a formal assessment should be considered because aggression is such a disruptive behavior and has the potential to lead to injury. A child study team may meet to consider the problem, or a meeting involving the child's parents could be arranged. It may be suggested that Karly shows evidence of a handicapping condition because she does not appear to benefit from regular instruction, but the available information is far from complete enough to justify any firm conclusion. What other questions should be answered in the process of developing an intervention plan?

First, it would be a good idea to look at Karly's academic performance. This means to evaluate each performance area and determine whether Karly is performing at or near grade level. Group testing and performance from previous years should also be considered. Any suggestion that a learning problem exists needs to be followed up with tutoring, assignment to remedial groups, formal testing, or other appropriate interventions. Children with behavior problems often have academic performance deficits.

After looking at academic performance, it would be helpful to develop a more detailed history of the problem behavior. Contacting previous teachers or schools should indicate whether the problem is a recent development or has been around for a long time. If the problem is a recent development, perhaps environmental stressors such as parental divorce are related to development of problem behaviors. Because aggression is a complex behavior with many potential underlying causes (e.g., Eron, 1980, 1986), a thorough formal assessment is desirable, especially in a relatively older child. The key issue, as information about Karly is gathered, is whether the aggressive behavior itself should be a target of a behavior management program or whether there are other interventions that could address the problem indirectly but effectively. A behavior management program that rewards completion of in-class assignments may lead to both improved academic performance and reduced aggressive outbursts. Identification of alternative intervention targets is one of the positive outcomes of a formal assessment.

Formal assessment may reveal that Karly is performing adequately in school and there is no evidence of a learning problem. Perhaps parental divorce is found to be in progress, which provides a psychological explanation for the outbursts but does not change the fact that the outbursts need to be halted. Under these circumstances, the assessment team might be inclined to agree that the aggressive outbursts (a behavior excess) should be reduced with a behavior management program. Chapter 7, "Management of Behavior Excesses in the Regular Classroom," describes several behavior management procedures that may be effective. In choosing from among these procedures, the guiding principle should be to use the least restrictive option. *Least restrictive* means the option causing the least disruption of Karly's daily academic program. Timeout is one of the most restrictive behavior management procedures. A coupon program might be a good choice in this situation because it causes little disruption of classroom activity, and it is very flexible. The coupon program described in Chapter 7 involves giving the child a predetermined number of coupons or tokens and removing one contingent on inappropriate behavior. If the coupon program proves ineffective after several modifications, other interventions may need to be considered. Family therapy to address issues surrounding the divorce may be an essential component of a successful intervention plan for Karly.

In the six chapters that follow, many different behavior management programs are described using the eight-step procedure explained in Chapter 3. The present chapter will guide the reader through the process of selecting the best behavior management options. It is designed to summarize issues discussed in previous chapters and to serve as a blueprint for using the programs described in the following chapters. When in doubt about how to proceed in the face of a particular problem, a review of this chapter may be helpful.

For students who have read Chapters 1 to 5, Chapter 6 will be a review. Some instructors may elect to skip this chapter without a major loss of content. The main purpose of the chapter is to provide a quick overview of important issues in selecting a behavior management program. I have included this chapter to make it easier to use *Behavior Management in the Schools* as a reference, so that those who are familiar with the book can obtain a quick overview anytime the need arises. Although behavior management programs are essential tools in the schools, a particular classroom teacher may need to refer to this book infrequently. Thus, I have summarized important issues in selecting a behavior management program so that it will be possible to review these issues quickly and then proceed directly to developing an appropriate program.

SELECTING A BEHAVIOR MANAGEMENT PROGRAM

As illustrated by the example that opened this chapter, selecting a satisfactory behavior management program is a process full of twists and turns. There is no linear, step-by-step program that will consistently enable an educator to remediate children's behavior problems. Even the eight-step procedure described in Chapter 3 acknowledges this fact with Step 7, "Modify the program if necessary." Many remediation strategies do not work the first time they are tried. Fortunately, in most cases, a few minor modifications are all that is needed for success. On the other hand, many problems need a radically different approach than originally

planned. The challenge in planning a behavior management program is to have the right mixture of persistence and flexibility. Persistence is needed to keep trying new approaches and seeking new information until an accurate and helpful picture of the problem behavior emerges. Flexibility is needed to be able to abandon an unsuccessful approach, modify a program that has not yet shown success, or plan a radically different approach when it is needed.

Table 6.1 has a summary of the major issues that need to be considered in the process of planning a behavior management program. These issues have been addressed in more detail in previous chapters, to which the reader should refer for more information. It would not be realistic to expect that every one of these issues has

Table 6.1. Key Issues in Planning a Behavior Management Program

1. Identify the problem.
2. Have classroom and schoolwide rules and consequences been appropriately and consistently enforced?
3. Decide on the appropriate level of assessment. Asking these questions may help you evaluate the need for more assessment.
   a. How disruptive is the behavior?
   b. Is there potential danger to the student or others?
   c. How many other interventions have been tried?
   d. How long has the behavior persisted?
   e. How unusual is the behavior?
4. Have signs of any of the following problems been observed?
   _____ learning problems
   _____ hearing problems
   _____ vision problems
   _____ physical abuse
   _____ sexual abuse
   _____ emotional abuse
   _____ intense unhappiness
   _____ suicidal thoughts or plans
   _____ hyperactivity, impulsivity, attention problems
   _____ anxiety that interferes with normal functioning
   _____ parental alcoholism
   _____ parental divorce
   _____ childhood or adolescent alcoholism
   _____ other substance abuse
   _____ unusual, strange, or bizarre behavior
5. Is the target behavior a behavior excess or a behavior deficit?
6. In what environment will the program take place: regular classroom, special classroom, or home?
7. Go to the appropriate chapter:
   Chapter 7: Management of Behavior Excesses in the Regular Classroom
   Chapter 8: Management of Behavior Excesses in Special Classrooms
   Chapter 9: Management of Behavior Excesses in the Home
   Chapter 10: Management of Behavior Deficits in the Regular Classroom
   Chapter 11: Management of Behavior Deficits in Special Classrooms
   Chapter 12: Management of Behavior Deficits in the Home
8. What is the least restrictive, developmentally appropriate program?
9. Remain flexible throughout the process, never losing sight of the primary goal of developing interventions that serve the child's best interests.

been thoroughly addressed before a behavior management program is begun. In fact, educators with experience in behavior management probably select a behavior management program because it has been useful in the past for solving similar problems. However, each of these issues and questions has the potential to influence the approach to a particular problem. In the remaining sections, each issue is briefly discussed.

Identify the problem. This is Step 1 in the eight-step procedure discussed throughout *Behavior Management in the Schools.* Chapter 3 discusses each of these steps in detail. Every process must have a starting point and a behavior management program begins with identification of the problem behavior. One way to view all the remaining issues that are raised in the process of designing a behavior management program is that they all pose the question of whether the focus should remain directly on the problem behavior identified at the beginning of the process, or whether the focus should shift to other issues.

Have classroom and schoolwide rules and consequences been appropriately and consistently enforced? Chapter 5 focused on prevention of behavior management problems. When a problem is first identified, it is both time- and cost-effective to ask whether school and classroom policies, rules, and consequences have been applied consistently to the present situation. If policies have not been followed adequately or if the policies themselves are not adequate, preventable behavior problems may develop. Review and revision of school and classroom policies may be an effective approach to a problem situation.

Decide on the appropriate level of assessment. All behavior management programs require that some assessment be performed. At a minimum, the problem behavior must be defined and its baseline rate of occurrence measured so a standard for judging improvement can be established. Every child in school also has an academic record that can be reviewed for problem areas. A decision to go beyond assessing the baseline rate and reviewing existing academic records is usually based on the perceived severity of the problem behavior. Serious problems require more assessment. Judging the seriousness of a problem behavior depends on a number of variables, such as how disruptive the behavior is, whether there exists any potential danger to the student or others, how many interventions have already been tried, how long the problem has persisted, and how

unusual the problem is. The more severe, resistant to intervention, persistent, disruptive, or unusual the problem, the more likely that a thorough assessment will be valuable.

Have signs of any of the following problems been observed?

_____ learning problems

_____ hearing problems

_____ vision problems

_____ physical abuse

_____ sexual abuse

_____ emotional abuse

_____ intense unhappiness

_____ suicidal thoughts or plans

_____ hyperactivity, impulsivity, attention problems

_____ parental alcoholism

_____ parental divorce

_____ childhood or adolescent alcoholism

_____ other substance abuse

_____ unusual, strange, or bizarre behavior

Although this list is not exhaustive, it contains common problems for which educators need to be alert as they plan a behavior management program or any other educational intervention. The occurrence of any of these signs suggests a need for consultation with a mental health professional, such as a school psychologist, physician, school social worker, or private practitioner. It is not necessary that school personnel conduct a thorough assessment to rule out any of these signs completely. However, discovery of one or more these signs could indicate a need for consultation and team involvement in the child's program. Detection of signs of suicidal intent or abuse should be priorities for all educators.

Is the target behavior a behavior excess or a behavior deficit? Behavior management procedures are of two basic types: those designed to increase behavior and those designed to decrease behavior. Behavior that occurs excessively is called a behavior excess—for example, fighting, crying, talking at inappropriate times, walking around the classroom, throwing objects, running in the hallways or classroom. Behavior deficits are the opposite: desirable behaviors that are not occurring frequently enough. Examples include lack of social skills, failure to complete in-class work, failure to answer when asked a question, inability to recite the alphabet, inability to read at grade level, failure to complete homework, and failure to participate in group activities. When a behavior deficit is the target behavior, the behavior management goal is to *increase* the deficit behavior. When a behavior excess is the target behavior, the behavior management goal is to *decrease* the excessive behavior.

Behavior deficits and behavior excesses run in tandem; for any identified behavior excess, there is an associated behavior deficit. For example, a child who is out of seat during work periods may appear to be showing a behavior excess. However, the problem can also be defined as a behavior deficit: The child is not getting assigned work completed. As pointed out in Chapters 3 and 4, it is best to define a problem in terms of a behavior deficit rather than a behavior excess because it is easier and more productive to reinforce appropriate behavior than to punish undesirable behavior.

In what environment will the program take place: regular classroom, special classroom, or home? Behavior management programs need to be compatible with the environment in which they are to be used. School personnel are likely to work in one of three environments: regular classrooms, special classrooms, and the home. Regular classrooms are typically structured around a lead teacher who may work alone or have a variety of assistants available. For the most part, regular classrooms demand behavior management programs that are compatible with teaching, easy to administer, and require minimal record keeping.

Special classrooms provide students with much more individual attention. Either classes are much smaller than the typical regular classroom, or more staff members are available. The result is that more contact with instructional and pupil support personnel is available. Pupils in special classrooms are usually receiving special education services as a consequence of their needs and the presence of a learning disability, emotional or behavioral disorder, developmental disability, or other condition that interferes with their ability to benefit from instruction in regular classrooms. The staffing available in special education programs means that more complex behavior management programs are possible in special classrooms.

At the present, there is a strong trend toward decreased use of special classrooms and increased efforts to keep students with special needs in mainstream classrooms. However, this trend does not eliminate the need to distinguish between regular and special classrooms for behavior management purposes. It is still useful to categorize behavior management programs according to the amount of staffing and supervision they require. In this context, *special classroom* merely means that staff are available to provide close supervision and data collection. Thus, availability of a behavior management aid or pupil support assistant in a "regular" classroom may make it possible to use one of the programs described for a "special" classroom. Flexibility in adapting programs to the student's needs will have the greatest impact on success.

The home environment has characteristics of both regular and special classrooms. A fair amount of one-to-one attention is available from parents. However, running a household can also be a very time-consuming task that leaves little time to spare, especially if both parents work. Behavior management programs in the home need to be flexible and compatible with the ability of parents to monitor behavior and provide consequences.

Although each of the next six chapters discusses behavior management programs that are most compatible with a particular environment, this does not mean that these particular programs are the only suitable options. The needs of the child must be given priority in deciding what program will work best under particular circumstances. Most of the behavior management programs discussed in this book can be adapted to any environment as long as needed support personnel are available. The organizational scheme of the book should not dictate choices—meeting the child's needs should dictate the choice of programs. The organizational scheme was designed to give educators convenient access to workable program options, but it is critical to remember that these are simply options and guidelines. As always, the key to success is to be flexible in meeting the child's needs.

Go to the appropriate chapter. For quick reference, the six remaining chapters are listed below. Once it has been determined whether the target behavior is a behavior deficit or a behavior excess and the environment in which the program is conducted is known, the next step is to read the available options in the applicable chapter.

Chapter 7: Management of Behavior Excesses in the Regular Classroom

Chapter 8: Management of Behavior Excesses in Special Classrooms

Chapter 9: Management of Behavior Excesses in the Home

Chapter 10: Management of Behavior Deficits in the Regular Classroom

Chapter 11: Management of Behavior Deficits in Special Classrooms

Chapter 12: Management of Behavior Deficits in the Home

What Is the Least Restrictive, Developmentally Appropriate Program?

The final step is to select the least restrictive, developmentally appropriate behavior management program that will meet the child's needs. The *least restrictive alternative* refers to meeting a child's needs with techniques and in environments that are as similar to the child's normal environment as possible—that is, to employ the rules and consequences that apply to all children in the classroom or entire school. The *most restrictive* alternative is to use a timeout that isolates the child from instructional activity. As a rough guideline, a list of behavior management procedures in approximate order of restrictiveness from least to most restrictive follows. Nelson and Rutherford (1983) described a similar hierarchy exclusively for timeout and related procedures.

Least Restrictive

Praise and natural contingencies

Consequences described in classroom rules

Consequences described in schoolwide rules

Reinforcing notes to parents

Reinforcement of specific behaviors

Ignoring of inappropriate behavior

Token programs

Monitoring of daily school performance with a checklist

Response cost programs

Brief chair timeout in the classroom

Removal of normal privileges

Timeout that isolates the child

Most Restrictive

Behavior management programming should begin with the least restrictive option that will meet the child's needs. As a general rule, isolation timeout, although it can be a very effective contingency, should always be planned by a team of individuals including all the educational staff who contact the child, a representative administrator, and the child's parents. Restrictions on the use of timeout vary from state to state. At least one state (Minnesota) requires that there be a written program, that the timeout room meet specific safety standards, and that review of the program by an outside committee be available prior to implementing timeout with a disabled child. Other restrictions on using timeout will be discussed in Chapter 7.

Once the least restrictive program has been selected, it must be designed to be developmentally appropriate for the child (see Chapter 4). Some programs are simply inappropriate for a particular age group. A complex point system is unlikely to work with a preschool child. However, many programs can be adapted to meet the needs of a developmentally diverse array of children. These issues are discussed as each behavior management program is described.

CONCLUSION: REMAIN FLEXIBLE

As I have emphasized, flexibility is an important asset for anyone planning a behavior management program. Flexibility is crucial to almost every aspect of behavior management, from initial assessment of the child's needs to program planning. In practical terms, it is necessary to adjust programs according to the information that they produce. A program that does not work can be a signal that the problem is more complex than originally thought, or it may mean that a simple modification such as using a more attractive reinforcer is needed. The primary goal is to develop interventions that serve the child's best interests. Persistence and optimism when programs do not work, combined with flexibility in changing programs and seeking new information, are key elements in developing such interventions.

REVIEW

Terms to Remember and Review

behavior excess

behavior deficit

least restrictive alternative

hyperactivity

alcoholism

abuse

developmentally appropriate

flexibility

corporal punishment

suspension

three-chance plan

Study and Discussion Questions

1. Do you think the coupon program was a good option for Karly? Why or why not?
2. Why is it usually better to focus a behavior management program on a behavior deficit instead of a behavior excess?
3. Explain the concept of *least restrictive program.*
4. Look at the list of behavior management programs shown in order of restrictiveness. Do you agree with the order of this list? Give your reasons for making any changes in the order.
5. Why is it important to remain flexible while planning and conducting a behavior management program?
6. What are some reasons for avoiding the use of timeout in a behavior management program?

Group Project

When children are placed in isolation timeout, they are removed from the classroom to another area where they receive no reinforcement for a brief period of time. Develop a policy for using timeout that would apply to all children in a particular school district.

CHAPTER 7

MANAGEMENT OF BEHAVIOR EXCESSES IN THE REGULAR CLASSROOM

This is the first of six chapters describing specific behavior management programs following the eight-step procedure introduced in Chapter 3. This chapter describes programs for controlling behavior excesses in regular classrooms where it is assumed that a teacher may be working alone or with the assistance of one or two aides or paraprofessionals. The chapter begins with a discussion of general considerations and then describes four specific programs for decreasing undesirable behavior: (1) extinction or ignoring, (2) the coupon program, (3) timeout in the regular classroom, and (4) the good behavior game plus merit.

DECREASING UNDESIRABLE BEHAVIOR

Almost all children engage in undesirable behavior at some time in their development, and all school personnel must occasionally decide how to deal with it. There are a host of effective ways, both formal and informal, for decreasing undesirable behavior. The least troublesome method is to ignore it. To ignore a behavior means to eliminate completely any response that might reward it. This includes positive attention that could be provided by peers, sarcastic comments ("That's really cute, Josh"), negative attention ("Josh, stop that right *now*!"), or even a quiet personal reprimand. Acceptable responses to a behavior that is being ignored are to turn away and walk to the other side of the classroom or to

praise another child who is behaving appropriately, which may cue the first child to behave correctly in the situation.

There are two common difficulties in attempting to eliminate behavior by ignoring it. The first is that it may be a relatively long time before the behavior is finally eliminated. This is especially true if the behavior has been followed by positive consequences, such as teacher or peer attention, in the past. The second difficulty is that ignoring a behavior may lead to a temporary increase in its frequency before it begins to decline. This increase is typically attributed to the frustration that results from the unfulfilled expectation of reward. The key to eliminating a behavior by ignoring it is to be patient and consistent.

Another method of decreasing undesirable behavior is to remove a privilege, reward, or access to a desirable activity when a child behaves in an unacceptable manner. This represents an application of negative punishment in that a positive stimulus is removed (subtracted) from the situation. For instance, the child who misbehaves in class or fails to complete work could be forbidden to go outside for recess. Parents and teachers typically control numerous rewarding activities that can be withdrawn when a child's behavior is unacceptable. However, this method will not work well if the child loses all or most privileges, because the child then has nothing to lose by misbehaving. In such cases, a concurrent program to reward appropriate behavior will be necessary.

When the consequence of an undesirable behavior is logically related to the behavior itself, one is employing a behavior change technique known as *logical consequences*. The technique involves letting the natural and logical consequences of behavior affect the child (Dreikurs & Grey, 1970). For example, if a child has spent the morning in off-task behavior and fails to complete seatwork, then a logical consequence might be that the child must miss a desired activity, such as recess, in order to complete the unfinished work. In the home, the parents of a child who refuses to pick up his or her dirty clothes might respond by refusing to pick up or wash the clothes. Dirty, unwashed clothes are the logical consequence of not picking clothes up. A child who carelessly or purposefully breaks an object could be required to pay for replacing the item. When logical consequences for misbehavior can be identified, they can be very effective in reducing the problem behavior.

Probably the most important aspect of decreasing undesirable behavior is to provide fewer opportunities for such behavior to occur by rewarding desirable behavior in the same situation. When desirable behavior occurs at a high rate, undesirable behavior is less likely in that situation. For example, if a child frequently behaves aggressively, the amount of aggression will decrease as the amount of cooperative play increases. In all cases where one is trying to decrease the frequency of an undesirable behavior, a concurrent program to increase preferable behavior in that situation should be in effect. Alternatively, if the behavior excesses are not dangerous or extremely disruptive, it might be desirable to implement one of the programs for dealing with behavior deficits in the regular classroom (Chapter 10) instead of using a program that directly reduces behavior excesses. This represents a broader application of the Golden Rule of Behavior Management, which says to ignore inappropriate behavior as much as possible and to provide positive attention to students behaving appropriately.

DESIGNING EFFECTIVE EXTINCTION PROGRAMS

Extinction refers to the gradual decrease in the frequency of a behavior that occurs when reinforcement is discontinued. The fact that extinction occurs is the reason that the initial advice to a teacher seeking consultation about a disruptive pupil is often "ignore the behavior and maybe it will go away." The usefulness of this advice depends on whether all sources of reinforcement can be eliminated. If the child receives no reinforcement for the behavior, extinction is likely to take place.

The reason that extinction or ignoring is such a useful behavior management technique is that children's behavior is often rewarded by "negative attention." Negative attention refers to the reprimands, admonishments, and orders to "Stop that!" that characterize some classroom discipline. Negative attention can also be provided by peers who laugh or snicker at misbehavior. For some children, negative attention is highly rewarding.

An interesting relationship exists between extinction and the proportion of responses that are reinforced. If every single occurrence of a particular response is reinforced, reinforcement is said to be *continuous*. When some responses are not reinforced, reinforcement is then said to be partial or *intermittent*. The effect of continuous versus partial or intermittent reinforcement is simple. When reinforcement is discontinued, an intermittently reinforced response will disappear much more slowly than a continuously reinforced response. That is, intermittently reinforced responses are said to be more *resistant to extinction* than continuously reinforced responses. When reinforcement is intermittent, the child has learned that many responses are needed to generate attention or reinforcement. Often, undesirable behavior subjected to an extinction program has been reinforced intermittently, so it requires a long period of time to extinguish or disappear.

Extinction appears to be such a simple procedure that it hardly seems to require the formality of a written program. However, my experience with decreasing problem behaviors via extinction or ignoring has convinced me that a written program is helpful. First, there is the crucial element of communicating the program to everyone who may come into contact with the child. A child's regular classroom teacher could be doing a great job of ignoring an annoying behavior and simultaneously giving positive attention and praise for appropriate behaviors. If the child's music or physical education teachers are not following the extinction program, however, the target behavior will remain strong or even gain strength through intermittent reinforcement. A second reason for developing written plans for ignoring a target behavior is that some behaviors are very difficult to ignore, and it helps to have specific written instructions for handling a particular incident. This ensures that all personnel are responding in the same way to the target behavior. A third reason for putting the program in writing is that ignoring or extinction is used with behaviors that are undesirable. If it is necessary to develop another program or provide additional services, documentation of the extinction program will be very helpful.

An extinction program can work for a child of any age or cognitive ability. It will be most effective when the person who was reinforcing the behavior undertakes to extinguish it by ignoring.

A model extinction program follows.

Step 1: Identify the problem.   Extinction programs are typically used to decrease behaviors that are annoying, irritating, or impolite, but not likely to be harmful or injurious. Bad language, speaking without permission, disrupting others who are speaking, making irrelevant comments, name calling, and other impulsive verbal behaviors often fall in this category. Thumb-sucking, nose-picking, or inappropriate scratching may also be targets of an extinction program. The target behavior is not dangerous or injury causing, may not even interfere with academic progress, but can disrupt the flow of teaching and lecturing. It is often effective to remind the child quietly and privately that the behavior is not allowed in the classroom. Some children, however, may find the attention rewarding or may have been rewarded for the behavior in the past. Extinction programs will be most effective when the adult who originally and inadvertently provided attention for the problem behavior is the same person who reverses the contingency and decides to try extinguishing the behavior by ignoring it.

Step 2: Refine the definition of the problem. Refining the definition of the problem behavior for an extinction program means writing down a definition of the problem behavior in as much detail as necessary. "Inappropriate verbalizations" would not be a complete definition because this is such a broad category. To refine the definition more precisely might mean noting what specific words or phrases are included in the definition. Although behaviors such as thumb-sucking do not occur in discrete units as verbal behavior does, to keep the program simple enough for a classroom situation, each episode should be counted once regardless of length. I suggest that each episode of the target behavior be recorded on a card or clipboard chart. A sample chart is shown in Figure 7.1.

This is a versatile recording procedure that provides both a numerical and a visual representation of the data (Fabry & Cone, 1980; Kerr & Nelson, 1989; Martin & Pear, 1988). If a more complex baseline measure is

needed, a time-sampling procedure (see Chapter 3) could be used if adequate time and staffing is available.

Step 3: Assess the baseline rate. Assessment of the baseline rate is just as crucial in an extinction program as in any other behavior management program. However, gathering baseline data may actually be the start of the program, because recording each incident of the target behavior is one way to ensure that it is not inadvertently reinforced. Furthermore, it would not make sense to continue reinforcing the target behavior during the baseline period because that would be counterproductive. Of course, the expectation is that the frequency of the target behavior will decline.

Step 4: Design the behavioral contingencies and write the program description. Unlike other behavior management programs, there is no reinforcer or contingency in an extinction program. Instead, the goal is to ensure that *no* reinforcement is available for the target behavior. This may not always be simple, and close observation will be needed to be certain that all sources of reinforcement for the target behavior are removed. Within the classroom, two sources of reinforcement are possible: instructional staff, and the student's peers. Instructional staff must be careful not to give *any* attention to the target behavior. Even a look or glance at the child may communicate annoyance that will reinforce the target behavior and lengthen the amount of time needed for a successful extinction program.

Control of the child's peers may be more difficult to establish, but it is crucial that smiles, giggles, looks, laughter, and other social attention, either positive or negative, be eliminated. A quiet reminder to other individual students not to attend to the behavior may be effective. Alternatively, instructional activities could be planned to keep students engaged in their own work so that attending to distractions is less likely. If the student's peers provide reinforcement for the target behavior, extinction is unlikely to occur. This situation may require abandonment of the extinction program in favor of other alternatives. Options include group contingencies or the coupon program discussed later in this chapter.

Another source of reinforcement for the target behavior undergoing extinction are peers and staff outside the classroom. It is important to eliminate reinforcement that might occur outside the classroom. This means communicating the extinction program to other teachers who have the student, playground and lunchroom supervisors, and administrators. Unless all sources of re-

Directions: Make an "X" in the first column each time the target behavior occurs on the first day of data recording. Continue by using the next column for the second day, the third column for the third day, and so on. The height of the column provides a visual indicator of the number of episodes of the target behavior each day.

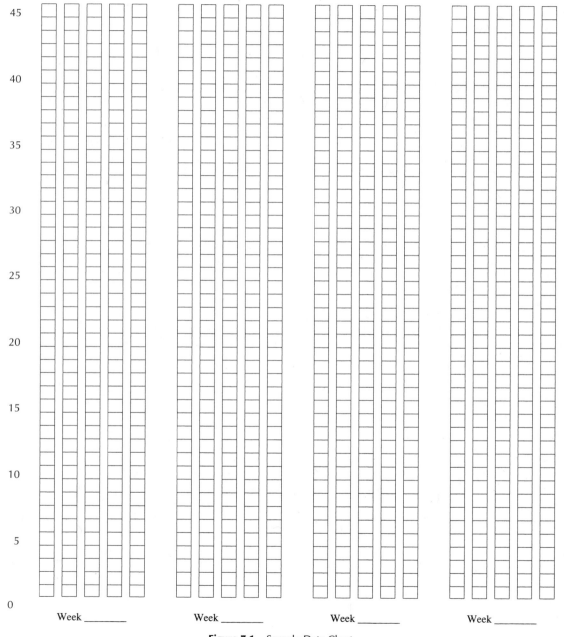

Figure 7.1. Sample Data Chart

inforcement are eliminated, the extinction process may be lengthened or not occur at all. It is possible that a target behavior could be eliminated in one setting, such as the child's primary classroom, while it is still occurring in other settings. In this case, it could be said that the child has learned that no reinforcement is available for the behavior in one setting. One would expect a lengthy extinction process under these circumstances.

In addition to ensuring that no reinforcement is available for the target behavior, the student should be given attention and praise when *not* engaged in the target behavior. This is simply following the Golden Rule of Behavior Management. If a child has developed an annoying habit as a consequence of peer or adult attention, a clear message is being communicated that the child has a need for the attention. Therefore, giving the child praise and positive attention for appropriate behavior will meet that need. Furthermore, reinforcement of alternative behaviors will make it less likely that the target behavior will occur. In some cases it may be necessary to develop formal behavior management programs to increase appropriate behavior. Several alternatives are described in Chapter 10.

The written description of an extinction program needs to be done carefully even though the program does not contain reinforcers and contingencies typical of other programs. It is particularly important that specific instructions for dealing with the target behavior be included in the program. "Ignore" is sometimes a difficult instruction to follow. For example, I once developed a program for a young developmentally disabled person who would lapse into inappropriate conversational topics. Designing a successful program to extinguish this behavior required that staff members received very specific instructions regarding how to react when the conversation turned to an inappropriate topic. Staff were instructed to say: "Stop! This is an inappropriate topic." Having said this, the staff person immediately turned and walked away.

In a classroom situation, it may be necessary for the teacher to engage in a specific activity, walk to another area of the classroom, or even look away from the student in order to ensure that no reinforcement is provided for the target behavior. A team meeting to discuss various possibilities, together with written instructions, will ensure that an optimally effective program is developed.

Step 5: Begin the program. As stated previously, the program begins as soon as collection of baseline data

begins. It is crucial that the number of episodes of the target behavior continue to be counted as the program continues, because this is the information needed to judge the effectiveness of the program.

Step 6: Observe the effects of the program and initiate steps to strengthen generalization beyond the training environment. When an extinction program is in progress, the expectation is that the target behavior will slowly decrease. It is important, however, not to be discouraged if the behavior shows a sharp increase shortly after the program begins. In fact, this is a common phenomenon in extinction programs and might even be interpreted as a positive sign that all sources of reinforcement have been successfully eliminated. A few days after this increase, a gradual decline in the frequency of the target behavior should begin to become evident. However, the graph will not usually be a perfect downward-sloping line. Instead, there will be numerous irregularities, with the frequency of the target behavior showing a lot of variability from day to day. Eventually, however, a downward trend should become noticeable and the behavior should ultimately cease to occur.

Step 7: Modify the program if necessary. There are a number of reasons that an extinction program might not be successful. The primary cause of failure for an extinction program is that the target behavior continues to be reinforced by unidentified sources. Although instructional staff, administrators, and support staff are likely to follow an extinction program, it is important to make sure each person who interacts with the child has been informed that the program is in effect. Peers may undermine even the most well planned extinction program. If this appears to be the case, consideration of alternative approaches to the problem may be needed.

Another source of reinforcement is that the behavior itself may be reinforcing to the child. For example, a child who views him- or herself as a future star drummer for a famous rock band may find it reinforcing to practice rhythms with a pencil, regardless of how others react to the behavior. Nose-picking, scratching, masturbation, playing with objects, or even vocal behaviors may fall into this category at various times. In this situation, a formal program to strengthen more appropriate behaviors may be indicated.

Step 8: Fade out the program. An extinction program is not faded out in the usual sense of the term because the target behavior should be ignored if it ever reoccurs. However, after a couple of weeks in which the target behavior does not occur, it makes sense to cease collecting frequency data. Once the program has ended, whether it is successful or not, all the relevant documentation should be saved for future reference.

THE "COUPON PROGRAM": AN EFFECTIVE SCHOOL- OR HOME-BASED METHOD OF USING RESPONSE COST TO REDUCE BEHAVIOR EXCESSES

As discussed in Chapter 2, a token is almost anything of little or no value that can be exchanged for something desirable. A token is analogous to money. Money itself can not be eaten or keep a person warm, but it can be used to purchase food and shelter . Consequently, both adults and children work very hard to obtain money because of the goods and services it can buy. Likewise, tokens themselves have no inherent value but can be used to "purchase" valuable rewards. Gold stars, points, marbles, specially marked pieces of paper, stickers, poker chips, or anything else that can be easily delivered to a child and then saved can be used as a token.

The main advantage of token programs is that they allow great flexibility in rewarding behavior. If highly motivating rewards are placed on the menu of items that can be purchased with tokens, then target behaviors can be changed within a relatively short period of time. It is particularly important that the reward menu be negotiated with the child. Without children's input, the token program may be destined to fail. Money is a nearly universal reinforcer, which almost always works. Other possible reinforcers include special field trips, a classroom party, school supplies, taking the family out for pizza, small toys, children's collectible items (baseball cards, marbles, etc.), large toys, special activities (sports camps, camping trips, fishing trips, etc.), or anything else the program administrator finds acceptable.

The best use of token programs is to reward a child's appropriate behavior. This application is given close attention in Chapters 10, 11, and 12. This is not always feasible, however, especially in a classroom situation where the teacher is busy with the needs of at least twenty-five other children. Also, for children who are easily distracted, the main behavioral goal is to keep them focused on their assigned academic tasks. If children are rewarded for paying attention to their work, the reward itself becomes a distracting stimulus that may draw the child off task. An alternative method of rewarding on-task behavior is to have children begin a time period with a several tokens. Then the contingency is that the child *loses* a token each time a classroom rule (such as "do your assigned work") is violated (see, for example, Iwata & Bailey, 1974; Rapport, Murphy, & Bailey, 1982; Sulzbacher & Houser, 1968). This is called a response cost contingency, meaning that certain responses end up "costing" the child something valuable, such as a token.

The program described next uses coupons as tokens because they are concrete, are easily stored, and bear a physical similarity to money. Teachers who have used the program in their classrooms have come to call it the "coupon program." A step-by-step description of the program follows.

Step 1: Identify the problem. The problem consists of keeping the hyperactive, disruptive, or attention-seeking child engaged in appropriate, on-task behavior in the regular classroom setting. What is required is a way of responding immediately and effectively to the child's off-task behavior while rewarding the child for completing academic tasks.

Step 2: Refine the definition of the problem. The child who is disruptive or off task usually is violating classroom rules that other children in the classroom obey most of the time. Therefore, a reasonable and concrete goal is for the child to obey classroom rules. Further refinement of the problem behavior requires that a concrete set of classroom rules be established. To keep things simple, the number of rules should be kept to a minimum. Three to five rules seems to work well with many children. Some examples of rules that I have found effective are:

1. Stay in your seat unless you have permission to leave.
2. Stay on task until all work is done.
3. No talking without permission during work time.
4. Obey the teacher.
5. Keep all four legs of your chair on the floor.

Rules 1, 2, and 3 are standard classroom rules that should be phrased according to the children's level of understanding. Rules will differ according to the needs of the teacher, the grade level of the children, and the subjects being taught. Rule 4 is a more general rule that can serve as a catch-all for unanticipated situations. If the child does something disruptive that is not covered by the rules, a warning can be given, followed immediately by the response cost contingency if the behavior continues. Rule 5 is an example of how a rule can be directed at a particular problem behavior. In this example, a teacher was concerned that a child might be hurt because he frequently tilted his chair backwards. Consequently, a special rule was used to cover this situation.

With a concrete set of established rules, the problem behavior can be defined as minimizing the number of rule violations. A secondary goal of the program is to improve the child's academic performance. Teacher records of assignments completed, attendance, test results, and other data can be used to monitor academic progress during the coupon program.

Step 3: Assess the baseline rate. Establishing a baseline rate merely consists of counting the daily number of rule violations for a given period of time, such as one week. The more detail contained in the baseline data, the easier it will be to modify the program if necessary. For instance, specifying the number of the rule that was violated and the time of day would give a more precise definition of the problem behavior. Also, it could reveal that certain times of the day or certain subject areas are most difficult for the child, which would suggest other interventions that may be helpful before the coupon program is implemented.

Step 4: Design the behavioral contingencies and write the program description. The contingency in the coupon program works like this: The child is given a predetermined number of coupons and loses one of them each time a rule is violated. The coupons themselves can be laminated paper with an original design on them. To get started, the teacher must select a block of time for running the program. At the beginning of the coupon program, the period of time should be relatively short, ranging from twenty minutes to no more than one hour. Then, using the baseline data, the number of coupons to give the child initially must be decided. The goal is to give the child enough coupons so that on a typical day, at least one coupon will be left at the end of the designated time period. A typical number is between five and ten coupons. A 5 × 8 card, taped on three sides to the child's desk, is a convenient way to store the coupons. Printing the rules on the 5 × 8 card and reviewing them regularly may assist the child in remembering them.

Some thought needs to be given to the design of the coupons. If the child carries the coupons around, they need to be counterfeit-proof. A unique design on colored paper, laminated to make it last, has the advantage of being nearly impossible to copy. A couple of teachers have suggested using a black-and-white picture of the child so the coupon resembles money. A system like this could prove helpful in situations where more than one coupon program is in progress at the same time.

Like all token programs, the coupon program depends on a menu of reinforcers. The reinforcers on the menu can be "purchased" by the child using the coupons that remain at the end of each time period. Experience indicates that two or three levels of rewards are effective in motivating the child. At the first level are small reinforcers that can be purchased for just a few coupons—a piece of candy, a sticker, a pencil, a pen, or some other small, inexpensive item. The use of these items is designed to keep the child from becoming discouraged in the early part of the program. Typical values for these items range from one to about five coupons. At the next level of reinforcer are items that require many more coupons to purchase, are somewhat more expensive, and typically require from one to several weeks for the child to save enough coupons to purchase these items. The cost of such items might range from twenty-five to several hundred coupons. A third level of reinforcer, first employed by a teacher using the coupon program, is a surprise reinforcer. Some children are highly motivated while working toward a surprise. The teacher who employed the surprise required the child to deposit coupons into separate envelopes, each representing a "bank" for one of three rewards. Deposits into the highly motivating "surprise" envelope were not allowed until deposits had been made into the other two envelopes. Using this rule, the child regularly received small reinforcers while steadily progressing toward more expensive rewards.

A fairly typical menu of rewards might look like this:

3 coupons	10 minutes' free time
3 coupons	Early dismissal for lunch
5 coupons	Eraser or pencil
8 coupons	"Cool" book cover or folder
10 coupons	Book or 30 minutes on the computer
20 coupons	Package of baseball cards
20 coupons	Bonus points added to next test score
50 coupons	Popcorn party for entire class
50 coupons	"Cool" T-shirt or jewelry
100 coupons	Money to treat family to dinner
200 coupons	Compact disc, tape, concert ticket

Selection of the reinforcer menu is crucial to the success of the program. The menu needs to be developed with the child's cooperation and input. Items on the menu also need to be appropriate to the child's age and developmental level. Compact discs and clothing may be favored by adolescents, whereas free time and sports cards are likely to be favored by younger children. Teachers need to be aware of what is popular with students and offer to include some "cool" items on the reward menu. It is also important to be aware that a reinforcer may lose its attractiveness over time and may need to be replaced on the menu.

The written program needs to describe carefully the program procedures (see the next section for a good summary), the classroom rules the child is expected to obey, and the reward menu negotiated with the child. A specific procedure for collecting data is also helpful. Fortunately, the coupon program takes care of this because the number of coupons removed by the teacher always equals the number of rule violations. Placing the confiscated coupons in an envelope corresponding to the rule violated will allow a precise tally. Some teachers feel uncomfortable taking a token or coupon away immediately and prefer to give one warning. If this is the case, the written program needs to reflect this procedure. Finally, it is also important to establish a time and place for exchanging tokens for rewards.

Step 5: Begin the program. The program may begin with a brief conference with the child to review the classroom rules, how the program works, and the reason for taping the card to the child's desk. At this time the reward menu should be reviewed after making sure the child has had ample opportunity to choose at least some of the rewards included on the menu. The meaning and value of the coupons should be carefully explained to the child. Also, it is a good idea to have the child explain the program back to you, which will clarify how well it is understood. Once the child has a reasonable idea of how the program works, it can be started. Do not worry if the child appears unmotivated or uninterested in the program. Children often need to exchange their remaining coupons for rewards once or twice before they really grasp the meaning and value of the coupons. Also, some children have few opportunities to earn positive feedback, so they may appear discouraged before the program even begins. Earning a few material rewards along with positive attention from the teacher will arouse the child's interest.

After explaining the program to the child, assembling the needed materials, and selecting a time period, you can start the program. The procedure is relatively simple:

1. The child receives a predetermined number of coupons for the designated time period. Five to ten coupons for a thirty-minute seatwork period is typical. Use the baseline data to decide the initial number of coupons.
2. Each time the child disobeys one of the established rules, the teacher takes away one of the coupons without any negative comments. However, it is appropriate simply to state the rule that was violated.
3. If the child runs out of coupons, then no more can be taken away. The child never goes into "debt" because this would lead to unnecessary discouragement. The best response to misbehavior after the child runs out of coupons is to ignore it.
4. At the end of the designated time period or as soon as convenient for the teacher, the child is allowed to deposit the coupons that remain into the "bank." These coupons, once earned, may not be lost regardless of the child's behavior. Again, the goal is to get the child going on a positive track.
5. Once the program begins to show positive effects during the designated time period, it is usually desirable to expand to other times during the school day. The child begins with a fresh set of coupons during each additional time period until acceptable behavior is well established. Later, when on-task behavior is well established, the child can be given coupons that are expected to last a longer time. Allowing the child to start fresh during each time period of the initial program will enable the child to make up for poor performance at one time with improved performance in the next period.
6. To monitor the effects of the program, it is necessary only to keep an accurate count of the number of coupons lost by the child during each time period. The expectation is that this number will steadily decline.

Step 6: Observe the effects of the program and initiate steps to strengthen generalization. If the coupon program is used in a special education or other small group setting, generalization to the regular classroom will be an issue. What has worked best so far is to use the coupon program in the regular education setting as described and then work to fade out the program.

Another option that has shown some success in regular classrooms is to have students monitor their own behavior (e.g., Rooney & Hallahan, 1988; Webber, Scheuermann, McCall, & Coleman, 1993). Lloyd, Landrum, and Hallahan (1991) provide a useful description of procedures for implementing self-monitoring programs, including a script for introducing the self-monitoring program to a student. The script begins by introducing the problem behavior to the student (e.g., paying attention). Then the teacher demonstrates both desired behavior (paying attention) and undesired behavior (being off task). The student is then asked to categorize several more examples of the teacher's behavior to ensure that the concept is understood. Next, students are told that they will hear a tape-recorded tone every once in a while. When they hear the tone, their task is to ask themselves immediately whether they were "paying attention" and to check the "yes" or "no" column on a prepared data sheet. The teacher then has the student begin a task, turns on the tape recorder, and observes the student, praising correct use of the monitoring procedure.

Rooney et al. point out that the signaling tone can be presented out loud without disrupting the remainder of the class. The tones should initially occur at random intervals averaging 45 seconds apart. According to Rooney et al., the tones are important for the success of the procedure. They can be removed or faded away once the target behavior improves. Self-monitoring procedures can be integrated with the coupon program by having the child take over the task of removing coupons for off-task behavior or rule violations. This is one of many techniques for fading the coupon program, and it may be necessary to determine empirically what is most effective for a particular child.

Step 7: Modify the program if necessary. If this program does not work, several options remain open. The first option is to review the reward menu. If the reward menu does not include reinforcers the child likes, the program may not work well. Also, a change in reinforcers may be needed to maintain the child's interest. Other parameters of the program that might be changed include the time of day the program is run and the program's rules. Research has shown that regular review of the rules for a token program can improve performance. One idea would be to review the classroom rules with the child at the beginning of each day. Also, the child could receive a bonus coupon if he or she is able to recite the rules from memory. Bonus coupons can also be awarded for completion of academic tasks or other exceptional behavior.

Step 8: Fade out the program. Fading out the coupon program may not work for all children. For example, problems associated with hyperactivity may demand a constant level of structure in order for the child to succeed. Therefore, in the process of fading out the program it may be found that the child is most successful at a certain level and that efforts to fade the program any further result in poor performance.

Experience indicates that the best way to begin the coupon program is to limit the time period for the program to around one-half hour. Once the child becomes successful during this time period, expansion of the program to other times is usually accomplished easily. The next step, once the program is working throughout most of the day, is to begin gradually to increase the demands on the child by giving him or her a larger number of coupons that are expected to last for a longer time period. For instance, the child could be given ten coupons in the morning to last for the entire morning and then another ten coupons for the remainder of the day. Next the child could be given fifteen coupons in the morning that are expected to last for the entire day. Once the coupons are expected to last the entire day and disruptive behavior remains at a low but acceptable level, the number of coupons given to the child can also be decreased gradually, perhaps on a weekly basis.

At this point it may be possible to have the student "graduate" from the coupon program, perhaps by earning a party for the entire class. Some students, however, may not be able to control their behavior without the benefit of the coupon program as a firm, consistent reminder to remain on task and inhibit disruptive behavior. An alternative approach is to involve the child's parents in the program by using a home note program of some kind. Home note programs are described in Chapter 10.

An effective variation of a response cost program was reported by Sullivan and O'Leary (1990). At random times during a twenty-minute period, a classroom teacher scanned students seated at their desks and recorded point losses on a public chart that all the students could see. Students who were off task lost points. Students began with four points that could be exchanged for four stickers or four minutes of extra recess time. To fade the program, the number of times the teacher scanned the students was decreased from three to zero per twenty-minute period. The students continued to receive their stickers or extra recess time noncontingently—that is, without regard to performance. In comparison to children who *received* tokens contingent on on-task behavior, the response cost procedure was equally effective at increasing on-task behavior above baseline levels. Behavior was much better maintained after the program was faded using the response cost contingency. Sullivan and O'Leary argued that the greater difficulty of discriminating the fading procedure from contingent loss of tokens was the main reason maintenance was superior for response cost.

Salend and Allen (1985) employed such a technique to modify out-of-seat behavior and inappropriate verbalizations in two second-grade boys with learning disabilities. In their procedure, each boy was given a predetermined number of tokens. If the boy had at least one token remaining at the end of a twenty-minute resource period, it could be exchanged for an agreed-on reward. The authors found that the response cost contingency was effective in reducing inappropriate behavior to zero occurrences at the end of the program. In addition, they found that the program was equally effective whether the contingency (removal of a token) was administered by the student or by the resource teacher.

Lewis and Blampied (1985) successfully employed a similar procedure to manage time on task and out-of-seat behavior of nine children. In this procedure, children self-administered tokens to themselves contingent on either being on task or being in their seats. The procedure was successful in increasing these behaviors to acceptable levels and illustrates an alternative method of employing token reinforcement procedures with older children.

Comment. The coupon program has been very popular with both regular and special education teachers with whom I have consulted. The reasons for its popularity seem to be related to the fact that the program gives the teacher an effective, active way of responding to misbehavior. Taking away a coupon substitutes an effective response for a verbal reprimand. Another advantage of the program is that it fits well into the daily routine of most teachers, who can remove a coupon without interrupting the teaching process. Although some effort is required to set up the program and introduce it to the child, it takes little effort to run the program after that. One teacher commented that it was great to be back "in control" of a child's behavior.

A disadvantage of the program is that other children sometimes become jealous or express a desire to be included in a coupon program. A teacher in this situation should approach it very carefully. In most cases, the request represents a desire to share in the rewards that the target child receives. This can be addressed by building in contingencies that allow the target child to earn a small party, free time, or other reward in which the entire class participates. On the other hand, a child who asks to participate in a coupon program or any other classroom behavior management program may really have a need for this type of reward. Careful observation may reveal that this child has other needs that should be addressed, such as lack of friends or social isolation.

TIMEOUT IN REGULAR CLASSROOM SETTINGS

Timeout has already been mentioned several times as a technique of nonviolent punishment. The essence of timeout is that a child is placed in a boring situation, with no access to interesting activities, immediately after undesirable behavior. Timeout can be considered punishment if it is assumed that placement in a boring situation is aversive, or it can be considered negative punishment if the operative contingency is denial of access to reinforcing activity. It is best to think of timeout as negative punishment because this emphasizes that reinforcing activities must occur during the nontimeout or "timein" period in order for timeout to be effective.

Timeout is a behavior management technique that must be used very cautiously because it has a high potential for misuse. The greatest danger in using timeout is that the child may lose access to valuable instructional time. Timeout can vary along a continuum of least restrictive to most restrictive procedures. The least restrictive timeout procedures involve brief separation from ongoing activities. For example, White and Bailey (1990) employed a procedure they called Sit and Watch, contingent on disruptive behavior during a physical education class. If a child was disruptive, he or she was seated in a special area for three minutes, after which the child could return to the physical education activities. Although students were removed from active participation for a short time, they still could observe the class. Consequently, most educators would agree that this procedure falls in the least restrictive area of the continuum. A similar procedure called "contingent observation" was used successfully by Porterfield, Herbert-Jackson, and Risley (1976) with two- to four-year-old children in a nursery school class.

On the other hand, in some situations, timeout consists of complete removal from a classroom for a period of time that may be extended by continued misbehavior.

The timeout area is an isolated room devoid of instructional materials. In these situations, the child may physically resist placement in timeout and may continue to act aggressively and disruptively while in timeout. Because it is important that the child be calm when released from timeout to prevent inadvertent reinforcement of such behavior, a timeout may be extended for a considerable amount of time under these circumstances. This timeout procedure completely removes the child from academic instruction for a significant amount of time and is regarded as highly restrictive. These procedures are typically used only in settings where sufficient staffing is available, such as residential programs for behaviorally disturbed children.

Wherry (1983) also cautions that the use of timeout involves the potential for violating the rights of the student. He advises that informed consent be obtained from the child's parents prior to the use of timeout, response cost, and overcorrection (a method used to suppress undesirable behavior). In addition, Wherry suggests the following guidelines for the use of timeout based on judicial proceedings:

1. Timeout should be employed in situations where the student's behavior creates "substantive" disruption.
2. The length of timeout should not exceed fifty minutes to one hour.
3. The child should be provided with books or lesson materials during timeout.
4. The student should be closely and directly supervised.

In general, it seems that the practitioner can avoid problems if timeout is employed only to decrease very disruptive behavior and concurrent programs to increase desirable behavior are implemented. However, laws in any state may impose additional restrictions and requirements.

It is also absolutely imperative to monitor the effect of timeout on the target behavior. Solnick, Rincover, and Peterson (1977) cite two attempts to use timeout that failed. In one instance, timeout was actually reinforcing to a girl who engaged in self-stimulating behavior during the timeout period. The opportunity to engage in such behavior during the timeout actually caused the target behavior to increase. Thus, in applying timeout, it is important to establish that it actually causes the target behavior to decrease. Within a classroom, this might fail to occur if the timeout allowed the child to escape from an unpleasant situation, such as doing difficult seatwork,

or if the child managed to obtain social reinforcement from peers during the timeout period. Observation of the child's behavior during the timeout period can provide some information about how the timeout period is functioning.

Solnick et al. also studied the effectiveness of timeout with a sixteen-year-old developmentally disabled boy. It was found that timeout was ineffective in reducing undesirable behavior until the nontimeout environment was enriched so that it included more reinforcing stimuli. Timeout should result in the loss of some reinforcement when it is applied in the regular school environment. If the nontimeout environment is not significantly more reinforcing than the timeout environment, timeout may be ineffective.

In my own consultation work, I was once asked to assist in developing an alternative program for a child who had been punished with timeout for a variety of behaviors over a twenty-four-week period. After examining informal timeout records and tabulating the frequency with which timeout was administered, I found that the number of timeouts had steadily increased over each six-week block of time. It was obvious that the timeouts were ineffective in reducing disruptive behavior. When timeout was discontinued, disruptive incidents dropped *below* the baseline level. Had the team more carefully monitored the effectiveness of timeout, it would have become apparent much sooner that the procedure was not working so that it could be modified or discontinued. This case convinced me that timeout should not be employed unless the administrators are willing to document precisely each timeout and tabulate the records so that it is apparent whether the procedure is effective. Figure 7.1 shows an easy method of summarizing frequency data.

A step-by-step plan for implementing a simple, least restrictive timeout in a regular classroom environment follows. Chapter 8 discusses the use of more restrictive timeout procedures and the special cautions that apply to them.

Step 1: Identify the problem. This formal behavior management program is designed to decrease disruptive behavior in a regular classroom setting. Timeout can be effective with a child of any age, but the procedures discussed in this program are best suited to children of preschool or kindergarten age. The Sit and Watch procedure was effective with fourth-grade regular and special education children. One reason for using these procedures with younger children is that the contingency can be administered immediately after disruptive behavior. As children get older and are able to respond to delayed contingencies, timeout may not be necessary because other procedures will work. When a kindergarten child is physically aggressive, however, an immediate, effective response is essential to prevent escalation of the problem.

When timeout is first considered, the disruptive behavior may be somewhat loosely defined but is likely to consist of shouting, physical or verbal aggression, blatant noncompliance, or other behaviors that have the potential to become serious problems. For example, kindergarten children must learn to respond promptly to adult directions for safety reasons. According to Wherry (1983), the target behavior should cause "substantive" disruption. Some kindergarten or preschool teachers may include a timeout or "thinking" chair as a component of their normal classroom discipline. As long as parents are aware of it, this approach to discipline is probably acceptable. However, I would recommend that *all* banishments to the "thinking" chair be documented, and, if a child is given timeout more than once, a formal written program should be instituted to document that the target behavior is reduced by the timeout procedure.

Step 2: Refine the definition of the problem. In this important step, a written description of the target behavior or behaviors should be developed. Consultation with other school staff members can be helpful to ensure that the behavioral descriptions are objective and well defined. For instance, assume that in Step 1, the problem behaviors were identified as aggression and loud shouting. The goal is to develop clear, workable definitions of these behaviors, which can be used throughout the remainder of the behavior management program. An acceptable definition of aggression might be any physical contact with another child or the teacher that would be considered aversive or unwanted. This might include pushing, shoving, biting, hitting, taking objects, and/or other behaviors observed to be disruptive and to which the victim reacts with avoidance or defensive behavior. Shouting would be easier to define and would include verbalizations that are much louder than the child's normal speaking voice occurring at times when such behavior is not authorized. It would probably be necessary to specify the places and times when shouting was to be punished with timeout.

If noncompliance was the target behavior, even more careful attention to a definition of the behavior would be needed. In general, it would be unreasonable to expect

any group of children to respond instantly to a general direction. Thus, failure to respond to general directions such as "take your seats" or "line up for recess" probably should not be punished with timeout. Instead, praise for correctly following the direction and delaying the next activity until compliance is obtained should be used. When all but one member of the class has complied, however, it is more than reasonable to expect that a specific, personal direction to a single child will be promptly obeyed (e.g., "Alex, sit down at your table!"). Thus, the target behavior could be defined as failure to obey a direct, personal command (using the child's name and ensuring the child is attending to the command) within five seconds. As a note of caution, a hearing problem should probably be ruled out before a program to decrease noncompliance is begun.

Step 3: Assess the baseline rate. If an adequate description of the target behavior was developed in Step 2, then a convenient recording system is all that is necessary to begin assessing the baseline rate. Because each instance of the undesired behavior must be recorded, a portable record sheet, such as a 3×5 card with blocks for each hour or half-hour of the school day, might be convenient. Alternatively, Figure 7.1 provides a convenient method of recording frequency data. Each time one of the target behaviors occurs, a single mark should be made in the correct time block. Additional notes, such as teacher responses to the behavior, should be made on the back of the card. The baseline period may extend for as long as necessary, but several days to one week should be adequate. In the case of high-magnitude aggressive behavior that may lead to injury of other children, it may be prudent to begin baseline observations and the management program at the same time. See Chapter 3 for more detailed descriptions of methods for recording baseline observations.

If noncompliance is the target behavior, collecting baseline data is a little more complex because the number of opportunities for misbehavior is limited to the number of commands the child is given. Therefore, each time a specific command is given to the child as described previously, it should be recorded. If the child obeys the command within five seconds, this also needs to be recorded. A convenient recording method is to use two columns of Figure 7.1 for each day. In the first column, place a slash (/) in the box if a command is given. In the second column, record a slash (/) only if the command is obeyed. The result will be two side-by-side columns, one showing the commands issued and the other showing whether each command was obeyed. The daily percentage of obeyed commands is easily calculated from this information. Other coding systems are certainly feasable.

Step 4: Design the behavioral contingencies and write the program description. This step takes place while the baseline observations are being conducted. The purpose is to formulate the rules for dealing with the target behavior. Two different procedures will be described: a chair timeout (e.g., Porterfield et al. 1976) and the Sit and Watch procedure (White & Bailey, 1990).

Implementing a chair timeout program requires, above all, good planning from the start. It is particularly important to have clear definitions of target behaviors, materials for recording baseline and treatment data, and a preselected location for the timeout chair. For a chair timeout in a regular classroom, a timeout or thinking chair should be located near enough to the group to allow the child to see and hear instructional and/or play activity but far enough away to communicate that the child is not part of the group during that immediate time. A timer may be needed to determine the length of timeout depending on the personal preference of the teacher. A timer is useful because the teacher does not need to focus on the details of monitoring the child.

The length of a timeout period can vary considerably. Some authors suggest one or two minutes of timeout for each year of age. Thus, a typical range might be between three and ten minutes. The exact length of the timeout should be determined beforehand and remain constant. A three- or five-minute timeout should be effective with young children. Timeout must be administered *immediately* after the undesirable behavior. The person administering the timeout should be calm but firm. The timeout may be accompanied by some brief explanation, such as, "You can't stay with the class if you (hit the teacher, don't follow my directions, etc.)." If the child continues to display undesirable behavior and/or fails to comply with the timeout procedure, the timeout methods discussed in Chapter 8 may be effective. These methods require someone to supervise the timeout and should not be implemented without full discussion among team members, including the primary teacher, administrators, the child's parents, and other interested staff or consultants. Once the child has been released from timeout, it may be useful to discuss briefly why timeout was administered and have the child think of alternative ways that the situation leading to timeout could have been handled.

Timeout can be carried out easily when advance preparations have been made. One key is to have a timeout area selected in advance, and for the teacher to be mentally prepared to administer timeout quickly and calmly whenever it is required. To summarize the requirements of effective timeout, remember that the timeout location must be a boring one that does not allow the child to participate in social interactions. Timeouts should be administered quickly and calmly, along with a brief statement of the reason for timeout. When the timeout period (three to ten minutes) expires, the child should be released. A method of timing the interval may also be helpful. An egg or kitchen timer is often used. If the child fails to comply with the timeout, a more restrictive procedure or different program entirely is needed.

The Sit and Watch procedure described by White and Bailey (1990) was used with disruptive fourth-grade children in a physical education class. The three target behaviors in this program were noncompliance, physical aggression, and throwing objects. When a target behavior occurred, the student was removed from the activity and the reason was explained. The student then obtained a timer, walked to the timeout area, and sat down on the ground with the timer. The timer was constructed from two plastic bottles, glued and screwed together at the mouths, and filled with enough sand that it took about three minutes for the sand to flow from one bottle to the other. A large timer was constructed so it would be visible from a long distance away. When the student reached the timeout area, he or she turned over the timer and was allowed to leave timeout when all the sand had flowed through.

As discussed, the written program should concretely define the target behavior(s) and clearly indicate the length of the timeout. The method and forms for recording baseline and treatment data also need to be described. It is also helpful to state what is to be said to the child when timeout is administered.

Step 5: Begin the program. After the careful planning in Steps 1 through 4, this step should be easy. It should not be forgotten, however, that data must still be collected so that Step 6 can be performed. For any behavior management procedure, data should continue to be collected in the same way as during the baseline period.

Step 6: Observe the effects of the program. This step, it will be recalled, is a continuation of Step 5, except that expectations of change should be confirmed. A period of one to three weeks, about two or three times the length of the baseline period, is a reasonable time within which to anticipate observable change. Of course, the careful baseline observations that establish the range of expected frequencies of the target behavior are very important at this time. Any decrease or downward trend in the frequency of the target behavior should be considered justification for continuing the program without modification.

Note that it is very important that generous reinforcement be available to the child. If academic and/or social skills are lacking, then the rewards that other children experience in the classroom will be unobtainable for the target child. A return to less desirable means of obtaining attention can be expected if the program is faded out while the child lacks other skills that contribute to success in the classroom. Therefore, a concurrent program to improve deficit skills may be an important part of the general approach to reducing the occurrence of disruptive behavior. Also, the effectiveness of a timeout depends on having a rich and rewarding "timein" environment.

Step 7: Modify the program, if necessary. What if, despite the best efforts of those involved, the timeout procedure does not work? First, it is important not to become discouraged, because initial efforts at implementing a behavior management program can fail, even when very experienced behavior therapists are involved. Second, it is also important not to attribute the failure to the child. The source of the problem is in the environment that has been structured, and failure is an indication that it is time to consider what adjustments may be necessary and beneficial.

White and Bailey (1990) included backup contingencies in their version of Sit and Watch. The first time students receive a timeout, they lose computer time later in the day; the second time, they also lose free time later in the day. The effectiveness of these specific contingencies was not evaluated, but this is one way that timeout could possibly be made more effective. However, this is most likely to be effective only with older children who will be able to understand the connection between their behavior at one time and the loss of a privilege or rewarding activity at a later time.

As noted, an important element in all timeout programs is that the nontimeout environment needs to be more reinforcing or interesting than the timeout environment. If this is not the case, the child in timeout may be escaping a more aversive situation, and this situation will actually increase the disruptive behaviors that are "punished" with timeout. This is one reason that White and

Bailey's Sit and Watch procedure is so effective. Talk to any school-age child and you will find out that one of the favorite school activities is physical education (PE or gym). Being seated in a timeout area and watching others participate in all the fun is almost certainly an unpleasant experience for most children. On the other hand, if it is more unpleasant to be *out* of timeout than *in* timeout, the child will work or misbehave in order to be in timeout and escape the unpleasant task. This situation could arise when the child is faced with academic tasks that are too difficult or disliked. When timeout is unsuccessful, it is wise to look at the nontimeout situation to see if that might be the cause of the problem.

Other potential reasons for the failure of a timeout program include the following:

1. The timeout is not administered immediately after the target behavior.
2. The student is able to socialize with peers while in timeout.
3. The child is being released from timeout while still engaging in disruptive behavior (see Chapter 8).
4. The timeout is not long enough to be aversive.
5. The child lacks skills needed to perform successfully in the situation where disruptive behavior is occurring.
6. The child is able to amuse him- or herself in some way during timeout, such as by playing with a toy kept in a pocket.

Step 8: Fade out the program. The general goal of fading out the program is to substitute the child's internal controls for the external controls provided by the behavior management program. A successful timeout program will cause the disruptive behavior to decrease to a less intense and frequent level. As the target behavior decreases, timeout is also less frequent so the program naturally fades as a consequence of its own success. However, a concurrent program to improve academic or social skills may be needed before the target behavior decreases to zero.

THE GOOD BEHAVIOR GAME PLUS MERIT

As noted previously, control of disruptive behavior does not guarantee that behaviors conducive to learning will increase. Thus, it is typically necessary to employ behavior management strategies specifically designed to improve academic performance in programs designed to control disruptive behavior. The following procedure is based on a study by Darveaux (1984). In this study, the disruptive behavior of two boys at risk for placement in a classroom for behaviorally impaired students was greatly decreased while the percentage of assignments completed almost doubled, using an intervention called the Good Behavior Game plus Merit. The intervention combined contingencies for reducing disruptive behavior with a contingency for increasing academic productivity. The study employed an ABAB design (baseline, intervention, return to baseline conditions, return to intervention conditions), which demonstrated that the intervention alone was responsible for the observed behavior changes.

The original Good Behavior Game (Barrish, Saunders, & Wolf, 1969) was targeted exclusively at disruptive behavior. Students in a regular classroom were divided into two teams. When the rules of the game were in effect, each time an individual student emitted a disruptive behavior (being out of seat or talking without permission), his or her team received a point (e.g., a demerit). The team with the lowest number of points was declared the "winner" for the time period in which the rules of the game were in effect. If both teams had fewer than five points, both were "winners." Privileges received by the winning team included free time, early dismissal for lunch, stars by their names on a chart, and the opportunity to wear a victory tag. The program "significantly and reliably" decreased the students' disruptive behavior. The effectiveness of the Good Behavior Game in reducing disruptive behaviors has been replicated by Harris and Sherman (1973), Medland and Stacknick (1972), and Salend, Reynolds, and Coyle (1989).

A major difference between this procedure and others is that it employs *group contingencies*. With a group contingency, each individual's behavior contributes to or detracts from the rewards given to the entire group. An advantage of group contingencies is that the entire group benefits from the performance of its members. This can create a cooperative climate where none existed prior to the program. For example, if one particular student is disrupting the class and the behavior is maintained by attention from peers, a group contingency can reverse the trend because the group's rewards now depend on acceptable behavior from all members. A disadvantage of group contingencies is that one individual can become the target of anger if his or her behavior causes the group to lose out. Thus, group contingencies

should not be used unless the behavior of the entire group is subject to close monitoring.

A brief description of the procedure follows.

Step 1: Identify the problem. The Good Behavior Game plus Merit is a flexible program that may be useful in a variety of situations. A particularly rowdy class that has a high frequency of violating classroom rules might provide an opportunity for one application. Although good classroom rules include effective consequences, it may not be practical to administer the consequences if it appears that the entire class or a persistent minority are violating rules. A group contingency is an efficient way to address these issues.

Step 2: Refine the definition of the problem. The core of the Good Behavior Game plus Merit is the classroom rules. Chapter 5 discussed classroom rules in general. A generic set of classroom rules might resemble these:

1. Stay in your seat unless you have permission to leave.
2. Stay on task until all work is done.
3. No talking without permission during work time.
4. Obey the teacher.

A fifth or sixth rule that covers the specific classroom situation might be added. Publicly posting the rules and discussing them with students should make them clear. As noted previously, reviewing the rules daily may improve compliance.

In addition to classroom rule violations, the program also targets deficit behaviors such as work completion. Some thought needs to be given to the deficit behaviors that might be rewarded during the program. In Darveaux's study, students received "merits" each time an individual completed a math task at or above 75 percent accuracy. However, there are an endless number of deficit behaviors that could be reinforced with "merits," including accurate completion of other academic assignments, being settled and ready to work right after recess, attendance, making a contribution to discussion, working an example at the board, or any other behavior that the teacher sees a need to improve. All that is needed is a concrete and workable definition of the target behavior.

Step 3: Assess the baseline rate. Two contingencies are involved in the Good Behavior Game plus Merit.

First, each team receives a point or demerit for each violation of classroom rules committed by any individual on the team. Second, merits are awarded to students who engage in predesignated behaviors.

It is important, though not absolutely crucial, to know approximately how many rule violations can be expected and how many merits might be awarded during the time period when the Good Behavior Game plus Merit will be used. This will assist in planning the economy of points and merits.

With respect to baseline observations, the simplest approach would be a count of rule violations prior to beginning the program. Presumably, classroom rules are objective, concrete, and measurable, but it may be necessary to give this component of the program careful attention. The count of rule violations could focus on both an individual child and the entire classroom, depending on the goal of the program. Additional data could also be included, such as the particular rule violated, the name of the rule violator, the time of day, and/or the type of activity in which the class was engaged. Alternatively, a time-sampling procedure may be used to obtain objective observational data regarding the behavior of a particular child (see Chapter 3). The baseline data would be useful in setting the criterion for acceptable behavior that results in access to a reward. In addition, it could prove important should a child study team be assembled to consider special services for the target child or children.

Step 4: Design the behavioral contingencies and write the program description. To begin the procedure, the class is divided into two teams. The intervention consists of two contingencies. First, for each violation of a classroom rule, the child's team receives a single point. If the entire team keeps its point total under five during a predetermined period of time, that team receives a reward such as candy, access to free time, or story time. Baseline observations, consultation with others, and previous experience should be used to determine an acceptable number of points. The rules in effect for the Darveaux study were not talking without permission, no excessive noise, staying in one's desk area, remaining still while seated, and not tattling on other children. Of course, one would expect this procedure to be effective with any reasonable set of classroom rules.

The second contingency involves a positive reward for desirable behavior. The children earn "merits," which consist of the words "one merit" printed on an index card. Five merits acquired by the children on a team result in the loss of one of the team's accumulated points. Thus, through good behavior, the children on a team can reduce their point total and thereby receive a reward for keeping that total below five. Merit cards were distributed for completing an arithmetic assignment at or above 75 percent accuracy and active class participation in Darveaux's study. However, "merit" cards could be awarded for any target behavior deemed important to an individual child or the group as a whole. Thus, in order to conduct this intervention, a minimum of prior preparation would be necessary. This would include a list of classroom rules and ways that children could earn merits, a supply of merit cards, plans for providing access to rewarding activities, and a method of conducting baseline observations.

Step 5: Begin the program. Since "merits" and points will not be effective unless students have some understanding of them, the basic rules of the program need to be explained to the students. Once the program is explained, it should be started as soon as possible. Remember, it will be helpful to review both classroom rules and the specific rules that apply to the Good Behavior Game daily for at least a few days and perhaps once a week thereafter.

Steps 6, 7, and 8: Observe the effects of the program and initiate steps to strengthen generalization beyond the training environment; modify, if necessary, and fade out the program. Once the Good Behavior Game plus Merit has been initiated and positive effects have been observed, the question of generalization must be considered. One strategy would be to make the intervention a permanent component of the classroom structure. A disadvantage of this strategy is that the children remain subject to external structure, when the ultimate goal of the classroom teacher may be to promote self-motivated behavior and independence. If this is the case, a couple of alternative approaches could be used.

First, the program could be slowly faded until most of its components had been removed entirely. Two variables can be manipulated in this respect. The number of merit cards necessary to erase one of the points could be slowly increased so that greater productivity would be required of the classroom as a whole in order to offset the penalty for disruptive behavior. Another variable that could be changed is the period of time between rewarding activities. That is, in the initial stages of the program, the children might receive access to a rewarding activity if fewer than five points were accumulated during a single day or independent work period. This could be changed in a number of ways. For instance, access to a rewarding activity could be made contingent on two or three days of having fewer than five points at the end of the day. Similarly, the students could be allowed access to a rewarding activity for having accumulated fewer than, say, ten points during an entire week. Using changes like these, the program could eventually be entirely eliminated, or a level of structure with which the classroom teacher was satisfied could be maintained with the Good Behavior Game plus Merit.

An alternative approach might be to fade out the group contingencies and focus the rules of the game only on children who are exceptionally disruptive. Then the same techniques discussed here could be used to fade out the game for the individual students.

Comment. The Good Behavior Game plus Merit represents one of many viable strategies for intervening when children are disruptive in school. The advantage of the procedure is that it combines negative contingencies (loss of access to rewarding activity) for disruption with positive rewards for desirable behavior. However, this could be accomplished in other ways as well. For instance, timeout for disruptive behavior could be employed concurrently with one of the behavior management programs described in Chapter 10. The choice of an appropriate strategy will depend on the particular needs of the target student and the needs of the classroom teacher.

REVIEW

Terms to Remember and Review

behavior excess	extinction
ignoring	coupon program
negative punishment	logical consequences
negative attention	continuous reinforcement
intermittent reinforcement	resistance to extinction
token	response cost
Sit and Watch	timeout
least restrictive procedures	

Study and Discussion Questions

1. What is negative attention, and why is it important to avoid using negative attention as a method of disciplining children in a classroom? Contrast negative attention with ignoring behavior.
2. Explain the meaning of the term *logical consequences* and give two examples of using logical consequences both in a classroom and at home.
3. Do you agree or disagree with the author's contention that extinction programs should be described in writing? Why?
4. What is intermittent reinforcement? What role does intermittent reinforcement play in the strength or resistance to extinction of a behavior?
5. What are some of the reasons that an extinction program might not be successful?
6. Explain what is meant by a *response cost* contingency.
7. In one or two paragraphs, summarize the basic elements of the coupon program.
8. Briefly summarize how a timeout procedure is implemented and give three key reasons that timeout might be ineffective.
9. Explain, in one or two paragraphs, the nature of the Good Behavior Game plus Merit.
10. Develop a written program to describe how one of the procedures discussed in this chapter could be implemented in a classroom situation.

Group Project

Divide into groups of two or three students and develop a behavior management program for the child described in the case study. Explain the program with enough detail that the child's parents will be able to understand it. Any of the interventions described up to this point in the text may be used.

Case study. Josh is a male in the second grade who is the third child of his still-married biological parents. His teacher describes Josh as having the potential to be an exceptional student based on his contributions to discussions, but he fails to complete much of the work assigned in class. The teacher's main behavioral concerns are:

1. Josh pushes other students, especially when getting into lines.
2. Josh often throws objects (books, pencils, other small objects) in class, posing a threat to other students.
3. Josh often swears and uses foul language in class.

4. He is frequently off task and does not seem to pay attention.

5. He appears "immature" in social situations.

Following the steps shown here may be helpful. Refer to Table 6.1 for a summary of issues in planning a behavior management program.

1. Identify the problem.

2. Determine what, if any, additional assessment might be helpful.

3. Refine the definition of the problem behavior(s).

4. Identify and explain the reinforcer and contingency.

CHAPTER 8

MANAGEMENT OF BEHAVIOR EXCESSES IN SPECIAL CLASSROOMS

The behavior management programs described in this chapter focus on the needs of children in special classrooms. In this context, *special classroom* refers to classrooms in which student–teacher ratios are more favorable than in regular classrooms. Programs described in this chapter may be appropriate for regular classrooms by either changing some features of the program or providing a pupil support assistant, a paraprofessional, or an aide whose primary task is to monitor the target child's behavior. Programs useful in regular classrooms can also be used in special classrooms. The division between regular and special classrooms is not meant to stifle creativity. The goal is to provide quick and efficient access to useful behavior management programs. The main distinguishing characteristics of programs described in this chapter is that they require more staff than is usually available in a regular classroom, and they are designed to reduce the occurrence of target behaviors. Teachers just beginning to organize a special classroom may also find Chapter 5 useful.

As discussed in Chapter 2, there are two basic techniques for reducing behavior excesses, presentation of an aversive stimulus and loss of access to an appetitive stimulus. The formal names for these techniques are positive punishment and negative punishment, respectively. Presentation of an aversive stimulus (punishment) is not a practical or effective procedure under most circumstances. This leaves negative punishment as the primary option for dealing with behavior excesses in school settings. Two programs are described in this

chapter: the response cost lottery (Witt & Elliott, 1982) and timeout. The chapter concludes with an introduction to cognitive-behavioral procedures that represent a very different approach to behavior excesses. Cognitive- behavioral procedures are a generic method of teaching the child cognitive skills to avoid or cope with situations that might lead to problem behavior.

THE RESPONSE COST LOTTERY

The response cost lottery is similar to the coupon program described in Chapter 7. A response cost lottery can be regarded as less restrictive than timeout because it does not cause removal of the child from classroom instruction. It is also similar to the assertive discipline technique but has the advantages of making a much more noticeable event contingent on disruption and providing more immediate consequences. This similarity may improve generalization of skills from special to regular classrooms. This program is designed for small groups of students and would be appropriate for smaller special education classes or a group of several disruptive students. The program requires the ability to understand classroom rules and tolerate a fairly lengthy delay between a consequence (loss of coupon) and the outcome. Also, the child needs to be able to understand that each loss of a coupon causes the odds of winning a raffle to decline. These types of cognitive skills are likely to develop in the later elementary grades and are typically well established by middle school.

A more detailed description of the program follows.

Step 1: Identify the problem. Behavior excesses can occur in a number of different forms. Those of greatest concern to teachers include any behavior that disrupts the teaching process, such as talking out of turn, failing to follow directions, being out of seat, other off-task behaviors, verbal or physical aggression, and not completing assignments. Some special classes may have automatic consequences for such behavior, whereas disruptive behavior may be unusual in other classes. The response cost lottery is an effective method for controlling disruptive behavior (Proctor & Morgan, 1991; Witt & Elliott, 1982). The technique is analogous to the coupon program described in Chapter 7. Students are given a predetermined number of slips of paper. As in the coupon program, slips or coupons are lost each time a student violates a classroom rule or emits one of the target behaviors. But this technique is unlike the coupon progam in that students do not trade in the remaining coupons for reinforcers. Instead, each student's name is written on his or her remaining coupons and they are placed into a container. At the end of a week, a slip is drawn from the container and the student whose name is drawn receives a substantial reward—a toy, game, T-shirt, compact disc, or other attractive reinforcer.

One disadvantage of this procedure is that students need to understand that the more slips with their name on them deposited in the container, the more likely they are to receive the large reward. Some children may have difficulty with the long time interval between behavior and a rewarding consequence. On the other hand, the procedure is effective with groups, of students, and it is much cheaper to provide a single attractive reward than to provide several such rewards to individual students.

Step 2: Refine the definition of the problem. The fairest way to conduct this type of behavior management program is to establish a set of classroom rules. A public and fair set of classroom rules is a core requirement for almost any classroom discipline system. Here are some examples of effective rules:

1. Stay in your seat unless you have permission to leave.
2. Stay on task until all work is done.
3. No talking without permission during WORK time.
4. Have arithmetic workbook and pencils ready when the 10 A.M. bell rings.
5. Obey the teacher.

Classroom rules should be tailored to the needs of the situation (e.g., Rule 4) and should include a generic component such as Rule 5 that gives the teacher flexibility in dealing with unique classroom problems. Chapter 5 includes a detailed discussion of rules for the school and classroom.

Developing a good set of classroom rules sets the standards for classroom behavior and provides a convenient way of defining target behaviors. However, effective classroom structure also depends on strengthening appropriate behaviors. Thus, it is also important to include praise, attention, and sometimes material rewards for appropriate behaviors such as meeting academic goals and completing assignments. A behavior reduction program will not be completely successful unless appropriate behaviors are strengthened at the same time.

Step 3: Assess the baseline rate. Figure 8.1 shows a sample data chart for monitoring the frequency of rule violations. Each classroom rule is given its own column, and each time a rule violation occurs, an X or the initials of the child violating the rule are placed in the next available square above that rule. The height of the column provides a graphic indication of the frequency with which each rule is violated. The graphs then provide the standard for judging the success of the program. Once the program has been in effect, a decline in rule violations should be evident.

Step 4: Design the behavioral contingencies and write the program description. The response cost lottery begins with each child in the target group receiving slips of paper, which are placed under a 5 × 8 card taped on three sides to the child's desk. The number of slips of paper given to each child is determined from the baseline data. Whenever a rule is violated (the rules could be written on the 5 × 8 card), the teacher removes one slip of paper from the child's supply. This should be done with minimum interaction with the child. A good technique is to tell the child what rule was violated and remove the slip without further comment. The number of slips with which each child begins the day should be equal to or somewhat below the average daily frequency of disruptive incidents, so that with some improvement in behavior the children are likely to end the day with at least a few remaining slips. At the end of the school day, each child's leftover slips are labeled with the child's name and placed in a jar.

If this program is used with large groups of children,

Directions: Make an "X" in the first column each time the target behavior occurs on the first day of data recording. Continue by using the next column for the second day, the third column for the third day, and so on. The height of the column provides a visual indicator of the number of episodes of the target behavior each day.

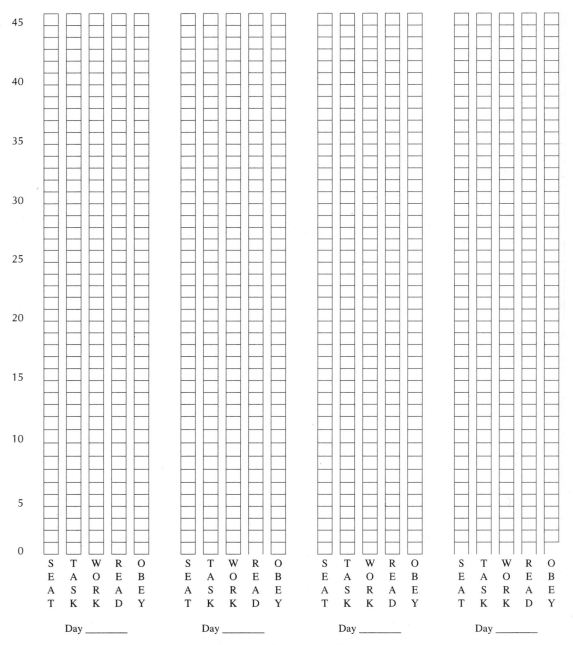

Figure 8.1. Sample Data Chart

it may be important to ensure that the slips can not be counterfeited. Colored papers with a unique identifier for each child will usually be sufficient to prevent counterfeiting and trading.

At the end of the week, a slip of paper is drawn from the jar and the child whose name is on the slip receives a predetermined reward. Thus, each time during the week that a child is discovered breaking a rule, his or her chances of winning the lottery decrease. This should be carefully explained to the children involved, although it may take them at least a week to understand what it means to lose one of their slips.

Important issues to resolve in the written program include the specific classroom rules along with definitions of key terms in the rules. It would also be important to specify the nature of the reward delivered to the individual whose name is drawn.

Step 5: Begin the program. A classroom discussion of rules and expectations along with daily review of the rules will help children learn and respond to the rules. An explanation of the lottery or raffle will also be needed. However, the children may not really catch on until a raffle has actually been conducted.

Step 6: Observe the effects of the program and initiate steps to strengthen generalization beyond the training environment. The predicted effect of this program is that rule violations will gradually decline. At the same time, teachers should observe that the classroom climate improves and that time is spent more productively focused on learning tasks rather than discipline issues.

The requirement of following rules should be a normal feature of all classrooms. Therefore, a program that improves this behavior will contribute to a student's success in regular classrooms. Should a student participating in this program be mainstreamed in regular classes, one option is to switch to the coupon program described in Chapter 7. An alternative strategy would be to use this response cost procedure for students in the early stages of a levels system. Students whose frequency of rule violations is about the same as is typical in a regular classroom setting could graduate to a program that is similar to discipline techniques employed in the regular classroom. For example, a student whose behavior under the response cost lottery program improved from a baseline of five rule violations per day to three rule violations per week, could be graduated to a less restrictive program. Students receive a warning for the first rule violation on any given day, and the consequence for a second rule violation is that they must remain in the classroom for three minutes after other students have left for lunch. This contingency could easily be used in a regular or special classroom and should succeed in keeping rule violations to an acceptable minimum.

Proctor and Morgan (1991) suggested that an interesting direction for research would be to test the efficacy of adding a self-management component to the response cost raffle. Their idea was that students could be trained to monitor themselves and administer the consequence. For example, Christie, Hiss, and Lozanoff (1984) used videotapes of a child's own behavior to train children to observe and code their own behavior. Each child participated in six hours of training during the summer to learn the recording procedure. Then, in the regular classroom, these children recorded their own behavior when signaled by the teacher to do so. The researchers obtained strong to modest changes in behavior as a function of the self-observation procedure. DiGangi, Maag, and Rutherford (1991) found that adding self-graphing to a self-monitoring procedure enhanced the positive effects of the technique. These results suggest that one method of promoting generalization of the response cost lottery would be to have students take over some of the monitoring tasks involved in the program.

One approach could be to instruct students to maintain a graph like the one shown in Figure 8.1, which shows the number of rule violations for each day of the program. Students could first record a rule violation whenever instructed to do so by the teacher . Later, students could be instructed to monitor their own behavior and record a rule violation whenever they caught themselves violating a rule. Eventually, it would be hoped that rule violations would occur infrequently enough that a response cost lottery could be slowly faded away (see Step 8), with discipline procedures that apply to the entire school substituted in its place. Accomplishing the transition from a teacher-directed behavior management program to a student-directed behavior management program would require at least three steps. First, the student should record behavior under the direction of the teacher. Second, the student and teacher should independently record rule violations and then meet to compare records. The student would then be reinforced for accurate recording. In the final phase, the student independently monitors behavior. Remember, at the same time the student is developing self-monitoring skills, on-task behavior should be rewarded. In fact, students could also graph on-task behavior or number of assignments completed. The main focus is to improve academic productivity. An improvement in productivity will be an indirect consequence of the declining rate of classroom rule violations.

Another way of promoting generalization of the skills learned when the response cost raffle is employed is to make this program a component of a levels system. When each individual child reaches a predetermined criterion, they "graduate" to a less restrictive level of classroom structure. For example, the "graduation" requirement could be that the individual child must lose fewer than two coupons per week for three successive weeks in order to graduate to the next level of the system.

Nelson, Smith, Young, and Dodd (1991) reviewed a number of self-management studies and concluded that generalization of positive effects to other settings did not occur unless specific training or instructions to use the self-management procedure was given. This implies that students who "graduate" from the resource room to mainstream classrooms may need additional training in monitoring their own behavior in order to bring about behavior changes that will be maintained in this environment.

Step 7: Modify the program if necessary. What elements of the response cost lottery would need to be changed if the program is unsuccessful or slow to have an effect? The most obvious problem might be that the reward given to the lottery winner is inadequate. Perhaps it is not attractive enough, or the odds of winning may be too low or not clearly understood by the students. Problems of this type could be resolved by discussing them with the students, who may have ideas of their own regarding tangible rewards for which they will work. A reward that is popular with students one year may not be "cool" the next school year. Keeping current with the popular culture and fads of schoolchildren is helpful in knowing what rewards they will value. On the other hand, some reinforcers are almost universal—for example, a can of soda or free time.

Another possibility is that a teacher may be uncomfortable with the concept of a lottery or raffle because of its association with gambling. A simple modification of the program would be to allow the contingency—loss of a coupon for each rule violation—to remain the same. Instead of or in addition to placing the slips or coupons in a container for a raffle or lottery, each coupon that remains at the end of the day could be equal to one point. A menu of rewards could then be developed on an individual or group basis. These rewards could then be purchased with the points represented by the coupons that the child does not lose. This would resemble a group version of the coupon program described in Chapter 7.

Step 8: Fade out the program. One suggestion for fading out the response cost lottery is to develop a criterion for "graduation" from the program so that students who meet the graduation requirement are allowed some measure of freedom or privileges denied to those whose behavior has not yet improved sufficiently. For example, a child could advance to a higher level within the classroom system when two or fewer coupons are lost each week for three weeks. Depending on the nature of the child's program, a specific goal may need to be stated in the IEP.

If the problem is to fade the response cost lottery for an entire group of students, there are two directions in which the process could go. First, the length of time between lotteries could be slowly increased. Second, the number of coupons with which each child begins the day could also be decreased. It is impossible to specify a precise procedure in this phase of the program because needs will vary from class to class and child to child. The basic principle is that the program administrator must continue to monitor the number of rule violations per day as the program is faded. If the number of rule violations remains at an acceptably low level, the fading process should continue. If the number of rule violations increases, it would be appropriate to go back to an earlier phase of the program. Eventually, it may be desirable to announce the end of the program by allowing students to earn a party or some other celebration to mark their progress.

TIMEOUT IN SPECIAL CLASSROOMS

I was once asked to consult with a special education teacher who was using a timeout program to decrease a child's aggressive attacks on smaller children in the classroom. The target behavior consisted of pushing smaller children hard enough so they fell and risked a serious injury. The timeout program was well planned and developed in consultation with the child's parents. Each time the child acted aggressively toward another student, he was placed in a small office area for ten minutes. The consultation was requested because aggressive behavior did not decline and the child was consistently destroying the timeout area. Examination of the documentation indicated that the program was soundly designed and was directed at a well-defined behavior. It was not until I had observed a couple of timeouts that the problem with the program became apparent. The child was placed in timeout contingent on any aggressive act and was released from timeout at the end of the ten minutes regardless of his ongoing behavior. The child emitted violent tantrum behavior as soon as the timeout began and the behavior continued until the timeout period expired. It seemed that tantrum behavior was reinforced by release from timeout.

By the time I was consulted, tantrum behavior had escalated to an extreme level, and aggressive behavior continued at a high rate. My first suggestion was to release the student from timeout only after ten minutes of calm behavior in the timeout room. This was bad advice, because tantrum behavior continued for over an hour. My next suggestion was to "shape" quiet behavior in the timeout room. This was accomplished by placing the child in the timeout room for ten minutes and then releasing him after an additional five seconds of quiet behavior. The goal was then to extend the required amount of quiet time until the entire ten-minute timeout was tolerated peacefully. Eventually, ten-minute timeouts were tolerated quietly and aggressive behavior was significantly reduced. A parallel program to reward on-task behavior, begun much earlier, also began having an impact on the student's behavior. At a later meeting to review the program, data indicated a decline in aggressive acts to about one every two weeks and substantial improvement in on-task behavior. The student's rate of academic progress also sharply increased. In short, after an important adjustment in the program, it was very successful.

This example illustrates two important points about the use of timeout. First, when used properly, it can be an effective tool for behavior management. Second, a timeout program is a serious undertaking, not to be taken lightly. It needs to be monitored carefully to ensure that it is having the expected effects, and any problems that develop need to addressed promptly. Timeout periods also subtract directly from the amount of instructional time available to address the child's academic needs. Consequently, the procedure is regarded as very restrictive. In fact, the restrictive nature of timeout procedures, particularly, timeout that removes the child from academic instruction, leads to a number of cautions and restrictions on its use in school environments.

Cautions and caveats in the use of timeout. The Council for Children with Behavioral Disorders (1990)

has issued a position paper on the use of behavior reduction strategies with behavior-disordered children. In their view, timeout is a "relatively harmless" procedure that consists of three "levels": (1) contingent observation procedures (i.e., "sit and watch") in which the child ceases participation in an activity while sitting and watching other children behaving appropriately; (2) "exclusion timeout" in which a child is excluded from seeing or being seen by others; and (3) seclusion timeout "in which a child is placed in a safe and secured room." The Council recommended eight guidelines for use of behavior reduction procedures, which are summarized next:

1. Prior consent for use of behavior reduction procedures should be obtained from a child's parents or guardians and from a human rights committee.
2. A careful analysis of the potential target behaviors should be conducted. The procedures for collecting baseline data discussed in Chapter 3 would provide this information.
3. Other, less restrictive interventions should be tried before using behavior reduction procedures. These include strengthening incompatible behaviors or perhaps using a response cost program to decrease the target behavior.
4. Local rules and guidelines for use of these procedures should be followed. This includes both schoolwide and state guidelines.
5. A detailed written program description should also be develop and included in the child's IEP if the child is handicapped. Modifications of the program in response to the data it generates should be written into the original document.
6. Only the least restrictive and effective behavior reduction procedure should be employed. Selection of a behavior reduction technique should be based on previous empirical findings.
7. People administering behavior reduction procedures should be appropriately trained to carry out the procedures described in the program.
8. Data regarding the efficacy of the program should be kept and discussed regularly with the team that is directing the child's program. The child's parents, administrators, and other professionals should all be regularly apprised of the child's progress.

In addition to these guidelines, it is crucial that any room used for seclusion timeout provide a safe environment. This would include a design that allows continuous monitoring of the pupil, a room that is large enough to be comfortable with good lighting and ventilation, and a room with tamper-proof fixtures. A room used for timeout must provide a safe place for the child to be, given that the child may become angry and/or frustrated and attempt to harm him- or herself or others.

Harris (1985) cautions that timeout is made effective by a large difference between the timeout and the regular (timein) environments. That is, the child must lose access to a generous amount of available reinforcement in order for the timeout to succeed in suppressing or punishing behavior. In fact, timeout can even be *reinforcing* when it is less aversive than the timein situation. This can occur when the child is working on a difficult or frustrating task, is bored, or receives social reinforcement from peers during the timeout period (Durand, Crimmins, Caulfield, & Taylor, 1989; Nelson & Rutherford, 1983; Solnick, Rincover, & Peterson, 1977).

The following sections describe step-by-step procedures for a timeout program. It is important to read the entire procedure carefully and thoroughly before attempting to use a timeout program. The first few times a timeout program is attempted, an experienced consultant should examine the written program and observe the program at the beginning and at regular intervals thereafter. A successful timeout program depends on a detailed understanding of several key principles. In the description that follows, these principles will be made as salient as possible.

Step 1: Identify the problem. Timeout is a serious, restrictive intervention. Therefore, it should be used only with serious behaviors that interfere with the academic progress of the student and others. Physical aggression is probably the only behavior that warrants a timeout program because it can result in harm to others, causes a great deal of stress for those who are directly involved and for observers, and because it has the potential to escalate to higher levels that can cause even greater harm. Generally, it would be difficult to imagine a situation in which suppression of aggressive behavior was not in the student's best interests.

Physical aggression can occur in a wide variety of forms—hitting, throwing objects, destroying property, spitting, pinching, kicking, biting, and, under some circumstances, kissing, hugging, and other unwanted physical contact. Aggression directed at oneself (self-injurious behavior) may also be considered a serious problem. Head-banging, slapping oneself, and biting oneself would be examples of such behavior. These behaviors

are more likely to be seen in severely disturbed children such as those with infantile autism and other developmental disorders, and they will not be given detailed treatment here. See Durand et al. (1989), Foxx (1982), Iwata, Pace, Kalsher, Cowdery, and Cataldo (1990), Loschen and Osman (1992), or Murray and Sefchik (1992) for a discussion of the unique problems of these populations.

Some behaviors are highly attention getting and may cause stress among staff and students. Behaviors such as swearing and calling others unprintable names may seem serious enough to justify a timeout program. In most cases, however, these types of behaviors are emitted for their shock or attention-getting value and are best ignored or punished in less restrictive ways, such as response cost, loss of a privilege, or a similar program. In my view, a timeout program is not appropriate for most verbal behavior. The key is to design classrooms so that appropriate behavior is frequently and genuinely rewarded. Thus, for present purposes, it is assumed that some type of physical aggression is the problem behavior when timeout is being considered.

Step 2: Refine the definition of the problem. When a restrictive procedure like timeout is being considered, refining the definition of the problem behavior is important because it may be possible to define the problem in a way that allows timeout to be avoided altogether. This would be the ideal outcome in this phase of the process. A good place to begin is with a thorough review of school records and all existing logs of behavior incidents. The logs should be examined to determine the potential target behaviors and to look for patterns in their occurrence. One way to approach this problem is to ask whether there is any way of predicting the occurrence of the target behavior. For example, it would be very useful to know that the target behavior occurs only during reading lessons, when the child is reviewing a list of advanced sight words. In such a case, timeout might not be an appropriate contingency. Instead, changing the environment to make aggression less likely would be a less restrictive alternative. A number of explanations for a reading problem might exist. Perhaps the child has a visual problem that leads to headaches while the sight words are reviewed. Alternatively, the child might benefit from a program to increase motivation and desire to participate in the activity. Finally, it may be that the word list is too difficult and its role in the child's academic program needs careful review.

As the definition of the problem behavior is reviewed,

it would be prudent to determine whether any other interventions had been attempted. Because it is a restrictive intervention, formally regulated in some states, the use of timeout should be avoided unless other, less restrictive interventions have failed. Other interventions might include environmental modifications, response cost programs, and rewarding of on-task or other behavior incompatible with the target behavior. These interventions should be thoroughly documented before using timeout.

Once a team has determined that the problem behavior has not responded to other interventions and cannot be predicted by environmental events, the target behavior must be carefully defined. The team developing the timeout program needs to reach a consensus on an objective, complete definition of the target behavior. Recall from Chapter 3 that an effective definition of a target behavior requires no interpretation on the part of the observer. This means that variables such as the intention of the child or whether provocation has occurred should not influence judgments of the observer or program administrator. If the definition is ambiguous, the program administrators may be uncertain about when to administer timeout. Furthermore, an ambiguous definition will lead to unreliable baseline data, so it would be difficult to assess whether the timeout contingency is effective.

Other issues that may emerge as the team develops a working definition of the target behavior deserve further discussion. First, it may become apparent as the assessment is conducted that certain behaviors of the student predict with a high degree of certainty that an aggressive act is about to occur. A verbal threat is the most likely cue. The team will then need to decide whether a verbal threat is counted as an aggressive act to be followed immediately by timeout. This might be a case where verbal behavior is appropriately punished with timeout. The team will need to make a decision based on the child's past history and the goals the team has developed for the child. One certainty is that intercepting the aggressive behavior will prevent harm to other children. If threats of aggression are punished with timeout, it would be helpful to keep separate records of verbal threats and actual physical aggression.

Another important issue is whether timeout should be a consequence for failure to obey a legitimate adult command. Again, a team consensus is the only way to decide the issue. Certainly, the decision of the team will depend on the nature of the adult command. If the child consistently engages in behavior that could result in

harm or injury to self or others, then an adult's command to cease should certainly be heeded. On the other hand, other failures to obey a command are less harmful and more correctable, such as a delay in assembling needed materials and beginning an academic task. In those cases where harm might result from failure to obey the command, a timeout might be justified. A brief warning that timeout will result if the behavior does not immediately cease should be built into programs that punish failures to obey a command with timeout.

Step 3: Assess the baseline rate. A baseline is the rate or frequency with which a target behavior occurs when the program contingencies are not in effect. A baseline of the frequency of the target behavior taken before a timeout program begins then serves as the standard against which the success of the program is judged. In the case of a timeout program, the expectation is that the frequency of the target behavior will decrease. An accurate baseline requires that the team reach a consensus on the precise definition of the target behavior. Without a precise definition, the target behavior's frequency will vary as a result of inconsistency in counting rather than actual changes in behavior.

Once the target behavior has been concretely and objectively defined, baseline data can be collected. Figure 8.2 shows a useful method of collecting baseline data. This method illustrates more than a simple frequency count because a detailed record allows the team to examine the data for patterns that might suggest program modifications. Also, it is crucial to document the length of each timeout, and this form includes space for doing so. In addition to a record of each incident and timeout, it would also be helpful to maintain a simpler graph of the frequency of incidents as is illustrated in Figure 7.1 (Chapter 7). The graph provides a visual representation, and any trends that develop will be easier to see. Collection of baseline data needs to be consistent across environments, which is why the form shown in Figure 8.2 includes space for recording where the incident took place. Any patterns that become apparent need to be investigated because they may indicate other directions for the program. For example, if the target behavior occurs only in a particular setting and not in others, this might suggest that some manipulation of the environment, such as separating the target child from a provocative peer, could succeed in decreasing the target behavior.

The length of time for collecting baseline data will vary with the situation. A relatively infrequent behavior

Directions: Each timeout should be documented by providing the information requested below. If no timeout is administered (such as during baseline observations), write NA in the space for "timeout length."

Student's Name: _____

Date: _____   Time: _____   Location: _____

Incident; _____

_____

Timeout Location/Method: _____

Starting Time for Timeout: _____   Ending Time for Timeout: _____

Timeout Length: _____

Comments: _____

_____

Student's Name: _____

Date: _____   Time: _____   Location: _____

Incident; _____

_____

Timeout Location/Method: _____

Starting Time for Timeout: _____   Ending Time for Timeout: _____

Timeout Length: _____

Comments: _____

_____

Student's Name: _____

Date: _____   Time: _____   Location: _____

Incident; _____

_____

Timeout Location/Method: _____

Starting Time for Timeout: _____   Ending Time for Timeout: _____

Timeout Length: _____

will require a longer baseline period, whereas a valid baseline for a behavior that occurs several times a day could be established within a few days. Another factor that may influence the length of the baseline period is the seriousness of the target behavior. The more serious the target behavior, the more urgent it may seem to begin the actual timeout program. Although it is possible to conduct a timeout program without preintervention baseline data, the disadvantage is that problems with the program may be less apparent in the absence of baseline data for comparison. For example, an increase in the target behavior above baseline levels would not be quickly detectable. On the other hand, the team may decide that an immediate response to the target behavior is more important than having precise baseline data. Also, it may be possible to develop a very good estimate of the baseline rate of the behavior by reviewing existing incident logs.

Step 4: Design the behavioral contingencies and write the program description. Before any timeout program is begun, the most important question to pose is: What reinforcers will this child be able to earn when *not* in timeout? The reason for this concern is that timeout needs to remove the child from a reinforcing environment to one that is boring and lacking in reinforcement. Many writers consider the use of timeout to be unethical unless parallel programs to strengthen desirable behavior are also in place. Thus, before developing a description of the timeout program, careful consideration of the timein environment is needed. The timein environment needs to be full of desirable reinforcement, positive attention, and interesting activities so that it contrasts sharply with the timeout environment.

Once it has been established that the timein environment is rich with opportunities to earn reinforcement, planning for timeout administrations can begin. Recall that timeout encompasses a range of interventions that vary in restrictiveness, ranging from the "sit and watch" procedure described in Chapter 7 to seclusion timeout in a special timeout room. The choice of procedure should be based on the criterion of using the least restrictive effective alternative. For example, imagine that a special classroom employs a group reinforcer of allowing the class to have free time at the end of the day contingent on acceptable behavior during the day. However, one student tends to become overexcited during this period and acts aggressively toward peers while engaged in some activities. In this case, the "sit and watch" contin-

gency might be adequate to decrease the frequency of aggressive outbursts.

On the other hand, a student may have explosive fits of temper during which she throws objects around the room and threatens both peers and teachers. Furthermore, the student doesn't respond to verbal commands to remain calm or stop the aggressive behavior. In this type of situation, removal to a secure timeout room may effectively punish the behavior while providing relief and safety to the remaining students. Regardless of the choice of procedure, the team must carefully consider the alternatives and plan for the actual administration of timeout. Two basic issues must be considered: the timeout location and adequate staffing.

The location where the child serves the timeout can vary from a seat just a few feet away from an activity to a special room where the child is isolated from all reinforcing activity. The most restrictive procedure, of course, is to remove the child completely to a special timeout room. A special timeout room must have tamper-proof fixtures, properly covered walls and floors, and adequate ventilation and light. It should be large enough to allow the student to stand, stretch, or lie down. The room must also be clean and allow for continuous monitoring by a staff member. Safety and protection of the child must be primary considerations. State and local regulations should be consulted to make sure all requirements are satisfied.

A timeout area within the special classroom allows timeout to be administered more quickly, but it is difficult to eliminate all sources of reinforcement such as attention from peers. A timeout area could consist of an isolated desk or carrel, or an area surrounded by sturdy partitions. The choice of a timeout area is up to the judgment of the team planning the program. The goal is to choose the least restrictive option that is effective. The team must consider how compliant the child is likely to be and whether unauthorized reinforcement from peers and other activity can be eliminated. The team must also consider whether the child will be resistant to the use of timeout, which may indicate a need to have additional staff members available. This may be an unpleasant possibility, but a child who is aggressively misbehaving may physically resist placement in a timeout room or area. Special training is needed for staff members who may find themselves in this situation. Dura (1991) describes a case study of such a situation.

Once the timeout contingency has been administered to a child, the student should remain in timeout until two criteria have been met: He or she is quiet, and it has been long enough to be unpleasant. One or two minutes of timeout for each year of age is usually sufficient (Barkley, 1987a). Children under four years of age require only a few minutes. Children between five and eight years may require five to ten minutes. Those over eight years may require ten to fifteen minutes, although shorter timeouts of around five minutes are likely to be effective with many children (Harris, 1985). McGuffin (1991) compared the effectiveness of timeout durations of one, five, ten, and twenty minutes with twenty children ranging in age from four to twelve years. The outcome was that the one-minute timeout was clearly less effective than the other timeout durations, which did not differ in effectiveness. The authors concluded that a five-minute timeout duration should be used in most cases. When there is the possiblity that several durations of timeout may be used, shorter durations of timeout should be used first because these shorter durations lose much of their effectiveness if used after longer durations of timeout (Harris, 1985).

Remaining in the timeout for the minimum length of time is only the first criterion for release from timeout. The second criterion is that the child must be calm when released from timeout. If the child is not calm when the minimum length of timeout expires, the timeout needs to be extended. If the child is complaining, tantruming, or otherwise misbehaving when released from timeout, these behaviors would then be reinforced by release from timeout. Delaying release from timeout until the child has remained calm means that the child will learn to be quiet immediately upon being sent to timeout.

Extension of the timeout as a consequence of continued misbehavior may cause the timeout to continue for a very long period of time. If the timeout extends for more than an hour, I would recommend that the timeout be ended and a team meeting be called to discuss whether the timeout program should be continued. Some state guidelines require that when timeouts of more than fifteen minutes are necessary, access to drinking water and a bathroom must be provided.

Here is a summary of steps in conducting a timeout program:

1. Thoroughly review the past history of the problem and ensure that less restrictive alternatives have been tried.
2. Carefully define the target behavior and obtain baseline data.
3. Develop a detailed written description of the timeout program, including the location and mini-

mum duration of timeout. Also, ensure that adequate staffing is available to administer the program. Under some circumstances the written program should be reviewed by an outside committee in order to ensure that the student's rights are not violated and that the program is soundly designed.
4. If a designated timeout room is used, ensure that it is safe and meets all relevant codes and regulations.
5. Obtain the informed consent of the student's parents.
6. Explain the program to the child.
7. Immediately administer timeout each time the target behavior occurs unless it has been agreed to issue a warning to the child before timeout.
8. When timeout is administered, it is acceptable to make a brief statement of the reason for timeout. However, avoid discussions or arguments with the child because they will only provide reinforcing attention for the target behavior.
9. Place the child in the timeout location with continuous monitoring by a staff member. The success of the timeout will depend on elimination of extraneous reinforcement such as peer attention.
10. When the minimum time has expired, release the student from timeout and allow him or her to return to the regularly scheduled activity. If the child is misbehaving when the timeout is scheduled to end, the timeout should be extended until the child has been quiet and calm for a minimum length of time specified in the program.
11. Maintain records of each timeout.
12. Maintain a graph of the frequency of the target behavior.
13. Schedule regular meetings with the team to review the effects of the program and make any needed modifications.

Step 5: Begin the program. As noted in previous sections, careful preparation and planning must precede a timeout program. Although it may be helpful to explain the consequences to the student before a timeout program begins, this is not mandatory. As explained, target behaviors may be intolerable, and a timeout program may be started without the benefit of baseline data. However, baseline data can play an important role in judging the success of the program, and every effort to collect baseline data should be made as long as it is safe to do so. Thus, the start of a timeout program may be somewhat abrupt. Once the team has reached agreement on the nature of the program, a starting point can be designated and the next occurrence of the target behavior is then punished with timeout. Administration of the first timeout requires that adequate staff be available to assist. Also, the first few timeouts may become very long if the child continues to resist or misbehave during the timeout period. A maximum length of timeout that is somewhat longer than might be acceptable at a later stage of the program may give the child time to adapt to the new contingency. On the other hand, removal from the classroom situation to a quiet area may have a calming effect.

Step 6: Observe the effects of the program and initiate steps to strengthen generalization beyond the training environment. A decrease in the target behavior is the predicted outcome of a timeout program. How quickly a decrease occurs will be a function of a number of variables, including the effectiveness of the timeout as a punishing event and the frequency of the target behavior. If the target behavior occurs only once or twice per week, it may be several weeks or more before a decrease is seen. If the target behavior occurs several times a day, one would hope for a noticeable decline within a week or two. Other variables that could affect the outcome include whether the target behavior was reinforced in the past on a continuous or intermittent basis, the age of the child, the intrinsic reinforcing value of the target behavior, and the immediacy of timeout administrations. A brief rise in the target behavior could occur after the start of a timeout program, but a significant and/or steady rise is cause to have a team meeting.

One serious problem that may be encountered in a timeout program is that the child may physically resist placement in the timeout area and may aggresively attempt to leave. Although blocking any exit from the timeout area may be effective in these circumstances (Roberts & Powers, 1990), a school-based team may find this alternative unacceptable. An alternative plan might be to begin timeout procedures in the home using the method outlined by Barkley (1987b) and to implement timeout in the school only after the child's parents have succeeded in reducing target behaviors at home. I am aware of no studies specifically demonstrating that this approach would work, but the approach would provide one avenue for improving behavior in both environments.

The most important assurance that generalization of behavior will occur is to provide the student with skills to succeed in other settings. Timeout is a method of suppressing or eliminating target behaviors that interfere with needed educational programming. However, suppression of behavior is no guarantee that appropriate behavior will take its place. Suppression of target behavior with timeout expands the opportunity to train needed skills. It is these skills that are most likely to help the student succeed in other environments.

If a child is moved to a mainstream classroom after a target behavior has been suppressed with timeout, the presence of a staff member who has previously administered timeout to the child may be all that is necessary to provide strong assurance that the target behavior will not reoccur. Focusing on improving deficit skills is probably the most important element of strengthening generalization to other environments. Another possible strategy is to have a slow transition from the timeout program to following the normal school rules and procedures for dealing with the target behavior (e.g., fighting). Such a transition would improve generalization of behavior to other settings and could be implemented by the team when the target behavior had declined substantially.

Step 7: Modify the program if necessary. There are several ways to modify an unsuccessful timeout program. As discussed before, one of the most important elements of a successful timeout program is to ensure that the timein environment is much more reinforcing than the timeout environment, which should not be associated with any reinforcement. Enrichment of the timein environment is one of the first modifications of a timeout program that should be considered.

To be effective, timeout must be at least mildly aversive. If observations show that the child is amusing himself or herself during the timeout period, the timeout location could be changed. Another possibility is that the timeout is too short. Lengthening the timeout period could be an effective adjustment, but timeouts beyond five or ten minutes require team discussion. If timeout is ineffective, it could also be that the timeout is a reinforcer because it allows the child to escape disliked seatwork or other activities. One option for dealing with this difficulty is to be sure that the child has an academically relevant activity to do in the timeout location. In extreme cases, it may be feasible for the child to earn his or her way out of the timeout by completing certain tasks.

Another way of occupying a child during a timeout period is to have him or her write or copy an essay about the incident or behavior that led to timeout. Workman (1982) and Swift and Spivack (1975) both describe a technique of giving the child a typed essay that describes the targeted misbehavior, its negative consequences, what the child should have been doing, and the positive consequences of the desired behavior. The typed essay is written to address the child's particular behavior problem and is copied by the child during the timeout period. Because it may be difficult for a teacher to prepare an essay for each anticipated behavioral problem or even to anticipate what problems may occur, it may be effective to assign the child the task of composing an original essay that would answer general questions about the incident that led to timeout, such as: What did I do wrong? Why is it wrong? What was I *supposed* to be doing? What good things will happen if I do what I'm supposed to do? The resulting essay could then be used as a basis for discussion of how to avoid problems in the future. A disadvantage of this method is that some teachers might object to making writing, itself, part of the punishing event.

If the target behavior actually increases or remains steady, it is possible that the student is avoiding something more aversive than the timeout. For example, a child who is fearful of changing in the locker room before physical education class might act out in order to avoid the situation. Timeout records should be examined carefully to ensure that this is not the case. If records indicate that the child is avoiding something, an alternative strategy might lead to improved behavior and obviate the need for timeout. It is also possible that aggressive behavior can be maintained by inadvertent reinforcement and that the same contingencies that maintain the aggressive behavior can be used to develop more functional behaviors (e.g., Northup et al., 1991).

Another modification of a timeout program is to increase its restrictiveness, either by increasing the length of the timeout or by using a more restrictive procedure.

Step 8: Fade out the program. Programs designed to decrease behavior tend to fade as a consequence of the decreasing frequency of the target behavior. That is, suppression of the target behavior leads to less frequent use of the punishment contingency. At some point in the program, the team must decide whether to discontinue the timeout in favor of a less restrictive alternative that is more compatible with mainstream education. Ideally, the eventual result of a timeout program is that inappropriate behavior occurs at a very low rate and that natural contingencies and school policies that apply to all children are sufficient to deal with misbehavior when it occurs. For example, delaying the child's departure for a reinforcing activity such as lunch, physical education,

or free time is an effective contingency that can be used as part of a classroom discipline program. See Chapter 5 for a more detailed discussion of this and other techniques. Suppression of the target behavior also presents the opportunity to develop the student's academic and social skills. Remember that a basic principle of behavior management is that a child who is behaving appropriately and receiving praise and other reinforcement for this behavior will be less likely to emit inappropriate behavior.

Foxx and Shapiro (1978), Foxx (1982), and Salend and Maragulia (1983) described a unique form of timeout that may be appropriate under some circumstances. For their procedure, each child was required to wear an object such as a ribbon that could be established as a discriminative stimulus for positive reinforcement. Whenever a student misbehaved, the ribbon was removed and the child was excluded from all forms of teacher-dispensed reinforcement and participation in rewarding activities. In this procedure, the child is in timeout but remains in the classroom. Foxx and Shapiro demonstrated that a three-minute timeout (extended if misbehavior continued) was effective in reducing misbehavior. They suggested that the procedure would be effective and convenient with lower functioning special education classes. An advantage of the procedure was that classroom visitors knew with which students they could interact and which students were to be ignored.

In order to implement such a procedure effectively, it would be necessary to establish the ribbons as discriminative stimuli for positive reinforcement. Foxx and Shapiro accomplished this by providing teacher praise and edibles to the students for good behavior and for wearing their ribbons. The procedure could also be faded out by substituting a less obvious discriminative stimulus such as a wristband.

In sum, timeout is a complex, restrictive behavior management procedure with many variations. Successful application of timeout procedures requires careful planning and attention to detail. Timeout should never be administered without due consideration to the rights of the student: a safe timeout area, programs simultaneous with timeout to increase appropriate behavior, and careful collection of data that will indicate whether timeout is successful in reducing the target behavior. Review of timeout programs by experts from outside the school system is also highly recommended. The team needs to consider the possibility that the student will physically resist placement in a timeout area. Where indicated, appropriate preparations, such as having individuals available who have been trained to deal with physical aggression, may need to be taken.

AN INTRODUCTION TO COGNITIVE-BEHAVIORAL TECHNIQUES FOR REMEDIATING INATTENTIVE AND IMPULSIVE BEHAVIOR

When teachers are asked to describe children having difficulty in school, they use phrases such as "doesn't follow directions," "doesn't get work done," "gets into trouble without thinking about the consequences," "impulsive," or "can't pay attention." When teachers say, "Pay attention!" they usually expect students to be cognitively engaged in the assigned task whether it is listening to a lesson or doing an assignment. However, the mere *appearance* of attending to task is not enough to ensure that information is being processed and academic performance is improving (Ferritor, Buckholdt, Hamblin, & Smith, 1972; Jones & Kazdin, 1981). An alternative strategy for improving "attention" and decreasing "impulsivity" is to focus directly on cognitive skills. This is the basic goal of an area of behavior management that has come to be known as cognitive-behavioral therapy.

The basic problem of inattentive or impulsive children is that they appear to act "without thinking"—that is, too quickly or illogically to have analyzed properly the particular requirements of a problem solving situation. Cognitive-behavioral therapy attempts to remediate impulsive/inattentive behavior by training children in verbal and cognitive skills necessary for analyzing a task and responding correctly. A substantial empirical and theoretical literature has developed around interventions designed to accomplish this with children. However, the overall effectiveness and optimal procedures of cognitive-behavioral therapy are not yet fully established (e.g., Abikoff, 1985; Ager & Cole, 1991; Dush, Hirt, & Schroeder, 1989; Gresham, 1985; Kendall, 1993). Consequently, rather than provide detailed step-by-step descriptions of several procedures, an overview of cognitive-behavioral techniques will be presented. I believe that these procedures will become a vital tool of behavior management within the next ten years or so.

Basics of Cognitive-Behavioral Therapy

One of the most frequently cited articles in the area of cognitive-behavioral interventions is by Meichenbaum and Goodman (1971) entitled, "Training Impulsive Children to Talk to Themselves: A Means of Developing Self-Control." The title accurately describes what these authors set out to do. The underlying theory is very simple: Much of what people do is mediated by self-generated verbal instructions. That is, we think or talk to ourselves while solving problems. Therefore, one way to learn a new skill or to improve an old one is to learn an appropriate set of verbal mediators to go along with that skill.

Meichenbaum and Goodman taught children to formulate questions about the nature and demands of a task, answer these questions in the form of cognitive rehearsal and planning, verbalize appropriately while performing the task, and reinforce themselves for good performance. The results of two studies in which the effects of such training were assessed indicated that the program was successful in modifying impulsive behavior. A similar procedure was used by Palkes, Stewart, and Freedman (1972). In their procedure, four cue words with illustrative line drawings were used: STOP, LISTEN, LOOK, and THINK. They showed that these self-directing commands could be used to modify the maze performance of hyperactive boys. Unfortunately, only the children's maze performance was assessed, so it is not known whether classroom behavior or academic performance was improved by this treatment.

Brown, Meyers, and Cohen (1984) employed a concrete sequence of cues using a schematic stoplight. The stoplight consisted of three colored circles against a black background. The top circle contained a picture of an owl, which served as a cue to "stop and think." The second circle contained a picture of a turtle with a checkmark below it, serving as a cue to go slowly, and look carefully, and then go back and check the answer. The third circle contained a smile face, which cued successful use of the procedure and self-praise. This self-instruction training technique was successful compared to two carefully matched control groups. It was also found that the training generalized to both similar and dissimilar tasks. The authors attributed their results to several factors, which may be relevant in planning such interventions.

First, they noted that the length of the intervention (nine sessions of about thirty minutes each), coupled with the use of a concrete, visual cue, may have enhanced retention of the self-instruction sequence. Second, the self-instructions were a combination of task-specific instructions and general instructions "not anchored to a specific task." The use of a general self-instruction strategy rather than a task-specific strategy would tend to enhance generalization to novel tasks and situations. This principle is supported by other research (cited in Brown, Meyers, & Cohen, 1984). Finally, the authors suggested that the young age of their subjects (four- and five-year-old preschoolers) may be related to the success of self-instruction training.

Other studies (Argulewicz, Elliott, & Spencer, 1982; Brown & Conrad, 1982; Kendall & Braswell, 1982b; Paniagua & Black, 1990) indicate that these types of training procedures can be useful in remediating problem behaviors of hyperactive boys, as well as academic deficiencies of teacher-referred (Thackwray, Meyers, Schleser, & Cohen, 1985), depressed (Reynolds & Coats, 1986), anxious (Kane & Kendall, 1989; Kendall, 1994), physically aggressive (Lochman, Dunn, & Klimes-Dougan, 1993), angry (Feindler & Guttman, 1994), and emotionally disturbed (Kazdin, Esveldt-Dawson, French, & Unis, 1987; Kazdin, Siegel, & Bass, 1992; Swanson, 1985) children. Harris, Wong, and Keogh (1985) edited a special issue of the *Journal of Abnormal Child Psychology* devoted to cognitive-behavioral modification with children. Furthermore, three detailed treatment manuals (Braswell & Bloomquist, 1991; Kendall & Braswell, 1985, 1993; Zarb, 1992) and an edited book illustrating the wide range of application of cognitive-behavioral procedures (Kendall, 1991) are now available.

For example, Kendall and Braswell (1982b) conducted a group-oriented training program for children (85 percent boys) in grades 3 through 6, who were referred by their teachers for "non-self-controlled" behavior. The experimental, cognitive-behavioral treatment group received twelve 45- to 55-minute sessions, two sessions per week. The treatment package consisted of a variety of tasks in which the emphasis was on training in verbal self-instructions via modeling, social reward for correct responses, response-cost contingencies for errors, and token reward for successes.

The self-instructional training was designed to teach a five-step problem-solving approach to the children. The steps were problem definition, planning an approach, focusing attention, selecting an answer, and self-reinforcing for correct performance. One interesting feature of the program is that the therapist met with the teacher of each child to determine what situations were likely to elicit non-self-control. These situations were then employed in role plays of problem solving in social situations.

A large number of dependent measures were em-

ployed in this study, but the results can be briefly summarized. First, specific skills were learned and general classroom behavior also improved. Second, the cognitive component of the program was shown to add to the effectiveness of the treatment package. Finally, these authors reconfirmed one of the most robust generalizations from the behavior management literature: that generalization of new skills and behavior to situations other than the treatment environment needs to be an explicit component of a successful treatment package.

Kendall and Braswell (1985, 1993) have elaborated their techniques in a book, that focuses on applying the technique with individual children. The program they describe consists of several components embedded within a token system. In each session, the child begins with 20 tokens. Whenever mistakes are made—such as going too fast, omitting a step, or getting the wrong answer to a problem—the child loses a token. The rationale for employing the response cost contingency is that the loss of a token is a potent cue to remind the child to stop and think before answering. In addition, the technique avoids the problem of rewarding the child for impulsive guessing, which occasionally results in a correct answer. An important component of the response cost procedure is that the child is given a brief explanation of why the token was taken away, so that future improvement is cued.

In addition to the response cost contingency, the child is given opportunities to earn bonus tokens. One way of earning bonus tokens is by accurate self-evaluation of performance within a training session. This is accomplished in the following way: First, the trainer evaluates the child on a "How I Did Today" chart, which consists of five alternatives: not so good, O.K., good, very good, and super extra special, with one point assigned to not so good and five points assigned to super extra special. After the trainer rates the child, the child rates him- or herself. The child receives a bonus token if his or her rating comes within one point of the trainer's rating. This procedure was implemented to enhance generalization of the training.

Another way for the child to earn bonus points is by completing homework assignments. These assignments consist of describing situations where the problem-solving procedures were or could have been used in real-life situations. The assignments are graded for accuracy and difficulty. The main function, again, is to enhance generalization from the training environment to other situations.

The recent treatment manual by Braswell and

Bloomquist (1991) views cognitive-behavioral therapy as one component of a multimodal approach to treatment that also includes medication and behavior management. Their manual is guided by an ecological or systems model emphasizing parental and school involvement in treatment. The goal is to ensure that treatment changes behavior in a variety of environments, produces changes that have a significant impact on the child's functioning, and are long-lasting. The program is recommended for children ranging in age from eight to twelve years, but only after appropriate behavior management programs have been implemented. For those wishing to learn more about cognitive-behavioral therapy, the Braswell and Bloomquist manual, along with the book edited by Kendall (1991), are highly recommended.

To illustrate the application of cognitive-behavioral techniques in a form that can be applied by the school-based practitioner, I have selected a case study by Berger (1981) and published in the *School Psychology Review*. Although the generalizability of the case study is in doubt because only a single child was involved, the program described by Berger provides a good illustration of cognitive-behavioral techniques. The procedure employs cognitive mediators to train a skill that is incompatible with impulsive, inattentive behavior. In addition, Berger's procedure has a design that allows ready transfer from the situation in which training takes place to the classroom. Also, the technique's procedures can be used and reinforced in the home. The basic procedure consists of training the child to shoot a basketball and build towers of blocks in a nonimpulsive manner. A description follows.

Step 1: Identify the problem. The general problem is defined as inattention or impulsive behavior, either as an isolated problem or in the context of other behaviors that accompany hyperactivity. For a complete review of relevant assessment techniques and issues, see Kendall and Braswell (1982a) or Braswell and Bloomquist (1991). One of the measures discussed by Kendall and Braswell is a rating scale for self-control in children. The scale (Kendall & Wilcox, 1979) consists of 33 items, which are rated on a seven-point continuum by a child's teacher. The scale covers a broad range of behaviors and was designed to measure generalization of behavior management programs beyond the specific training environment. The measure could be a valuable assessment tool because it can easily be used to assess both a target child and a control child. Also, it would be a good way of determining the broad effects of a treatment program.

Impulsive behavior occurs when a child acts too quickly to have processed the relevant components of a problem and, in addition, typically makes mistakes when work is completed too quickly. This may happen in a variety of situations, ranging from completion of seatwork to social situations that result in anger and fights. The child who requires a lot of individual instruction in order to understand the nature of an assigned task is also likely to approach schoolwork in an impulsive or inattentive manner. Inattention can be indicated when the child is unable to repeat or perform the essential elements of a task that has been presented via group instruction. Of course, behavioral indicators—not looking at the teacher, bothering other students, playing with objects in and around his or her desk, being out of seat during group instruction—are all behavioral indicators of inattention and impulsive behavior.

A key element in any definition of impulsivity and inattention to schoolwork is the concept of ability level. It is important to know whether the child is capable of doing the assigned work. If a child is incapable of doing the work, he or she is likely to appear inattentive and/or impulsive, when the actual problem may be an academic handicap. What is necessary in identifying inattention and impulsivity is independent evidence that the child is capable of doing the assigned work. The accepted way to answer this question is to conduct an individual assessment of the child. Such an assessment could consist of an individual intelligence test or a period of individual instruction in which attention to the task can be closely monitored. It is important that a child be taught at a level that does not produce frustration, so that any program to modify academic habits will work.

The problem in Berger's case study was the behavior of an eight-year-old boy, medically diagnosed as being hyperactive. Observations indicated that he was very disruptive and spent only 30 percent of his time engaged in assigned tasks. Medication significantly reduced off-task and disruptive behavior, but accuracy of completed seatwork dropped to near zero. A preliminary observation indicated that the boy could control his high rate of activity when rewarded with candy for doing so. According to Berger (1981), the ability to exhibit self-control is an important prerequisite for using this procedure.

Step 2: Refine the definition of the problem.
Successful performance of schoolwork is the ultimate indicator of proper attention and reflection. However, lack of success in performing schoolwork may be the

result of a variety of problems. As discussed by Meichenbaum and Goodman (1971), who were among the earliest to apply these techniques, previous research has suggested that children learn to use internal speech to guide their behavior in a gradual progression. Early in development, adult speech serves to guide and direct a child's behavior. Later, the child's own overt speech serves this function. Finally, the child's inner speech (thoughts) serve to guide and regulate behavior. Given that this is a universal progression, it might be hypothesized that impulsive and/or inattentive children have failed to learn to control their behavior via covert verbalizations. This is the essence of how the problem of inattention/impulsivity is viewed from this perspective. The question for the school staff member to ask is whether this model might have validity for remediating a particular child's behavior.

What, then, are some specific indicators that training in verbal mediation of problem solving might be beneficial? Meichenbaum and Goodman (1971) employed a pretest in which children were given instructions to slow down while performing a task. Those children who did not slow down were included in the treatment group. This informal test might serve as a general indication that a child could benefit from training that teaches him or her to control behavior verbally. Other indicators might include inaccurate responses or an inability to respond to questions about the nature of an assigned task, an inability to respond accurately to a request to "tell me what you're doing," or any of the signs of impulsivity or inattention discussed in Chapter 4. A teacher might also be requested to answer the questions on the Kendall and Wilcox rating scale.

Berger conceptualized the problem as the absence of self-control skills. The emphasis, however, was not on verbal mediation of problem solving but on establishing external controls for inhibiting hyperactive and disruptive behavior. At the same time, the program emphasized learning to anticipate the consequences of actions and make appropriate behavioral adjustments to compensate for predicted results.

Step 3: Assess the baseline. Berger did not specify his procedures for recording classroom observations. The goal of the program, however, was to improve classroom behavior and academic performance so that tracking academic performance and on-task behavior in the classroom would be appropriate. Teacher-maintained records can be used to track academic performance, and time-sampling can be used for tracking

on-task behavior. In a time-sampling procedure, a period of about ten to thirty minutes is selected, during which the class is regularly engaged in the same assigned activity. Observations are recorded by dividing the observation period into equal intervals and noting on a prepared data sheet whether the child was on task at each observation point. These data are then used to compute the percentage of time the student was on task. See Chapter 3 for more discussion of these procedures.

Step 4: Design the behavioral contingencies and write the program description. The training in this case involves teaching the child how to shoot a basketball and how to build a tower out of blocks. For a highly impulsive or inattentive child, these are difficult tasks, and the goal of training is to teach the child a nonimpulsive, attentive approach that could generalize to the classroom. The child is taken to the school gym or playground and given the opportunity to earn candy, points, or tokens for making three shots in a row or six out of ten. The child is then given specific instruction, including how to push off using his or her legs, how to hold the ball, how to aim, and how to "think the ball through the hoop." The child is also told to wait ten seconds between shots.

In the following sessions, the child is conditioned to respond to the words "Stop! Think!" accompanied by a hand signal, whenever he or she is about to shoot "impulsively." Here, impulsiveness is defined as not waiting ten seconds between shots and not following the other instructions. As the child's skill improves, the requirement for being rewarded is increased, and other games (including challenging the instructor) are added for variety. Two contingencies are involved in the training: the natural contingency of making baskets and the reward for successful shooting. Both rewards are more likely to occur if the hand signal and verbal prompt ("Stop! Think!") are obeyed or if a nonimpulsive approach to shooting is taken.

In the second phase of the program, the child is required to earn basketball time by building towers from wooden blocks. Berger's criteria were that the tower either had to be taller than two feet or had to use all of the blocks. Only one block was allowed to touch the floor as a base. During this phase, the child is coached just as during basketball shooting. This includes reminders to "Stop! Think!" about what is being done, the current status of the tower, and how another block will affect its balance.

Step 5: Begin the program. Once baseline data concerning academic performance and behavior have been collected, the actual training begins. Berger experienced success using 3 twenty-minute sessions of basketball shooting per week for 17 sessions, followed by 35 additional sessions, which also included tower building. The number and timing of sessions for other children would vary with both performance during training sessions and performance in the classroom.

Step 6: Observe the effects of the program and strengthen generalization beyond the training environment. These steps rely on the sound judgment of the instructor for their success. It is not possible to provide objective criteria against which to judge the success of the program. However, both classroom observations and behavior within the training situation should be observed. To promote generalization from the training environment to the classroom, Berger taught the hand signal and verbal prompt to the classroom teacher, who was to use them when the child left his seat, was not attending to work, or was playing with other students. Once the hand signal and verbal prompt have been learned by the classroom teacher, they should be used at the teacher's discretion.

Other steps could be taken to promote generalization of learning beyond the school gym. One method would be to employ the training procedure with worksheets and other academic projects. This may require additional individual training. As with all programs in this chapter, it may be useful to refer to the programs in Chapter 10 if academic performance does not improve.

Step 7: Modify the program if necessary. As Berger notes in his article, the success of his program depends in large part on the interaction between child and instructor. This interaction, which was neither described in detail nor monitored by Berger, consisted of encouragement, physical skill training, "challenges," and "conditioning" of the hand signal and verbal prompts. Unfortunately, the exact meaning of "conditioning" in this case is not clear. Presumably, it means that the signals began to be associated with reward whenever the child followed the instructions. That is, reward is much more likely to follow a carefully planned and executed shot than an impulsive or careless one. Success at tower building was also likely to be governed by similar rules.

It seems that the most appropriate modifications of the procedure would involve the nature of the signal and the interaction between child and instructor. More specific instructions or prompts, such as "Stop and aim!" or "Stop! What will happen?" may work better at first. In addition, the success of the verbal prompt and hand signal in the classroom depends at least partially on the child's level of academic functioning and maturity. If the child's skills are weak, more specific training may be beneficial, as described elsewhere in this book.

Step 8: Fade out the program. Fading out the individualized portion of the program can be accomplished by initially skipping an occasional session and then slowly scheduling less frequent meetings. As the end of the program is reached, monthly sessions on an irregular schedule can provide booster training. The hope is that success experienced in academic performance and peer relationships will provide intrinsic rewards for the child.

One of the advantages of Berger's program is that the activities on which it is based can easily be used by the parents at home. It requires some caution to give parents the information necessary to execute the procedures in this chapter. I recommend that parents be introduced to simpler procedures, such as a home-note program. If parents can master and understand this simple, straightforward procedure, then they and their child might benefit from instruction in more sophisticated procedures. If the parents appear cooperative and concerned, extending some of the techniques discussed in this chapter to the home may be helpful. Ideally, parents should observe training sessions both early and late in the school's management program, and then be instructed in techniques similar to the ones they have observed.

If a decision to proceed with parental training is made, several important issues must be considered. Initially, the parents must be given a simple but accurate introduction to the basic principles of child management as explained in Part I. Two general points are of particular importance: First, the parents must be made aware of the need for consistent application of behavior management techniques. Second, an awareness of the nature of their child's behavior problem in strictly behavioral terms should improve their understanding of general principles and lead to more consistent use of management techniques at home. Ideally, with experience, the parents will see the value of behavior management and share responsibility with the school for dealing with their child's problem behavior.

Conclusion and Comment

All the techniques described here have empirically demonstrated validity, but the techniques for decreasing impulsive and inattentive behavior are fairly recent additions to behavior management technology. Thorough study of the current research literature should be undertaken before these techniques are applied. When these or related techniques are implemented, continuous observations of classroom performance and behavior are necessary to ensure that the procedures are useful in the context in which they are applied.

Addressing the broader issues in using techniques to reduce behaviors, it is crucial to remember that the first option is to strengthen the more desirable behaviors that are absent. In the context of conducting a behavior reduction program, it remains vitally important to have parallel programs to strengthen desirable behaviors.

REVIEW

Terms to Remember and Review

behavior excess	timeout
behavior deficit	self-monitoring
pupil support assistant	self-graphing
contingent observation	exclusion timeout
seclusion timeout	response cost lottery

Study and Discussion Questions

1. Describe the response cost lottery. What are its advantages and disadvantages?
2. Why is it important for most classrooms to have a clear set of classroom rules that apply to all students?
3. Give examples of situations or specific behaviors that might justify use of a timeout program.
4. Explain why is is best to describe behavior problems in terms of behavior deficits rather than behavior excesses.
5. What are the key principles that contribute to a successful timeout program?
6. Find out whether the state in which you plan to work has any regulations regarding the use of timeout.
7. Explain the basic principles that underlie cognitive-behavioral therapy, and summarize briefly how these principles are put into practice.

Group Project

Conduct a mock team meeting in order to plan a behavior management program for the following case study:

Case Study.

Ned was a nine-year-old boy referred to the team by his fourth-grade teacher and his parents. He is receiving special education services for a learning disability in the area of reading. The team meeting was called to address concerns about Ned's behavior.

Evaluation revealed that the main concerns of the teacher (as reported on a standardized behavior rating scale) were: (1) being off task most of the time, (2) refusing or failing to complete class assignments, (3) refusing to obey classroom rules, (4) being rejected by peers as a consequence of his behavior, (5) directing physical aggression at peers (about once per week), and (6) failing to follow teacher directives.

Prior to the team meeting, Ned had been moved to a seat in the front of the classroom and had been placed on a home-note program for three weeks. Both interventions were unsuccessful in changing Ned's behavior. In the week before the team meeting, Ned had two incidents of physical aggression toward a peer. In one incident, the other student received two stitches to close a wound that occurred when Ned hit the other student with a ruler.

CHAPTER 9

MANAGEMENT OF BEHAVIOR EXCESSES IN THE HOME

Although the main focus of *Behavior Management in the Schools* is on solving behavior problems in school settings, there are many good reasons for broadening a school-based approach to include the home. First, for many parents, a primary, cost-effective source of mental health services may be school-based professionals. Second, when behavior problems are observed in school, even the best behavior management programs are likely to be more effective if the child experiences similar contingencies at home. Third, by working together cooperatively to solve common problems, the school staff and parents can learn more about each other. Parents can learn about the skills and parental support that a child needs to succeed in school, and the school staff can learn about the child's unique family and cultural background. For these reasons, I believe it is important for schools to provide behavior management consultation to parents whenever possible.

The main goal of this chapter is to describe programs for reducing behavior excesses in the home. The sections cover parent training programs, ignoring and extinction, the use of the coupon program at home, and timeout at home.

PARENT TRAINING PROGRAMS

Schools are in an excellent position to offer a variety of training programs to parents. Parent training programs actually begin as soon as parents walk through the school door. As discussed in Chapter 5, schools have policies and rules that need to be communicated accurately to parents. If school rules and policies are properly presented and clearly explained to parents, they will provide a model of appropriate and effective discipline techniques. A school can also arrange to provide parents with more direct instruction and guidance in handling the challenges of parenting.

Swap (1992), citing Epstein (1988), has suggested that one of several areas of parental involvement in schools is education programs for parents. Swap argues that the most critical elements in successful parent education programs are accurate assessment of parent needs and provision of long-term opportunities to try out new ideas. This means that parents should be surveyed to determine their needs and interests. One-day workshops on topics such as behavior management techniques, school-related problems such as learning disabilities, or ADHD may be requested by significant numbers of parents. The resulting workshops may be interesting and informative and will be even more effective if a follow-up meeting is scheduled to provide an opportunity to try out new skills and techniques and discuss the outcomes. When programs in behavior management are designed with the flexibility to meet the needs of individual parents, they provide the kind of reinforcing feedback that can encourage a cooperative and professional relationship between home and school. Many parents can benefit from training in child management techniques (e.g., Patterson, Chamberlain, & Reid, 1992; Ramsey, Walker, Shinn, O'Neill, & Stieber, 1989; Sheridan, Kratochwill, & Elliott, 1990), and parent training can be an important component of programs to interrupt the chain of circumstances leading to problem behavior (e.g., Mulvey, Arthur, & Reppucci, 1993; Yoshikawa, 1994).

School practitioners have many resources on which to draw when working with parents to modify child behaviors. Numerous informative books about child problems and child management techniques are available. Several of them are listed in Table 9.1.

Other formats for conducting parent training include videotaped programs (Webster-Stratton, Kolpacoff, & Hollinsworth, 1988; Webster-Stratton, Hollinsworth, & Kolpacoff, 1989), combining parent training with family therapy (Brunk, Henggeler, & Whelan, 1987), and various workshops (e.g., Barkley, 1987a, 1987b). For an excellent overview and history of parent training techniques, see Schaefer and Briesmeister (1989).

To close this section, I will review three parent training programs. These programs represent only a fraction of what is available, but each has a strong behavior management emphasis and could prove useful to the school-based professional.

SOS! Help for Parents (Clark, 1985) is the core of a program developed by Lynn Clark. It consists of the *Help for Parents* book, an audiotape on the effective use of timeout, a sixty-five-minute video for parents, and a kit for professionals including the parent book, the audiotape, flip cards on using timeout effectively, and other materials. The program's emphasis is on helping parents handle "common everyday behavior problems." The materials are amusingly illustrated, deal with a wide range of common problems, and are written in a style that parents should find interesting and informative. This program is suitable for parents who are interested in improving their general behavior management skills.

Hyperactivity (ADHD) is one of the most commonly diagnosed behavior problems of school-age children. School staff often find that even a single presentation on hyperactivity may be one of the most well attended events for parents. Among the school psychologists, special education teachers, social workers, and clinical psychologists in your community are likely to be several individuals who could make presentations on this topic.

At the regional or national level, too, speakers are available who could also make an informative, entertaining presentation to parents.

The ADD Hyperactivity Workbook for Parents, Teachers, and Kids (Parker, 1988) is a workbook that contains information about hyperactivity, suggestions for both parents and teachers who are coping with hyperactive children, and a useful appendix of materials (charts, stickers, forms) that can be used for behavior management programming. A very good training program for parents or teachers of hyperactive children could be constructed around this workbook.

For more severe cases of ADHD-related behavior problems where professional leadership is available, the manual and workbook developed by Russell Barkley (Barkley, 1987a, 1987b) may be appropriate. For a more thorough discussion of Barkley's program and a comparison with two other parent training programs, see Newby, Fischer, and Roman (1991).

In sum, a variety of resources exist that could be used to develop school-based parent training programs. This review was far from exhaustive, but I hope the reader who sees a need to develop such programs has been given a good start. In the remaining sections of this chapter, specific programs for managing children's behavior at home will be described.

IGNORING AND EXTINCTION AT HOME

Chapter 1 introduced the most important principle of child behavior management, the Golden Rule of Behavior Management. It is the most effective way to approach general classroom and home discipline. Following this rule not only prevents many minor problems but can also alleviate existing problems. The Golden Rule of Behavior Management is this:

> Ignore, as much as possible, all minor annoyances and misbehavior and spend as much time as possible giving positive attention to students who are behaving correctly.

For parents, the Golden Rule of Behavior Management could be rewritten as follows:

> Ignore, as much as possible, all minor annoyances and misbehavior and spend as much time as possible giving positive attention to your child's desirable behavior.

Table 9.1. Books for Parents

The Difficult Child by Stanley Turecki, M.D., and Leslie Tonner (1985, Bantam Books) is an excellent manual for parents of difficult or hyperactive children. It describes the typical difficult child and provides guidelines for disengaging from conflict and regaining control.

Effective Parents/Responsible Children by Robert Eimers and Robert Aitchison, Ph.D. (McGraw-Hill Book Company, 1978). This book, subtitled *A Guide to Confident Parenting,* provides a general look at the skills needed for effective and confident child rearing. It is a very helpful guide for those who desire to establish consistent rules and consequences for their children.

Training and Habilitating Developmentally Disabled People: An Introduction by Richard M. Wielkiewicz and Christiane R. X. Calvert (1989, Sage Publications, Inc.) emphasizes the practical issues surrounding implementation of behavioral programs for developmentally disabled people. The book is written for parents, paraprofessionals, and others who work with this population.

Sign Here: A Contracting Book for Children and Their Parents by J. C. Dardig and W. L. Heward (1981, F. Fournies and Associates, Inc.) tells the story of a family who needed to develop some rules and consequences for their household. It then explains in simple terms, complete with forms, step-by-step procedures, and concrete examples, how to write simple contracts to perform household duties and fulfill responsibilities.

The ADD Hyperactivity Workbook for Parents, Teachers, and Kids by Harvey C. Parker (1988, Impact Publications, Inc.) contains information on ADHD along with suggestions for teachers, information about medication, a children's story, descriptions of behavior management programs, and other useful material.

SOS! Help for Parents by Lynn Clark (1985, Parents Press) gives detailed instruction on a variety of techniques useful in managing children's behavior. Humorously illustrated, this book provides the parents of any child with concrete, useful information on how to avoid and cope with many common behavior problems.

Hyperactivity: Why Won't My Child Pay Attention? by Sam Goldstein and Michael Goldstein (1992, John Wiley & Sons, Inc.) is described as "a complete guide to ADD for parents, teachers, and community agencies." This thorough, up-to-date book provides information about hyperactivity in adolescents and adults that is not covered in most other books for nonprofessionals.

How to Discipline without Feeling Guilty (Silberman & Wheelan, 1980) is a guide for parents that integrates parenting techniques with a consideration of the principles of assertiveness.

The Good Kid Book (Sloane, 1979) and *How to Help Children with Common Problems* (Schaefer & Millman, 1981) are resources that discuss a wide variety of childhood problems and how parents can cope with them.

A Parent's Guide to Child Discipline by Rudolf Dreikurs and Loren Grey (1970, Hawthorn/Dutton) is a classic book on parenting that covers the entire age spectrum from birth to twenty-one.

"Making the Grade as Parents" (Meyerhoff & White, 1986) is an article that appeared in *Psychology Today.* It discusses how parents can provide their children with an intellectually stimulating environment that allows children to grow independently.

Your Hyperactive Child: A Parent's Guide to Coping with Attention Deficit Disorder by Barbara Ingersoll (1988, Doubleday) describes how medication and behavior management can help parents cope with a hyperactive child.

Childswork Childsplay is the title of a catalog of "materials addressing the mental health needs of children and their families through play." Most of the books described in this table can be ordered through this catalog. It is available from the Center for Applied Psychology, Inc., 441 North 5th Street, Third Floor, Philadelphia, PA 19123. A wide variety of books, games, and other educational and instructional materials are listed in this catalog. School staff members or parents looking for resources on issues such as behavior management, coping with loss, self-esteem, prevention of drug abuse, adjusting to family changes, and other topics are likely to find what they need in this catalog. The ordering phone number is 1-800-962-1141.

Following this rule at school and at home is the best way to prevent behavior problems.

Under many circumstances, however, parents may find it difficult to follow the Golden Rule. Perhaps their own parents modeled ineffective discipline techniques, which they are emulating without realizing just how ineffective they are. Perhaps marital problems interfere with the parents' ability to parent effectively. Perhaps the parents simply lack knowledge and experience in child-rearing practices. Whatever the circumstances, it may be helpful to provide parents with instruction and guidance in how to ignore a problem behavior. A step-by-step description of such a program follows. The core of the program is a parent handout that describes how to apply the Golden Rule of Behavior Management in the home.

Step 1: Identify the problem. Numerous methods for improving children's behavior at home are discussed in this chapter and in Chapter 12. Many parents also could benefit from school-based consultation regarding their children's behavior at home. The perspective taken in this chapter is that one should proceed from the simplest to the most complex solutions. One of the simplest ways to deal with a behavior excess is to ignore the behavior and hope that it goes away. As discussed in Chapter 7, extinction programs may not always work for a variety of reasons, but they are relatively easy to implement. If presented properly to parents, extinction programs may be an effective way to help parents solve a behavior management problem while simultaneously improving the child's functioning in school.

A behavior excess is a behavior that is undesirable and occurs too often. The behavior excesses that parents are most likely to find disturbing include whining and complaining, fighting, excessive yelling, crying, temper tantrums, bothering parents while they are talking on the phone, watching too much television or spending too much time playing electronic games, making excessive demands of parents, refusing to take "no" for an answer, indulging in inappropriate personal habits (e.g., thumb sucking), or eating excessively. Obviously, not all of these behaviors can be reduced simply by ignoring them. Eating and watching TV are behaviors that, themselves, are reinforcing to most children and are not likely to be affected by adult attention. Fighting may be impossible to ignore because it is more important to prevent injury. Some behaviors, however, such as crying, temper tantrums, and complaining, might respond to an extinction program, especially if it is combined with a conscious

effort to provide positive attention for appropriate behavior.

Consultations with parents mean that the consultant must depend on parental reports as the primary source of data. The problems associated with depending on parents as the source of data are outweighed by the advantages of working directly with parents. Although parents may be unable to provide precise baseline data, their long-term experience with the child should enable them to judge with fair accuracy whether a problem behavior occurs with a great enough frequency to warrant some kind of behavioral intervention. Ultimately, parental satisfaction with the intervention is the primary barometer of success.

To gain the trust of parents, an objective, nonaccusatory approach to discovering parental concerns needs to be developed by the consultant. Probably the most important principle to remember is that parents are likely to become uncomfortable and defensive if they are approached in an accusatory or blaming manner. Research into the issue of how people attribute causes indicates that people tend to take credit for positive outcomes and deny responsibility for negative outcomes (Harvey & Weary, 1984). It is particularly important to avoid forcing the parents into making what would be called "internal and stable" attributions. An internal attribution ascribes the cause of an event to some internal characteristic of the individual; a stable attribution is one that cannot be changed. Research into the origins of depression indicates that people who tend to make internal and stable attributions regarding the cause of negative events are good candidates to become depressed (Seligman, Abramson, Semmel, & Von Baeyer, 1979). In other words, if parents come away from a conference feeling that they are "bad parents" (an internal and stable attribution), they may also feel helpless about dealing with the problems of their children. Instead, parents need to leave a conference feeling confident that problems are temporary and solvable.

On a more practical level, the main goal in conferring with parents whose child presents a behavior problem in school and/or at home is to listen carefully to their concerns. Acknowledging the parents' expertness and giving them the opportunity to share information about the child is one of the best ways to accomplish this. Listening to parents (or anyone else) is not just a matter of being polite and quiet. It also means that the listener must truly gain some understanding of the ideas and feelings being communicated. One technique for gaining understanding of another's ideas is to rephrase what has been said and repeat it back to the parents with particular emphasis on acknowledging the feelings that were expressed. By saying things back to the parents in different words, one can check on the accuracy of their own interpretation of what has been said.

Sometimes, of course, important thoughts and feelings are left unsaid. For this reason, it is also important to attend to the body language of the parents. If they appear uncomfortable or hostile, it may be fruitful to inquire whether they are satisfied with the conclusions or direction of the consultation. This can often be most easily accomplished by making an indirect inquiry rather than approaching the potential problem head on. For instance, asking parents how they have been coping with a particular behavior may reveal that many things have been tried unsuccessfully or that they feel helpless and have given up trying to cope with the problem. In either case, it is up to the school staff to come up with fresh approaches, instill confidence in the plan developed by the team, and ensure that the parents have input into the final plan.

Development of the plan begins with developing an understanding of the child's behavior from the parents' perspective. It may be helpful to begin by asking parents to complete a brief assessment instrument or checklist, such as the Home Situations Questionnaire (Barkley, 1991). This instrument can then serve to structure the discussion with the parents. Once potential target behaviors are identified, the next step is to determine whether it is appropriate to use an extinction program to decrease them.

Step 2: Refine the definition of the problem. The handout shown in Table 9.2 is meant to help parents and the school-based consultant to arrive at a common understanding of how to ignore a behavior. As discussed previously, a behavior that is reinforcing in itself (e.g., watching TV, avoiding chores, continuing to play outside after parents have summoned you home) is likely to continue even if it is ignored by both parents. However, behaviors that cause conflict between child and parent (e.g., repeatedly making an unreasonable request), lead to sympathy (e.g., being hurt in a wrestling match with a sibling), or cause irritation (e.g., bothering parents when they are talking on the phone) may be appropriate behaviors for parents to ignore. If the target behavior or behaviors are not dangerous to the child, ignoring can be an effective, easy-to-use intervention that may lead to improved behavior.

Part of the role of assisting parents to effectively manage their children's behavior is to help them specifi-

cally define behaviors that need to be changed. The idea of carefully considering the nature of the target behavior may be new to some parents. Parents may have a tendency to use global labels—"good," "bad," "hyper," "lazy," "annoying," "disobedient," "mean." As discussed in Chapter 3, target behaviors need to be defined in terms that are concrete and measurable so that the conditions for applying the rules of the behavior management program can be consistently applied to the same behaviors.

For example, if the problem behavior is labeled as "disruptiveness" by the child's parents, they will likely need some help in specifying just what this means. For some parents, "disruptive" may mean that the child bothers them while they are on the phone , whereas other parents may define "disruptive" as watching TV instead of getting ready for school in the morning. The precise nature of potential target behaviors can be established by asking parents for examples. Parents also need to understand that a concrete definition of target behaviors will enable them to perform the behavior management program in a consistent manner. This is particularly important when ignoring a behavior.

Step 3: Assess the baseline rate. Parents may lack the motivation, time, or organizational skills to do a baseline assessment. The program described in Table 9.2 attempts to get around this problem by combining the beginning of the program with collection of data on its effectiveness. Consultants need to impress upon parents the importance of having some means of evaluating the effectiveness of any intervention. Reference to programs conducted in the school may be helpful as an illustration of this point. However, parents are likely to be most cooperative when data collection is combined with the start of the actual program. As discussed in Table 9.2, parents are instructed to write down each occurrence of the target behavior(s) as a means of collecting data and removing themselves from the situation where behavior is to be ignored. Parents can be given copies of Figure 8.1, the Sample Data Chart, to help them with their record keeping.

Step 4: Design the behavioral contingencies and write the program description. When an extinction or ignoring program is used, the reinforcer is adult attention provided contingent on the undesirable behavior. The goal is to reverse this contingency so the child now receives parental attention contingent only on desirable behavior, and all occurrences of the undesirable behavior are ignored. It is important to emphasize to parents that once an ignoring program is started, it is crucial not

Table 9.2. Sample Parent Handout for an Extinction/Ignoring Program (Richard M. Wielkiewicz)

When children misbehave, the instinctive response of many parents is to say something like "Stop it!" This almost always leads to instant gratification for the parent because the misbehavior comes to an immediate halt. However, some children have a need for adult attention that is greater than their need to avoid negative words from their parents. In this case, it is actually possible for the child's behavior to get worse as a consequence of being scolded for misbehavior.

Here is what happens. First the child misbehaves and is scolded for the behavior. Then the child immediately stops the misbehavior. Children who need a lot of adult attention, however, may do the same thing again after a short time in order to receive the attention they crave. The result is that the misbehavior actually occurs *more* often. As time goes on, the child is scolded more and more often without any long-term effect, and what began as a small episode of misbehavior grows and grows until it is a frustrating behavior problem.

What can a parent do in this situation? Possible answers include using timeout, setting up a complex sticker or point system, or taking away privileges such as television when misbehavior occurs. Before the more complicated procedures are attempted, however, there is something much simpler that parents can try. *They can ignore misbehavior, and it just may go away without any other effort.* Ignoring behavior is a simple strategy that can be used without much effort, although it does take a lot of discipline. Because ignoring behavior is relatively easy to do, it makes sense to try this simple technique first before attempting other, more complicated, interventions.

How to Ignore Misbehavior
1. The first step in ignoring misbehavior is to decide exactly what misbehavior(s) to ignore. This needs to be considered carefully because any inconsistency in ignoring behavior will cause problems later on. Also, both parents, whether living together or separated, need to agree to ignore the selected behaviors consistently. Use the spaces below to write down exactly what behaviors are to be ignored. Make your descriptions as concrete and specific as possible.

    Behaviors to be ignored:
    A.
    _____
    B.
    _____
    C.
    _____
    D.
    _____
    E.
    _____

2. The second step is to decide exactly *how* behavior is to be ignored. To ignore behavior effectively means to do nothing that may give attention to the misbehavior. One effective method of ignoring misbehavior is to leave the immediate area where misbehavior is occurring and go make a notation that one of the misbehaviors has occurred again. This has two very important advantages. First, leaving the immediate area ensures that the behavior has been effectively ignored. Second, by taking time to note which of the misbehaviors occurred, you construct a record that can be used to judge whether ignoring is effective. If the number of times the behavior occurs slowly decreases, the strategy is effective and should be continued. Parents who use this strategy should be cautioned that behaviors may actually *increase* early on. This is actually a positive sign because it indicates that the ignoring is effective and that decreases in misbehaviors will soon be seen.

3. Ignoring behavior, by itself, is only one of two things that need to happen to make success as likely as possible. The second thing is that positive attention needs to be directed at acceptable behavior. This means putting extra effort and energy into giving the child attention when he or she is playing alone, performing chores, doing homework, or doing any other acceptable activity. By directing more frequent attention toward positive behavior, you help the child to learn more acceptable ways of getting attention from adults. When giving attention to the child's good behavior, be sure to be specific and immediate. That is, tell the child exactly what it is you like, and do so immediately—don't wait until later.

to attend to any instances of the target behavior. Attention that a child sees as reinforcing may consist of saying "Stop that," giving the child a "dirty look," or even sighing in exasperation. The result of providing any attention may be a behavior that is even more frequent and resistant to any attempts to eliminate it by ignoring or other means.

Step 5: Begin the program. Table 9.2, the Sample Parent Handout, should be thoroughly reviewed with the child's parents before they are allowed to begin the program. It is particularly important that clear definitions of the behaviors to be ignored be developed, along with a clear and workable plan for actually ignoring the behavior. Although a plan for how to behave while ignoring behavior may seem unnecessary, most parents will find ignoring behavior much easier when they have a specific activity to perform. Walking away and recording the occurrence of the behavior has the dual advantage of being a behavior that is unlikely to reinforce the child's behavior while simultaneously providing the information needed to judge the success of the program.

Step 6: Observe the effects of the program and initiate steps to strengthen generalization beyond the training environment. Parents must accomplish two key things to ensure that their program is a complete success. The first is to be sure that the child receives plenty of reinforcement when he or she is *not* engaging in the behaviors that are being ignored. The second is to be sure that other adults (grandparents, neighbors, friends) do not reinforce the target behaviors. If ignoring is consistently applied in all environments into which the child goes, it is unlikely that the target behavior will return.

Step 7: Modify the program if necessary. As the program proceeds, parents are likely to tire quickly of recording data on its success. Fortunately, when a behavior excess is targeted for change, this is often not a major problem. However, the school-based consultant should make a sincere attempt to assess whether the parents are subjectively satisfied with their attempt to ignore the behavior excess. If they are not satisfied, perhaps a more structured program involving response cost or timeout is needed. On the other hand, a successful program is likely to enhance the status of the school-based consultants and make it more likely that other problems can be solved.

Step 8: Fade out the program. As with most programs for reducing behavior excesses, fading out the

program is not a major problem because a decline in the target behavior is accompanied by a parallel decline in the use of the program. However, it is important to continue a steady diet of positive attention and reinforcement for appropriate behavior. Otherwise, the child may resort to inappropriate behavior to gain lost attention.

RESPONSE COST CONTINGENCIES AT HOME

Ignoring behavior is the easiest way to eliminate some behavior excesses. Another approach is to use response cost or other negative punishment procedures. Recall that negative punishment is defined as removing something desirable contingent on undesirable behavior. For example, if a child is devoted to playing electronic games, removing access to these games contingent on misbehavior should lead to a decline in the frequency of the misbehavior. Many parents successfully employ this discipline strategy with their children. It is relatively simple and very effective.

Some parents may need assistance in developing an effective response cost program for their misbehaving child. This section describes two response cost strategies that parents can use. The first, an extension of the coupon program described in Chapter 7, is described using the eight-step procedure. Table 9.3 shows a parent handout that can be used in conjunction with this program.

Step 1: Identify the problem. As discussed in Chapter 7, a coupon program can be effective with a variety of undesirable behaviors, ranging from being off task to failing to comply with adult commands. Coupon programs are flexible and can be used to reduce several target behaviors at the same time. Selection of appropriate target behaviors for a home-based program will depend on the needs of the parents and on what behavior management programs are already used in the school environment. Virtually any inappropriate behavior could be the target of a coupon program. Developing a definition of such behaviors will require an open, frank discussion with the child's parents.

For younger children, some of the most common behavior problems include engaging in play at inappropriate times such as when the child should be getting ready for school, failing to obey parental commands, fighting with siblings of similar age, teasing or hitting younger siblings, disobeying specific household rules, playing carelessly or dangerously, having temper tantrums, or intentionally damaging toys or household furnishings. As suggested previously, it may be helpful to ask parents to complete a brief assessment instrument or checklist such as the Home Situations Questionnaire (Barkley, 1991).

Step 2: Refine the definition of the problem. Basically, I suggest one of two approaches to refining the definition of the problem behavior. One approach is to develop a working definition of one or two important problem behaviors and focus the behavior management efforts on them. An alternative approach is to help the parents develop a set of household rules that covers all or most of the misbehaviors that concern them. An effective set of household rules might consist of the following:

Rule 1: (child's name) must be ready to catch the school bus at 7:35 A.M. every weekday morning.

Rule 2: No running, screaming, or baseball playing in the house.

Rule 3: No hitting or teasing your younger sister.

Rule 4 _____ must obey the commands of his parents.

Once a set of household rules has been developed, misbehavior is defined as any violation of the rules. Parents are likely to need assistance in developing a set of household rules or in defining a target behavior for a coupon program. See Chapter 5 for a discussion of the characteristics of good rules.

Step 3: Assess the baseline rate. Assessment of the baseline rate is one of the most problematic phases of developing a home-based behavior management pro-

---

Table 9.3. Sample Parent Handout for Timeout and Other Discipline Techniques

---

Some Practical Discipline Techniques for Parents of Children with Difficult Behavior Problems

Richard M. Wielkiewicz, Ph.D.

The best general approach to children's behavior is to ignore undesirable behavior whenever possible and give lots of positive attention AND reinforcement for the behaviors you like. Most interactions with your child should be positive rather than disciplinary. If this approach is followed, many problems can be avoided. However, some children are likely to be "in trouble" at least sometimes, and parents need to respond effectively so the child is less likely to repeat the behavior. This handout outlines some general guidelines and specific techniques that parents can use for responding to misbehavior.

Things to Think about Before Attempting to Discipline Your Child

Always remember the "golden rule of behavior management," which states that the best general approach to child discipline is to *ignore* inappropriate behavior and pay attention to good behavior. Keeping this simple idea in mind will allow even the most conscientious parents to avoid unnecessary or unproductive confrontations with their child. The sections below offer additional guidelines.

Consistency
It is not possible or realistic to be a perfectly consistent parent. The concept of consistency has caused a lot of unnecessary guilt for parents who sometimes lack the energy or time to respond in the same way to each misbehavior of their child. *It is not necessary to respond in the same consistent manner to each misbehavior. However, once parents have decided to confront their child's misbehavior, they must then consistently follow through until the problem is resolved and the child has complied with all commands.* It is entirely O.K. for parents to walk away from their child's misbehavior when it is impossible to follow through because of lack of energy or time. In fact, ignoring misbehavior often will make it *less* likely in the future. On the other hand, it is important for parents to communicate that they are a source of authority that their children must obey.

Consider an example. If a child comes home and tosses his jacket on the floor of the living room, it is perfectly O.K. for his parent(s) to ignore the behavior and avoid a confrontation. On the other hand, it is not acceptable to tell the child to hang up the jacket unless you are ready and able to follow through on the problem until the child has hung up the jacket. The child must learn that when a parent gives a command, he or she must eventually comply. Telling the child to hang up the jacket without enforcing the command just teaches the child that it is O.K. to ignore parental commands. Parents need to be selective in giving commands to their children, because once a command is given, it is important to follow through until it is obeyed.

Behaviors to Discipline
Parents determine what behaviors are to be punished and what behaviors should be ignored. This decision needs to be made before behaviors actually occur, especially with children who are impulsive and have difficulty learning to follow rules. Parents who find themselves overwhelmed by the prospect of gaining control of their child's behavior need to be very careful and selective. Not every problem can be solved right away. Instead, setting limited goals such as eliminating one or two important misbehaviors is the best way to maintain reasonable consistency and regain control.

Rules

The best way to begin a discipline program is to establish at set of household rules for your child. The rules should be simple and easy to understand, and it should be very easy for either parent to judge whether the rule has been broken. A maximum of three or four rules is best for young children. Rules can be added for older children. One rule can be a catch-all that covers a variety of situations, such as "follow all your parents' commands." The other rules should be directed at the most important problems. Using rules as the basis of your discipline program enables your child to learn that behavior has consequences. Learning to anticipate the consequences of actions and then make a decision about what to do is one of the key skills that children need to learn. Giving children a set of consistently enforced rules helps them learn this lesson. However, because a rule has the force of a parental command, do not make a rule unless you intend to enforce it as consistently as possible.

How to Enforce the Rules

When a child violates a household rule, there are essentially three ways that the parents can reduce the child's tendency to do the same thing again. First, they can present something unpleasant to the child, like a spanking or a brief period sitting in a chair with nothing to do. The second way of responding to misbehavior is to take something desirable away from the child. Paying a fine for an overdue library book is a good example of this method. The third response is to have the child restore the environment to its original condition or a condition that is better than it was before the child misbehaved.

Timeout

Timeout has been shown to be a valuable technique for disciplining children with behavior problems. Like all discipline techniques, it can be difficult to administer under some circumstances. For instance, if the child refuses to go to or remain in timeout, parents do not have very many options. For this reason, parents who wish to use timeout may want to attend a workshop where individualized supervision and discussion of problems are available. In this way, any problems that occur can be resolved within a short time. The instructions for administering timeout given in this handout will be effective for most parents, but some parents will need additional help in developing strategies to cope with their child's responses to it.

It is important to begin a timeout program with a clear idea of what behaviors will result in timeout. A set of clear, fair household rules can be a great help in this regard. Also, parents should avoid giving commands to their children when they are not prepared to administer consequences. When a child complies with a command or is behaving appropriately, he or she should be praised and should receive positive attention for it. When the child does not comply with a command or breaks an important household rule, he or she should receive an immediate consequence. It is *not* effective to scold or nag the child because this gives a lot of attention and makes the misbehavior more likely to occur in the future. Sending the child to a timeout for failing to obey commands or breaking important rules is a very effective method of punishment. Behaviors that are not confronted can be ignored, and all parents should remember that ignoring a behavior is a very effective and acceptable way of making it less likely that the behavior will occur again.

If you plan to use timeout with your child, the first thing to do is select a location. A hard kitchen chair in a dull, boring area of the house will work best. Place the chair so the child is not able to reach anything or see a television while sitting in it. The chair should be in a place where it can be seen from other places in the home, so the parent can continue other activities while watching the child. Sending children to their own rooms is not as effective as using a chair, laundry room, stairway, or bathroom because many playthings are available in the child's own room. Choosing a good location for timeout makes it easy to enforce when needed.

If the child engages in inappropriate behavior or fails to obey a command, parents may give the child a single warning, count silently to five, and take the child to the timeout area or order him or her to go there alone. The sequence goes like this (adapted from Barkley, 1981, 1987b; Clark, 1985; Eimers & Aitchison, 1978):

1. When you give your child a command, use a firm but pleasant voice and do not phrase the command as a question. Make a direct, assertive statement. It may be helpful to have the child repeat the command to ensure it has been heard and comprehended. If, after five seconds, the child has not started to comply, repeat the command along with a warning that the child will be in timeout if he or she does not do what you ordered. Alternatively, the child may have broken a household rule that both parents agree should result in a timeout.
2. If the child has broken a household rule (e.g., hitting a younger sibling, swearing, or talking back to a parent) or has failed to heed a command after one warning, he or she should immediately go to the preselected timeout location. The more quickly the child goes to timeout, the more effective the timeout will be, because it will be clear to the child exactly what behavior is being punished.
3. The rule is that once a punished behavior occurs, the child goes *directly* to timeout. The child does not say "No!" And he or she does not collect any positive attention.
4. Once placed in the preselected timeout location, the child remains there until given permission to leave by the parent. An alternative method, highly recommended by Clark (1985), is the use of a portable timer to gauge the timeout length. When the bell of the timer rings, the child may leave the timeout area. The disadvantage of this method is that if the child continues to tantrum or misbehave during the timeout, it is more difficult for the parent to extend the timeout.

Table 9.3. Continued

5. When the child is *quiet,* and the appropriate *length of timeout* has been served, you may go to him or her and repeat the original command. If the child still refuses, timeout may be continued until the child complies with the command. When the child complies with the comand, he or she is to be praised in a neutral voice without any apology for the timeout. If the child is in timeout for something that cannot be corrected, he or she may be allowed to leave the chair once the time is up and he or she has been quiet. If the child refuses to go to or remain in timeout, the individual(s) who provided this handout should be contacted for advice.

6. After the child has completed the timeout, watch for his or her next desirable behavior. Then go to the child and give positive feedback for behaving appropriately. This shows your child that you are not angry and are willing to praise good behavior. The child also learns that *behavior* leads to punishment or praise; therefore, a choice of behavior is also a choice of consequences. This also balances the program so the child is never punished more than he or she is praised.

The child stays in the chair until he or she is quiet *and* the timeout has been long enough to be unpleasant. One or two minutes of timeout for each year of age is usually recomended. Children under four years of age require only a few minutes. Children between five and eight years may require five to fifteen minutes. Those over eight years may require ten to thirty minutes. The child does not leave the chair until he or she is quiet, even if this extends the timeout to an hour or more. Eventually, the child will learn to be quiet immediately upon being sent to timeout. The child also misses any activities that happen while he or she is in timeout. This is what makes timeout so effective.

To begin using timeout, punish only one or two specific behaviors for the first couple of weeks. This will prevent overuse of punishment and enable you to see some immediate progress. Use one of the timeout record forms that appear at the end of this handout to keep a record of the length and reason for each timeout. As time passes, the punished behaviors should decrease. As this occurs, timeout can be used with a wider number of behaviors. If you experience difficult problems, such as the child leaving the timeout chair without permission, consult with a professional before continuing to use timeout. Also, keep in mind that timeout is an abbreviation of the phrase "time out from positive reinforcement." Timeout is effective only if the child receives a lot of positive feedback and reinforcement when he or she is behaving appropriately, doing what is expected, or obeying commands.

If fighting between siblings is the problem behavior, placing both children in timeout is probably the best solution because it is next to impossible to determine fairly "who started it." By placing both children in timeout, you are letting them know that they share responsibility for getting along peacefully.

Restoring the Environment
Another effective way to deal with misbehavior is to make the child restore the environment to the condition it was in before the misbehavior. This is appropriate when the child has made a mess, forgotten to clean up after a project, broken something in anger or out of carelessness, or done something else that spoils the environment. Logical consequences and restitution are other names for this method. For instance, if it is a household rule to wipe your feet or take off shoes before entering the house, a logical response to breaking the rule is to make the child mop the dirty floor. The first few times you try this, the child may need to spend time in the timeout chair before complying.

Taking Away Something Valuable
Another way to respond to misbehavior is to take away something valuable when the child misbehaves. An ideal application of this technique is found in a token program. If the child violates one of the rules of the token program, an appropriate number of tokens can be taken away. Another way of applying this technique is to reduce the child's allowance by 10 or 20 percent when he or she misbehaves. A problem with this method concerns how immediate the "response cost" or fine is. A fifty-cent fine on Monday may not work if the allowance is not given until later in the week. On the other hand, children need to learn that their behavior has long-term consequences, so with the right child this technique could be effective.

One way to bridge the gap between a fine and the later loss of money or another reward is by using what I call the coupon program. A variation of the coupon program works well in public places such as a shopping mall, church, or anyplace where it is difficult to administer timeout. On a shopping trip, for instance, three rules could be established: (1) Stay right next to me unless you have permission to go somewhere else, (2) do not touch anything without permission, and (3) obey all commands of your parents. Give the child eight coupons and say that each time a rule is broken he or she loses a coupon. If five coupons are left when it is time to leave, the child can have a valuable reward; if only one coupon is left, the child can have a much smaller reward. If all the coupons are taken away, the trip is immediately ended and the child spends time in the timeout chair at home. Parents who use this program with their child need to be fairly strict and prepared to end a couple of shopping trips prematurely. Later, a real improvement in the child's behavior in public should be noticeable.

Directions: Each timeout should be documented by logging the following information. If no timeout is administered (such as during baseline observations), write NA in the space for "timeout length."

Child's Name: _____

Date: _____ Time: _____ Location: _____

Incident: _____

_____

Timeout Location/Method: _____

Starting Time for Timeout: _____ Ending Time for Timeout: _____

Timeout Length: _____

Comments: _____

_____

Child's name: _____

Date: _____ Time: _____ Location: _____

Incident: _____

_____

Timeout Location/Method: _____

Starting Time for Timeout: _____ Ending Time for Timeout: _____

Timeout Length: _____

Comments: _____

_____

---

gram. The most successful approach is to keep the baseline measurement as simple as possible. Even then, many parents express a desire to begin a program immediately rather than wait until a baseline is established. The school-based consultant will need to consider carefully what is in the child's best interests in developing a plan with parents. In some cases, establishing an accurate baseline may be imperative. In other cases, establishing a friendly relationship with parents may dictate that the proposed program be begun as soon as possible. If it is possible to establish a baseline, parents may find the form presented in Figure 8.1 to be a useful and convenient way to record baseline information.

Step 4: Design the behavioral contingencies and write the program description. The coupon program gives a child a number of coupons that can be exchanged for attractive rewards or prizes. The child keeps these coupons as long as he or she is behaving appropriately. When misbehavior or a rule violation occurs, one of the coupons is taken away from the child (hence, the negative contingency). The loss of a coupon is a mild negative punishment that makes it less likely that the child will repeat the undesirable behavior. This contingency can be just as effective at home as in the school environment.

The contingency in the coupon program works like

Directions for using the Record of Timeouts
Each time your child emits a physically aggressive behavior, put a *slash* through the next number on the chart. If timeout is administered, *circle* the number
For purposes of this program, physical aggression is defined as any of the following behaviors:

—hitting —spitting
—kicking —throwing objects toward another person
—biting —slapping
—pushing —unwanted physical contact

Day	Number of Aggressions	Comments	Week _____
Mon	1 2 3 4 5 6 7 8 9 10		
Tue	1 2 3 4 5 6 7 8 9 10		
Wed	1 2 3 4 5 6 7 8 9 10		
Thur	1 2 3 4 5 6 7 8 9 10		
Fri	1 2 3 4 5 6 7 8 9 10		
Sat	1 2 3 4 5 6 7 8 9 10		
Sun	1 2 3 4 5 6 7 8 9 10		

Weekly Total for Aggressions _____

Day	Number of Aggressions	Comments	Week _____
Mon	1 2 3 4 5 6 7 8 9 10		
Tue	1 2 3 4 5 6 7 8 9 10		
Wed	1 2 3 4 5 6 7 8 9 10		
Thur	1 2 3 4 5 6 7 8 9 10		
Fri	1 2 3 4 5 6 7 8 9 10		
Sat	1 2 3 4 5 6 7 8 9 10		
Sun	1 2 3 4 5 6 7 8 9 10		

Weekly Total for Aggressions _____

Day	Number of Aggressions	Comments	Week _____
Mon	1 2 3 4 5 6 7 8 9 10		
Tue	1 2 3 4 5 6 7 8 9 10		
Wed	1 2 3 4 5 6 7 8 9 10		
Thur	1 2 3 4 5 6 7 8 9 10		
Fri	1 2 3 4 5 6 7 8 9 10		
Sat	1 2 3 4 5 6 7 8 9 10		
Sun	1 2 3 4 5 6 7 8 9 10		

Weekly Total for Aggressions _____

Timeout Record

this: The child is given a predetermined number of coupons and loses one of them each time a rule is violated or a designated misbehavior occurs. The coupons themselves can be made of laminated paper with an original design on them. In consultation with the child's parents, the day can be divided into time blocks such as morning, afternoon, evening, and bedtime. The child begins each time block with a predetermined number of coupons, typically around five to ten. A wallet, small purse, or holder taped to the refrigerator can be used to store the coupons. Prominently displaying the household rules and reviewing them regularly with the child may improve the effectiveness of the program. Little and Kelley (1989) used a sheet of paper with "smile faces" printed on it. When misbehavior occurred, a smile face was crossed off, and rewards were determined by the number of smile faces remaining at the end of the designated time period.

The specific contingency is that a coupon is taken from the child or a smile face is crossed off when parents see a designated misbehavior. If a parental command is issued, the child loses a coupon or smile face if he or she fails to comply with the command after a single warning. Typically, loss of a coupon should be accompanied with a brief description of the misbehavior. For example, "you lose a coupon (smile face) when you tease your sister." Alternatively, when either parent issues a command, the sequence may be like this: "Tammy, it's nine o'clock and time for you to go to bed." If the child fails to comply within five seconds or so, a warning is issued. "Tammy, if you don't go to bed right now, you will lose a coupon (smile face)." If the child fails to comply, a coupon or smile face is taken away after five seconds. The command can then be repeated and the sequence begun again. It may be very helpful to role-play a couple of sequences with the school-based consultant playing the role of the child and the parents responding to the "child's" misbehavior.

Like all token-based programs, a coupon program depends on a menu of reinforcers. The reinforcers on the menu can be "purchased" by the child using the coupons that remain at the end of each time period. Families should control access to a number of activities and material rewards that can be used.

A fairly typical menu of rewards might look like this:

3 coupons	Access to TV or electronic game
	Small amount of money added to allowance
5 coupons	Small school supplies
	Stay up half an hour later on Friday
10 coupons	Candy or favorite snack
	Receives 50 cents
15 coupons	Parents perform assigned chore for child
	Allowed to stay out past usual curfew
20 coupons	Package of sports cards
	Small toy or game
50 coupons	Movie rental and popcorn
	Stay overnight at a friend's house
100 coupons	Receives money to treat family to dinner
	Invite several friends to stay overnight
	Money to buy tape or compact disk

The reward menu needs to be adjusted to the needs of the child and the parents. Direct negotiation with the child is essential to develop the most effective menu of rewards. It is crucial to remember that rewards are specific to the individual . Rewards that are very motivating to one child may be boring and uninteresting to another child. At the same time, one child's preferences in rewards may also change. The success of any behavior management program based on rewards depends on the flexibility of this aspect of the program.

A variation of the coupon program can be used in public. It works especially well in places such as a shopping mall, church, or grocery store. On a shopping trip, for instance, three rules could be established:

1. Stay right next to me unless you have permission to go somewhere else.
2. Do not touch anything without permission.
3. Obey all commands of your parents.

Give the child eight coupons and say that each time a rule is broken, the child loses a coupon. If five coupons are left when it is time to leave, the child can have a valuable reward; if only one coupon is left, the child can have a much smaller reward. If all coupons are taken away, the trip is immediately ended and the child spends time in a timeout chair at home. Parents who use this program with their child need to be fairly strict and prepared to end a couple of shopping trips early. Later, a real improvement in the child's behavior in public should be noticeable. The program can be used alone or linked to a reinforcer menu and coupon program at home.

Step 5: Begin the program. Table 9.4 presents a handout that can accompany a home-based coupon program.

Table 9.4 Sample Parent Handout for a Home-Based Coupon Program (Richard M. Wielkiewicz)

A token is just like money—something of little or no value that can be exchanged for something desirable. Money cannot be eaten and won't keep a person warm, but it can be used to purchase food and shelter. Both adults and children work hard to obtain money because of the goods and services it can purchase. Likewise, tokens have no inherent value but they can be used to "purchase" valuable rewards. Gold stars, points, marbles, specially marked pieces of paper, smile faces, stickers, poker chips, or anything else that can be easily delivered to a child and then saved can be used as a token. When children learn that tokens can be exchanged for valuable rewards and activities, they will work hard to earn and keep them.

The main advantage of token programs is that they allow great flexibility in rewarding behavior. If highly motivating rewards are placed on the reward menu, desired behavior will increase and undesirable behavior will decrease within a relatively short period of time. It is particularly important that the reward menu be negotiated with the child. Without the child's input, any token program may fail. Money is one nearly universal reinforcer that almost always works. Other possible reinforcers include a party, school supplies, taking the family out for pizza, small toys, children's collectible items (baseball cards, marbles, etc.), large toys, special activities (sports camps, camping trips, fishing trips, etc.), clothing, tapes, compact disks, or anything else parents find acceptable. More tokens are needed to "purchase" more valuable or desirable rewards.

A fairly typical menu of rewards might look like this:

3 coupons	Access to TV or electronic game
5 coupons	Small school supplies
10 coupons	Candy or favorite snack
15 coupons	Parents perform assigned chore for child
20 coupons	Package of baseball cards
50 coupons	Movie rental and popcorn
100 coupons	Receives money to treat family to dinner

The reward menu needs to be adjusted to the needs of the child and the parents. Of course, money or an allowance can be "purchased" with coupons. Direct negotiation with the child is essential to develop the most effective menu of rewards.

The program described in this handout involves a simple rule. When the child misbehaves or fails to obey a command after one warning, a token or coupon is taken away. The loss of the token, which represents desirable rewards, serves to punish the misbehavior. The basic procedure is described below.

1. The child receives a predetermined number of coupons for a designated time period. Dividing the day into three or four time periods should work well. The number of coupons given to the child during this period should approximately correspond to the typical number of misbehaviors the child emits. Thus, if the child is able to improve by just a small amount, a few coupons should remain at the end of the time period.
2. Each time the child disobeys one of the established rules or fails to obey a parental command, one coupon is taken away without any negative comments. However, it is appropriate simply to state the rule that was violated.
3. If the child runs out of coupons, then no more can be taken away. The child never goes into "debt" because this would be unnecessarily discouraging. The best response to misbehavior after the child runs out of coupons is to ignore it.
4. At the end of the designated time period or as soon as convenient, the child is allowed to deposit the coupons that remain into a "bank." These coupons, once earned, may not be lost regardless of the child's behavior. Again, the goal is to get the child going on a positive track. Another important aspect of any behavior management program is to record the number of coupons lost during each time period. This daily record provides a yardstick for measuring how much behavior is improving.
5. To monitor the effects of the coupon program, it is only necessary to keep an accurate count of the number of coupons lost by the child during each time period. The expectation is that this number will steadily decline.
6. Although this program depends on loss of coupons, tokens, or smile faces for misbehavior, the importance of giving positive attention and reinforcement to children at every opportunity must be emphasized. Learning *not* to misbehave is only part of any child's task. Children also must learn what behaviors are expected and admired by parents. Parents communicate this by praising and rewarding behavior.
7. A variation of the coupon program can be used in public. It works especially well in places such as a shopping mall, church, or grocery store. On a shopping trip, for instance, three rules could be established: (a) Stay right next to me unless you have permission to go somewhere else, (b) do not touch anything without permission, and (c) obey all commands of your parents. Give the child eight coupons, and say that each time a rule is broken he or she loses a coupon. If five coupons are left when it is time to leave, the child can have a valuable reward; if only one coupon is left, the child can have a much smaller reward. If all the coupons are taken away, the trip is immediately ended and

the child spends time in a timeout chair at home. Parents who use this program with their child need to be fairly strict and prepared to end a couple of shopping trips early. Later, a real improvement in the child's behavior in public should be noticeable. The program can be used alone or linked to a reinforcer menu and coupon program at home.

8. As the program begins to show positive effects, it can be faded out in a number of different ways. The goal is to fade away the program to a level at which the parents are satisfied. There are numerous ways to accomplish this. First, the child can be given fewer coupons, expected to last a longer period of time, and the prices on the reward menu can be increased so that longer periods without misbehavior are necessary to earn rewards. Another approach is to announce an end to the program after the child has earned enough coupons for a major reward and to make the reward a celebration of the child's accomplishment. A new set of household rules can then be established using a more natural group of mild punishers such as loss of television privileges or some other attractive activity when misbehavior occurs. A more typical allowance can also be substituted for the coupon program. If misbehavior that cannot be ignored occurs, a reduction in the amount of the weekly allowance or a more acceptable or appropriate mild punishment can be used.

Again, the school-based consultant must make every effort to be sure that the program is well understood and that parents have made the decisions needed to run the program effectively. A phone call or meeting a couple of days after the program is begun may help clear up misunderstandings or iron out the wrinkles in the program.

Step 6: Observe the effects of the program and initiate steps to strengthen generalization beyond the training environment. As briefly explained in Table 9.4, one advantage of a coupon program is that the confiscated coupons provide a quick and easy record of the frequency of target behaviors. All parents need to do is write down how many coupons were taken away during each time period to provide an excellent measure of progress. The expectation is that fewer and fewer coupons will be taken away from the child as time passes. As the target behaviors are eliminated, the consultant will need to help the parents articulate their expectations regarding acceptable discipline methods and then develop a plan for fading the coupon program. If misbehaviors are infrequent, natural contingencies or logical consequences can be substituted for the formal program. For example, failure to obey a parental command could result in loss of TV privileges for the evening, temporary confinement in the child's bedroom, or any other mild punishment was acceptable to the parents.

Step 7: Modify the program if necessary. If the program is unsuccessful, several avenues can be explored. The first part of the program to examine is the menu of rewards. Perhaps this needs to be renegotiated with the child. Another potential problem is whether the program is being properly administered. Finally, it may be possible that family issues such as marital distress are preventing the parents from devoting the necessary energy to the behavior management program. It may be necessary to refer the parents to a family therapist, child clinical psychologist, or other mental health professional if factors beyond the expertise of school-based professionals are found to be involved in the child's behavior problems.

Step 8: Fade out the program. As discussed previously, fading out the program depends on what the parents consider acceptable in the way of informally dealing with the common misbehaviors of children. The coupon program itself can be faded out with the usual techniques. That is, the child can be given fewer coupons expected to last a longer period of time, and the prices on the reward menu can be increased so that longer periods with fewer misbehaviors are necessary to earn rewards. Another approach is to announce an end to the program after the child has earned enough coupons for a major reward and then to make the reward a celebration of the child's accomplishment. A new set of household rules can then be established using a more natural group of mild punishers, such as loss of TV privileges or some other attractive activity when misbehavior occurs. What is important is that alternatives for handling misbehavior effectively, including ignoring whenever appropriate, be developed.

TIMEOUT AT HOME

Timeout can be as effective in the home as it is in schools for reducing behavior excesses (e.g., Allison & Allison, 1971; Barkley, 1981, 1990; Pisterman et al., 1989; Roberts & Powers, 1990; Williams, Williams, & McLaughlin, 1991b). In most cases, administering timeout at home is a simple, practical, and effective discipline strategy that parents can quickly learn. However, timeout *can* be difficult to administer, even for experienced behavior management technicians. Thus, teaching parents to use timeout needs to be approached cautiously, depending on the circumstances. For example, parents of a kindergarten child may be disturbed that their child frequently fights with a sibling. If the parents have never used timeout to punish fighting, they may find it to be an effective, easily administered technique. Books such as Clark (1985) or Eimers and Aitchison (1977) may be very helpful under these or similar circumstances. Other parents may learn to use timeout via magazine articles in the popular press (e.g., Hamilton, 1993), one-day workshops, or similar educational opportunities.

On the other hand, parents may need close supervision and training in the use of timeout. This might occur in dealing with persistent, difficult discipline problems that parents have already tried to control using a number of different strategies such as scolding, loss of privileges or allowance money, unsuccessful timeouts, or spankings. Parents are likely to need the supervision and support available in individual or group therapy, child guidance clinics, or workshops lasting several months. For example, the behavior management program described by Barkley (1987a, 1987b) for children with ADHD involves about nine weekly sessions plus a booster session one month after completion of the core program. This type of instruction gives parents detailed, highly structured presentations and enables the clinician to provide help and feedback when problems arise. The instruction in Barkley's program deals with a wide range of issues, such as paying attention to good behavior, that will increase the chances of success with timeout and behavior problems in general.

One serious problem that can arise when timeout is administered is that the child refuses to remain in the timeout chair or area. This can happen in either a home- or a school-based timeout program. If it occurs at home, it leaves the parents in an extremely uncomfortable position, unable to enforce even a simple command to remain in one place. When parents are unable to enforce a timeout, it is likely that they have little control over their child in any other situation, either. Before parents can have realistic hope of regaining control, it is crucial that they learn to use timeout effectively. In school, the problem is just as serious and schools are given even less flexibility in handling the situation than parents. However, neither situation is intractable given careful planning and preparation.

At home, several authors (e.g., Barkley, 1987a, 1987b; Clark, 1985; Forehand & McMahon, 1981) recommend that a child who leaves the timeout without permission receive a brief spanking. Barkley (1987b) provides detailed instruction on how this procedure can be carried out. Although some parents and professionals are opposed to spanking, the procedure does have some advantages. First, as already mentioned, parents who cannot enforce a timeout are in an extremely difficult situation that needs to be helped because a child who will not comply with a directly supervised timeout will have essentially no constraints on his or her behavior. Such children would be at a severe risk for a multitude of behavior problems. A second advantage is that using a spanking to enforce timeout presents the punishment under conditions that are likely to be maximally effective. The punishment is immediate, directed at a well-defined behavior, and is likely to be administered when the parents are in a relatively calm state of mind. Furthermore, when a spanking is used only to back up the timeout, as advised by Barkley, spankings are actually less likely in the long run because timeout becomes the primary punisher and the spanking is only a rarely used backup.

For parents and professionals who prefer to avoid spankings completely, the most commonly recommended alternative is to restrain the child in the chair by holding him or her around the waist area while grasping the forearms. However, Roberts and Powers (1990) researched the relative effectiveness of four different methods of enforcing timeout with preschoolers. In a clinic analog setting it was found that spanking and "barrier" conditions were superior to restraint and child-determined release from a chair timeout. The "barrier" condition consisted of placing the child in a small (4×5 feet), carpeted, empty room with the door open and a four-foot-high barrier slid into the door slot and held there by the child's parent. When the child left the timeout chair, he or she remained in the barrier room for sixty seconds and was then placed back in the timeout chair. The restraint procedure consisted of holding the child for a count of ten and then releasing the child while he or she remained in the timeout chair. Of course, this is not the same as restraining a child until he or she is calm and accepts the timeout. The authors pointed out that successful use of restraint procedures requires release only when the child ceases all struggling, followed by gradual fading out, procedures that may be difficult for parents to learn or use but could be practical in a school setting where trained personnel are available. Thus, with preschool children, the barrier technique may be the most practical alternative when a child refuses to comply with timeout.

Given the potential complexities and problems with the use of either home- or school-based timeout, school personnel face some difficult decisions regarding when to help parents use timeout at home. Table 9.4 provides a sample handout that can become the basis for helping parents learn to use timeout and other techniques at home. The handout only describes placing the child in a chair timeout and states that the parents should contact those who provided the handout for advice if the child will not remain in the timeout. If the parents experience difficulty in enforcing timeout, there are several options. One is to give them a copy of Clark (1985) or an additional handout describing how to use a spanking to enforce timeout—for example, Barkley (1987a). Another option is to refer the parents to a clinic or other professional who can provide assistance.

In my own experience, timeout is a bottom-line procedure. If parents cannot successfully use timeout as a discipline technique when it is necessary, it is a sign of the potential for major problems both at home and at school. School personnel who are concerned about the welfare of students need to be persistent in giving parents the help they need to discipline their children at home. Help can be provided in a number of ways, ranging from direct instruction in the use of timeout to making a referral to a family therapist to address problems that may exist within the family system as a whole. Whatever the choice of intervention, school behavior is likely to be affected positively if parents receive the help they need to succeed with their children at home.

CONCLUSION

Working directly with children's parents is an essential component of providing effective, school-based behavior management consultation. The increase in consistency that results when school personnel and parents work on the same behavioral goals vastly improves the power and effectiveness of behavior management techniques. At the same time, supporting parents with effective behavior management consultation makes a positive contribution to home–school relationships and provides a "systematic" intervention that will be more likely to succeed over the long term. Consistency is maximized when the two systems or environments in which the child spends the majority of his or her time are focused on the same goals.

REVIEW

Terms to Remember and Review

behavior excess	behavior deficit
ignoring	extinction
learning disability	hyperactivity
ADHD	Golden Rule of Behavior Man-
response cost	agement
timeout	coupon program

Study and Discussion Questions

1. If you were developing a school-based library for parents, what books and materials would you purchase?
2. Discuss how you would approach a single parent whose third-grade son was a severe discipline problem because of excessive aggression.
3. Go to the mall, ask children, watch TV, read the newspaper and use any other available sources to develop a menu of reinforcers suitable for a second-grade child and a tenth-grade child.
4. When a child refuses to remain in timeout at home, what are the parents' two main options? Discuss the advantages and disadvantages of each of these options. What option would you prefer? Why?

Group Project

A list of several books about child problems and behavior management techniques, suitable for parents, is provided in Table 9.1. An interesting and valuable project is to ask small groups of two or three students to read one of the books and report their impressions of it to the class. In this manner, several books can be reviewed efficiently. Written book reviews could also be assigned to all students as a part of their regular grade or extra credit.

CHAPTER 10

MANAGEMENT OF BEHAVIOR DEFICITS IN THE REGULAR CLASSROOM

The disruptive and sometimes dramatic quality of behavior excesses makes their treatment a top priority of educators. For every behavior excess, however, there is an equal and opposite behavior *deficit* that is just as deserving of treatment. Also, many schoolchildren do not call attention to themselves with behavior excesses but have performance deficits that need to be remediated if they are to experience the success they deserve in school. We now turn to these problems.

Recall from Chapter 2 that negative reinforcement and positive reinforcement are the two basic methods of increasing behavior. Negative reinforcement involves *taking away* an aversive stimulus. This method is rarely programmed purposefully but sometimes explains how undesired behavior may be strengthened. For example, if a child is confronted with a difficult and frustrating reading exercise, behavior that leads to escape from the situation (e.g., a tantrum) may be negatively reinforced. That is, disruptive behavior leading to escape from the aversive reading task becomes more likely to occur in the future. Similarly, most adults can remember at least one teacher in their past whose classroom was structured around fear of severe negative consequences for misbehavior. The classroom may have been characterized by satisfactory behavior and reasonable productivity, but the goal of students was to *avoid* negative consequences. The result may have been an unpleasant learning experience. The practical and ethical problems of presenting an aversive stimulus that can then be taken away make negative reinforcement an impractical procedure that is rarely used purposefully. However, negative reinforcement can often explain the development of behaviors occurring under natural contingencies.

On the other hand, positive reinforcement is the sine qua non of behavior management procedures. Positive reinforcement means to present a desirable stimulus or event as a consequence for desirable behavior. Praising an accurate answer, rewarding good grades with money, and awarding free time to those who finish an assigned task are just a few examples of using positive reinforcement. Although the basic definition of positive reinforcement is straightforward, a wide variety of specific programs employ the procedure. This chapter will focus on procedures using positive reinforcement that can be used in regular classroom settings to remediate behavior deficits. The chapter begins with a basic program for increasing appropriate classroom behaviors, followed by discussion of a program for remediating school refusal or school phobia. Programs that use school–home notes, a behavior monitoring form, and behavior contracts are also described.

A BASIC REGULAR CLASSROOM BEHAVIOR MANAGEMENT PROGRAM

Most schools, particularly elementary schools, have what may be called a "difficult" class or group of children. This group may be described as "wild," "impossible to manage," "out of control," or "a pain." These are not "bad" children, but there is a core group of students who have the ability to lead a major segment of a classroom down the wrong path. Teachers of these students may become frustrated and distracted from their primary task, teaching. The program described in this section is meant to provide an example of how this situation can be remediated. The program is an independent group contingency program. This means that the contingency applies to the whole group, but each student is individually rewarded (Shapiro & Goldberg, 1986).

Brantley and Webster (1993) described the application of independent group contingencies to a fourth-grade classroom of twenty-five children. The study makes for an interesting example because the teachers involved believed that nine of the students in the class should have been placed full time in a special education class because of their conduct problems. The study not only illustrates the effectiveness of behavior management interventions, it also shows how important behavior management procedures can be in maintaining difficult students in mainstream classes. The eight-step program described here is loosely based on Brantley and Webster's study, but the description is presented in a more flexible format to facilitate the task of adapting it to a particular need.

Step 1: Identify the problem. In the Brantley and Webster study, the identified target behaviors were talking without permission, noisiness, not paying attention to teacher presentations, refusing to work on assignments, physically touching others, and leaving seats without permission. These behaviors are probably typical for nonproductive students in many classrooms. Other behaviors, such as failing to raise a hand before speaking, not having materials ready for activities, minor physical aggression, attention-getting behavior, tardiness, and inaccurate completion of assignments, could be added to the list. Individual teachers are also likely to vary in their definition of appropriate behavior in the classroom. For instance, some teachers may structure their rooms so students are encouraged to work at learning centers and are allowed to leave their seats without permission. Other teachers may demand that students remain in their seats unless given permission to leave. If a behavior management program is needed in either classroom, allowance for these kinds of differences must be made.

Step 2: Refine the definition of the problem. Although a behavior reduction program of some kind (see Chapter 7) could be designed to provide effective consequences for misbehavior, it is also possible to eliminate misbehavior by rewarding incompatible appropriate behavior. The goal is to increase the amount of appropriate behavior, which causes inappropriate behavior to decline.

In the Brantley and Webster program, three classroom rules were written specifying appropriate behaviors incompatible with the target behaviors. The strategy was to reward students who exhibited behavior consistent with the classroom rules. The key is to develop classroom rules that concretely specify for students what is meant by desirable classroom behavior. A wide variety of variations on what is considered appropriate classroom behavior could be developed. As noted, the final set of rules would depend in large part on the personality of the teacher, her or his model of how a classroom should be structured, the grade level of the students, and schoolwide discipline policies. Chapter 5 includes an extensive discussion of developing a good set of classroom rules.

Step 3: Assess the baseline rate. Determining the baseline rate can be a difficult task in a regular classroom setting, mainly because most teachers have little time in their day for extra record keeping tasks. Therefore, any method of recording baseline data in a regular classroom must be simple and highly efficient unless extra staff people are available to observe classroom behavior or review a videotape of the class at a later time.

There are many simple and efficient approaches to counting behaviors that can be used in a regular classroom situation. One method begins with categorizing inappropriate behavior in categories such as aggression, disobedience, off-task behavior, and being out of seat. Then each category is assigned a number. Each time a behavior in one of the categories occurs, that number is written down. At a later time the frequency of each category can be counted. Alternatively, a form can be prepared that simplifies the task even more. Figure 10.1 provides one example, and Figure 8.1 (Chapter 8) shows another example of how this could be accomplished.

It is not always necessary to focus on inappropriate behavior as suggested here. Instead, it would also be reasonable to count the occurrences of appropriate behavior. Using this strategy, suggests counting the number of reinforced behaviors. If the program is successful, the number of reinforced behaviors (i.e., the number of

Directions: Each time a behavior in the categories designated below occurs, cross off the next number in the sequence. The last number crossed off at the end of the day is the total of incidents for the day.

Date: _____   Class: _____

| Aggression | 1 2 3 4 5 6 7 8 9 10 1 2 3 4 5 6 7 8 9 20 1 2 3 4 5 |
| | 6 7 8 9 30 1 2 3 4 5 6 7 8 9 40 1 2 3 4 5 6 7 8 9 50 |

| Disobedience | 1 2 3 4 5 6 7 8 9 10 1 2 3 4 5 6 7 8 9 20 1 2 3 4 5 |
| | 6 7 8 9 30 1 2 3 4 5 6 7 8 9 40 1 2 3 4 5 6 7 8 9 50 |

| Off-Task | 1 2 3 4 5 6 7 8 9 10 1 2 3 4 5 6 7 8 9 20 1 2 3 4 5 |
| | 6 7 8 9 30 1 2 3 4 5 6 7 8 9 40 1 2 3 4 5 6 7 8 9 50 |

| Out-of-Seat | 1 2 3 4 5 6 7 8 9 10 1 2 3 4 5 6 7 8 9 20 1 2 3 4 5 |
| | 6 7 8 9 30 1 2 3 4 5 6 7 8 9 40 1 2 3 4 5 6 7 8 9 50 |

Figure 10.1. Sample Data Collection Form

times students are observed behaving according to the rules) should gradually increase along with academic productivity. The difficulty with this approach is that appropriate classroom behavior does not necessarily occur in discrete, countable units. Instead, the typical pattern is that a student engages in appropriate behavior (i.e., remaining in seat and on task) for an indefinite length of time, which is only occasionally disrupted by inappropriate behavior such as leaving an assigned seat. Thus, the more practical approach is to count the number of inappropriate behaviors.

Step 4: Identify the reinforcer and contingency and write the program description. In the Brantley and Webster study, students were awarded a checkmark next to their name if they exhibited behaviors consistent with two of the three posted classroom rules: (1) pay attention and stay on task, (2) get the teacher's permission before saying anything, and (3) stay seated without touching anybody. The school day was divided into forty-five-minute intervals and a student could earn up to seven checkmarks per day, one per forty-five-minute interval. Charts showing each student's name and the number of checkmarks earned were posted in a prominent location in the classroom. The backup reward for checkmarks was a rewarding activity at the end of each week. Students who earned four out of five checkmarks in the morning sessions and two out of three checkmarks in the afternoon sessions for the entire week could attend the activity. Students who did not meet this criterion worked on academic tasks in another room during the activity.

The program began with a less stringent criterion that had an "immediate positive impact," but the criterion was changed to increase classroom structure even fur-

ther. In actual practice, there are likely to be a number of different ways the criterion for participation in the rewarding activity could be structured. Those who implement such a program need to develop a criterion with which they are comfortable and then let the incoming data tell them whether or not the program was successful. Also, it was not precisely clear how the checkmarks were awarded within each forty-five-minute interval. However, it appeared that the teachers continued to maintain frequency counts of the original problem behaviors. Then they used these data to determine who had earned a checkmark. If a student violated more than one rule, a checkmark could not be awarded. Obviously, there would be considerable flexibility in this regard. For example, teachers could note rule violations on a privately maintained chart and award checkmarks only to students who had zero rule violations in a given time interval. Also, the time interval could be shortened or lengthened to meet the needs of the situation. Shorter intervals have the advantage of giving students more frequent, and therefore more accurate, feedback regarding their behavior.

An important component of this program is that the teacher needs to be generous in praising the appropriate behavior of students. Although it is not practical to praise every instance of behavior consistent with the classroom rules, praise needs to be frequent and genuine.

The written program description needs to address all of the key issues in a format that is simple and easy to follow. A sample outline of a written program follows:

1. What classroom rules have been established? The program needs to begin by establishing a clear set of classroom rules that specify appropriate behav-

ior. It may be helpful to develop the rules in the context of a classroom discussion so students have greater "ownership" of them. The rules should be prominently posted in the classroom as well as being part of the written program.

2. How will rule violations be recorded for each student? There are two data-recording problems to be addressed. First, this program depends on keeping an accurate record of each individual student's behavior. One approach is to duplicate a copy of the class list with space to record rule violations. Each time a rule is violated, the number of the rule is placed next to the student's name. The second problem is to generate data measuring the overall progress of the class. A graph of the grand total of rule violations for the entire class each day should provide excellent feedback to indicate whether the program is successful.

3. How will individual student progress be communicated? A prominently displayed poster with each student's name has the advantage of being efficient and clear, but an individualized note is more private and confidential. An individualized note could be constructed using the same class list on which rule violations are recorded. By recording the student's name twice, the functions of a record form and feedback form can be combined. The example below shows this more concretely.

Name	Rule Violations	Name/Points
Jason S.		Jason S.

Constructing an entire class list in the manner provides a convenient way of recording rule violations. The space for rule violations can be divided into sections for each period of the day. The reason for recording each name twice is that at the end of the day or period a paper cutter may be used to give students slips of paper with their name and the number of points or checkmarks earned. Alternatively, the entire list could be publicly posted.

4. What criteria will determine which students earn a privilege? The answer to this question depends on the number of opportunities to earn points or checkmarks. For example, if students could earn up to four checkmarks per day, this would equate to twenty per week. At the beginning of the program, it may be reasonable to allow students who earn at least fourteen checkmarks to participate in the rein-

forcing activity. This criterion could be raised as student behavior improves.

5. What reinforcing events will be made available at the end of the week? This is a critical question. The success of the program depends on the attractiveness of the reward at the end of the week. An hour or so of free time at the end of the day on Friday may be sufficiently rewarding to motivate most students. Alternately, special activities such as movies, art projects, or guest speakers could be arranged. Students who do not meet the criterion to participate should spend their time making up the academic work they missed during the week.

Step 5: Begin the program. A program at this level of complexity probably needs to be explained carefully to the students involved. A careful review of the classroom rules, clarifying the meaning of key words and providing concrete examples of appropriate and inappropriate behaviors, will also increase the chances of success. The explanation needs to be adjusted to the developmental level of the students.

Backup rewards are crucial to the success of a program involving token reward (the checkmarks or points function in the same way as tokens) and need to be discussed carefully with the students to ensure that the backup reward is attractive to as many students as possible. Movies, videos, popcorn parties, free time, an extra recess, a softball game, various treats, and field trips are just a few rewarding activities that students may suggest. Once a menu of rewarding activities has been developed, students could be allowed to choose the reward to be used for the first week of the program. Another review of how students' behavior will gain them access to the activity may be helpful. On the Monday that the program begins, asking students to sign a contract that explains the program could increase their commitment to change. Daily review of classroom rules, especially in the early stages of the program, could also improve compliance.

Step 6: Observe the effects of the program and initiate steps to strengthen generalization beyond the training environment. This program is designed mainly for use in a regular classroom setting, but it could also work effectively in a special classroom. Transferring the positive results of this program to another environment should be relatively straightforward. The first step would be to present students with a set of classroom rules identical to those to be experienced in the new classroom. If the program could be completely faded in the old or training classroom, transfer to the new classroom should be easy to accomplish because dependence on the program would be eliminated. On the other hand, it may be necessary to give students some feedback as they adapt to the new classroom. This could be done by using an individualized version of the program and then fading it, sending a note between the new and old classroom, involving the student in self-monitoring, or using the coupon (response cost) program or any number of different strategies. Successful transfer of skills to the new setting will depend in part on the day-to-day behavior management strategies employed by the regular classroom teacher. If the principles discussed in Chapter 5 are fully utilized, transfer will be easily accomplished.

Of course, if the program is being conducted in the students' regular classroom, transfer to another environment is not a crucial issue unless there is a concern with special classes such as art, music, and physical education. Brantley and Webster found that the program was needed only in regular academic classes. As long as other teachers are willing to cooperate, however, there is no reason that the program could not be run in other settings.

Step 7: Modify the program if necessary. If student behavior does not improve, several modifications can be attempted. The first place to look is the backup rewards, particularly when a single reward is given to an entire group of children. Every effort to provide an effective reward must be made. Holding a brainstorming session, talking to individual students, or asking teaching colleagues may provide some ideas on how to make the reward more attractive.

Another option for modifying the program is to provide more frequent rewards. Brantley and Webster designed a program with a weekly reward. Students with difficult behavior problems may need more frequent reward and more precise feedback regarding their behavior in order to change. Allowing students to exchange their checkmarks for rewards on a daily basis could be an effective modification. For instance, students who earn six checkmarks on any one day could be given ten or fifteen minutes of free time at the end of the day, a note to take home to their parents, or another small reward. This could be done at the same time the weekly reward was available. Numerous combinations and permutations of the procedure for providing backup rewards are possible, and the one that is best suited to the particularly classroom and situation needs to be discovered, often through trial and error. Behavior management programs

work best when the task is approached in a flexible manner with the intent of finding out what works best.

Step 8: Fade out the program. One theme of this book is that all children need to receive reinforcing consequences for their appropriate behavior. The program described by Brantley and Webster is relatively easy and efficient to use in an elementary classroom. There is no reason that the program could not continue as a semipermanent component of the classroom structure. On the other hand, it may be desirable to simplify the program to provide a better fit with the classroom environment. Consistent application of the Golden Rule of Behavior Management (ignoring inappropriate behavior as much as possible and providing consistent positive attention to students behaving appropriately) will contribute to the success of this approach. Simplification could consist of moving toward one of the approaches to classroom management discussed in Chapter 5 or making adjustments to the Brantley and Webster program.

One clear option is to move toward a biweekly or even monthly rewarding event. One advantage is that bigger rewards such as particularly interesting field trips or more elaborate parties can be planned. Care will be needed, however, to bridge the gap between reinforcing events with lots of praise, positive attention, and other small rewards. The final decisions on how to structure a classroom must remain with the classroom teacher, but this program provides one approach that can serve as the beginning.

BEHAVIOR MANAGEMENT OF SCHOOL REFUSAL AND SCHOOL PHOBIA

The most basic condition for benefiting from school is to attend regularly. The chronically absent child is at risk for academic failure, and the child's parents are subject to legal consequences. Frequent, long-term, or chronic absence from school is not a behavior excess, although occasional absence or tardiness is often treated as such and punished. Instead, school refusal is best viewed as a behavior deficit, where the deficit behaviors are coming to school and participating in the academic and social activities it offers. Programs for improving school attendance focus on rewarding, supporting, and encouraging school attendance and the associated academic and social behaviors.

Durlak (1992) states that little agreement exists among writers regarding the basic elements of school phobia—its correct name, primary characteristics, treatment, and prognosis. He attributes some of the confusion to the variety of different manifestations of the problem. Two important distinctions can be helpful in guiding the approach to school phobia. The first is between an underlying fear focused on the school environment, in which case the problem is called school phobia, and "separation anxiety," which is focused on fear of leaving parents rather than on a fear of going to school. The second distinction is between acute and chronic school phobia. Acute school phobia, which typically occurs suddenly in young children, often in response to a specific event in the school environment, responds well to treatment. Chronic school phobia develops more slowly, usually in preadolescent or older children, and is associated with other serious academic and personality problems. Chronic school phobia is more difficult to treat than acute school phobia.

The basic technique underlying programs for remediating school phobia is to reward appropriate coping behavior that takes the place of fearful behavior. For example, if a child showing signs of school phobia is rewarded for completing schoolwork, increasing the amount of time spent on academic work has the effect of leaving less time for behaviors associated with fear. Thus, a phobia may be eliminated by increasing the frequency of more desirable behavior. Specific techniques involving positive reinforcement include reinforcement and shaping, teaching various coping strategies, modeling, and vicarious extinction. See Doll (1987), Biran and Wilson (1981), Hatzenbueler and Schroeder (1978), Last (1992), Morris and Kratochwill (1985), Phelps, Cox, and Bajorek (1992), Richter (1984), and Ross (1981) for more discussion and examples of techniques for treating children's fears and phobias.

Several essential elements are involved in the treatment of children's fears and anxieties (L. C. Miller, 1983; Reed, Carter, & Miller, 1992). They are establishment of a relationship, stimulus clarification, desensitization to the stimulus, and confrontation of the stimulus. The first element, establishing a relationship, refers to the process of learning about the child, the child's family, and the characteristics of the problem as they see it. Empathetic listening and the development of trust and confidence in the interviewer probably make strong contributions to establishing a helping relationship.

The second element, stimulus clarification, consists of determining the stimulus conditions related to the debilitating fear. The importance of thorough assessment prior to beginning a behavior management program has already been discussed, but it is important to reemphasize the necessity of determining the stimulus conditions that control the problem behavior. It is these stimuli to which the child must eventually be desensitized, so it is important that they be well understood by those planning a behavior management program.

The third element, desensitization to the anxiety-producing stimulus, consists of implementing an appropriate behavior management program.

The last element in the management of anxiety and fear is confrontation of the stimulus. Miller (1983) states that confronting the stimulus is an "absolutely necessary" part of treatment as well as an indicator of treatment success. The attitude of the parents toward forcing a confrontation of the stimulus is one of the key elements in the success of the management plan. Parents may, to some extent, reinforce the child's fear for a number of reasons, such as a history of similar fears or empathy for the discomfort of their child. Miller believes that at least one parent must resolve this ambivalent attitude toward a confrontation of the fear-evoking stimulus and decide that, regardless of the consequences, the child will go to school, sleep in his or her own bed, or otherwise face the stimulus.

This is particularly true for school phobia. Regardless of the severity of the child's fear, it will be necessary that the child be returned to school as soon as possible after treatment is initiated. Under some circumstances, this may prove to be an extremely difficult task. Resistance can be so strong that one parent alone finds it impossible to bring the child to school without the risk of serious injury. However, regardless of the strength of resistance, the child must return to school at some point in the course of treatment. Although it may be possible to ease the transition for some children, for others it may be necessary to go to the child's home and physically bring the child to school.

Because of the prevalence and serious consequences of school phobia, a step-by-step procedure will be used to describe remediation techniques for this problem.

A REMEDIATION PLAN FOR SCHOOL PHOBIA

Sometimes a case of school phobia comes to the attention of school personnel in a dramatic way. A nearly frantic call comes from a classroom teacher asking *some-*

one to please do something about a student who is crying uncontrollably and disrupting the entire class. In other cases, school phobia is identified when a secretary's comment that a particular student has been missing a lot of school lately prompts a call to the parents, which reveals that they are experiencing great difficulty in getting the child to school. Some parents may be relieved that someone from the school has taken an interest in their problem, but other parents may be consciously or unconsciously reinforcing the problem behavior.

As noted in Chapter 4, school phobia is characterized by avoidance of school, sometimes accompanied by physical symptoms such as complaints of headaches, vomiting, stomach aches, or nausea. The child is also likely to express unrealistic fears about attending school. In younger children, school phobia usually occurs with the consent and knowledge of the parent(s), who are aware that the child is remaining out of school. Older children may be absent from school without the consent of their parents, who may be unaware of the child's whereabouts during the day. Differentiating school refusal or truancy from school phobia is not difficult but will certainly influence the nature of the remediation program.

Blagg and Yule (1984) studied a series of consecutive referrals for school phobia. They compared the effectiveness of a behavioral treatment that emphasized returning the child to school as quickly as possible versus hospitalization versus home tutoring. Their findings were that the group treated behaviorally showed a superior outcome to the other two groups. The superiority of the behavioral treatment extended to attendance, separation anxiety, self-esteem, personality indices, and the amount of therapist time involved in the treatment. The formal behavior management program that will be outlined has much in common with the techniques used by Blagg and Yule (1984) and Houlihan and Jones (1989), especially in its emphasis on returning the child to school as quickly and efficiently as possible. It differs from Blagg and Yule's approach in that immediate confrontation with school attendance can be delayed, while the child is gradually accustomed to stimuli associated with school attendance and rewarded for mastering these situations. The latter technique was successfully employed by Houlihan and Jones (1989), in which the school psychologist provided support and social reinforcement for gradual increases in school attendance.

Step 1: Identify the problem. School phobia is fairly easy to identify. Once it is identified, however, assess-

ment should not come to a halt. Other problems may be present as well. For instance, academic difficulties and failure could be major contributors to the development of school phobia. In such a case, getting the child to attend school would be only the first step in the process of improving school performance. Other problems may also be potential targets for remediation, such as a poor self-concept, a learning disability, or poor social skills.

Three sources of information are likely to be involved in the initial identification of school phobia. First, and probably most important, are the school's attendance records. Frequent absences are one of the major characteristics associated with school phobia. A second source of valuable information is the child's classroom teacher, who may observe signs of anxiety in the classroom or provide other information relevant to identifying the nature of the problem. The third source of information is a phone conversation with at least one of the child's parents. This phone call is very important because the parents eventually must see that the child attends school. Thus, any problems they experience are going to be crucial in identifying school phobia and formulating a remediation plan.

It may also be helpful to take a look at the school environment from the child's perspective. As pointed out in Chapter 5, there are many ways that the school environment can be constructed to make it pleasant for students. Clear rules, reasonable and fair consequences, consistent enforcement, and plenty of opportunities for children to be recognized for their positive accomplishments will contribute to the type of school environment that minimizes children's fears. A critical look at classroom management will may also be helpful. Lack of flexibility, an emphasis on harsh punishment, or lack of sensitivity to the needs of individual children can create a classroom that magnifies children's problems. Finally, children can sometimes be very cruel to their peers. The bathrooms, playground, lunchroom, bus, and other areas where close supervision is typically not available may allow bullying, extortion by older children, and other behaviors that can create a truly fearsome environment for some children. When chronic absences become a problem, it may be essential to assess these aspects of the school environment.

Step 2: Refine the definition of the problem. Refining the definition of school phobia is simple. There are two basic issues. First, the child must return to school as soon as possible and maintain an acceptable attendance record. Second, problems secondary to the school phobia, but also interfering with school performance, should be considered potential targets for remediation. This could include poor academic performance, test anxiety, disruptive behavior, or any other significant behavior problem in school.

If excessive fear is the problem, then the primary goal of assessment is to specify as completely as possible the stimulus conditions associated with fear. However, because the child's parents are responsible for initiating the process of getting the child to school, it is equally important to determine the family systems factors related to the problem of school phobia.

Several specific areas need to be assessed if the behavior management program is going to address the key issues and have a reasonable chance of success. The first of these is the child's behavior. The main question is: How does it come about that the child does not attend school? Does the child complain of physical symptoms that cause the parent to keep him or her home for health reasons? Does the child physically resist efforts to transport him or her to school? What kinds of resistant behavior are noted? Does the child resist with crying, tantrums, running away, hiding?

Information about the child's behavior in the classroom should also be obtained. An observation of on-task behavior may be very helpful and could become part of the baseline observations. In addition, observations of any behaviors that interfere with accomplishing assigned work should be made informally, and precise frequency data should be obtained. If the child has not been attending school, it may be necessary to depend on secondhand reports until the child has actually returned to school.

Information about the stimulus conditions associated with fear of school is also a necessary component of the assessment. The following information should be obtained: When and where does the child first begin to show signs of fear? Does the child show signs of separation anxiety; that is, does separation from the parents for any reason result in signs of fear from the child? What specific behaviors do the parents and teachers observe that are associated with fear? Does anyone else in the family behave similarly to the target child? What steps in the process of getting to school do not elicit signs of fear? Does the child express worry about school in the evening or on weekends? This information is needed to construct a hierarchy of stimulus events beginning with events that elicit no fear and moving in gradual steps to the most threatening stimulus conditions.

Once the stimulus conditions surrounding the fear have been completely specified, it is then necessary to determine how others, particularly parents and teachers, react to the child's behavior. A second question is whether any other member of the family is experiencing problems similar to those of the child. If so, it may be necessary to encourage the family to seek treatment for that individual because the target child may be learning to show fear as a result of modeling by a significant other. The goal is to determine what sources of reinforcement, if any, may be contributing to the maintenance of the problem behavior. Naturally, whether or not a formal behavior management program is undertaken, it will be necessary to arrange that undesired behavior is ignored and desired behavior is rewarded.

It is often possible to deal with some milder cases of school phobia via a phone conversation with the child's parents. In such cases, one might expect the child to be attending school but showing signs of discomfort and fear prior to leaving home. The parents may need professional support to do some of the things they realize may be necessary to force school attendance. In discussing this issue with parents, one should obtain a description of the child's behavior and parental reactions to it. Then one would encourage the parents to ignore inappropriate behavior and reward behavior that is appropriate and realistic. A classroom observation or secondhand report from the child's teacher can be very reassuring to a parent if it turns out that the child is showing no evidence of a problem in school.

When the child is avoiding school by reporting physical symptoms—such as stomach pain, headaches, or fever—one should first encourage the parents to have the child examined by a medical doctor. If the doctor discovers no physical basis for the child's complaints, a few simple rules can be instituted to assure appropriate attendance. First, the parent should be instructed to ignore the child's complaints of physical problems. If the child persists with a complaint, then a temperature should be taken and the child allowed to stay at home only if a fever is present. Alternatively, the child could be sent to school every day, regardless of complaints, and the school nurse asked to decide whether the child is sick enough to justify remaining at home. Of course, this should be done only with the consent of the nurse. Finally, the days that the child actually remains at home should not be loaded with fun. Since the child is sick, remaining in bed to rest is the most appropriate activity.

Occasionally, it will be discovered that the child's school phobia is deeply entangled within the structure of the family. In such cases, it may be very difficult to implement a successful behavior management program because the child's parents play a role in getting the child to school. Referrals to appropriate social agencies or a family therapist may be appropriate. In extreme cases, it may be necessary to take legal action if the child is being deprived of educational rights.

Step 3: Assess the baseline rate. The most important baseline measurement is the child's record of attendance and tardiness. However, this should not be the only behavior of interest. If the child is attending school, then formal classroom observations will be helpful. The percentage of time on task is a basic measure, discussed in Chapter 3, that could be of some value. If the child disrupts the classroom with tantrums or crying, the frequency and/or duration of these behaviors should also be recorded. It may not be possible to take baseline measurements before a behavior management program is begun if the child is not attending school. In such cases, baseline data can be obtained from school records and during the early stages of the program.

Another component of the baseline assessment is construction of a stimulus hierarchy, a list of stimulus situations surrounding school attendance ranging from least to most threatening. I recommend that a stimulus hierarchy be constructed around the following categories and adjusted as necessary to meet the needs of individual children: nonthreatening practice at school attendance (e.g., driving by the school on a weekend), school-related weekend and evening activities, getting up and getting ready for school, leaving the home to go to school, traveling to school, arriving at school and entering the building, entering and remaining in the classroom, and participating in other events that may occur in school (e.g., a fire drill). A specific example of such a stimulus hierarchy follows.

1. The child is riding in a car that passes by the school on a Sunday afternoon.
2. The child is at home watching TV on Sunday evening.
3. It is time to go to bed on a school night, and the child is instructed to get his or her school supplies ready for the next day.
4. The child is ready for bed on a school night.
5. The child is in bed trying to fall asleep on a school night.
6. It is time to awaken on a school morning.
7. It is time to get out of bed on a school morning.
8. The child is eating breakfast on a school morning.
9. The child is getting dressed on a school morning.
10. The child goes through the front door on the way to begin the walk to school.
11. The child passes by various points en route to school.
12. The child crosses the last street on the way to school.
13. The child enters the schoolyard.
14. The child enters the school building.
15. The child is walking down the hallway.
16. The child pauses at the entrance to his or her classroom.
17. The child enters an empty classroom.
18. The child is remaining alone in an empty classroom.
19. The child is the only child in the classroom with the teacher.
20. The child is in a crowded but quiet classroom.
21. The child is in a crowded, noisy classroom with a number of different activities taking place at once.

Step 4: Design the behavioral contingencies and write the program description. School phobia is a problem that must be handled flexibly enough to deal with the variety of its manifestations. As noted, milder cases that are in the early stages may be remediated via phone consultation with the parents. At the other extreme are cases that require referral to outside agencies. In this example, it is assumed that the child's phobia is moderate to severe and the parents are concerned and cooperative.

The general approach outlined in this formal behavior management program involves the use of positive reinforcement to reward the child for gradual mastery of the steps involved in attending school. Variations on this procedure and other techniques that may be used to supplement the program will be discussed in Steps 6 and 7.

One thing that must be kept in mind is that the goal of any remediation program for school phobia is to get the child back in school. This sounds very simple and concrete, but in practice it can also be very difficult. The case study and experimental literature on the treatment of school phobia contains a variety of procedures that have successfully returned children to school. These procedures range from programs involving shaping, gradual exposure, relaxation training, and a variety of behavioral contingencies to those that simply have one of the parents bring the child to school until voluntary attendance is no longer a problem. The strategy described begins with token reward for gradual approximations of school attendance, followed by reward for attendance and completion of schoolwork. In actual practice, the form of the program will depend greatly on the judgment of the person implementing the program and the severity of the problem behavior.

The central feature of the program is a hierarchy of stimulus conditions associated with fear and refusal to attend school. Although the specifics of the hierarchy will vary from situation to situation, its general form will remain the same from case to case. The key to implementing a particular program is to select a satisfactory point of entry into the stimulus hierarchy. The major risk to be considered in this decision is the negative consequence of entering the hierarchy at a point that elicits behavior beyond the tolerance of the person responsible for the program. For example, if a step in the hierarchy calls for one or both parents to escort the child to school, one must be sure that they are capable of coping with the child's responses. If the child's crying and tantrums cause the parents to take the child home instead of to school, the avoidance behavior of the child is rewarded and those responses actually gain in strength (another example of negative reinforcement).

The specific reinforcer and contingency are tokens and social praise from significant adults provided for mastery of the steps in the stimulus hierarchy. In addition, the adult conducting the program can also be a model of appropriate behavior. As described in Chapter 2, a token reward program rewards a child for appropriate behavior with tokens, such as points, poker chips, or marbles that can be exchanged for some desirable reward. The value of the tokens as a reward comes from the fact that they can be used to "purchase" backup rewards. Usually, a menu of several different backup rewards is offered to the child so that the tokens maintain their usefulness as rewards over a long period of time. The number of tokens required to purchase a reward will vary with the value that the child places on a particular reward.

Alternatively, it may be possible to reward the child effectively with praise or perhaps with a consumable reward, such as potato chips. As noted previously, younger children will respond best to rewards that are concrete and immediate. Garvey and Hegrenes (1966) described a case study in which a school phobia was eliminated in a ten-year-old boy by developing a graded hierarchy of stimulus situations related to school attendance. The therapist accompanied the boy to school and provided social praise for mastery of succeeding steps

in the stimulus hierarchy, beginning with being seated in a car outside the school. When the boy reported being afraid, the boy and the therapist returned to the car. Over twenty days (weekends included), the school phobia gradually dissipated and had not returned at a two-year follow-up. Thus, a variety of procedures can be used to successfully reinforce a return to school.

The exact nature of the formal behavior management program is this: First, a thorough assessment of the problem is conducted and the information is used to construct a stimulus hierarchy like the one shown earlier. Then, using praise, token rewards, consumable rewards, or a combination of the three, the child is rewarded for mastering the elements of the stimulus hierarchy. This phase should probably last about five to ten days. The final goal of having the child enter school is accomplished by escorting the child on a Monday following the original identification of the problem. Numerous variations are possible. However, an important characteristic of the program's implementation is how well the various components of the system work together. Remediating school phobia requires the full cooperation and trust of the child's parents.

The written program description for remediating school phobia needs to be developed in conjunction with the child's parents. In fact, the best approach may be to put the program in the form of a behavioral contract (see the discussion later in this chapter). A sample outline for the written program follows:

1. What is the stimulus hierarchy? A stimulus hierarchy should be developed over the course of the assessment process. It should begin with school-related activities that do not elicit fear and end with the most threatening school-related situations.

2. What specific rewards and contingencies will be employed? A token program that rewards the child for attempting or mastering successive steps in the hierarchy is the recommended procedure. The type of token to be dispensed and the backup rewards will need to be specified. See Chapters 11 and 12 for detailed discussions of token programs. It is also important to specify the criterion for advancing to the next step in the stimulus hierarchy. Options range from advancing to the next step only when the child is completely comfortable and fearless to setting a date and time for completing the step.

3. What are the specific responsibilities of parents, teachers, administrators, and consultants? Many of these responsibilities can be spelled out in the proc-

ess of developing the stimulus hierarchy. For example, one step in the hierarchy may state that the child will come to school accompanied by one or both parents. Another step may state that the child will remain in the classroom in the presence of the school psychologist.

4. What is the scheduled date for a return to school?
5. Finally, what support programs are needed once the child returns to school? This is a crucial element in the program. If the child has academic problems or social skill deficits that are not addressed, a pattern of school absences may reoccur.

Step 5: Begin the program. Beginning an intervention procedure for school phobia is somewhat different than for other techniques. Parents, teachers, other school staff members, and the child must be appropriately prepared for the child's reentry into school. First and foremost, all interactions with the child should refer to the child's eventual return to school, thereby communicating to him or her that the return is inevitable. That is, the question is not *if* but *when*. Second, the child's teachers and other school staff who might be in contact with the child should welcome him or her and not overload the child with work or aversive activities. Likewise, a method for handling complaints of physical symptoms, such as ignoring them or taking the child's temperature, should be arranged ahead of time.

Preparation of the child's parents will require the greatest care, particularly if it was decided to bring the child directly to school. The child may show a great deal of resistance, and it may require some planning to ensure that an escort is available for quite a period of time. If it is necessary for school personnel to go to the child's home and bring him or her to school, two people should always be involved. This is necessary mainly to prevent injury to the child because resistance can be so strong that one individual would find it impossible to control the child. Most authors recommend that the child's return to school be scheduled for the Monday following the identification of the original problem.

The child's parents could be inadvertently rewarding some or all of the problem behaviors associated with resistance to attending school. Great care must be taken to establish a cooperative relationship with the child's parents because they are the most important element in the long-term success of the program. Reframing the child's behavior in terms of a desire to remain in the secure environment of the home and reframing the parents' behavior in terms of their desire to provide a secure

environment for the child may enable them more easily to adjust their behavior to the task of getting the child to attend school without absences (see Chapter 3). An advantage of gradual exposure to the stimulus elements of the hierarchy is that the parents can be retrained in methods of rewarding school attendance and associated behaviors while they learn to ignore behaviors that interfere with attending school. With this approach, it is possible to ensure that the parents have some of the necessary skills when it is time to confront the stimulus and actually attend school regardless of the consequences.

A program to remediate school phobia begins as soon as the responsible person from the school system makes contact with the child's family. The school staff should communicate confidence in the child's ability to return to school and in the parents' ability to participate in the program and bring it to a successful conclusion. The emphasis in all conversations must be on when, not if, the child returns to school. Once all pertinent data about the problem have been gathered and a stimulus hierarchy has been constructed, the actual program can begin. Consider a concrete example.

Assume that a child has been absent from school for a week and a phone call to the child's parents on a Monday reveals that the parents just cannot manage to get the child to school. The first step is contact the parents personally and obtain all the necessary assessment data. An interview with the child's teacher, inspection of attendance records, and a search of the child's cumulative file should also be conducted. The data from these sources should be used to construct the hierarchy of stimulus conditions. On Tuesday, a plan for returning the child to school on the following Monday should be formulated and discussed with the parents. For example, the agreed-on program might involve gradual exposure to the stimulus elements in the hierarchy on Tuesday through Friday, having the parents escort the child to school on Monday through Wednesday, and having the child come to school with a school staff member on Thursday and Friday.

The following week can be devoted to continuing the child's successful pattern of attendance, consulting with the parents, and determining whether additional interventions might be necessary, such as implementing a home note program as explained later in this chapter. A period of close supervision of the child's attendance should continue for approximately six weeks. Also, a return to former patterns of behavior on Mondays and on the first day of school following a holiday or a genuine illness should be anticipated.

Step 6: Observe the effects of the program and initiate steps to strengthen generalization beyond the training environment. The major effect of the program should be to get the child to attend school. However, this may be accompanied by behaviors such as tantrums and crying that require some special handling. If tantrums and crying are disruptive enough to interfere with the classroom routine, isolation in a quiet area or office until the child calms down may be necessary. It will be necessary to keep a record of how long it takes the child to settle down if any form of isolation is employed. Remember that avoidance is the problem, so the child should not be allowed to escape the classroom without some penalty or contingency, such as having to complete the same work as other students in the class.

Since the goal of the management program is to return the child to the regular classroom as soon as possible, generalization to other environments is not an issue. However, the problem of promoting generalization can appear in two different forms. First, it is possible that returning the child to the classroom is not followed by optimum performance. That is, the child may engage in other behaviors, such as seeking attention and reassurance from the classroom teacher or being off task for an unacceptable percentage of the time. In these cases, a supplementary behavior management program to deal with other behaviors may be helpful.

A second issue involving generalization of coping behaviors concerns the possibility that the child may be all right in the presence of certain conditions but show signs of fear and anxiety in the absence of these conditions. The most likely manifestation of such a problem comes from using one or both of the child's parents to escort the child to school. Occasionally, under these circumstances the child behaves appropriately as long as the parent is present in school but shows signs of distress as soon as the parent begins to leave. One solution to this problem is to fade out the presence of the parent slowly over one or several days. An example should clarify how this can be accomplished.

On the first day that the child is escorted to school, the child's parent might begin the day remaining very close to the child. As the day goes on, the parent can be instructed to move away, perhaps sitting in the back of the classroom by midday. Then, as the afternoon progresses, the parent can move outside the classroom for short periods of time, which are gradually lengthened. On the following day, the parent could begin by sitting in the back of the classroom and could leave the room again for increasing periods of time. The goal would be for the parent to drop the child off at school with no need to remain in the school. As time passes, the escort to school may also be faded in gradual steps, perhaps beginning with having the parent bring the child and a friend or neighbor of the child. With successive trips to school, the length of the escorted portion of the trip could be slowly decreased. This procedure, known as stimulus fading, can be useful in any circumstance where behavior is appropriate in the presence of a particular stimulus but inappropriate in its absence.

Step 7: Modify the program if necessary. The description of this behavior management program has been complicated by the fact that so many variations in the nature of the referred problem are possible. Once it has been decided to bring the child to school on a certain date, the options for modifying the program become somewhat limited because the avoidance behaviors will be strengthened if the child is not kept in school. However, it is possible to modify the program to enhance its effectiveness.

Doll (1987) described a treatment protocol, successful with four children, ages ten to twelve years, that is similar to the program described here. It deserves detailed description because it includes many useful components that could be integrated with the program just described. The central element in Doll's protocol is a subjective anxiety scale completed by the child. The subjective anxiety scale is developed with the cooperation of the child by presenting him or her with a line divided into seven numbered segments, labeled at both ends with descriptive terms, 1 being "very calm" and 7 being "very anxious." The child then provides representative incidents, based on his or her own experience, at each level of anxiety (going in the order 7, 1, 6, 2, 4, 5, 3), which are written down on the scale. The resulting scale, complete with examples, becomes the child's subjective anxiety scale. The child is then asked to rate the steps in a typical school day using the subjective anxiety scale. This scale can be used to identify the most difficult parts of the school day and to provide a method of monitoring progress during the course of treatment because the child is asked to provide ratings for each day.

Beginning at a level of school attendance the child had already demonstrated, a series of goals were developed. Each goal represented an incremental step toward daily attendance. The children were then rewarded for meeting daily or weekly goals. A unique component of the program was that the children monitored their own behavior and comfort levels (using the subjective anxiety scale). Two other components of the program were therapeutic support from the psychologist and relaxation training based on procedures described by Morris and Kratochwill (1985). The program described by Doll could be very useful by itself or in conjunction with the procedures described earlier.

Step 8: Fade out the program. Fading out the program refers to the process of removing the artificial supports for school attendance, leaving the child able to go to school without problems. Although the procedures just described are demonstrably effective in accomplishing this, it is possible for them to miss the main point, that school should be a positive experience for any child. Thus, once the child has been successfully returned to school, monitoring the child's classroom behavior should be continued with this in mind. The fact that the child is once again in school does not mean that the problem has been completely solved. Additional intervention of either a behavioral or academic nature may be helpful. For instance, the child may show signs of an academic handicap or social skills deficits. Assessment and, if needed, intervention may be the best ways to prevent future avoidance of school.

OTHER WAYS OF REMEDIATING ANXIETY

Although the formal behavior management program just outlined can be useful under a variety of circumstances, other techniques may be employed by themselves or in conjunction with this program. Relaxation training, systematic desensitization, self-monitoring, positive self-statements, and cognitive-behavioral training are four such techniques. These techniques will be discussed in this section.

Relaxation training can be a useful addition to the formal behavior management program that was outlined for school phobia. In addition, it could be used alone to remediate specific fears, such as test anxiety. As discussed earlier, the research evidence for the value of these techniques is slim at this time, although numerous successful case studies exist. Thus, those who opt to use such techniques should monitor their effectiveness carefully and be prepared to change treatment strategies, if needed. Also, reviewers (e.g., Forman & O'Malley, 1984; Reed, Carter, & Miller, 1992; Richter, 1984; Ross, 1981) seem to agree that relaxation training appears most effective when used in conjunction with other

methods, such as skill training and practice in coping with the problem situation. For instance, in treating test anxiety, it would make the most sense to work on both learning to relax and improving study skills.

A variety of methods can be employed to induce relaxation in children, but few of these methods can be easily administered in school, where space is limited and quiet rooms with soft chairs are often nonexistent. Within the restrictions imposed by typical school settings, it is possible to teach a child some relaxation skills. Two elements are particularly important in such teaching. First, it is often necessary to give the child some instruction in the meaning of relaxation. Not all children understand what the word means nor do they necessarily have any experience with the behaviors involved in relaxation. Furthermore, they may not know when it would be appropriate to use such skills. Thus, it may be possible to help children greatly by giving them the vocabulary to label their own feelings (of both relaxation and anxiety), training in relaxation skills, and training in how to apply relaxation skills in problematic situations.

Saigh and Antoun (1984) compared the effects of systematic desensitization, imagining a series of pleasant images counterposed with a hierarchy of anxiety-evoking scenes, and a control condition, on levels of anxiety and grade point averages of a group of test-anxious subjects. The findings were that systematic desensitization was as effective as the imaging technique, both of which were superior to the control condition. The technique they employed was to select a group of pleasant images based on group ratings. Five images were selected to be counterposed with a ten-item hierarchy of anxiety-evoking images related to test anxiety. Then, a group of test-anxious students of high school age were instructed to imagine alternately one of the pleasant scenes and one of the scenes from the hierarchy of anxiety-evoking scenes until they reported being able to imagine the anxiety-evoking scene without experiencing any anxiety. This training was conducted in seven fifty-minute treatment sessions. In addition, all of the subjects received three fifty-minute sessions of training in study skills.

Because study skills training was given to all subjects, including those in the control group, the effects of the treatment conditions can be attributed to the use of imagery and desensitization. In fact, the control group showed a slight decline in grade point average and a slight increase in reported anxiety, indicating that study skills training alone was not helpful.

In applying this technique with individual children,

several considerations must be kept in mind. First, it is important to consider the chronological age and cognitive skills of the child. Elliott and Ozolins (1983) concluded from an examination of the relevant research that seven- or eight-year-old children are able to produce and manipulate images. Younger children are also able to use imagery, but these authors question whether they can manipulate images in the ways required by systematic desensitization. Given the ease with which the behavior of children from four to about seven years old can be changed with reinforcement techniques, it would seem prudent to reserve imagery techniques for those age seven and older.

A second consideration concerns the specific imagery that a particular child is encouraged to employ. Research shows that imagery seems most effective in controlling behavior when its content and elaboration are at least partially determined by the child. Elliott and Ozolins suggest that children may interpret therapeutic instructions in ways not intended by the therapist, so it is important to monitor the meaning that any particular child assigns to an image he or she is encouraged to conjure up.

A method I found useful in helping children to form images is to have them draw a picture of themselves doing something that is relaxing, makes them feel good, or makes them feel happy. As the drawing is produced, the child can be questioned about its details and encouraged to elaborate on various aspects of the drawing. Then it is a relatively simple matter to ask the child to imagine the scene. The child's drawing can then be used to guide the trainer in helping the child form a concrete and relaxing image. As training progresses, every effort to monitor the child's behavior must be made to assure that relaxation is the net result.

Following the procedure employed by Saigh and Antoun (1984), a well-elaborated, relaxing image could then be imagined by the child in alternation with items from a hierarchy of anxiety-evoking scenes related to the child's specific problem. In Saigh and Antoun's procedure, the relaxing image was alternated with the test-anxiety-related image until the subjects reported that the image related to test anxiety no longer evoked any anxiety. Although this might be fairly easy to establish in subjects of high school age, younger children may need some additional training in order to learn to monitor their subjective feelings of anxiety. Alternatively, behavioral indicators of discomfort could be monitored by the person conducting the training.

For readers who wish to learn more about the treatment of anxiety, Morris and Kratchowill (1983b) have written an excellent book on the behavioral treatment of children's fears and phobias. They provide a thorough review of the research support for techniques plus the necessary detail to apply them. This book is highly recommended to those who wish to know more about the treatment of children's fears. Cautela (1982) provides a description of general procedures useful in the application of techniques involving imagery, along with a couple of case study examples. Ross (1981) and the books edited by Walker and Roberts (1983, 1992) and Reynolds (1992) also contain interesting and relevant chapters. The application of cognitive-behavioral techniques in treating anxiety is described Kendall et al. (1991).

USE OF HOME NOTES TO MONITOR SCHOOL PERFORMANCE

It is not always convenient for school personnel to provide rewards and monitor the performance of children. The use of home-based behavior management programs can be one method of decreasing the burden on school personnel (see reviews by Atkeson & Forehand, 1979; Kelley, 1990). The simplest method of conducting such a program is for the teacher to communicate with parents via a home note. School performance can then be rewarded by the parents, thus relieving the teacher of most of the tasks involved in conducting a behavior management program (e.g., Schumaker, Hovell, & Sherman, 1977). A potential problem with home-based programs is that parents may not be skilled in the application of behavior management techniques. Thus, it is important that the parents' behavior be monitored to ensure that they follow the rules of the program (cf. Blechman, Taylor, & Schrader, 1981). If problems develop as a consequence of parental inconsistency or lack of understanding, it may be necessary to suggest additional training in parenting skills or family counseling.

The mechanics of a home note system are simple. A printed note (see Figures 10.2 and 10.3) is filled out once a day or once a week by the child's teacher(s). The child receives points according to the quality of academic and behavioral performance, which are tabulated by the child's parents. The child can use the points to "purchase" from a menu of rewards. Alternatively, the notes can be used as a basis for a behavior management program that does not directly involve the child's parents. For example, children placed in special education

Student's Name: _____   Date _____

The student's academic perfcormance was (initial appropriate space)

_____ Excellent (30 points)

_____ Good (20 points)

_____ Acceptable (10 points)

_____ Unacceptable (0 points)

The student's general behavior was

_____ Exccellent (30 points

_____ Good (20 points)

_____ Acceptable (10 points)

_____ Unacceptable (0 points)

Teacher's comments: _____

_____

_____

_____

_____

Figure 10.2. Daily/Weekly Report Card

programs who are being mainstreamed into regular education classes can be monitored with a note system. This can be used as a basis for rewarding mainstream behavior in the special education classroom. Detailed descriptions of the various programs follow.

Step 1: Identify the problem. School–home or within-school notes can be effective with a variety of behavioral and academic problems, such as completing classroom work, staying on task, avoiding disruptive behavior, and following classroom rules (Kelley, 1990). With respect to academic performance, this type of program is most likely to be successful when the student shows inconsistent performance, doing well in "interesting" subject areas and poorly in "boring" subjects, or when the child shows variable performance in the same academic area from day to day. This type of performance would indicate that the student is capable of doing well but is poorly motivated. The situation that must be approached cautiously is one where the child may have an academic problem such as a learning disability. The addition of a behavior management program to an already frustrating situation may not be in the child's best interests. When academic performance is the target behavior, it is often the case that other disruptive behaviors will decrease because being disruptive is not compatible with being engaged in academic tasks.

School–home notes can be constructed to address behavioral and academic problems. A child who has "good days" and "bad days" with respect to complying with school and classroom rules would be a good candidate for success with this type of program. Note that the underlying principle for designing successful home note programs is that the child shows some evidence of having the requisite skills for success. If the child lacks the skills necessary for academic and behavioral success, then a home note program is less likely to succeed. In such a case, it may be necessary to intervene more directly to improve the deficit skills.

Step 2: Refine the definition of the problem. In the real world of the classroom, it is not always possible to

Student's Name: _____   Date _____

The student's academic perfcormance was (initial appropriate space)

_____ Outstanding (30 points)

_____ Good (25 points)

_____ Above average (20 points)

_____ Improvement shown (15 points)

_____ Improvement needed (10 points)

_____ Acceptable (5 points)

_____ Not acceptable (0 points)

Teacher's comments: _____

_____

_____

The student's general behavior was

_____ Outstanding (30 points)

_____ Good (25 points)

_____ Above average (20 points)

_____ Improvement shown (15 points)

_____ Improvement needed (10 points)

_____ Acceptable (5 points)

_____ Not acceptable (0 points)

Teacher's comments: _____

_____

_____

Figure 10.3. Daily/Weekly Report Card

take the time and energy to define undesirable behavior and deficit academic skills precisely. Instead, from the teacher's point of view, the problem is that the student disobeys classroom rules and fails to complete assigned work. The home note program described here is designed for this situation, where the simplest possible behavior management program is desired. Of course, a potential problem is that the program will fail because the problem has not been defined concretely. Under many circumstances, however, this program will work very well. In those cases where the program does not work well, it is always possible to reassess the situation and switch to a program that more directly addresses the problem behavior.

Step 3: Assess the baseline rate. It would be most desirable if the precise number of rule violations could be tabulated along with an accurate record of the child's academic accomplishment. Again, such precision may not always be possible. If this is the case, a useful baseline measurement can be obtained if the teacher fills out the home note for a week without providing any feedback to the child. In this way, a reasonably objective record of the teacher's impressions can be obtained, and it will be possible to determine whether the program results in any positive change in the child's behavior from the perspective of the classroom teacher. Also, this record will provide an excellent basis for determining the number of points that will be required for the rewards provided by the child's parents.

Step 4: Design the behavioral contingencies and write the program description. The rules for implementing a home note program are very simple. At the end of each school day, the child's teacher fills out a note to the parents, such as shown in Figures 10.2 and 10.3. The child then takes the note home, and the parents tabulate the points earned for that day. The points earned are then exchanged for rewards as negotiated between the child and parents. Given that the child can earn up to 50 or 60 points per day, a reasonable starting point might be about 300 or 400 points for a reward of moderate size, such as a movie or small toy. Alternatively, a reward menu like the one described in Chapter 4 might be set up to provide varying rewards at a range of point values. To get the program off to a good start, it may be helpful to provide one or two small rewards that can be earned with relatively few points.

An important element of the home note program is the role of the child's teacher in providing social reinforcement for good performance and feedback regarding unacceptable behavior. Because the target behaviors are not precisely specified and, in addition, may vary from day to day, it is important that the child's teacher provide feedback to the child regarding the reasons behind the points, if any, awarded for each day's performance. For example, if the child failed to complete an in-class assignment or failed a spelling test and therefore received a low rating for the day's academic performance, this should be carefully explained to the child at the end of the day. Likewise, if the child's behavior was rated as "unacceptable" for a day, the exact reasons for the rating should be explained. The hope is that knowledge of what behaviors resulted in poor ratings will motivate the child to improve her or his behavior the following days. At the same time, feedback regarding the reasons for positive ratings also needs to be a regular part of the program. Concrete and immediate positive feedback during the day will also help the child learn what is expected.

A written program is particularly important for a home note program because information needs to be communicated from teachers to parents. Table 10.1 provides a sample handout that can be used for both teachers and parents. The handout can be either copied or modified to meet the needs of a particular situation.

Step 5: Begin the program. Several elements need to come together in order for a home note program to begin. First, an appropriate format for the note must be determined. Two examples are provided in Figures 10.2 and 10.3. Figure 10.2 shows the simplest format, whereas Figure 10.3 is more detailed. A detailed format is appropriate when the child's behavior is generally poor and much improvement is needed. The additional rating levels allow the child to earn some points for less than optimal performance. Note that both formats request a rating of behavior *and* academic performance. Because each affects the other, it is recommended that both ratings be used even when improvement in only one area is needed, to allow the child to receive at least some positive feedback. Finally, I suggest that the note be typed on the school's letterhead to give it a more official appearance.

Another alternative is to use a commercially available home note system. Parker (1991) has developed a program intended for children diagnosed with Attention-Deficit Hyperactivity Disorder designed to track five behaviors: (1) attentiveness in class, (2) completion of classroom work, (3) homework completion, (4) general behavior, and (5) neatness. The program comes with instructions and preprinted forms for rating these behaviors several times a day or once a day, depending on the child's needs. A calendar that parents can use to record the total number of points earned by the child is also provided. A disadvantage of using this program is that five specific behaviors are targeted and this may not meet the needs of all children with whom it may be desirable to employ a home note program.

Once a format for the home note has been determined, the next step is to meet with the child's parents to discuss the classroom situation and options for handling it. Those involved, particularly the classroom teacher, should have met with or at least talked by phone with the parents on previous occasions. During the conference, the home note system should be offered as one method of dealing with the child's behavior, and the parents' willingness to cooperate should be assessed. If the parents are willing, then a date to begin the program should be set, allowing for a one-week baseline period. Alternatively, the baseline data could be gathered prior to the

Table 10.1. Sample Written Program Description for a School–Home Note Program

1. The goal of this program is to assist _____ in developing improved behavior in school.

2. Each school day, a school–home note will be completed by the student's primary teacher. The student is responsible for bringing the note home to his./her parent(s), who will tabulate the total number of points earned each day and dispense the agreed-on rewards. If the note is lost or forgotten, no points can be earned that day.

3. The student may exchange points earned for the following rewards of his/her choice:

    30 points _____

    50 points _____

    100 points _____

    200 points _____

    300 points _____

    500 points _____

    1000 points _____

4. If the student earns 275 points or more for three weeks in a row, he/she will receive a special "graduation" present consisting of _____ .

5. After meeting the criterion in #4, the school–home note will be completed once each week by the teacher, and the menu of rewards will be renegotiated. If the program results in acceptable behavior for four successive weeks, another "graduation" award consisting of _____ will be given and the program wil be ended.

6. Signatures:

    _____
    _____
    _____
    _____
    _____
    _____

conference to and used during meeting with the parents to set "prices" on the reward menu.

A few days prior to the start of the program, both the parents and the teacher should explain the program to the child. On the first day of the program, nothing more need be said, although a blank copy of the home note might be shown to the child. At the end of the school day, the teacher should have a brief conference with the child to present the note and provide feedback regarding the day's accomplishments. Under no circumstances should the teacher get into arguments with the child over the appropriate rating for the day, although the teacher must also make every effort to be consistent and realistic in the standards that are applied. At the start of the program, a couple of phone contacts between the teacher and the child's parents are to be expected, to clarify rules

and the operation of the system. In my own experience, one aspect of the program that frequently needs clarification is the nature of the point system. Children are likely to want to collect their rewards while still holding onto the points they have earned. A good way to clarify this issue is to explain that the points, like money, are gone once they have been spent. Alternatively, the rewards could be tied to points by a rule that states that successively higher numbers of total points are followed by specified rewards. For example, 5000 points may be required for the child to earn a major reward, such as a new bicycle, while at the same time each 200 points earned toward the grand total results in a small reward, such as a pencil, sticker, or other school supply.

An alternative method of administering a home note program calls for less involvement on the part of the parents. This may be necessary when the family system has problems that preclude accurate, consistent administration of the program. The classroom teacher, tutor, special education teacher, or school principal could be responsible for keeping records of points earned and awarding items supplied by the parents. Some parents are capable of providing large rewards, such as a new bicycle, but others do not have the resources to supply even the smallest item. This should not prevent implementation of such a program. Even the smallest rewards, such as a pencil or eraser, can be effective. Occasionally, I have administered programs where it seemed that the positive feedback was much more important than the specific reward for which the child was working.

Step 6: Observe the effects of the program and take steps to strengthen generalization beyond the training environment. Once the program begins, the child's parents or other administrator of the program should keep a record of the number of points earned each day and the total number of points earned each week. As the number of points earned increases, subjective reports of classroom behavior should reflect the improvement represented by the points. If not, the purposes and goals of the program should be reviewed.

Because the training environment is the classroom, it is not necessary to be concerned with generalization. However, it is desirable that the program be faded out. Techniques for accomplishing this are discussed under Step 8.

Step 7: Modify the program, if necessary. If the program fails to produce the expected changes, the first question is whether the child and his or her parents understand the program. Sometimes, parents will take away a reward that has been earned with good behavior in school when the child misbehaves at home. Such behavior on the part of the parents is a sign that they need additional help in learning to manage the behavior of their child. Another possibility is that the child does not understand the connection between the points earned in school and the promised reward. This could be remedied by a careful explanation or by lowering the total number of points necessary to earn a smaller reward.

As in almost all behavior management programs, it is possible that the rewards offered to the child are not powerful enough to bring about behavior change. A conference with the child may reveal what incentives are likely to be effective. It is also possible that the material reward is not the issue from the child's point of view.

When the child's behavior shows improvement, significant adults should respond with obvious pride in the child's accomplishment. Without this element, the program could be doomed to failure. An examination of the motives of the parents and their role in maintaining the child's behavior may be in order. For instance, if the parents are in the middle of an acrimonious divorce or separation, the child's behavior may be an issue with which they are not able to cope effectively, given the extent of even larger problems in the marriage.

Because of its simplicity, a home note program may not be effective in every case. If either the child's ability or skill level was overestimated at the beginning of the program, the feedback provided by the home note points may be insufficient to improve performance. In such cases, more thorough assessment and new behavior management programs might be necessary.

Step 8: Fade out the program. Home note programs are not meant to be faded out completely given that periodic report cards and parent–teacher conferences are a regular occurrence as the child progresses through school. The goal, then, is to fade out the daily notes from the teacher and the reliance on the reward system to maintain good behavior. As noted previously, an important part of making the transition to a reward-free system is that the adults involved in the original program must provide the child with positive attention and praise for good performance. As the child begins to excel, the number of points required for a reward can be increased while the frequency of home notes is decreased. If good performance can be maintained with a weekly home note, then it would be reasonable to discuss with the child the possibility of eliminating the point system entirely. If both parents and teachers respond positively to the child's accomplishments, it can be expected that the formal behavior management program can be completely replaced by informal behavior management techniques.

MONITORING AND REWARDING DAILY SCHOOL PERFORMANCE

Often, children having problems in school appear to possess adequate ability but apparently lack the motivation and organizational skills to function at an acceptable level. These students may, as a consequence of a disorganized approach to schoolwork and achievement–ability discrepancies, be labeled as learning disabled or as having an attention deficit. Such students may respond well to systematic monitoring of school performance on a subject-by-subject basis. Such a system can be backed up by either school- or home-based rewards and is similar to a home note program. The difference is that a home note program does not provide such a detailed monitoring of performance. A step-by-step outline of such a program follows. It is a token reward program in which points are awarded to the student for emitting the component behaviors, which contribute to school success. The points are added and converted to a daily percentage (total earned divided by total possible). A percentage rather than total number of points earned is suggested to eliminate the effects of the variability likely to be found in the academic schedule of junior and senior high school students.

Step 1: Identify the problem. Like the home note program just described, this program is designed to improve behavior and academic performance. Unlike the home note program, it is designed to monitor all potential problem areas. Thus, this program is designed for students who are not doing well in school as a result of disorganization, poor attendance, poor study habits, inappropriate behavior in class, production of low-quality work, or any other problem that can be defined concretely. The program is specially suited for the junior or senior high school resource setting, but it requires the cooperation of the student's teachers, who must provide daily or weekly ratings of the student's performance.

Step 2: Refine the definition of the problem. Unlike the home note program, which assumes that the student possesses the crucial skills needed for success, the daily monitoring program can be used as a tool for teaching and rewarding academic survival skills. A Daily Performance Record is used to record the points earned by the student in each academic subject or period. Each category of behavior is worth from 1 to 5 points, with 1 point representing unacceptable performance and 5 points representing outstanding performance. It is up to the teachers involved to establish the criteria for each level of performance. These criteria should be discussed with the student so that he or she receives daily feedback regarding the acceptability of his or her behavior. Thus, the definitions of acceptable and unacceptable behavior are defined by the teachers while working directly with the student.

The sample Daily Performance Record shown in Figure 10.4 is designed to be as flexible as possible. It allows

for monitoring attendance, homework, preparation for class (having books, note-taking materials, pencil or pen, etc.), completion of in-class assignments, quality of completed work, and other behaviors relevant to acceptable performance. The Daily Performance Record is meant to be the responsibility of the student, who should carry the record and present it to each teacher for completion at the end of the academic period. Because the Daily Performance Record provides reminders and detailed criteria for acceptable behavior, it is possible that the student can learn new skills, such as appropriate organizational habits, as a consequence of this behavior management program.

Step 3: Assessment of the baseline rate. Several methods of establishing a baseline can be employed with this behavior management program. The simplest method would be to use the records of the student's academic performance that are regularly kept by her or his teachers. This approach has some validity, even though the behaviors that are the direct target of the behavior management program may not be directly monitored, because the ultimate goal is to improve academic performance. Another approach to establishing a baseline is for the monitor of the program to survey each teacher to determine the frequency of the behaviors directly targeted for change. Finally, each teacher could be asked to complete the Daily Performance Record every day for a week before the program begins. This can be done by giving a copy to each teacher and collecting them at the end of the baseline period. The result is a detailed baseline record that is useful in setting the criteria for rewards once the program is begun.

Step 4: Design the behavioral contingencies and write the program description. In this program, the contingency concerns the relationship between the number of points earned and whatever rewards can be mutually agreed on by those involved in planning the program. As shown in Figure 10.4, each of the behaviors monitored in the program is given a rating of 1 to 5, with 5 representing outstanding performance and 1 representing unacceptable performance. For each day that the program is in effect, one of two methods can be used for computing the total number of points earned. If there is little variability in the behaviors expected from day to day, then the total number of points earned can simply be added up. A second method is to use a percentage instead of the sum. Percentages are computed by dividing the total number of points earned by the total number

Name: _____

Date: _____

Points earned: _____

Total possible: _____

Percentage: _____

Points
5 = Outstanding performance
4 = Good performance
3 = Acceptable
2 = Improvement needed
1 = Unacceptable

	Period or Subject						
	1	2	3	4	5	6	7
Attendance							
Homework completed							
Has needed materials							
In-class assignments complete							
Quality of completed work							
Teacher's initials							

Comments and upcoming assignments

_____

_____

_____

_____

Figure 10.4. Daily Performance Record

of possible points for a given day. The total possible points is equal to five times the total number of behavior categories that were rated summed across subjects or periods. This method is most useful when the number of applicable behavior categories changes from day to day, such as when homework is assigned irregularly in one or more classes. An additional advantage of using per-centages is that each student whose behavior is monitored on such a program will be able to earn a minimum of about 30 percentage points and a maximum of 100 points. Keeping all students on the same scale should simplify record keeping and program design.

Percentage points alone have little or no value to most students. When percentage points may be exchanged for rewards, however, behavior change can be expected to take place. For younger children, stickers, small toys, school supplies, and the opportunity to run errands should be sufficient to promote behavior change. For older students, the rewards used to back up the daily percentage points may include privileges, prizes, or rewards negotiated with individual students. The backup reward may be provided by parents, school personnel, or both. Flexibility in the selection of the backup reward is a key to success.

The choice of whether the backup reward is provided on a daily, weekly, monthly, six-week, or nine-week basis depends on the age of the student, his or her maturity, and the size of the reward for which the student is working. When doubt exists as to how the backup reward should be delivered, it should be remembered that behavior change is easiest to obtain when the interval between rewards is shortest. Once the time interval and back-up reinforcers have been selected, their precise relationship must be determined. If a 1-week time interval has been selected, then the student could earn a maximum of 500 percentage points per week. A reasonable starting point for the management program might be that the student earns a small reward for obtaining 250 percentage points, a larger reward for obtaining more than 300 percentage points, and a highly desirable reward for obtaining 400 or 500 percentage points. One contingency for obtaining 400 or more percentage points might be that the student could gain some relief from the monitoring system.

There are a number of ways to approach the written program, but the most helpful and realistic may be to negotiate a behavioral contract that all involved parties sign. The sample program shown in Table 10.1 provides a good example of the essential elements in such a contract.

Step 5: Begin the program. To begin the program, a good supply of the Daily Performance Records should be available. Records could be custom designed for each student, or one generic form could be employed for all students. To begin the program, the adult in charge may simply announce the rules of the program to the student and set the day on which the rules will take effect. Alternatively, a meeting at which a behavioral contract is negotiated could precede the start of the program. Some students will complain about possible embarrassment involved in taking the Daily Performance Record to each teacher. One response to this potential weakness of the program is to give students an opportunity to correct their behavior (perhaps during the baseline period). If students are sufficiently motivated, it may be possible for them to remain off the program. Alternatively, if the team agrees that the problem is beyond the student's control, a copy of the Daily Performance Record can be given to each teacher and collected by the program monitor at the end of each day or week.

Steps 6, 7, and 8: Observe, strengthen generalization, modify if necessary, and fade out the program. Once the program has begun, two issues become important. First, the backup reward must be powerful enough to motivate students to improve their behavior. This issue may require repeated negotiation with students before an adequate system is developed. The second issue is strengthening generalization of the skills so that the student can function in school without the monitoring program. This is accomplished by employing the usual procedures for fading out a reward system and through careful evaluation, and modification if necessary, of the particular behaviors included in the monitoring program. The behaviors monitored should contribute to the student's eventual independent functioning in the school.

One fading strategy that deserves consideration is for the student to take over the monitoring functions of the program. That is, once students learn what behaviors are needed to meet the requirements of the program, they can complete the monitoring form themselves after each class or period. At the same time, the monitoring form cues the student's appropriate behavior. Self-management of the program can be used from the beginning of the program if the student is cooperative and mature enough to accurately record his or her own behavior. Some students may be unable to manage the program themselves without a lot of training and prompting from adults. The steps in developing a student-managed version of this program are described next.

1. As with all behavior management programs, a baseline rate of target behaviors needs to be established. Baseline data can be obtained by asking the student's teachers to complete the monitoring form at the end of each of the student's classes or periods for about a week.

2. Once baseline data have been obtained, the program could proceed as described previously or the self-monitoring procedure could be implemented. For the self-monitoring procedure, students continue to carry the form with them. Instead of asking the

teacher to complete it, however, each student completes the form by themselves at the end of each class.

3. Rewards are based on the student's self-reported behavior. However, as a check on the student's accuracy, the student's teachers should be asked to complete the monitoring form independently for the student on a randomly selected day each week that is unknown to the student. The student would be aware that this was occurring about once each week but would not know on which day it was to occur.

4. On the designated day, teacher-completed monitoring forms are collected by the teacher monitoring the student's program. Then the student- and teacher-completed monitoring forms are compared. If the student's self-rating is within one point in either direction of the teacher's rating, the student should receive verbal praise or points depending on the program. However, the major contingency is that failure to match an adequate number of ratings can result in a return to teacher-based monitoring. In the early stages of a student-managed program, the criterion for matching can be liberal, such as being within one point in either direction of the teacher's rating for at least half the behaviors being monitored. Later, this criterion can be raised to include more of the monitored behaviors.

5. The hope is that students' skill at monitoring their own behavior will continue to improve so that even this aspect of the program can be faded by decreasing the frequency with which the student completes the monitoring form. For example, instead of daily, the form could be completed every other day or once a week. At some point in the program, the daily monitoring form could then be exchanged for an assignment notebook, calendar, or other organizational system. Some students may need to remain on a monitoring program at some level in order to maintain a particular level of performance.

For more discussion of self-management interventions in the schools, see Cole (1992), Lam, Cole, Shapiro, and Bambara (1994), Lazarus (1993) or Webber, Scheuermann, McCall, and Coleman (1993). Ninness, Fuerst, and Rutherford (1991) provide a detailed description of a similar program based in a special education classroom. This program included self-instruction in appropriate behavior and a levels system built into the reinforcement contingencies (see Chapter 5). An interesting finding of this study is that the stu-

dents' greatly improved behavior did not generalize to a situation outside the classroom until the students were given explicit instructions to apply their self-management skills in the new setting.

BEHAVIOR CONTRACTS

As children become older and more independent, behavior management programs need to be more flexible in meeting their needs. In some situations, it is possible to have enough control over access to reinforcers that even teenagers are likely to comply with program rules. In most other cases, however, teenagers have almost as much control as adults. For example, children over the age of sixteen have the option of leaving school. If a behavior management program designed to increase their academic performance does not meet some of the teenager's needs, the teenager may choose to leave school rather than comply. One way of addressing the situation where it is desirable to formalize a child's input into a behavior management program is to negotiate a behavior contract with the child.

Behavior contracts can be effective with a wide range of ages, not just adolescents. Allen, Howard, Sweeney, and McLaughlin (1993) reported success with behavior contracting for three students in the second or third grade. They used a reversal design in which the treatment was withdrawn several times to demonstrate a causal link between contracting and improved behavior. An interesting finding was that when the third baseline period was begun, the three students showed a high rate of the target behaviors. The authors suggested that the data showed evidence of maintenance effects across the baseline conditions. Although more research would be needed to substantiate this point, it does suggest that withdrawal, reinstatement, and withdrawal of the contingency may have contributed to the generalization effects that were demonstrated.

Behavior contracts include a wide range of interventions. In some cases they consist of negotiated written agreements between two parties, who agree to engage in a mutual interchange of privileges and responsibilities where each privilege specified in the contract is earned by fulfilling a specific responsibility. At the other extreme, behavior contracts can be informal verbal agreements in which one person agrees to change certain specified behaviors (Kirschenbaum & Flanery, 1984). Behavior contracts differ from other behavior management techniques in that they may specify privileges and responsibilities for *both* of the involved parties, whereas in most other methods parents or teachers are administrators of contingencies, which they dictate. Behavior contracts can be a valuable tool for negotiating mutually satisfactory agreements between two parties who desire behavior change from each other.

Behavior contracts are useful under a variety of circumstances. Any behavior management program can be improved by involving the child in its design and putting its provisions into writing so that all who are involved can refer to it. Signing a contract may also strengthen the child's commitment to changing his or her behavior. Programs that involve the child's parents can be more effective in contract form because communication is made more concrete and the rules may be looked at and discussed at any time.

Another application of behavior contracts is in both self-contained and resource special education classes. In these settings, a standard behavior contract that outlines the teacher's expectations, rules of conduct, academic expectations, consequences of both desirable and undesirable behavior, and other aspects of the program relevant to the student's success can be signed by both the teacher and the student. The student's contribution to the contract can be to set personal goals for academic accomplishment and behavior. Although student input into these contracts is limited, by signing such a contract, the student indicates an understanding of the rules governing behavior in the room and a commitment to following those rules.

At the most sophisticated level, behavior contracts can be used as a negotiating tool for resolving conflicts between children and adults. Successful conflict resolution normally requires a series of several behavior contracts, because the first draft rarely captures the essential needs of those signing it. Instead, several drafts may be needed before the parties feel comfortable enough to reveal their most important needs within the context of the negotiating process.

Good behavior contracts, like good behavior management programs, state the specific responsibilities to be performed by each party and the specific privileges earned by each party as a consequence of performing those responsibilities. Of course, the more concrete and specific the definitions of the behaviors are, the more effective the contract is likely to be. However, the definitions of behaviors can require repeated negotiation. Careful attention to baseline observations before the contract is in force and continued measurement of these behaviors after the contract takes effect are provisions

that should be included in a contract. Also, behaviors of *both* parties who sign the contract may need to be monitored.

Clauses that specify a bonus for complying with the contract and sanctions for failure to comply may also be included in a behavior contract. Finally, a monitoring and feedback system, which informs each party when responsibilities have been fulfilled, should be included. The last clause in a contract should specify when the contract will be reviewed and renegotiated, if necessary. Sample behavior contracts are presented in Tables 10.2, 10.3, and 10.4. A summary of guidelines for effective behavior contracts (Kanfer & Schefft, 1988; Martin & Pear, 1988; Shelton & Levy, 1981; Sulzer-Azaroff & Mayer, 1991; Wells & Forehand, 1981) follows:

1. Emphasize behaviors to be increased.
2. Contract for improvements in small steps.
3. Ensure that the terms of the contract are concrete and clear. It is especially important to define target behaviors and methods of keeping track of their occurrence carefully so all participants know whether responsibilities are being met.
4. Ensure that reinforcement is delivered as soon as possible after target behaviors occur and that it is clear when reinforcement will be delivered and by whom.
5. Include clauses specifying penalties for failure to meet goals, but emphasize reinforcing appropriate behavior. Contracts may also include bonus clauses for performance above the minimal goals.
6. Strike a balance between the costs and benefits of the contract for all participants.
7. Include a clause that allows for review and/or renegotiation of the contract on a specified date.
8. Include signatures of all participants and the specific date that the contract begins. Each participant should also receive a copy of the contract.

Behavior contracts have several features that can be important in the success of a behavior management program. One of their main advantages is that they clarify the roles of those involved with the student, such as teachers, biological parents, and stepparents. When a written agreement has been distributed to all involved, misunderstandings, misinterpretations, and mistakes are less likely than if the rules are described to parents over the phone. Occasionally, parents will learn new ways of dealing with their children from a written contract. Other advantages of behavior contracts are that they allow for

Table 10.2. Sample Behavior Change Contract

The purpose of this contract is to help Annie complete daily homework assignments. Annie has been doing less than 25 percent of her assigned homework, and she is in danger of failing fifth grade if she does not improve.

1. Annie's teacher will provide her parents with a weekly report of progress in completing homework for the previous week, along with upcoming assignments for the current week. The listing of coming assignments may not be complete, and it is Annie's responsibility to keep track of other assignments given during the week. The report will be provided each Monday and will report the percentage of homework completed and the percentage accuracy for the previous week (Monday through Friday). The note will go home with Annie every Monday.

2. On Sunday through Thursday evenings, Annie is required to spend at least forty-five minutes each night working on her homework. If she finishes all homework, the remaining time is to be spent reading a book of her choice.

3. Annie may start her homework any time before 7:00 P.M. Once started, her work period is to last the full forty-five minutes.

4. At the beginning of the homework period, Annie will tell her mother what she intends to accomplish for the evening. At the end of the homework period, Annie will show her completed work to her mother or tell her about the book she is reading. If Annie meets the goals stated at the beginning of the period, her mother will prepare her a small snack such as popcorn or cookies and milk. Annie may also elect to receive 10 points. Annie's mother also agrees to ensure that Matt, her younger brother, does not enter her room during study time.

5. Each Monday, Annie is responsible for showing her mother the note from the teacher regarding her accomplishments for the previous week and her future assignments. For each week that Annie meets her weekly goal, she receives 100 points, which can be spent as described in #8. The weekly goals are:

    Week 1:   50 percent of assignments complete; 30% accuracy.
    Week 2:   70 percent of assignments complete; 50% accuracy.
    Week 3:   90 percent of assignments complete; 70% accuracy.
    Week 4: 100 percent of assignments complete; 75% accuracy.
    Week 5: 100 percent of assignments complete; 80% accuracy.

    For the remaining weeks of the program, the goal remains 100 percent of assignments complete and 80 percent accuracy.

6. Annie's mother will keep a graph showing the percentage of assignments complete and accuracy. Total points earned will be posted weekly next to the graph.

7. Annie may earn bonus points in the following ways:
    a. Each time the weekly accuracy exceeds 80 percent, Annie receives 5 bonus points for each 1 percent above 80 percent. (*Example*: If Annie completes assignments with 87 percent accuracy, she receives 35 bonus points.)
    b. If Annie receives reports stating she completed 100 percent of her assignments with 85 percent accuracy or better for three weeks in a row, she receives 500 bonus points.

8. The points that Annie earns through this program may be spent on any of the rewards shown below. Every Monday, Annie and her mother will discuss the total number of points available and Annie's plans for using the points.

    100 points . . . . trip to shopping mall with a friend
    250 points . . . . purchase a new compact disc
    250 points . . . . go to a movie
    500 points . . . . new pair of jeans
    500 points . . . . new blouse or shirt
    1000 points . . . . new shoes
    1500 points . . . . have hair professionally cut and styled

    Other rewards may be negotiated with Annie's mother.

9. This contract will begin next Monday and will be reviewed in one week, at which time it may be revised or remain in force. Thereafter, it will be reviewed every two weeks.

10. Signatures:

    Student   _____

    Mother   _____

    Teacher   _____

    School psychologist   _____

Table 10.3. Sample Behavior Change Contract

Name _____

The purpose of this contract is to help learn to do the following: (1) Obey classroom rules, (2) complete seatwork for each day.

A. _____ can earn stickers by following classroom rules. The first time a rule is violated each day, his/her name will be written on the board. For each additional time a rule is broken, a checkmark will be placed by the name. The student can earn his/her name and checkmarks off the board for following the teacher's instructions. At the end of each day, a sticker will be awarded if the student's name is not on the board:

Name *not* on board . . . . 1 sticker
Name or checkmarks on board. . . . . 0 stickers

B. Stickers will also be given for completing assigned seatwork. One sticker will be awarded for completing arithmetic worksheets. One sticker will be awarded for completing all reading worksheets. One sticker will be awarded for completing all other worksheets and projects for the day. If all written work for the day is finished, a bonus of two more stickers will be awarded.

Finish arithmetic work . . . . 1 sticker
Finish reading work . . . . 1 sticker
Finish all other work. . . . . 1 sticker
Finish all work for the day . . . . 2 bonus stickers

C. If 28 or more stickers are earned in 1 week (Monday–Friday), 5 bonus stickers will be awarded. If 30 stickers are earned in one week, an *additional* 5 stickers will be awarded.

D. Stickers earned in school may be used to "buy" rewards supplied by the student's parents from the following menu:

_____ 10 stickers

_____ 30 stickers

_____ 40 stickers

_____ 50 stickers

_____ 100 stickers

_____ 200 stickers

E. The student's teacher agrees to keep a daily and weekly record of the number of stickers earned.

F. This contract will be reviewed on _____

G. Signatures:

Student _____

Mother _____

Teacher _____

Father _____

input from all involved; they can point to problems that go beyond the immediate issues, such as abuse or chemical use or abuse; they have a wide range of potential applications; and they are effective tools for changing the behavior of adolescents.

We now turn to a step-by-step description of how to develop a behavior contract.

Step 1: Identify the problem. As noted, behavior contracts have a wide variety of applications. They can be used to document the specifics of virtually any behavior management program. For example, a regular classroom teacher could have a handout describing classroom rules, consequences for misbehavior, and other expectations. This could be presented as a formal contract to be

Table 10.4. A Sample Behavioral Contract

1. Mike agrees to come home before 9:00 P.M., Sunday through Thursday nights, and before 12:00 midnight Friday and Saturday nights. For each night he is on time, Mike receives $1.00 from his parents. Mike also receives a bonus of $5.00 for seven consecutive nights of being on time.

2. If Mike accumulates a total of more than two hours of tardiness from Saturday through Friday nights, he will wash the car and mow the lawn on Saturday.

3. Mike's parents agree to question Mike regarding his whereabouts and activities for no more than two minutes on nights when he is late and not at all when he is on time. In exchange for a perfect week of not exceeding these time limits, Mike agrees to attend church and eat dinner with the family on Sunday.

4. Mike's parents will maintain a record of Mike's evening arrival times, and Mike will keep a record of the amount of time his parents question him regarding his whereabouts and activities.

5. This contract remains in force for two weeks. At the end of two weeks, the contract may be extended or renegotiated.

6. Signatures:

   Mike:

   Mother:

   Father:

signed by the teacher and by each student, with each student retaining a copy. For some students, the formal nature of signing a contract may encourage a strong, sincere commitment to meeting the contract's terms. In this sense, the contract is a significant step above a handout or poster.

At the other extreme, a behavior contract can be a therapeutic tool that helps the participants improve communication and clarify their own needs. For example, an adolescent and his parents might engage in conflict over the issue of a curfew. Parents are upset when the adolescent comes in after 9:00 P.M. on weekday nights and the adolescent claims that he comes in late because he wants to avoid being vigorously questioned by his parents regarding his whereabouts during the evening. It may be possible to negotiate an agreement in which parents agree to limit their questions and the adolescent agrees to come home on time. If the contract fails to bring about behavior change, not unusual for the first contract, it would normally be renegotiated. Perhaps the adolescent views "just a few questions" as "nagging," whereas the parents see it as "being involved" in their son's life. Further clarification of the needs of each participant may eventually result in behavior changes that each family member views as positive.

To illustrate the wide range of behavior contract ap-

plications, a typical situation employing a behavior contract will be described. This situation will illustrate both the general behavior management approach and the specifics of writing effective behavior contracts. The primary issue is completion of homework by a fifth-grade girl.

Step 2: Refine the definition of the problem. The first two guidelines for writing effective behavior contracts are to focus on behaviors to be increased and to contract for improvement in small steps. In the case of the fifth-grade girl, whom we will call Annie, it seems evident that the logical behavior to increase is homework completion. Teachers maintain detailed records of academic performance for grading purposes, so it would be relatively easy to establish the history of the problem. As in all situations involving academic performance, however, considerable caution is needed because failure to complete homework could reflect either a lack of motivation or the presence of a handicapping condition such as a sensory problem (hearing or vision deficiency), a specific learning disability, or perhaps Attention-Deficit Hyperactivity Disorder. Any such suspicions need to be followed up with a complete academic assessment to rule out the presence of problems that may be beyond the control of the child.

Assuming that Annie shows no signs of academic or behavior problems, a plan for improving homework completion may be developed. The first step would be to meet with Annie's parent(s) to discuss the situation and develop a plan to solve the problem. According to Olympia, Jenson, Clark, and Sheridan (1992), forty-five to ninety minutes of homework per night with two to four assignments per week is a reasonable amount for a fifth-grade student. Furthermore, these authors note that rapid feedback, good in-class preparation, and relevance to classroom topics are crucial variables in making homework an effective learning tool. Annie's fifth-grade teacher would be expected to fall within these guidelines, and Annie's parents would need to understand the teacher's specific expectations. From the parental perspective, the main issues are being aware of the teacher's expectations and providing a suitable study environment for the child. These parameters can then be used to develop an acceptable behavior contract.

Thus, the main issues that need to be addressed in the contract are as follows:

1. Define expectations regarding amount of homework to be completed and approximate time to be spent per night on homework.
2. Develop a systematic method of communication between the child's parents and the classroom teacher.
3. Ensure that Annie's parents make an appropriate study area available to her.
4. Reach agreement on rewards for homework completion.

In line with Guideline 2, it is suggested that the first contract goal be to improve homework completion to an acceptable level over a one-week period.

Step 3: Assess the baseline rate. It is unlikely that an assessment of the baseline rate of homework completion will be needed, because the classroom teacher's records will provide the needed information. However, for purposes of communicating with parents and documenting the child's progress, it may be helpful to transcribe records from the gradebook to another format. It would also be helpful to describe homework completion using a measure that remains constant from week to week despite changes in the amount of homework assigned. One method is to keep a record of the *percentage* of assigned homework completed and its *accuracy*, also

expressed as a percentage. Both quantities could be plotted on the same weekly graph.

Computations of the percentage of homework completed need to make sense to everyone involved. If each assignment is given a point value, computation of these percentage will be easy. For assignments that involve problems or questions, the percentages completed and the percentage correct can be based on the problems completed. Assignments such as reports should be graded using the same criteria that apply to all students, with a percentage assigned according to the grade. For example, a report that receives a grade of "C" might be regarded as 100 percent complete with 75 percent accuracy. A report receiving an "A+" might be regarded as 100 percent complete with 100 percent accuracy. By contrast, a report that receives a "D" might be regarded as 75 percent complete with 65 percent accuracy. Although such a system would not be perfectly consistent, it should accurately reflect the student's performance and the contribution of homework toward the final evaluation.

Step 4: Design the behavioral contingencies and write the program description. Homework completion is not really a negotiable issue between a fifth-grade child and her parents. The expectation is that homework *will* be completed. Some issues are negotiable, however, such as the time and place for working on homework, specific goals, the level of parental supervision, and rewards for meeting goals. Also, the long-term issue is developing the responsibility and organizational skills to complete necessary tasks without adult supervision. A behavior contract is just one of many possible techniques for accomplishing these goals.

Assuming that the baseline for homework completion has been around 10 to 25 percent completion and around 15 percent accuracy (based on the total amount of homework assigned), a reasonable goal for the first week might be to improve completion to 30 percent and accuracy to 20 percent. This would be consistent with Guideline 2, contracting for improvement in small steps. The precise goal for the first week of the contract can be negotiated with the student. Other issues that will need to be decided include establishing a study time and location, the types of parental support to be offered, and a means of communication between home and school.

Another crucial element of the contract is the contingency designed to reward the child for success. This component needs to be negotiated carefully and honestly with the child. Rewards must be within the financial means of the family while also providing the child with sufficient motivation to exert effort toward fulfilling her portion of the contract. A mixture of short-term rewards, larger long-term rewards, and bonuses for exceeding expectations will help maintain interest in the program. A complete contract is shown in Table 10.2.

Although homework is not a behavior that the child will be allowed to choose to do or not do, the behavior contract should have plenty of flexibility in allowing input from the child. It is particularly important that the child be given as much flexibility as possible to choose the rewards because the success of the program depends on selection of highly motivating reinforcers. Note that the contract shown in Table 10.2 also allows new rewards to be negotiated without revising the entire contract.

Step 5: Begin the program. Once a satisfactory contract has been negotiated, a starting date needs to be agreed on. Because the contract shown in Table 10.2 depends on weekly teacher reports brought home by Annie every Monday, it would make sense to begin the program on a Monday evening. With the student's active participation in developing the contract, no difficulties should be encountered in starting it on the date specified in the contract.

Step 6: Observe the effects of the program and initiate steps to strengthen generalization beyond the training environment. The contract shown in Table 10.2 calls for the first review after one week and reviews every two weeks thereafter. If the first week's goals were met or substantial progress has been made, the contract may continue to be in force. A successful contract can remain in force for as long as all parties agree to abide by it. At some point, however, the contract may be seen as having served its initial purpose. Then it may be time to renegotiate, and to encourage the student to become more independent and self-directing. This can be accomplished in a number of ways.

First, the amount of daily supervision could be decreased. That is, instead of checking with Annie before and after each homework session, her mother could depend on the weekly reports from the teacher. Also, Annie could become responsible for keeping track of upcoming homework assignments entirely on her own so her teacher would not need to list upcoming assignments on the weekly report. If Annie is able to handle the responsibility of budgeting study time and keeping track of assignments on her own, other components of the contract could be gradually faded. The most crucial component is the weekly teacher report of assignments completed and degree of accuracy. The first step in fading this aspect of the contract might be to ask the teacher to send home reports every other week or to make reports to the mother by telephone instead of in writing. These changes could be made gradually in successive contracts. Another step could be to ask the teacher to contact the parents by phone only when an assignment is missed. This would alert parents to any problems but would keep the responsibility for homework clearly focused on Annie. Eventually, the contract could include a date for final termination, perhaps after a major reward was earned.

Steps 7 and 8: Modify the program if necessary and fade it out. An early review of any behavior contract is crucial to success because dealing with problems early in the process increases the chances of eventual success. For example, if Annie did not reach her goal in the first week, this might be an indication that the contract needs to proceed in even smaller steps. Perhaps a daily note from the teacher is needed so that Annie's parents will know what tasks need to be completed every night. Also, Annie's access to television, electronic games, or other after-school activities may need to be made contingent on completion of homework. Closer parental supervision during homework time may also be needed to ensure that the time is used productively. The possibility that learning or behavior problems are interfering with the goals of the contract also needs to be reconsidered. Finally, a review of the rewards of the program may point to weaknesses. Perhaps Annie did not understand how much time and effort would be required to earn 1000 points, and smaller, more easily earned rewards need to be added in order to bridge the gap.

Table 10.3 shows another sample contract, a fairly complex contract designed to help a child improve classroom behavior. The main purpose is to illustrate how a contract could be written for a younger child. The complexity is deliberate in order to illustrate a wide range of possibilities. Of course, many changes are possible. One of the most obvious changes is that points could be substituted for stickers, resulting in some savings of time and money. Stickers would have the advantage of providing some degree of immediate reinforcement for younger children. The provisions for bonus stickers could also be deleted with little loss in the effectiveness of the program, depending on the child involved. Finally, the number of behaviors targeted by the program could be reduced. For instance, if the student is busy doing assigned work, it may not be necessary to include rewards for following classroom rules, and this aspect of the contract could be deleted.

Should this version prove ineffective, two major modifications could be attempted. First, the definitions of desired and undesired behavior could be made more specific and concrete. For instance, the classroom rules could be specified in the contract and rewards could be made contingent on following these rules. Likewise, annoying and/or disruptive behavior not covered by classroom rules could be defined in the contract, along with ways of rewarding the absence of such behavior. If the child lacks the necessary skills for succeeding in the classroom, it may be possible to define the deficit skill carefully in the contract and to reward its occurrence, although other formal behavior management programs may be better suited to this type of problem.

The second way to modify this contract is to change the time interval over which behavior is counted and rewarded. At one extreme, the requirement for acceptable behavior could be increased and rewards delivered on a less frequent schedule, such as once a week. At the other extreme, the time interval could be shortened so that the child begins anew after perhaps one hour, receiving stickers for each hour of acceptable behavior.

Behavior contracts can be effective tools for changing children's behavior. The number of possible variations in the form and specific provisions of contracts is infinite. Virtually any of the techniques discussed in this book can be put into a behavior contract. In the course of using behavior change contracts, school personnel should be aware that their first efforts may not be successful. However, this should not be interpreted as failure. Instead, it indicates that the contract needs renegotiation and change. As the age of the child with whom the contract is negotiated increases, the amount of input from the child should also increase. Adolescents, for example, may have legitimate needs from parents and teachers that can be included in a behavior contract.

A CASE STUDY: JACK

In order to illustrate the principles and interventions just described, a case study is presented. The case is intended to illustrate both the nature of deficit behaviors and the wide variety of interventions that may be necessary to help children.

Jack, a seven-year-old first grader, was referred to a school psychologist for an evaluation by his teacher, who noted that he did not do his schoolwork unless closely supervised, did not attend to classroom instruction, and showed signs of frustration and emotional upset, including crying and excessive self-criticism. An interview with Jack's teacher indicated that her major concern was Jack's apparent inability to organize the components of a task and focus his attention on completing it. Jack's mother also reported problems managing his behavior at home.

A behavior rating scale completed by the child's teacher revealed a multitude of problems in the classroom. The most serious problem was off-task behavior. Other areas of concern were self-blame, poor impulse control, poor academic achievement, excessive suffering, and resistance to adults. A classroom observation confirmed that Jack spent most of his unsupervised time engaged in irrelevant, off-task behaviors. In addition, Jack seemed to lack the ability to cope with frustration and failure. This was illustrated succinctly by his behavior during an intellectual assessment. When he was unable to complete one of the tasks in the examination, Jack pushed away the materials, thereby losing points he could have gained for partially completing the task. Other behaviors that interfered with his test performance included attempting to engage the examiner in conversation, perseverating on his errors, and giving up on tasks before time limits expired.

Jack also indicated a lack of confidence in his ability to perform, criticized his own performance, and appeared anxious. He inquired about his times on many timed tasks and wanted to read all the notations recorded by the examiner on the test protocol. It was concluded that the results of the assessment probably represented a minimal estimate of Jack's ability and that in the absence of interfering behaviors he could be expected to perform somewhat better. However, Jack scored just above average (61st percentile) on the intellectual assessment, and no signs of learning problems were revealed. It seemed, then, that Jack was capable of satisfactory performance but that a variety of behaviors were interfering with classroom achievement.

Many of the behaviors shown by this child were suggestive of the cluster of behaviors associated with childhood depression. Theses behaviors included self-criticism, poor academic performance, crying, and an apparent inability to concentrate on academic tasks. Jack was living with his divorced mother and had recently moved to a new town. School records indicated that he had been referred for behavior problems by his previous school. Thus, it is possible that his behavior could have been related to the turmoil surrounding the divorce of his mother and the consequent loss of his father, who was living and working in a distant city.

A variety of interventions were chosen to remediate Jack's behavior. Several of them were very practical. First, to help Jack organize his work and complete tasks, a schedule of daily activities was taped to his desk. This schedule listed both the task and the materials required for it. A second intervention was to obtain a new pair of sneakers for Jack. Observations indicated that his old pair was too big for him, which caused him to appear awkward and uncoordinated in physical education class and while walking around. Finally, Jack's desk was crowded with unnecessary supplies, such as an excessive number of crayons and tablets. Some of these items were eliminated or replaced.

Two formal behavior management programs were initiated. First, Jack occasionally would emit tantrums. Jack's classroom teacher was instructed to present him with a brief timeout or "cooling off" period whenever such behavior occurred. Jack's mother was also given instruction in the use of timeout. (See Chapter 7 for a detailed guide to using timeout.) In addition, Jack's classroom behavior was monitored with a checklist of desirable behavior, and good behavior was rewarded by his mother. Chapter 10 discusses the implementation of such programs.

Jack's teacher was also given detailed instruction in how to apply informal behavior management procedures to some of Jack's behavior problems. We worked mainly at defining Jack's undesirable behavior in concrete terms and developing some strategies for dealing with them. This included ignoring inappropriate behavior, looking for and prompting positive self-evaluations so they could be praised, and discussing alternative ways of handling situations that resulted in tantrums. Finally, it was also recommended that Jack's second-grade teacher be informed of his behavior problems and the methods of dealing with them that had been effective so that some degree of continuity and consistency would be maintained from year to year.

The general impact of these interventions was positive, as indicated by the teacher's report. However, it would not be possible to identify which components of the intervention were most effective. It was my impression that the informal behavior management procedures and practical interventions had the greatest immediate impact.

CONCLUSION

Positive reinforcement is the most important component of any behavior management program. Regardless of the definition of the target behavior, an intervention is not successful until the child is academically productive in the least restrictive educational environment. This means that eliminating behavior excesses only partially meets the needs of children. It is also necessary to ensure that the skills needed to be socially and academically productive are strengthened. The main goal of the programs described in this chapter is to help students adjust to the demands of regular classrooms. These programs can also serve an important role in preventing more serious problems that could lead to placement in more restrictive environments. As always, the programs described in this chapter are meant to be starting points for developing successful interventions. Remaining flexible and adjusting programs to meet the needs of individual children ensures the best chances of success.

REVIEW

Terms to Remember and Review

positive reinforcement	negative reinforcement
escape	avoidance
school phobia	timeout
separation anxiety	relaxation training
school–home note	behavior contract
least restrictive environment	

Study and Discussion Questions

1. What is the meaning and significance of this statement: For every behavior excess, there is an equal and opposite behavior deficit?
2. Negative reinforcement is rarely programed purposefully, but it can explain how some behaviors are reinforced in the natural environment. Make up an example of how negative reinforcement may maintain an otherwise undesirable behavior.
3. How can positive reinforcement be used to eliminate a behavior excess?
4. Develop a list of rewarding activities that are a natural part of an elementary school classroom. Do the same thing for a high school classroom.

Group Project

A good exercise that I believe students can really enjoy while they learn a good deal about behavior contracts and group processes is to have students form groups of four to seven students each and then role-play the process of negotiating a behavior contract. In my own classes, I have students form groups and then give each group member a short description of the role he or she will play in the group. The descriptions that follow illustrate one of the role-play situations I have used:

Consultant: Your job is to negotiate a behavioral contract between the parents and their teenager. Be sure you have a commitment from all parties to follow the rules of the contract. As the consultant, you must take a leading role in the negotiation process. You must determine why the parents have come to you and just what goals they wish to accomplish.

Teenager: As far as you are concerned, this is just a bunch of BS. You don't see any problems except that your parents won't leave you alone. Sure, you've been out drinking a few times with your friends, but you haven't been caught. It's so easy to make up some stupid story for your parents. They'll believe anything. And who cares about school?

Those teachers don't know anything anyway. You can't wait to get out of this meeting and tell your friends about it. Maybe somebody will bring some beer?

Parent #1: You aren't sure what the problem is, but there is something seriously wrong with you child's behavior. You even suspect that your child stole a $10 bill from you yesterday. Here are the specific problems you have noticed: (1) academic performance is well below potential, (2) your child doesn't spend any time on homework, (3) your teenager stays out late on weeknights, and (4) you don't like the teenager's peer group because they're always getting into trouble. The most crucial problem is that you believe your child may be drinking too much alcohol. You are afraid to confront this issue because it could lead to a dangerous confrontation with your spouse, who also drinks a lot.

Parent #2: You don't know what all the fuss is about. You have been more or less dragged to the school by your spouse, who exaggerates your teenager's problems.

This example illustrates a complex and emotionally charged situation. Instructors and students are encouraged to develop their own scenarios.

CHAPTER 11

MANAGEMENT OF BEHAVIOR DEFICITS IN SPECIAL CLASSROOMS

Behavior management programs described in this chapter focus on the needs of children in special classrooms. This does not necessarily mean special education classrooms. The only assumption is that student–teacher ratios are more favorable than in the typical regular classroom. Programs described in this chapter may be made appropriate for regular classrooms by either changing some features or providing a pupil support assistant, paraprofessional, or aide to monitor behavior and administer consequences. Programs useful in regular classrooms can also be used in special classrooms. The main characteristics of the programs described in this chapter are that they may require more staff and time than are usually available in a regular classroom, and they are designed to increase target behaviors. Teachers just beginning to organize a special classroom may also find Chapter 5 useful.

As discussed in Chapter 2, there are two basic techniques for increasing behavior: presentation of an appetitive or reinforcing stimulus and removal of an aversive stimulus. The formal names for these techniques are *positive reinforcement* and *negative reinforcement,* respectively.

Presentation of an appetitive stimulus (positive reinforcement) is the most practical and effective procedure for remediating most behavior problems. Negative reinforcement, by contrast, has only limited use. For example, some behavior management programs give children negative points or demerits as a consequence for misbehavior. A child who accumulates a predetermined number of demerits, receives a consequence such as after-school detention. Typically, demerits can be canceled out or taken away by appropriate behavior such as a week of perfect attendance with no tardiness. Removal of a demerit (a negative contingency) under these circumstances is an example of negative reinforcement.

This chapter begins with two programs using token reinforcement, which is one of the most flexible ways to employ positive reinforcement. The first program is based on concrete tokens and is designed to remediate deficits in basic skills. It would be most appropriate for children in preschool or in first, or second grade. The second token program is based on a point system. It is suitable for older children and adolescents and is designed to apply flexibly to a wide variety of designated target behaviors.

A BASIC TOKEN REWARD PROGRAM FOR TEACHING SKILLS

Token reward programs are among the most useful procedures available for behavior management programs. Token rewards can be delivered without interfering with ongoing tasks, and their effectiveness is not tied to a single reward. Because the implementation of a token reward program is very similar to being paid for work, the concept is easy to communicate.

A token is almost anything of little or no value that a child can exchange for something desirable. A token reward is analogous to money. Money cannot be eaten or keep a person warm, but it can be used to purchase food and shelter. Likewise, tokens have no inherent value, but they can be used to "purchase" rewards that are valued. Gold stars, points, marbles, specially marked pieces of paper, poker chips, or anything else that can be conveniently delivered and saved can be used as a token. Concrete objects that can be handled are best for younger children; points usually work well with older children. The simplest token reward programs can be implemented by telling the child, "If you earn five of these, then you can trade them in for anything in this box!" The success of the program will depend on the child's understanding of the instructions and on the value of the rewards contained in the box.

It may be helpful, when a token program is begun, to be flexible in defining the target behavior (an excellent opportunity to practice shaping behavior) and to be generous with tokens until the child has earned enough to turn them in for a reward. In this way, by showing the child what has been accomplished and how to exchange the tokens for a reward, you increase the likelihood that he or she will understand the system.

When children enter school, they are expected to have several skills that are important to the learning that will take place in kindergarten. Staats (1971) labels these skills *basic behavioral repertoires*. A child who is lacking in basic skills, such as being able to attend to a stimulus on command, will almost certainly have difficulty in the early years of school. The child is also likely to present a behavior problem because he or she will be engaged in other activities while the remainder of the class is working on an assigned task or attending to lessons.

When a child lacks basic attending skills, an indirect way of dealing with the situation is to use a behavior management program to teach the same skills that are being taught in the classroom, but using more powerful rewards than are received by the typical child. Using more powerful rewards and, perhaps, one-on-one instruction can serve the dual purpose of helping the child to acquire specific skills, such as learning the alphabet, and to acquire the more general attentional skills that will be needed for success throughout his or her academic career. Learning to attend appropriately comes about

because earning rewards requires both responding correctly and being able to attend to the relevant stimuli. For instance, the child will not be rewarded for learning letters unless he or she learns to attend to the characteristics that differentiate letters from one another.

In addition to the development of attention skills, one might also expect other disruptive or nonproductive behavior to disappear as a result of a token program to teach academic skills. If the child is working hard to earn rewards for desired behavior, the opportunity for undesirable behavior is significantly lowered. As noted in earlier chapters, an important consideration is the magnitude of the child's disruptive or nonproductive behavior. If the child is extremely disruptive or inattentive, a program to teach academic skills may be unsuccessful until other behaviors are brought under control. On the other hand, even a very disruptive child may respond immediately to the offer of a concrete reward for academic performance.

Much of early learning in school consists of memorized lists of individual facts, such as letters of the alphabet, state capitals, countries, arithmetic facts, continents, or vocabulary words. Failure to master certain basic facts can cause a child to fall farther and farther behind in areas where the facts are important. Because a teacher rarely has time to drill individual students in these unlearned facts, it is often up to a tutor or the child's parents to provide the necessary practice. The formal behavior management program that follows is one way to help a child attain mastery of important basic facts. A major advantage of the program is that it is very simple to implement.

The following step-by-step procedure for implementing a token reward system has broad generality and usefulness. Token programs can be effective in numerous situations and with children of any age.

Step 1: Identify the problem. For this example, two similar programs will be described. The first problem will be defined as a deficit in kindergarten reading readiness skills. Basically, this translates into not knowing the alphabet. Learning one's ABCs is no easy task to accomplish in kindergarten. Not only is the child required to recognize fifty-two different symbols (the upper- and lower-case letters), but the sound of each letter must also be learned along with how to write it. Considering how similar some letters appear (e.g., *b* and *d, F* and *P*), it is easy to see how difficult the task can be from the viewpoint of the child. Furthermore, without thorough knowledge of the alphabet, the child is likely to have great difficulty learning to read.

There are numerous reasons that a child in kindergarten may not be learning basic skills at the same rate as his or her classmates. The child's intelligence may fall in a range that means she or he will learn at a slower rate than those of average intelligence. Another possibility is that the child entered kindergarten without basic attending skills because of environmental factors. It is also possible that the child shows the cluster of behaviors associated with hyperactivity or ADHD. The child may have a physical problem that interferes with learning, such as an illness resulting in a large number of absences, ear infections that interfere with normal hearing, or an untreated visual problem. In any of these cases, it could be very beneficial to work individually with the child using the token program to be described, but concurrent remediation of other problems may also be necessary.

As a second example, a program will be described for a child who needs to learn basic multiplication facts.

Step 2: Refine the definition of the problem.   The primary goal of a token reward program is to increase appropriate responses. In this example, the desired responses are accurately naming letters, giving their sounds, copying them, writing them from memory, and so forth. The most important point to remember in conducting these programs is that *responses,* not stimuli, are reinforced. That is, rewards should be forthcoming only when the child has responded appropriately, such as by correctly naming a letter or by giving the correct response to a multiplication problem. Note how this contrasts with teaching in a group setting, where the teacher often points to a stimulus and describes its characteristics, then uses worksheets to confirm individual mastery. In an individual tutoring program, the tutor can directly monitor the child's behavior. This assures efficient learning because the tutor can monitor what has and has not been learned so that stimulus presentations can be repeated and other adjustments can be made as needed. During group instruction, the teacher cannot be sure that each child has learned the material until later.

An efficient way to implement such a program is to purchase or construct a set of flashcards, each of which contains one of the basic facts to be learned. Then, the refined definition of the problem becomes responding correctly to each flashcard. It may also be reasonable to specify an initial time limit for responding, such as five or ten seconds, which can be decreased as the child's mastery improves.

For the child who needs help with the alphabet, a set of fifty-two cards containing the upper- and lower-case letters can serve as the stimulus materials. For a child who needs to learn multiplication facts, a set of flashcards containing the facts to be remembered will be needed.

Step 3: Assess the baseline rate. Assessment of the baseline rate merely involves determining the child's level of knowledge in the skill area to be trained. If the target skills are recognizing the letters of the alphabet or remembering multiplication facts, the child's percentage of mastery of the skill can be determined by presenting each flashcard and asking the child to respond by naming the letter or giving the correct response to the multiplication problem within the time limit. A convenience that results from the use of flashcards is that separate piles of cards can designate correct and incorrect answers and can be easily counted after the entire deck has been presented to the child. The number of correct answers during the first pass through the set of flashcards is the baseline level of knowledge. An alternative method is to employ a computer program for presenting the stimulus problems. As always, it is important that the conditions of the baseline assessment be carefully noted so that they can be easily repeated when the child's progress is assessed. Important variables might include the method of presenting the various stimuli, and how the questions are posed to the child.

If the child shows evidence of other behavior problems in the classroom, such as inattention or disruptive behavior, it may be useful to determine the baseline rate of these behaviors even though they are not directly targeted by the management program. Any of the time-sampling procedures described in Chapter 3 would be appropriate for this purpose. Information about the child's behavior in the regular classroom could be particularly helpful in the final stages of the behavior management program, when the goal is to program events so that the child is capable of learning in a regular classroom without the benefit of individual tutoring.

Step 4: Design the behavioral contingencies and write the program description. The mechanics of a token reward program can be set up in a number of different ways. The tokens can be stickers, pennies, play money, marbles, or any other small objects. For young children, I have found that marbles work well as tokens. They can be easily given to a child, and various sizes of containers can be filled with them in order to earn the backup reinforcer. Plastic baby bottles work well as the container because they come in different sizes and their tops (minus nipples) are designed so that the marbles are not likely to spill out. Alternative methods of implementing token programs include filling various sized sheets of paper or cardboard with stickers and letting the child "buy" rewards with play money or points. The younger the child, the more concrete the progression toward the reward must be. For this reason, filling a container with marbles may work best with children of age five or six, and filling a chart may be acceptable to children of ages six to eight years, whereas a point system is more suitable for older children. If the child keeps the tokens for any length of unsupervised time, tokens will need to be designed so they cannot be counterfeited.

Once a suitable token system has been developed, the next step is to identify the backup rewards. This is an important element in the program because these are what the child actually earns. Therefore, the rewards must be powerful enough to gain the child's attention and motivate him or her to remain on task. The variety of possible rewards is endless: candy, snacks, trips, special activities, small toys, compact discs, clothes, and so forth. It is advantageous to offer a group of rewards from which the child can choose. With this method, the program is not likely to fail because the child has become bored with a particular reward. The child and the child's parents are the best sources of information about effective rewards. The reinforcer preferences of children and adolescents can change very quickly, so it is crucial to review the available reinforcers frequently and add new ones whenever possible.

The contingency in this token program is simple. The child is rewarded with tokens for correct responses to stimuli presented by the tutor. When the required number of tokens has been earned, they can be traded in for the backup reward. In practice, it is not so simple because of the wide variety of skill levels a child may have at the beginning of such a program. At the highest levels of skill, the tutor may find that the child is attentive, at least attempts a response to each question, and has already mastered at least some of the target skills. At the other extreme, the child may be disruptive, inattentive, and lacking all the target skills. In the latter case, it may be necessary to employ the tokens to reward behaviors that are prerequisite to effective instruction, such as remaining seated, looking at each stimulus, and giving appropriate responses to questions.

As noted earlier, it is crucial that the child's *responses* be rewarded. This is easy enough when the child responds correctly, but it is important to remember that a learning trial takes place for certain only when the child responds. When the child does not know the correct response or gives an incorrect response, it is important to have the child repeat the correct response while looking at the stimulus. One way to use the token system to accomplish this with ease is to give the child two tokens for a correct response without help and one token for a correct response with help.

When the child begins such a program with a high level of mastery, such as responding correctly to 70 percent of the stimuli, an alternative approach to rewarding performance can be used. First, the child may receive a small reward for sitting down with the tutor and going through the flashcards. Second, the child may receive a small reward for each increment in the total number of facts that are mastered. For example, the child might receive five tokens for each review of the flashcards plus two tokens for each individual fact mastered above the previous best performance. A decrease in the number of correct facts (and these are to be expected) is simply ignored, although the child still receives the scheduled reward for the review session.

The written description for this kind of token program is relatively simple, mainly because the target behavior (a correct response to the stimulus item) is so straightforward. Issues that need to be resolved include the method of obtaining the baseline data and making stimulus presentations, the type of tokens to be used, the precise nature of the contingency, the nature of the backup reinforcers, and the criteria for ending the program.

Step 5: Begin the program. In essence, the program begins with baseline measurements of the child's current knowledge. To place the token system in operation, the child is told a very simple rule, such as, "If you fill this with marbles, then you can have _____." It is possible, of course, to elaborate by telling the child how marbles can be earned, but this can just as easily be demonstrated. If the child does not appear to understand immediately, continue with the program as planned anyway. Once the child has filled up the container a couple of times, he or she may get the idea.

Older children may benefit from a more complete description of the rules of the program. For example, the child may be told that he or she will receive tokens for reviewing flashcards with the tutor. For each fact that is missed, the child should be required to recite the missed fact (e.g., "6 times 8 equals 48"), so the tutor can be certain that a learning trial has taken place. The child should then be informed that each correct response to the stimulus presentations will result in a token. It is also possible to give the child a bonus of additional tokens each time the total number of learned facts increases above the previous high point. Note that the bonus would depend on the *number* correct, not on which particular facts were learned. Since 100 percent mastery is the goal, noting exactly which items were missed would not be crucial. If missed items are placed in a separate pile, however, they can be reviewed quickly before another pass through the entire pile. It is important that all the facts be reviewed regularly because the additional practice will improve speed and confidence and will help the child perform better in the classroom. Also, each correct response should be followed by verbal praise from the tutor. The first time the child correctly recites all the facts, it would be appropriate to reward the accomplishment with a special treat or bonus.

Step 6: Observe the effects of the program and strengthen generalization beyond the training environment. If the program is effective, two things should be observed. First, the child should be learning the material as expected according to the goals of the program. This can be tested by readministering the baseline measurements. The second observation should be that the child is, in general, learning more efficiently. That is, the child works well, stays on task, and begins to show signs of being motivated to please the tutor. Behaviors that interfered with learning prior to the beginning of the program may be observed less often. Depending on the child's level of accomplishment prior to the start of the program, varying amounts of time may be required before positive effects are observed.

Generalization of the specific facts to other situations should occur readily. That is, the child would be expected to make use easily of the facts in other contexts, such as solving arithmetic problems. Again, if difficulty is evident, other explanations should be sought.

However, dependence on individual tutoring may become a problem if it appears that the child is not ready to benefit from the group instruction that is a major component of many regular education classrooms. Because a token reward program is usually implemented via one-on-one tutoring, generalization to the regular classroom will require some special effort. The first step is to wean the child from dependence on the token reward program. This is accomplished by slowly increasing the amount of work required in order to earn a token. In addition, the tutor can offer challenges to the child, such as five tokens if he or she answers a series of review questions without error. The eventual goal is to have the child working at a high rate for minimal material rewards. However, praise and positive attention from the adult tutor should continue at a high rate.

The problem of moving the child's learning activities from the tutoring environment to the classroom is not an easy one and may involve some trial and error to discover a program that works. A first step might be to offer a reward to the child for successful performance of a classroom activity, such as completing a worksheet or art project. As the child begins to experience success with simple classroom projects and the tutoring program brings the child's level of accomplishment into line with the regular class, the child can be given the responsibility of learning things in the regular classroom. With careful planning, the tutor can test the child's acquisition of classroom material and eventually provide reinforcement only when classroom material is mastered without the help of the tutor. As the child reaches this level of competence, the classroom teacher can take over the functions of the tutor in a manner that begins to approximate the regular classroom.

If the program does not appear to have a positive effect—that is, the child's mastery does not improve—one would probably look beyond the program itself for the reasons. It may, for instance, be possible that one of the academic problems discussed in Chapter 4 is interfering with progress. Alternatively, the child's behavior during the training sessions may be interfering with learning. If progress is not made and no explanation can be found, it would be advisable that one of the tutoring sessions be observed by a person who has experience in behavior management.

Step 7: Modify the program, if necessary. If the program is not effective, there are several alternatives. First, if the child appears not to grasp the value of the tokens, their relationship to the reward can be made more direct by decreasing the number necessary for earning a reward. In the most extreme case, it may be necessary to employ a consumable reward, such as a piece of candy or a banana chip, in the initial stages of the program. Then, the child can be taught to exchange a single token for a consumable reward. Once this concept has been mastered, it should be possible to increase the number of tokens required for a reward so that learning can proceed at a reasonable rate without having to wait for the child to eat after each stimulus presentation.

If the child's nonproductive behavior interferes with

the learning process, it may be necessary to target the undesirable behavior directly, using any of the programs described elsewhere in this book. For instance, high-magnitude disruptive behavior could be reduced by using timeout or a response cost contingency. It is very likely that a child unable to learn in the regular classroom will show more than one behavior problem. Thus, more than one contingency may be required to teach the child the skills necessary for academic survival in the regular classroom.

Pavchinski, Evans, and Bostow (1989) successfully employed a behavior management program similar to the one described previously with a twelve-year-old learning-disabled male who had been retained twice because of poor academic performance. These authors used a token program to increase mastery of a group of 220 basic sight words and simple arithmetic problems. They employed two techniques that could enhance the effects of such a program. One such technique was setting an overall level of performance necessary to earn the points awarded for each individual answer. For example, at the beginning of the program, the student needed to have at least 60 percent correct responses in order earn the points that were awarded for each individual correct answer. The overall criterion was raised in 10 percent increments as the student reached each successive level. Another technique employed by Pachinski et al. was that the student was required to write the word or arithmetic problem three times when he gave an incorrect answer and one time when the answer was correct. Either of these two elements could be added to the token program described here.

Step 8: Fade out the program. Fading out the program involves continuation of the techniques discussed under Step 6, such as fading dependence on the rewards and promoting generalization to the regular classroom. An issue that could be important to integrating the child fully into the regular classroom is the child's relationships with peers. If the child was not functioning well in this environment or had been absent for long periods each school day, the child's social status among his or her peers may be low. Part of the program for integrating the child back into a regular classroom could be targeted at this issue. One possibility is that the child could earn treats or snacks for the entire classroom for reaching milestones in his or her learning. Any part of the program that makes the regular classroom a more rewarding place will pay great dividends as the program is faded out.

The program can be faded out in a number of ways

once the child has attained one perfect pass through the flashcards. First, the contingency could be modified so that the reward for merely sitting down and participating in a review session is received only for a perfect pass through all the flashcards. This would ensure that the facts were well learned and unlikely to be forgotten. Then, the number of perfect passes through the flashcards required for receiving a reward could be increased slowly until the program is finally halted because the facts have been thoroughly mastered. When the child attains five or ten perfect sessions in a row, a special treat and a "graduation" certificate could be awarded.

A TOKEN REWARD PROGRAM FOR GENERAL CLASSROOM USE

A token reward system works with children in the same way that wages and salaries work for adults. No reasonable adults would continue working at a regular job without pay because they would not be able to purchase the essentials and luxuries that money can buy. Similarly, children cannot always be expected to work hard in school to receive the long-term benefits of education, such as vocational opportunities. Sometimes it is necessary to motivate them with more immediate consequences. A token program is one method of providing immediate consequences for academic productivity and related behaviors.

A token program rewards behavior with points, marbles, special coupons, stickers, poker chips, or anything else that can be easily delivered and saved but is resistant to counterfeiting. The tokens themselves have no inherent value but can be used to "purchase" desirable rewards—toys, snacks, CDs, clothes, or privileges. Because tokens can "buy" a variety of rewards, children and adolescents find them desirable for a long time and in a wide variety of situations. This flexibility makes token programs an effective way of dealing with many behavior problems.

The program described in this section is designed for older children and adolescents. Its design is deliberately flexible to make it applicable to a number of different situations. The program is based on points rather than physical tokens, although this aspect of the program could be modified.

The initial setup for a token program can be accomplished fairly easily, but it is important to remain very flexible, especially in the early stages of the program, because it is likely that adjustments and modifications will be needed to increase the program's effectiveness. Many questions will need to be answered regarding the initial structure of the program. Some of the issues that will arise as a token program is developing are listed next (Allyon & Azrin, 1968; Kazdin, 1977, 1983; Martin & Pear, 1988):

1. The first step is to make decisions about the overall structure of the token program. This entails deciding which behaviors to reinforce, what types of tokens to use, and the nature of the backup reinforcers. A written manual describing the rules and operation of the program should be developed. Keeping this manual up to date and publishing revisions should be a high-priority task because the manual will help substitute teachers and new staff learn how the system operates. Putting a summary of the system in contract form for students may be a helpful way to introduce them to the program.

2. Select concrete, easily observable behaviors to be reinforced to ensure that the focus is on desired behavior. Behaviors that will be rewarded by the natural environment will make the best target behaviors. In school settings, academic productivity, such as completion of worksheets, passing quizzes, and homework completion, should be priority target behaviors. Social skills and other nonacademic behaviors may also be rewarded. For special education students, careful review of each student's IEP will reveal many of the target behaviors that should be included in the token program.

3. Backup reinforcers must be relevant to the needs of the students. Activities that students do on their own (talking in class, eating snacks, etc.) can often be used as backup rewards (the Premack principle). Regularly surveying the pupils may be helpful in determining what reinforcers are desirable. The selection of backup reinforcers is crucial to the success of the program and needs to be approached in a flexible, open-minded manner. A wide variety of backup reinforcers should be available to prevent satiation.

4. Design tokens that can not easily reproduced or counterfeited by the students. The use of unique "paper money" on colored paper with space for a staff member's initials, the date, the nature of the behavior being rewarded, and the student's name has proved successful in many programs.

5. Ensure that the rules and operation of the program are clearly understood by all staff. A summary of

rules and procedures should be posted in the classroom and easily available for review by students.

6. Elimination of inappropriate behavior can be speeded by using fines or a response cost contingency, but the primary emphasis should be on rewarding appropriate behavior.

7. Making a token program the lowest component of a levels type program (see Chapter 5) can be one way of directly encouraging generalization of behaviors improved by the token program.

8. When individual students fail to respond to a token program, it may be helpful to individualize the program by improving the backup reinforcers. Allowing the student to select backup reinforcers (within reason) may be particularly helpful.

9. Successful token programs need to be carefully monitored to ensure that the program is having the expected effects and continues to be administered consistently. Continuous data collection focusing on student behaviors and proper administration of tokens will boost the chances of a successful program.

The process of developing a token program for a special classroom begins with defining the purpose of the program. There are two major purposes for which a token program might be developed. First, a token program might be used as a completely individualized behavior management program for a particular child. A second purpose would be to provide the total structure for a special classroom. In this case, the token program would structure the classroom operations to maximize student success and bring about behavior change. Often, this might be accomplished in the context of a levels system where the student is expected to progress from a tightly structured token program administered by adult supervisors through several levels until the child is able to spend most of the school day in regular classes. Chapter 5 provides a detailed discussion of a levels system.

If a completely individualized program is desirable, the token program described in Chapter 12 for use by parents may be acceptable. The focus of the remainder of the present section will be on describing a token program for a special classroom setting with several students. The program described is generic and will not succeed in every situation. All behavior management programs need to be adjusted so they provide a good fit to the environment in which they are expected to function. Thus, the description provided here should be regarded as a rough draft that will need significant changes before it works smoothly in a particular setting.

Development of this model token program will proceed using the eight-step organizational structure employed throughout the book.

Step 1: Identify the problem. Token programs may be used for the widest variety of behavior deficits, ranging from self-help skills like dressing and bathing to complex social skills like asking a person of the opposite sex for a date. They have been used across the entire age range from toddler to elder adult. The basic function of token programs is to shape, develop, and strengthen desirable behaviors that the individual either lacks or emits at an unacceptably low rate. Although school-based behavior management programs may be concerned with the entire range of behaviors, the most common focus is on academic productivity and social skills.

Although children may emit a variety of behavior excesses such as refusing adult requests, aggression, and so forth, the main reason they are assigned to special classrooms is because their academic progress is inadequate. If the child's academic productivity improves, many of the peripheral behaviors will become significantly less frequent because the child will spend more time engaged in academic tasks and therefore will have less time to engage in unacceptable behavior. Thus, in most settings, the primary goal of a token program is to strengthen academic behavior.

Step 2: Refine the definition of the problem.   Academic productivity can be defined in many ways. For some teachers, it may mean being attentive to instruction or reading a book. For other teachers, it may mean passing a test. Still others may define academic productivity as actively participating in a group discussion. All three of these definitions would be valid in a particular context, but children assigned to a special classroom need more concrete guidance because they are likely to lack some of the component behaviors associated with reading a book, passing a test, or participating in a discussion. For example, children assigned to special classes often are reading well below their assigned grade level, may lack the study skills needed to pass a test, and may be argumentative and impulsive while participating in discussion. To succeed in mainstream classes, these children need to learn to emit consistently the component skills that go along with academic productivity.

Exactly what are these skills? A detailed answer is impossible in the few paragraphs available here. Any teacher who has participated in the task of developing the outcomes required by outcome-based education (OBE) already understands the problems involved in defining the behaviors associated with learning the curriculum of any grade. However, most children assigned to special classrooms have been identified as handicapped under the Individuals with Disabilities Education Act (IDEA) and have been thoroughly assessed in both the academic and behavioral domains. Then, after a team meeting involving the child's parents and school personnel, an Individualized Education Plan (IEP) complete with both academic and behavioral goals is written. Thus, in most special classrooms the specific goals and objectives for each individual student have already been established by the educational team. In cases where the special classroom is a transition room or prevention program, academic goals for students will need to be established that are appropriate to their grade level and expected level of functioning after completion of the program.

Once the issue of specific academic goals has been addressed through planning the goals of the room or reviewing students' IEPs, the function of the token program is to advance these goals by providing a context within which learning can take place. Presumably, each student in the program has definite tasks that need to be completed so that defining behaviors associated with being on task will help establish at least some of the behaviors to be rewarded. Another event that can be rewarded with tokens is completion of the products required of each student at a minimum level of accuracy, such as 80 percent. On-task behavior and productivity are probably the two most important behaviors that may be addressed by a school-based token program. Other areas that individual teachers might wish to include in token programs are timely arrival at the classroom, having needed materials (books, pencils, notebooks, assignments, etc.), social interactions, responding to teacher commands, grooming, and appropriate behavior in mainstream settings. The sample handout shown in Table 11.1 provides a list of reinforced behaviors in the context of a student handout describing a token program. This entire handout is a model draft that should be changed as needed to meet the needs of a particular classroom.

Step 3: Assess the baseline rate. Recordkeeping in a token program is crucial to its success. Both regular and

Table 11.1. Student Handout for a Classroom Token System

A. *Introduction*: Welcome to the Washington Intermediate School Resource Room. The main goal of teachers in this room is to help you raise your academic performance to the highest level possible. The class is structured just like a job. You work for points, which are paid out like money for following class rules, getting your work done, and working on IEP goals. You use the points to buy privileges, prizes, and to graduate to higher levels of the program which will allow you more freedom to make choices in how you use your time. All students begin the program at Level I, which is the Structured Token Program.

B. *Level I Rules:*
   1. Students shall remain on task when work is assigned. Student receives 5 points for each ten minutes of on-task behavior. Student receives 20 points for each assignment completed with 80 percent accuracy or better.
   2. Use polite language and behavior toward others. No putdowns, name calling, yelling, screaming, swearing, threats, or other verbally aggressive behavior. The student loses 5 points for each incident.
   3. No physical aggression. Student loses 20 points for each incident.
   4. Students must comply with all teacher directions within ten seconds. Ten points are lost each time the student does not follow a direction within ten seconds.
   5. Students must remain in their seats unless given permission to leave.
   6. No out-of-class privileges (assemblies, library, lunch, etc.)
   7. On any necessary out-of-class trips (office, bathroom, etc.), the student is accompanied by a staff person.
   8. No free time except that a student may select reading material from the class library to read quietly
   9. During group discussion periods, students are expected to (a) wait until they have been recognized by the group leader before speaking, (b) be fair to other students, and (c) be good listeners. Each student receives 20 points for following the rules. A student can receive 5 bonus points for making a "helpful" comment.

C. *Level I Procedures:*
   1. A copy of each student's individual schedule will be posted in the classroom and on the front cover of his or her work folder. The schedule will also list the materials needed for each work period.
   2. Students on Level I must be in their assigned seat and ready to work before the second bell rings.
   3. "Ready to work" means having the materials needed for the work period on top of the desk.
   4. Two minutes before the first bell signaling the end of the period, Level I students will prepare for the next period by putting away unneeded materials and getting out work materials needed for the next period. Students going to another classroom may not leave until dismissed by an adult supervisor.
   5. Discussion group will be held each Friday morning to review the week and plan for the following week. Friday afternoon will be used to tabulate and distribute paychecks.

D. *The Levels System:*
   Students entering the Washington Intermediate School Resource Room will find that there are actually several levels of privileges available. All students begin at Level I, which is the most strictly supervised level. Eventually, it is possible to earn your way to higher levels, which allow you more freedom to choose activities and make your own decisions. However, each higher level also requires that you be able to demonstrate greater responsibility for your behavior and completing your work. It is possible to move both up and down the levels in this system. Each level is briefly described below.

   Level I: This is the structured token program. Students receive points for following classroom rules, staying on task, and working on IEP goals. You will be closely supervised at all times, and points or tokens are awarded only by the lead teacher and support personnel in the classroom. You must remain in your seat and on task for at least eight out of every ten minutes.
   Level II: In order to move to Level II, you must earn 85 percent or more of the available points for at least two weeks, and the move must be approved by your lead teacher and your IEP team. The rules at Level II are the same as for Level I except that students at Level II may leave their seats without permission to get materials, sharpen pencils, and, when appropriate, use the bathroom. They are also allowed to "buy" free time with their points and choose from a longer list of reinforcers.
   Level III: Level III students may leave the classroom on unsupervised trips to the bathroom, library, or to visit other teachers. A mutually agreeable time limit for each trip will be set. Level III students may use their points to purchase a soda on Friday afternoon, have lunch with a teacher or staff person, leave class early to go to lunch, or other rewards as negotiated with the staff.
   Level IV: Level IV students learn to monitor their own behavior using the token program. You will eventually be completely responsible for all the tasks necessary to keep track of tokens earned, lost, and spent. For the first few weeks, you will have frequent conferences with teachers and staff to discuss your ratings. Eventually, you will be completely responsible for rating your behavior and work time. As you make progress, student–teacher conferences will be less frequent. The goal is to have a once-a-week conference.
   Level V: At this level, students are completely free of the token program. The rule for earning privileges is that you must have complete all assigned academic work for the period. Once work is completed, you may engage in activities without the necessity of purchasing them with points. When students graduate to this level, they are ready to leave the resource room.

special classrooms are busy places. Most teachers find their time almost entirely occupied by teaching tasks and have little time left over for the administrative tasks involved in a token program. Thus, a simple and efficient data collection system is needed. Three separate areas need to be monitored in a classroom token program: (1) academic productivity, (2) tokens earned and lost, and (3) frequency of crucial behaviors.

Academic productivity is, in my view, the most important behavior to assess because encouraging academic success is the main mission of school. An academically successful student is less likely than other students to engage in misbehavior. Because all IEPs for disabled students address academic goals and objectives, the typical special classroom will have very good records of each student's academic accomplishment. The teacher's task is to translate these academic records into a metric that provides useful feedback about each student's progress and, in combination with the records of other students, also allows a fair assessment of the efficacy of the token program. I suggest that two measures be used: (1) percentage of assigned work completed, and (2) total time on task.

The percentage of assigned work completed is defined as the amount of work accurately completed divided by the amount of work assigned. *Work* in this context means any product (worksheet, answers to questions, homework, practice problems, etc.) that has been assigned to the student. For example, imagine that on Monday, Josh has been given a spelling test with 10 words (1 point each), assigned a worksheet worth 20 points, and had a homework assignment worth 30 points. If Josh had 3 words correct on the spelling test, 18 points on the worksheet, and only 5 points on the homework assignment, his percentage accomplished would be 26 divided by 60, or 48 percent. Repeating this process daily would provide an indication of how much assigned work was being accomplished and should be an excellent barometer of academic production. Implementing this kind of measure would require that assignments be given some point value based on the teacher's judgment of the value of the assignment. This can be approached in a flexible way. For example, if a spelling test has 10 words, it is not always necessary to assign 10 points to the test. Each word could be worth 3 points, for a total of 30, if the assignment was considered relatively important. On the other hand, if the spelling test was a pretest, each word could be worth 3 points, but the total given for the entire test could be 15 points, meaning that 5 out of 10 words correct on a pretest was regarded as acceptable perform-

ance. In applying this approach to assessing academic productivity, teachers would need to be flexible and use their best judgment regarding the scoring of each assignment.

For teachers who do not want to take such a quantitative approach, there are certainly other ways to approach this issue. Many teachers record assignments as being completed at a satisfactory level ("S") versus unsatisfactory ("U"). If this is the case, the number of "S" grades divided by the total number of grades for a day or week would also provide a convenient measure of academic production. There are other efficient and easy ways to keep track of the academic production of individual students, such as the number of successfully completed units in an individualized packet of instruction. The easiest approach that accurately summarizes the data in the teacher's gradebook is all that is needed. These data should then be plotted on a graph so they can be interpreted easily and shared with members of the child's educational team.

It is also desirable to keep a record of the approximate amount of allotted time that the child spends engaged in academic tasks. In most settings, however, this task may require more time than staff have available. An alternative approach would be to use the total number of tokens earned for on-task or work behavior as a measure of progress in this regard. The program description shown in Figure 11.1 states that one way of earning tokens is for the student to remain ontask, engaged in assigned tasks, for 10 minutes. If 5 points are awarded for each 10 minutes of on-task behavior, 30 points per hour would be available. Keeping a record of the total number of points earned per day for on-task behavior would provide a good measure of the child's "work" behaviors. If a more precise measure of on-task behavior is needed, an observer may be used or the student's behavior could be videotaped and scored for on-task behavior at a more convenient time (e.g., King, Marcattilio, & Hanson, 1981). In recording the number of points earned for on-task behavior, it is important that the student receive full credit for on-task time. If the student is fined for misbehavior, the resulting loss of points should not be subtracted from on-task time because this would distort the total. Points lost through fines should be tabulated separately. Also, if the student's program is subject to change as mainstream classes are added or subtracted or time in the special classroom is changed, computing a percentage of on-task time or percentage of points earned will allow comparison across the changing schedules.

Name: _____   Period: 1 2 3 4 5 6 7 8 9

Points Earned:

	Time Block								Time Block					
	10	20	30	40	50	60			10	20	30	40	50	60
Points Earned														

Other points: On time (5 pts)   Materials ready (5 pts)

Points Lost

Rule Number														
Points															

Other Points Earned/Comments/Other Target Behaviors:

_____

_____

_____

Swearing	01	02	03	04	05	06	07	08	09	10	11	12	13	14	15	16	17	18	19	20

Total points earned   _____

Total points lost   – _____

Net points   = _____

Figure 11.1   Student Record Form

In addition to tabulating points earned for time on task, it would also be important to tabulate the total number of points earned for appropriate behavior and lost as a consequence of rule violations. Again, it would be most helpful to tabulate points earned and fines separately because each reflects very different classes of behavior. The more detail that can be maintained in the data-recording system, the easier it will be to make needed adjustments to the program. Of course, a separate tabulation of the net points earned (points earned minus points lost) will be needed so the student can exchange points earned for backup rewards.

Finally, it will be important to tabulate behaviors incompatible with on-task work behavior. One efficient method to accomplish this is to base tabulations on the classroom rules (see Figure 11.1 for an example). Rule violations should result in a fine or loss of points. By recording each loss of points according to the particular rule that was violated, the frequency of key problem behaviors may be determined. Frequencies of violations can be tabulated separately for each rule, or the total number of rule violations can be counted.

Figure 11.1 shows an example of a form suitable for recording the points earned and lost by a student during a two-hour time block. Readers are welcome to copy the form for their own use and make any changes needed for use in a particular classroom. The form consists of sections for recording on-task behavior in ten-minute blocks across a total of two hours. Students who remain on task for an acceptable portion of any ten-minute block (eight minutes or 80 percent would be an acceptable criterion) receive five points. If they are on task for less than 80 percent of the ten-minute block, zero points are entered. Any other behaviors to be rewarded can be entered in the area labeled "Other Behaviors." When these behaviors occur, they can be circled to indicate that the associated points were earned.

The next section of the form provides space for recording points lost due to rule violations. When a rule violation occurs, simply record the rule number and number of points lost in the space provided. The last section of the form is for comments and miscellaneous points that may be earned. Some students may have individually designed behavior management programs. This section of the form could be designed to record data relevant to these programs. Figure 11.1 includes space for tabulating the frequency of "swearing." To use this part of the form, merely place an "X" over each successive number each time the target behavior occurs. At the end of the time period, the last "X" will be over the total frequency, which can be transferred to a graph or another form.

Step 4: Design the behavioral contingencies and write the program description. It should be clear by now that the contingencies in token programs consist of rewarding appropriate behavior with tokens or points and subtracting them for rule violations. This can be accomplished with physical tokens, actually handed to and taken away from students, or with a more abstract point system in which the student is informed verbally of the status of his or her earnings. Younger children will do best with physical tokens, whereas older children should be able to comprehend the more abstract points. If physical tokens are used, they need to be unique enough to be counterfeit-proof. Laminated "dollars" with unique designs should be cost-effective to produce, yet unique enough that unauthorized duplication is avoided.

The reinforcers vary according to what is available in the classroom, the needs of the students, and the ingenuity of staff running the program. However, a few issues remain to be discussed. The first is computation of the net amount of points. This can be done in one of two ways. First, the points lost can be subtracted from points earned regardless of the result. In some cases this may mean that students earn a negative total. If this occurs, they can then be required to earn their way out of "debt" before accumulating a positive total that can be exchanged for reinforcers. The disadvantage of this approach is that a student could go so far into debt that the situation seems hopeless. This might lead to a deterioration of behavior and make the program ineffective because the student sees no chance to participate in the rewarding aspects of the program.

An alternative approach is never to allow the student's point total to fall below zero. Although this is economically unrealistic, it may preserve the positive aspects of the program for those students who might go too far into debt. Several compromises are also possible. Indebtedness can be limited to, for example, 50 or 100 points, ensuring that a student can always see some hope in working off the debt. Another approach is to keep an accurate tabulation of points earned and lost while resetting the total back to zero (i.e., wiping out the debt) at regular intervals. For instance, regardless of behavior during the previous week, all students could begin each new week with zero points. This may be a good compromise because it provides realistic feedback for behavior, while giving each student an opportunity to come in contact with the positive aspects of the token program at the beginning of each new week.

Another crucial aspect of a token program is the menu of reinforcers and their costs. Let's assume that the typical student spends four hours per day in the resource room or special classroom. This would mean that a total of 120 points are available for on-task behavior. Add to this 120 points available for completing six assignments during four hours and perhaps an additional 50 points for other behaviors, and the total available points is about 300 per day or 75 points per hour. Thus, as a rough guideline, the cost of the smallest rewards should be about 25 points, allowing purchases to be made within a class period. The cost of larger rewards could range upward from 25 points. A student in the classroom for four hours per day could earn about 1,500 points per week. A major reward such as a compact disc or clothing could cost as much as 5,000 to 50,000 points and would take three to thirty days of excellent behavior to accumulate.

A sample menu of reinforcers and their costs follows:

Young Students	Adolescents	Tokens/ Points
Early dismissal (1 minute)	Early dismissal (1 minute)	25
Pencil	Pencil	25
Toy eraser	Pen	50
15 minutes of computer time	15 minutes of computer time	50
Snack item	Can of soda	100
Pack of sport cards	Comic book	300
Action figure toy	Compact disc	1,500
New video game	New video game	1,500
T-shirt	Sunglasses	3,000

This list is not complete and it omits fads that may enjoy a short burst of popularity and can be effective reinforcers during the time they are popular. The list of backup reinforcers needs to be one of the most flexible elements in the program. If the backup reinforcers are not desirable, the entire program is at risk. Thus, every effort must be made to develop a menu of backup reinforcers that consists of popular items and activities, meeting the needs of as many students as possible. When a new student enters the token program, it would be prudent to discuss the backup rewards with him or her and make sure that the student finds one or more items on the menu attractive. If not, adding an item or two to the menu would be a good idea. Also, the reward menu should be adjusted according to the age of the students in the program.

Finally, after all the major decisions about the program have been made, a written manual, detailed enough that a substitute teacher or new staff member could accurately run the program, needs to be prepared. As suggested previously, the manual should be composed on a word processor so additions and changes are easy to process. Each draft should be dated to avoid confusion, and it would also be helpful to refer directly to the latest draft in the posted classroom rules. A sample handout is shown in Table 11. 1.

Step 5: Begin the program. Introducing a new student to an established token program needs to be done carefully because token programs are somewhat more complex than many behavior management programs. A prepared handout, rules posted in the classroom, and a meeting to review the rules and procedures of the program are the first steps in introducing a new student to the program. Asking the student to sign a contract that summarizes the rules and procedures of the program may assist them in making a commitment to participate actively. If new students are present to see peers trade in their tokens or points for reinforcers, this may enhance the effectiveness of the program. As students begin the token program, it will also help if they are able to trade in tokens or points for at least a small reward as soon as possible, even if it means ignoring a rule violation or changing the usual class schedule.

A second situation that deserves some discussion is starting a token program with an entire class. This task should be undertaken with a great deal of care and preparation with a goal of giving the students some ownership of the program before it begins. Setting a starting date for the program and then using the prior two or three weeks to introduce it and solicit student input will provide an opportunity to iron out any problems.

Introducing students to the program by asking them to read the handout and offer suggestions will give them a sense of ownership while valuable critical feedback is obtained. Of course, the menu of reinforcers is crucial, and the teacher should be certain that the menu is varied enough that all students will find something on it for which they will work hard.

Step 6: Observe the effects of the program and initiate steps to strengthen generalization beyond the training environment. The program described here could be a component of a levels system designed to promote the return of students to a fully mainstream program as soon as they are ready. The decision to move student to the next level of the program should be made by reviewing their performance at their current level and consulting with the special education team. As in all behavior management programs, it is absolutely crucial that data regarding each student's performance be easily available for regular review. Graphs of on-task time, percentage of academic work completed, points gained, and points lost due to rule violations will greatly assist in the decision-making process.

At some point in the student's program, a limited return to the mainstream environment may be recommended by the team. Alternatively, a student may be placed in a special classroom while still attending one or more mainstream classes or periods. Students in the mainstream can often be served well with one of the programs discussed in Chapter 10 as they participate in the token program while in the special classroom. A behavior contract and/or a daily or weekly report card can be used effectively to monitor and reward appropriate behavior in the mainstream.

Chadwick and Day (1971) studied the effects of rewarding academic production and related behaviors with a point system plus praise and attention from teachers and staff. When the token system was discontinued and students were working only for praise and attention, both work completed and accuracy remained at the high levels produced by the token system plus praise. This result underlines the importance of providing praise and attention for appropriate behavior during distribution of tokens or points and suggests that continuing to provide contingent praise and attention is one method of strengthening generalization of gains produced by a token program.

Another approach to strengthening generalization of the gains associated with a token system is to allow students who do well on the structured token program to graduate to a self-monitored token program. Kazdin (1977, 1983) concluded from an extensive review of the available literature that having clients themselves administer tokens is one method that may contribute to generalization and maintenance of behaviors learned in a token program. However, Kazdin also noted that it may be necessary to include some external feedback loop to ensure that self-administered tokens are not administered noncontingently—that is, without any relationship to the target behaviors.

Rhode, Morgan, and Young (1983) studied six children from grades 1, 2, 4, and 5 who had moderate to severe behavior problems characterized by disruptive classroom behavior, refusal to work, noncompliance, aggression, and being out of seat. The authors first provided resource room treatment to the six children to remediate inappropriate classroom behavior and then taught the students to use self-evaluation procedures so the changes would generalize to each student's regular classroom setting. Although the study used techniques that may not be successful under all circumstances, such as with the most severely disruptive students, it provides concrete guidance in how to employ self-evaluation procedures to enhance generalization and maintenance of behavior gains in regular classroom settings. The core of the program was a point system. Students were awarded 0 (totally unacceptable) to 5 (excellent) points for both their academic work and their behavior in the resource room. Points could be used to purchase small rewards at the end of each session (e.g., small toys, candy).

The study began with a baseline period in which teachers were instructed to use their normal classroom management procedures. The intervention began with establishing classroom rules and introducing the point system. Points earned were recorded on cards held by the students for the one-hour session. Ratings were assigned by the teacher for each fifteen-minute interval. In the next condition, behavior and academic performance were rated by both the teacher and student. If the teacher and student ratings were within 1 point of each other (higher or lower), the student kept the rating they had assigned to themselves. If the teacher and student ratings matched exactly, the student received a bonus point. If the ratings were different by more than 1 point, the student earned no points for that fifteen-minute interval. During this condition, both the teacher and student explained their ratings to each other. Over the next several conditions, matching of student and teacher ratings was slowly faded while the time interval between

ratings was slowly increased from 15 to 30 minutes. At the end of this condition, student and teacher ratings were matched every two or three days and students could not anticipate when they would be matching their ratings with the teacher's.

The remaining conditions were designed to increase generalization of behaviors learned in the resource room to each student's regular classroom. Rhode et al. required that students average at least "80% appropriate classroom behavior in the resource room over a 4-day period" (p. 176) before being returned to their regular classroom. When the return to the regular classroom occurred, students rated their own behavior and academic performance every thirty minutes and ratings were matched with the regular classroom teacher on a random basis every two or three days. Points could be exchanged for the backup reinforcers once a day. Over the next 30 sessions or so, the formal self-evaluation procedure was gradually eliminated by extending the time period from thirty to sixty minutes and providing less frequent opportunity to exchange points earned on a particular day for the backup reinforcers. Eventually, the students were told they did not need the points anymore. Instead, they rated their performance verbally with feedback from the teacher. This procedure was also discontinued, but students were encouraged to use the self-evaluation procedure by themselves. If a student's behavior deteriorated, a "booster" session was provided by one of the authors. This session consisted of a discussion of classroom rules and whether the student had been able to follow them. Then, a discussion of plans for coping with difficult situations was developed and the student was asked to verbalize it.

Four of the six subjects were returned to their regular classrooms and maintained an average of 93 percent appropriate behavior as measured by independent observers. The other two subjects were never totally weaned from the self-evaluation procedures in the regular classroom, but both students did show substantial improvements in behavior compared to the baseline condition.

Rhode et al. were able to use independent observers to assess student behavior. In applying these techniques to less generously staffed school settings, it would be necessary either to depend on the teacher ratings, which were continued daily regardless of whether the ratings were matched with those of the students, or to employ a less frequent schedule of independent observations to assess the outcome.

Smith, Young, West, Morgan, and Rhode (1983) conducted a similar study with four junior high school students and successfully demonstrated that the technique was effective across a wide age range. The study also showed that asking the regular classroom teacher to match ratings with the student after a half-hour independent work period was a successful method of obtaining generalization of skills.

Ninness, Fuerst, and Rutherford (1991) used a procedure similar to that of Rhode et al. to train students in behavioral self-management. One of the main goals of the study was to train students to use the skills when no adult supervisor was present in the classroom. Two elements of this study deserve particular attention. First, during the training sessions, students were occasionally given particularly difficult situations in which to practice their self-management skills, such as being given a particularly difficult academic task or being distracted by a student confederate. A second feature was that students given explicit instruction to use their skills in another unsupervised setting did not apply the skills until instructed to do so. Both of these techniques—instruction to apply new skills in a new setting, and using particularly difficult situations ("red flags") as probes or tests of whether new skills were being applied—may enhance generalization and maintenance of skills.

For a good summary of issues in using self-monitoring procedures, see Lloyd, Landrum, and Hallahan (1991).

Step 7: Modify the program, if necessary. What if a student or students fail to respond to the classroom token program? Kazdin (1983) points out that it is probably best to look at elements of the program rather than characteristics of the individual in determining why an individual fails to respond to a token program. He also offers several strategies that may enhance responsiveness to a token program. One of the most obvious is to increase the magnitude of reinforcement. This can be accomplished by increasing either the frequency of token delivery or the value of the backup reinforcers. If the program is not succeeding with one or more students, it would be important to look at the rate of reinforcement they are experiencing. If reinforcement is occurring at a low rate because rule violations are causing loss of many points or tokens, it may be helpful to modify this aspect of the program to ensure that some tokens are available to purchase backup rewards.

If students are failing to emit responses that can be reinforced, priming, prompting, or shaping the responses may enhance performance (Kazdin, 1977).

Prompting consists of providing verbal or written cues to guide performance of reinforced responses. For example, a student who is low in on-task behavior may need very specific instructions to cue the behaviors involved in being on task. This might include prompts to take out needed materials, find the correct page of a workbook, read the instructions, and perform the required task. The cues to perform these steps could be given verbally, written on a card taped to the student's desk, or even modeled by a neighbor. Immediate, specific feedback may also be needed to encourage students and ensure that they are doing the task correctly. Review of previously studied material may also be needed if students lack the academic skill or knowledge to complete the task.

Shaping was discussed in Chapter 2. Shaping a behavior means rewarding successive approximations of the target behavior. That is, one begins by rewarding less accurate or expert responses than are acceptable later in the learning process. The criterion for reward is raised in small steps until only a polished performance is rewarded. A performance that was acceptable and rewarded early in the training is not rewarded at a later time, because the criterion has been raised so that the child's performance must be closer to the goal. One of the main ways of earning tokens or points in the token program described here is to be on task for eight minutes out of every ten-minute block of time. For this, the student receives 5 points. For some students, remaining on task for the full eight minutes may have a low probability of occurrence. On-task behavior could be shaped in this situation by lowering the criterion of on-task time that will result in a reward. It may even be necessary to begin rewarding the student for accomplishing anything during a ten-minute time block or for remaining on-task for just a minute or two. Then, as the student's ability and motivation to stay on-task improve, this criterion could be increased until eight minutes of on-task behavior was required to receive the full 5 points or tokens.

Another strategy suggested by Kazdin (1977) is to use individualized contingencies or group contingencies. Individualizing contingencies may require developing a separate behavior management program using plans discussed in other chapters or modifying the contingencies of the token program to better suit the needs of an individual student. Developing group contingencies is another possible strategy. Group contingencies are a form of cooperative learning in which an entire group can benefit from the behavior of individuals within the group. For instance, bonus points, extra privileges, or other rewards could be made contingent on the performance of an entire group. If five students were in a special classroom for two successive one-hour periods, a group privilege in the second period could be made contingent on group performance in the first period. If all students, for example, earn 25 points or more for on-task behavior during the first period, each member of the group could be allowed to have a can of soda during the second hour. Numerous variations in the way that group contingencies are programmed and administered are possible. Refer to the discussion of the "Good Behavior Game" in Chapter 7 for more ideas.

Kehle, Clark, Jenson, and Wampold (1986) reported on a method of improving performance of individual children who had failed to respond to a classroom token program. These authors showed each of four particularly disruptive children videotapes of themselves from the previous day from which all inappropriate behavior had been edited out. The result was a videotape that allowed children to view themselves behaving appropriately for eleven minutes. The decline in inappropriate behavior continued at a six-week follow-up observation. The self-observation procedure was used to supplement the classroom token system. Woltersdorf (1992) demonstrated that this procedure alone could decrease disruptive behavior. Clark, Kehle, Jenson, and Beck (1992) suggested that the procedure (called self-modeling) would be most effective with children who have the cognitive ability to imitate independently and in cases where the goal is to increase the frequency of deficit behaviors. For practitioners who have access to the equipment, this procedure could be a helpful way of improving the performance of children who do not respond to a classroom token system or other behavior management program. See Meharg and Woltersdorf (1990) for a review of studies employing this method.

Step 8: Fade out the program. The token program described in this section is meant to remain as a more or less permanent part of the classroom structure rather than being faded out. Instead, individual students are expected to progress to higher levels of the program until they are ready to return fully or partially to the mainstream environment.

In conclusion, token programs are among the most useful behavior management techniques. They are flexible and can be used successfully in a wide variety of situations. The keys to success are to ensure that the backup reward is attractive and that target behaviors have been well defined. Once these two components are in place, it is important to remain flexible and to make other adjustments in the program according to the needs of the students and the data generated by the program.

BEHAVIOR MANAGEMENT OF CHILDREN'S SOCIAL SKILLS

Ask any adult what he or she remember about his or her school years. Most will reminisce about their friends, their teachers, and the significant others who passed through their lives. Social experiences are a large part of our school memories. A brief visit to any school will reveal that when students are not engaged in learning experiences, they are socializing. Even learning activities have a social component because children who ask appropriate questions, smile at the teacher, and seek help when needed will be more successful than children who do not do these things (Cartledge & Milburn, 1986). Social skills are an important component of overall school success. The purpose of this section is to discuss major issues in remediating social skills deficits. The section begins with a general discussion of techniques for assessing and remediating social skills deficits. Then the focus shifts to the more specific problem of social isolation in childhood, including a model behavior management program for remediating this behavior deficit.

Under what circumstances should school personnel consider programs to remediate social skills? This is a difficult question because social skills training is usually considered a parental responsibility, and the range of acceptable social behavior is very wide. Some parents encourage their children to treat others with kindness and fairness, whereas other parents encourage their children to be competitive and pursue their goals aggressively. These approaches to child rearing represent different values, and neither is inherently wrong. The socially aggressive behavior of some children, however, leads to social rejection by peers, academic problems, and conflict with adult authority figures, which may lead to even more serious problems as the child grows up (Feindler, 1991; Hops & Greenwood, 1988). In contrast, other children tend to be isolated from their peer group as a consequence of social anxiety and negative self-perceptions of their social competence. This behavior pattern has been associated with internalizing difficulties such as loneliness and depression (Rubin & Mills, 1988). Both of these patterns of social isolation may require intervention.

Social skills consist not only of an overt, behavioral component, there is also a covert, cognitive component that needs to be considered. The cognitive component consists of the thoughts that mediate social behavior. For example, a child may be accidentally bumped while in line for lunch. One child may interpret the event as an accident and not react at all, whereas another child may see it as purposeful aggression and respond by punching and fighting. Still another child may impulsively strike back without making any attempt to interpret the event. The fact that the child was bumped is less important than the covert reasoning and thinking that occurred, or did not occur, in the situation. Research has indicated that popular children are able to generate more and better quality solutions to problem situations than children who are aggressive, isolated, or unpopular (Asarnow & Callan, 1985; Ladd & Oden, 1979; Richard & Dodge, 1982). The cognitive and behavioral dimensions of social skills may both need to be addressed in some situations. This can be accomplished using the cognitive-behavioral techniques that were introduced in Chapter 8.

Kendall and Braswell (1985, 1993) describe a complete program for providing cognitive-behavioral therapy for impulsive children. This program consists of teaching impulsive children to slow down and think about both academic and social problem situations. The children are taught to use a problem-solving procedure consisting of defining the problem, listing possible strategies that will lead to a solution, focusing attention on the problem at hand, choosing and implementing a possible solution, and, finally, rewarding themselves for a good job or uttering a coping statement that cues better future performance. The affective or social component of the treatment consists mainly of role playing problematic social situations, such as tearing their pants at recess and being teased about it. After being introduced to the role-play situation, the child then uses the problem-solving steps to generate a series of possible responses to the situation, evaluate them, and choose a course of action. The idea is to teach the child to slow down and think about the situation rather than respond impulsively.

Butler, Miezitis, Friedman, and Cole (1980) also employed a role-play format in the treatment of depressive symptoms in preadolescents. The main objective of the treatment was to teach children a problem-solving approach to threatening or stressful situations that emphasized learning to generate as many potential solutions to problem situations as possible. The greatest amount of favorable changes was observed in the role-play treatment compared to control conditions. This type of intervention seems to represent a useful approach to a variety of social skill deficits (e.g., Asarnow & Carlson, 1988). Thus, in formulating strategies for remediating social skills deficits, it can be helpful to focus on both the overt behaviors and the cognitive component of the skill deficit.

Kendall and Braswell (1982a) point to another dimension for evaluating an intervention strategy, the general impact level. The general impact level consists of the conspicuous effects of a particular intervention, such as in parent or teacher ratings of behavior, sociometric ratings, or the return of deviant behavior to within normal limits. The distinction is useful because it alerts the practitioner to the importance of conducting relevant interventions. One technique for defining the relevance of a particular social skill is to assess its importance in the target child's peer group. Skills that popular, socially successful peers use should improve the social adjustment of the target child. If interventions result in training prosocial behaviors that are high in their general impact, they should be "trapped" (that is, rewarded and shaped) by the natural environment. The result will be a long-lasting and significant change in the child's social adjustment.

Thus, in designing school-based social skills interventions, three issues need to be considered. First, what specific deficit skill is the child lacking? Second, is there a cognitive component to the social skills deficit that needs to be addressed? Finally, what is the likely general impact of intervening to increase the frequency of a particular social behavior. In other words, is the target behavior one that socially successful peers employ, and is it likely that training this particular skill will have a long-term, positive impact? Cognitive-behavioral approaches to behavior deficits can be useful but may require referral to an agency outside the school district unless personnel with the expertise to conduct such interventions are available.

Further reading on the assessment and treatment of social skills deficits from the behavior management and other perspectives is provided by Cartledge and Milburn (1986), Conger and Keane (1981), Dodge, McClaskey, and Feldman (1985), Elliott and Ershler (1990), Gresham and Nagle (1980), Hops and Greenwood (1988), Horan and Williams (1982), Kendall and Braswell, (1982b), LaGreca and Mesibov (1979), LeCroy (1982, 1994b), Vogrin and Kassinove (1979), and Wanlass and Prinz (1982). Instruments for measuring social behavior, such as the Vineland Adaptive Behavior Scales (Sparrow, Balla, & Cicchetti, 1984), the School

Social Skills Rating Scale (Brown, Black, & Downs, 1984), the School Social Behavior Scales (Merrell, 1993a, 1993b), or the Behavior Assessment System for Children (BASC; Reynolds & Kamphaus, 1992) may also be useful.

A PROGRAM FOR IMPROVING SOCIAL ISOLATION

One of the few generalizations to come out of the literature on socially isolated children is that there is little agreement among clinicians and researchers as to its nature and taxonomy (see reviews by Conger & Keane, 1981; Kratochwill & French, 1984; Wanlass & Prinz, 1982). The ambiguity lies in the measurement and dynamics of social isolation in any particular child. Social isolation can be assessed by either observing the extent of the child's interactions with peers or using sociometric measures in which the child's peers are asked to supply information, such as with whom they like to work or who they consider their best friend. Unfortunately, the effects of interventions on these measures are frequently contradictory, with few studies showing improvement in both measures.

Another important issue is whether isolation results from a performance deficit or a skill deficit. A performance deficit means the child is capable of social interactions but does not emit such behavior for some reason; that is, the child possesses the necessary skills but is not performing. A performance deficit should respond to a formal or informal behavior management program in which the child is rewarded for social interactions with peers.

On the other hand, a program simply to reward the occurrence of social interactions may be unsuccessful when the child lacks the needed skills. If this is the case, a detailed observation and analysis of the child's behavior is necessary because the dynamics that underlie the child's isolation will influence intervention strategies. Consider the following possible explanations of the child's isolation:

- The child fears social interaction and therefore withdraws from it.
- The child is teased by peers for wearing dirty clothes, being uncoordinated, having a bad smell, or other reasons.
- The child is aggressive, annoying, or obnoxious, and is avoided by others.

- The child has specific social skill deficits such as not knowing how to play cooperatively, ask questions, or take a turn in a game.
- The child is a recent arrival in a class with established cliques.
- The child interacts frequently with adults but not with peers.
- The child could be categorized as depressed, developmentally delayed, hyperactive, psychotic, autistic, physically ill, or as having other problems that result in social isolation.

The various hypotheses on this list, which is meant to be suggestive rather than exhaustive, can require different actions on the part of the professional. Basically, three courses of action are possible. First, social isolation may suggest other problems such as child abuse or neglect or a handicapping condition, which should be ruled out by further assessment. Second, social isolation may result from a skill deficit, which suggests that the child needs to learn new social skills. Third, it is possible that social isolation or withdrawal reflects a performance deficit, which can be effectively managed by rewarding social interaction with peers.

The behavior management program that follows is designed to remediate social isolation that results from a performance or skill deficit. As noted above, a number of factors may underlie a social skill deficit. One of these might be that the child is depressed. However, child abuse, a recent move to a new school, aggressive behavior, a loss in the family, or fear are alternative causes of social isolation. Although other assessment and intervention might be required, it is reasonable to focus a formal behavior management program directly on the problem of social isolation. The program described next is based on procedures described by Cartledge and Milburn (1986), Conning and Head (1990), Hops (1983), Sheridan, Kratochwill, and Elliott (1990), and Stark, Brookman, and Frazier (1990).

Step 1: Identify the problem. Social isolation or withdrawal is relatively easy to identify once attention is focused on the issue. On the other hand, a socially isolated child is not likely to attract much attention and would be easy to miss in a typical crowded classroom. Initial concerns are likely to center around issues such as the child spending too much time alone or being excluded from social interactions and play. However, further assessment may reveal that other, more serious or pervasive problems underlie the child's isolation and may indicate that these problems should also become a focus of intervention.

Step 2: Refine the definition of the problem. Although the initial concern is social isolation, the goal is not to decrease social isolation but to increase normal social interactions. This goal, of course, requires more than observation of the target child.

Assessment of the baseline rate of a problem behavior is not always a simple matter of counting occurrences of a discrete behavior. Assessment of social isolation/withdrawal requires at least two formal measures and consideration of at least two additional issues. Thus, I suggest that assessment of social isolation be conducted in two stages. In the first stage, several issues must be addressed simultaneously, so a running behavior record is the most reasonable assessment method. A running behavior record consists of writing a narrative of behavioral events as they occur. The goal, vague though it may be, is to gain an understanding of the nature of the child's isolative behavior. This is accomplished by taking special note of the sequence of behavioral events and how they relate to each other.

The initial observation should at least provide answers to these questions:

- Does the child's behavior cause other children to stay away?
- Is the child teased or harassed by others? If so, why?
- Does the child interact normally with anybody at any time, such as with adults in the classroom or a sibling on the way to school?
- How does the child behave outside the classroom?
- Does the child make unsuccessful attempts to approach other children?
- Is the child aggressive?
- What seems to be the most important characteristic of the child that leads to isolation?

Once these questions and any others that arise have been answered, it should be possible to decide on a course of action. One alternative is to revise the hypothesis that social isolation is the primary problem. Perhaps the child is rejected by peers because of excessive aggression, shows signs of depression that deserve immediate attention, or needs to have better personal hygiene. In these instances, it may be helpful pursue other courses of action such as implementing a program to decrease behavior excesses, or referring to a mental health professional or school psychologist for a thorough diagnostic assessment. A standardized measure of social skills such as the School Social Skills Rating Scale (Brown, Black, & Downs, 1984) may also be very helpful in providing a broad picture of the child's social functioning.

Step 3: Assess the baseline rate. Given the time limitations of most school personnel, a time-sampling procedure is the most reasonable approach to establishing a baseline for isolative behavior. The important variable in time sampling is to select an appropriate period during which to conduct observations. Because the concern is social isolation, a period of time with many opportunities for socializing would be required. For young children, a free time period or recess would be good; for older children, a discussion period, recess, or lunch might present a good situation in which to observe. It may also be wise to consider using a multiple baseline approach. A multiple baseline design consists of recording observations from two or more different environments while focusing treatment on only one environment. If improvement over the baseline occurs in the environment without treatment, it suggests that the results of the management program have generalized to that environment. For example, observations could be conducted on the playground and during a classroom free time. If treatment occurs during free time, observations on the playground will reveal whether generalization to the other setting has occurred.

Once a setting and time for recording observations have been determined, a recording scheme must be devised. Such a scheme should be based on mutually exclusive categories (i.e., a behavior fits only one category) and should include any behaviors that were observed significantly often during the initial observations plus those that are desirable to increase. The behaviors should be operationally defined, using the information in the narrative record. Such a scheme might include all or some of the following categories:

IPP: Initiation of positive interaction with peers
IAP: Initiation of aggressive interaction with peers
ARPP: Appropriate response to a peer attempt to initiate a positive interaction
IRPP: Inappropriate response to or ignoring of a peer attempt to initiate a positive interaction
IP: Isolated play

An alternative recording scheme is to observe the number of social interactions in which the child participates and the number of social interactions initiated by the child. In order to develop age-, sex-, and grade-appropriate intervention goals, it is helpful to observe socially competent control children of the same age and sex as the isolative child. These observations can then be used as standards against which to judge the effectiveness of the intervention program for the socially isolated child. Various techniques can be used. Continuous observation of the target child and a selected peer has the advantage of being simple but may or may not result in a comparison with validity across the child's entire peer group. Observation of two or three randomly selected peers may make for a more valid comparison.

The final step is to combine all of these elements and proceed with the actual baseline observations. This is accomplished by dividing the observation period into four- or five-second intervals and recording the behavior occurring during each interval, alternating between the target child and the peer(s) selected for comparison. The most convenient method is to use a prepared sheet divided into the appropriate number of squares, recording the code for the behavior category in which the child is engaged during each interval. During the baseline period, any inadequacies in the coding system should be corrected by eliminating uninformative categories and adding new ones as necessary. The percentage of intervals during which the child was engaged in each of the categorized behaviors can be computed daily and recorded or plotted to summarize the observations. Chapter 3 contains a more detailed discussion of observation methods.

Although this intervention is intended to focus on isolative behavior, it may also be informative to use a sociometric measure of the child's popularity and peer relationships. A variety of methods exist for conducting sociometric assessments. One method is to reproduce several dozen copies of a list of pupils in the class and ask all students to circle the names of their peers in response to questions such as, "Whom do you like to play with?" or "Who are your friends?" The sociometric status of the target child is measured by counting the number of times his or her name is circled in response to each question. The sociometric measure is administered before and after the behavior management program.

Step 4: Design the behavioral contingencies and write the program description. It is, or should be, intrinsically rewarding for children to interact socially with their peers. The aim of programs designed to improve social skill performance is to allow the naturally reinforcing consequences of peer interactions to come into play. In other words, initiation of social interactions is likely to be "trapped" by the natural environment.

Hops (1983) recommends employing a combination of procedures in interventions with socially isolated children. The techniques mentioned most frequently in the research literature are contingency management, symbolic (filmed) modeling, coaching, structuring of activity and play material, and peer socialization. My recommendation is that the formal behavior management program focus on rewarding increased duration and quality of social interactions, coaching the child in ways to initiate social interactions, setting and monitoring goals, and structuring the environment to enhance the probability that interactions will be rewarded and new skills learned.

The general goal would be to reward the isolated child for increasing initiations of social interactions and for developmentally appropriate duration and quality of the interactions. Some caution is necessary because it is possible to produce behavior that appears artificial, if the frequency of initiating interactions is emphasized rather than the duration and quality of interaction (Conger & Keane, 1981). A variety of approaches to providing contingent reward for appropriate nonisolative behaviors are possible. It may, in fact, be necessary to try several approaches before one is found that produces positive effects. One possible cause of isolative behavior resulting from a *performance deficit* is that adult attention is inadvertently being paid to the child when he or she is alone. If this is the case, it is necessary to reverse the contingency, paying attention to the child only when he or she interacts appropriately with peers. Naturally, operational definitions of preferred behaviors are those established during baseline observations of the isolated child and a same-sex peer. If adult attention does not have the desired effect, either a token system or a consumable reward could be tried.

The reward structure in this program can be varied according to the needs and maturity of the child. Its basic structure is that isolative behavior is ignored and socializing at appropriate times is rewarded with adult attention, points, or, if necessary, a consumable reward. The definition of appropriate socializing will also vary with the context, but concrete, operational definitions should be established prior to the start of the program using observations of socially competent control children. Recall, also, that the child's isolative behavior is presumed to be the result of a performance deficit, meaning that the child is demonstrably capable (i.e., at home) of emitting appropriate social behavior.

If the child has a *skill deficit*—that is, there is little or no evidence that the child possesses the skills for initiating or maintaining a social interaction—these skills will need to be learned via a process of coaching, prompting, shaping, role play, and rehearsal. Sheridan, Kratochwill, and Elliott (1990) employed a "Goal Sheet" in the first phase of their study on which children recorded daily goals, whether they met the goal, with whom they interacted, and when they interacted. The goal sheet also included space for teacher comments and feedback. Backup rewards were also provided. Later, the Goal Sheet was replaced by a personal journal in which the student recorded instances of attempting to initiate interactions with peers.

Although some children might be able to initiate an interaction successfully once they have set a specific goal to do so, other children will need additional help. For example, in a private session with the child, it may be necessary to help him or her practice the behaviors needed to reach the goal. If the goal was to ask another child to play ball during recess, the child could be coached in how to approach the peer, what to say, and how to proceed to performing the activity. It can also be helpful to enlist a peer as a confederate who expects to be approached by the target child and will respond positively. This makes it more likely that the child's behavior will be rewarded by his or her peers. Later, the target child can be encouraged to approach others who have not been prompted on how to respond.

The written program needs to include a format for the Goal Sheets and personal journal, and reminders to all staff who contact the target child to praise the child for initiating social interactions. If individual sessions are scheduled for coaching and goal setting, the time, place, and responsible person (who could be a school social worker, school psychologist, teacher, or aide) needs to be established.

Step 5: Begin the program. Once sufficient baseline data have been collected, the program can begin. If the program consists of rewarding appropriate socializing with adult attention, it is not necessary to inform the child that a change in contingencies is about to occur. However, it may be helpful to suggest to the child a couple of times that it might be more pleasant to join in group activities rather than staying alone. It may be even more helpful to suggest a specific activity and how the child might be able to participate. Caution must be exercised

that these interactions do not continue to reward the child's isolative behavior.

If individual coaching and goal setting are employed, the teacher and child need to reach agreement on the goals to be pursued and the rewards for meeting them. A token system using points for older children and stickers for younger children, backed up by age-appropriate rewards, will need to be explained to the child before the program is begun.

Step 6: Observe the effects of the program and initiate steps to strengthen generalization beyond the training environment. Periodically, the child's behavior should be observed using the same technique employed to collect the baseline data. Obviously, the expectation is that isolative behavior will decrease. Informal observations should indicate that the child is being reinforced by his or her peers and that social interactions are being maintained by these natural contingencies.

If the multiple baseline technique was used to gather baseline data, determining the generalized effects of the intervention program will be a simple matter of comparing more recent observations to the baseline data. Again, the expectation is that positive change will be found. The key to generalization of socializing to other environments lies in the natural contingencies that one hopes will affect the child. That is, other children should be rewarding the child's attempts at social interaction, so that adult attention or other rewards become unnecessary for maintaining the behavior.

On the other hand, generalization to other settings and across time may not be found until specific training is provided. Sheridan, Kratochwill and Elliott (1990) compared teacher-only consultation with conjoint consultation with teacher and parents. The conjoint treatment produced superior generalization across time and settings. In the conjoint condition, both teachers and parents of the target child were included in the consultative process, and both were active participants in the behavioral program. Thus, one method of enhancing generalization is to involve the child's parents in the program.

Step 7: Modify the program, if necessary. If the program does not result in positive effects within a reasonable time period, perhaps two or three weeks, various modifications can be considered. The most basic modification would be to change the reinforcer. If a token system is being used, renegotiation of the reward menu could improve performance. Similarly, adult attention may not be particularly rewarding for some socially isolated children, who would consequently show no improvement in social interactions. For such children, a change in the reward may be needed.

One aspect of this behavior management program that should be carefully monitored is the way the child's peers react to attempts at initiating social interactions. If the child is unable to initiate and maintain a social interaction successfully, even after coaching and rehearsal, it may be necessary to refer the child to a more comprehensive program for improving social skills or to provide additional training in the component skills.

Step 8: Fade out the program. The goal of any program to decrease a child's social isolation should be to intervene as necessary to modify the child's behavior to the extent that natural contingencies take over and the child fits into the social scheme of the classroom. As this occurs, the formal behavior management program can be faded out by decreasing the frequency of reward and raising the criteria for reinforcement.

Careful monitoring of the effects of fading out the program should be performed, especially in the early stages. As noted before, the expectation is that social interactions with peers will continue at a reasonable rate and that the child will gain some positive reinforcement from these interactions. If this does not occur and the target behavior returns to an unacceptably low level, other approaches to the problem may be worth consideration. These approaches might include reexamining the role of environmental factors in the child's behavior, revising the goals of the program, seeking the assistance of a clinical psychologist or psychiatrist, or making a referral to other professionals within the school system.

OTHER RESEARCH ON SOCIAL ISOLATION AS A SKILL DEFICIT

A socially isolated child might not respond to the behavior management program just described if he or she lacks the skills needed to participate in social interactions. In such cases, simply rewarding social interaction will not be successful because the quality of the child's interactions will not lead to rewarding responses from other children. Thus, the child will remain isolated. The solution is to teach the child some skills as well as reward social interaction.

Rather than attempt to teach every component of socializing with peers, it may be more efficient to teach

general strategies for interacting effectively. Oden and Asher (1977) studied the effect of coaching children's social skills on peer acceptance. The basic approach consisted of giving socially isolated children specific coaching in how it might be fun or enjoyable to play a game with another person, followed immediately by an opportunity to practice the same skills with a peer. Afterwards, the effectiveness of the strategies was reviewed with the child. Peer ratings of the desirability of the target child as a play partner showed improvements across time and at a follow-up assessment a year after the intervention.

Finch and Hopps (1982) suggested an intervention program for socially isolated children involving four components. The first component consists of tutoring the child in social skills necessary for successful interaction with classmates. The second component consists of giving the child an opportunity to earn rewards during recess by practicing the skills taught in the tutoring sessions. In the third component, the child is given a peer partner and assigned to an academically related task, which provides additional practice in social interaction. Finally, the child is given practice in predicting his or her own behavior on the assumption that those children who are taught to do what they say will actually increase their rate of social interaction. Each of these four components will be examined in some detail (see also Ladd and Mize, 1982, for a general discussion of social skills remediation from a social learning perspective).

Tutoring a child in social skills basically means to use informal behavior management techniques to help a child develop social skills that will result in positive feedback from peers. These techniques would include shaping, prompting, rewarding with praise, modeling, and ignoring inappropriate behavior. The program described by Finch and Hops includes training in how to initiate an interaction with others, how to respond to an initiation, how to keep an interaction going, how to praise others, and how to be cooperative. Reams could be written detailing the definitions and behavioral components of each skill. On the other hand, pretreatment observations of both the target child and a socially skilled counterpart should be sufficient to clarify the problem area and indicate which skills the child needs to learn.

In the second component, the child is given an opportunity to practice skills learned in the tutoring session. Points are awarded for playing and interacting with others during recess. Special helpers are selected to help the child earn the rewards, which can be exchanged for activities or treats shared by the child's classmates. A more formal structure could be added to this portion of the intervention by gathering pre- and postintervention data regarding the child's level of social interaction on the playground.

Finch and Hops call the third component of the program *joint task*. In this component, partners are assigned to the target child, who then work together on an academic task requiring social interaction, taking turns, and cooperation. This provides the child with additional structured opportunities to practice the newly acquired skills.

The last component of the program consists of having the child tell the instructor what he or she is going to do in the upcoming period of recess or free play and then report back to the instructor after the period to discuss what occurred. A partner is assigned to the child to corroborate the reports and provide a definite opportunity to engage in social activities. Giving the child practice in predicting his or her own behavior should increase the child's ability to formulate strategies for dealing with various social situations.

In sum, the program described by Finch and Hops (1982) may be helpful in remediating social isolation when lack of social skill underlies the isolative behavior. The success of such a program would depend on an assessment that accurately describes both the nature of the skills deficit and the skills shown by the child's socially successful peers. Then, skillful application of informal and formal behavior management techniques should help the unskilled child acquire at least some of the social behaviors of his or her socially successful peers.

A case study of an intervention technique similar to the general model described by Finch and Hops was described by Petersen and Moe (1984). The Petersen and Moe study was conducted with a nine-year-old girl, whose bossy, aggressive behavior resulted in rejection by her peers. The preintervention assessment consisted of interviews with the child's parents and teachers, a sociometric assessment, and behavioral observations of the child's inappropriate social behavior.

The intervention consisted of several strategies designed to both decrease inappropriate behaviors and improve social skill. The major portion of the intervention was conducted in a one-on-one structured teaching situation. The emphasis in the early sessions was on identifying the negative consequences of being bossy or aggressive and teaching positive social behaviors, such

as how to approach other children, smile, take turns, play with others, make requests, and let others do what they want. The emphasis was on teaching the child the consequences of her negative and positive behaviors so she "could learn the effects of her behaviors on other children's feelings and behavior."

After instruction was completed, various situations that had occurred recently were role played. Praise and smiles were used to reward correct responses. In addition, positive consequences of correct actions and negative consequences of incorrect actions were pointed out. Specific feedback was also given for correct and incorrect responses. When an incorrect, inappropriate response to one of the role-play situations was emitted, the situation was repeated until all behaviors emitted in that situation were correct.

Another aspect of the role-playing exercise was that role plays of negative social behavior were practiced, with the child playing the part of another child and the instructor playing the role of a child showing the negative behaviors. Then the negative consequences of the instructor's behavior were discussed, emphasizing how the child felt about the actions of the adult. It is important to emphasize the cognitive component of this intervention. The child was given specific training in anticipating the consequences of her own behavior and emitting appropriate social behavior.

The next phase of the training consisted of observing a "good" model of social behavior and discussing her behavior and what she did to which other children responded positively. The next two phases consisted of a supervised game with peers during recess. Initially, the child was given feedback in the same manner as in the role-playing exercises. Then direct supervision of the game was eliminated.

One interesting aspect of the procedure was that the child was reminded to look at the faces of other children to see whether they liked what she was doing or saying. The authors noted that the discovery that information about another's feelings could be gained through nonverbal cues was a revelation for their subject. This is an intriguing clinical observation that deserves additional follow-up.

Petersen and Moe reported strong effects of their procedure which persisted through follow-up observations conducted at the beginning of the next school year. However, interpretation of this demonstration should be done cautiously because only one subject was involved. Nevertheless, the techniques employed were sound and the results were highly favorable. It seems that both informal techniques just described may have some utility in remediating social skill deficits.

CONCLUSION

As noted in Chapter 10, the most effective use of behavior management techniques is to reinforce appropriate behaviors. The programs described in this chapter were designed to be used in classrooms with adequate staff for close monitoring of behavior. They can be adapted to other settings by either adding the needed staff or simplifying the program. Also, it should be remembered that each program is meant to be a "rough draft" of the final program. Remaining flexible and ready to try new strategies will lead to the greatest amount of success.

REVIEW

Terms to Remember and Review

positive reinforcement	negative reinforcement
token reinforcement	social skills
satiation	response cost
levels program	IDEA
basic behavioral repertoires	coaching
prompting	shaping
IEP	performance deficit
multiple baseline design	skill deficit

Study and Discussion Questions

1. Describe in your own words how a token system works.

2. What are some of the advantages of employing token reward programs?

3. What are the two major components of social skills discussed in the text? Give a concrete example of each component.

4. What is meant by the general impact level of an intervention? What makes this concept an important component of programs designed to improve social skills?

5. Design your own Goal Sheet that could be used in the program for remediating social isolation.

Group Projects

1. Have students assemble into groups of three to five students each. Assign each group a particular age range or developmental stage. The project for each group is to develop a description of social skills expected of children at the age their group was assigned. The lists from all groups can be combined into a broad list of social skills for the entire developmental range.

2. Imagine that you are working with a child who is extremely shy and socially anxious and who spends most of his time in solitary activity. He has no friends and is sometimes teased by other students because he has little athletic skill. Develop a written description of a program for improving this student's social skills. In groups of two or three, role-play a session of coaching this child in how to initiate a social interaction.

3. Imagine that you are a lead teacher of a resource room for behaviorally disordered students. Develop a handout for parents describing the levels system you or your group would implement in this setting. Remember that this is a handout for *parents*.

CHAPTER 12

MANAGEMENT OF BEHAVIOR DEFICITS IN THE HOME

As discussed in Chapter 1, the main focus of *Behavior Management in the Schools* is on solving behavior problems in school settings. However, helping parents solve behavior problems at home can increase the effectiveness of school-based programs, lead to improved communication with the family, and provide parents with a cost effective source of professional services. A good illustration of the helpfulness of extending behavior management programs to the home was provided by Sheridan, Kratochwill, and Elliott (1990). They found that the best generalization of skills across time and settings was obtained when behavioral consultation was done jointly with both teachers and parents being active participants in the behavior management program. School–home notes, discussed in Chapter 10, are another example of effective collaboration between home and school. For a broad perspective on home and school collaboration, the volume edited by Christenson and Conoley (1992) is suggested.

The main goal of this chapter is to describe programs for remediating behavior deficits in the home. The sections cover helping parents with common problems at home, homework, behavior contracts at home, simple token programs at home, and complex token programs at home.

HELPING PARENTS WITH COMMON CHILD-REARING PROBLEMS

Parenting is a complex and difficult task. Many of the common problems of children such as bedtime routines, nighttime soiling, aggression, and getting ready in the morning can become major areas of conflict between parents and children. The main purpose of this section is to suggest some strategies for handling common childhood problems and to direct the reader toward more comprehensive sources when appropriate. Table 12.1 lists some of the most common childhood problems, suggested strategies for dealing with them, and more comprehensive sources of information.

When parents ask for help in coping with child behavior problems, one of the most cost-effective methods of consultation is to provide them with resource materials to study on their own (Sloane, Endo, Hawkes, & Jenson, 1991). Several references for parents are listed in Table 12.1. These resources can be very helpful in providing both a competent overview of behavior management techniques, written in nontechnical language, and concrete advice on handling specific problem behaviors. Another excellent resource is the book published by the National Association of School Psychologists (1992).

Table 12.1. Common Childhood Behavior Problems, Remediation Strategies, and References

Aggression	Timeout; reinforcement of other behavior	See Chapters 9, 12
Bedtime problems	Ignore inappropriate behavior; reward appropriate behavior	See text; Clark, 1985; Eimers & Aitchison, 1977; Sloane, 1979
Bedwetting	Bell and pad; dry bed training	Azrin & Foxx, 1974; Christopherson & Rapoff, 1992; Houts, 1991; Van Londen et al., 1993
Communication	Negotiated behavior contracts; family therapy	See text; Foster & Robin, 1992; Dardig & Heward, 1981
Daily chores	Praise; token programs	See text; Clark, 1985; Eimers & Aitchison, 1977; Sloane, 1979
Disobedience	Reward obedience; timeout; loss of privileges	See text; Clark, 1985; Eimers & Aitchison, 1977; Sloane, 1979
Fears and anxiety	Reward coping behavior; cognitive-behavioral therapy; medication; biofeedback	Morris & Kratochwill, 1983b; Reed, Carter, & Miller, 1992
Fighting among siblings	Reward appropriate interactions; timeout for all fighters	See text
Homework	Good home–school communication; school–home notes; parent involvement; goal setting	See text; Kuepper, 1990; Miller & Kelley, 1991; Olympia, Jenson, Clark, & Sheridan, 1992; Gleason, Colvin, & Archer, 1991
Hyperactivity	Rewards; token programs; timeout; cognitive–behavioral techniques	See text; Abramowitz & O'Leary, 1991; Barkley, 1990; Braswell & Bloomquist, 1991; Parker, 1988
Lying	Correspondence training	See text; Paniagua, 1989; Stokes & Osnes, 1990
Morning routine	Rewards; token programs; timer	See text; Clark, 1985; Eimers & Aitchison, 1977; Sloane, 1977
Thumb-sucking	Reward other behavior; self-recording	Matthews, Leibowitz, & Matthews, 1992; Bernstein, 1994
Unhappiness and depression	Rewards; self-monitoring; cognitive-behavioral therapy; family therapy; individual therapy	Grossman & Hughes, 1992; Milling & Martin, 1992; Reynolds, 1992; Sheras, 1992; Stark, Rouse, & Livingston, 1991

This book contains about a hundred short articles designed to be used as handouts for teachers, parents, and others on such topics as nail biting, shyness, sleepwalking, divorce, adopted children, and many others. In many cases, parents will be able to solve problems on their own when they are provided with effective resource materials. On the other hand, some problems and situations are more resistant to change. A few of these are discussed below.

Obedience

Obedience is a crucial ingredient of successful parenting. Children need to obey the commands of their parents in order to remain safe and healthy, to develop a sense of responsibility, and to grow into productive adults. Children who disobey the commands of their parents can be a source of frustration to parents and may actually be exposed to physical danger such as automobile traffic or household hazards.

Although a brief timeout for disobeying a command is an effective consequence, a better strategy is to ensure that obedience is followed by praise and attention. Like any other desirable behavior, obedience is more likely when it is rewarded. This is one of the most basic rules of child behavior management.

What can be done when parents complain that their child is consistently disobedient? If a child is consistently disobedient at home, it is helpful to begin by taking a general look at the child's behavior both at home and at school. Problems such as a parental separation, academic problems, hyperactivity (ADHD), conflict with a sibling, a personality conflict with a teacher, or a physical illness such as an ear infection may be related to the child's behavior. On the other hand, the child's parents may need assistance in developing more effective parenting skills. Resources such as Clark (1985), Eimers and Aitchison (1978), or Parker (1988) can provide a starting point for improving effectiveness. The emphasis in these resources is on rewarding obedience with attention and praise, issuing commands that are clear and age-appropriate, and following through with commands in a consistent manner.

Ducharme and Popynick (1993) described an innovative approach to obtaining compliance with parental requests. In their study, parents and their children were observed to determine compliance rates for a wide range of requests. Then parental requests were divided into four groups ranging from those with which the child was least likely to comply to those with which the child was most likely to comply. Parents were then instructed in how to provide enthusiastic praise and physical contact for compliance and how to ignore the child when he or she did not comply. The innovative component of their training method is that training began with requests that the child was *most* likely to obey. Subsequently, requests from the other three groups were slowly introduced in succession while maintaining a high rate of compliance. The authors concluded that proceeding through a graduated series of requests ranging from high compliance to low compliance was needed to obtain compliance with all four groups of requests. The study involved four developmentally disabled children, so caution must be exercised in applying the procedure with other groups of children. However, the method has an intuitive appeal because it ensures a high rate of reinforcement for compliant behavior and avoids the complications of administering a consequence for noncompliance. A disadvantage of the technique is the large amount of therapist time involved. The procedure certainly deserves additional study.

Fighting among Siblings

One problem that often concerns parents is fighting among siblings. Bennett (1990) has suggested that ignoring sibling fighting may be an ineffective approach because it may allow one sibling to establish dominance over the less powerful sibling. This in turn causes the subjugated sibling to experience a state of helplessness characterized by the belief that he or she is incapable of positively influencing the environment. Instead, Bennett urges a more proactive approach such as timeout, particularly when a clear aggressor is identified.

Adams and Kelley (1992) compared the effects of timeout versus restitution for managing sibling aggression. The restitution procedure consisted of an apology and practice of appropriate behaviors similar to the aggression—for example, appropriately exchanging a toy, saying something nice, or offering a friendly touch. Timeout and restitution had similar positive effects and were rated as equally acceptable by parents. An advantage of the restitution procedure is that parents can prompt and reward appropriate behaviors. Parents should also be alert for spontaneous examples of nonaggressive behavior and should reward instances of these behaviors with attention, praise, or via a more formal behavior management program.

In discussing sibling aggression with parents, I often find that the sibling who "started" the fight is punished with timeout or some other method. This approach can be ineffective because it is often impossible to determine accurately what happened. Even when the parent witnesses one sibling apparently making an unprovoked attack on the other sibling, one never knows just what preceded the "unprovoked" attack. When parents are not witnesses to the start of the fight, they may listen to each sibling's explanation, try to sort out who started the fight, and punish the instigator. This often has the effect of rewarding the child with the best verbal skills. A simple solution to sibling fighting is to send both fighters to timeout. Although this has some elements of unfairness, it does teach that it takes two to fight, and many parents have reported almost instant success with this strategy. A conscious effort to help the siblings develop negotiation and conflict resolution skills (see Deutsch, 1993) should lead to a low level of aggression.

Lying

Another relatively common problem is lying. Children sometimes lie to avoid negative consequences for their behavior. When asked if they did something wrong, few children are likely to provide the truth voluntarily and then submit to punishment if an effective lie or half-truth allows them to escape or avoid punishment. As discussed throughout this book, an action that leads to escape or avoidance of a negative event is likely to occur more frequently in the future. This behavior then becomes a concern to parents who wish to see their child be truthful. If lying itself is punished, the child does not necessarily learn not to lie. Instead, he or she may try to lie with greater skill, because a successful lie still allows complete avoidance of punishment (Paniagua , 1989). One strategy for minimizing lying is to avoid placing the child in a situation where lying may be seen as a possible means of avoiding punishment. If a child has misbehaved, what is gained by forcing him or her to admit to it? Perhaps punishment, such as a brief timeout, should be administered without extracting an embarrassing confession from the child. This allows the parent to focus on the misbehavior without the complication of dealing with the child's verbal report.

Instead of punishing lying, some authors urge parents to reward truthfulness and honesty (Paniagua, 1989; Stokes & Osnes, 1990). This is accomplished by rewarding children for making what they *say* correspond with what they *do*, hence the name *correspondence training*. Paniagua suggests that parents ask their children whether they will perform a particular behavior such as being on time and then reward them only if the child follows through with the promise. Similarly, children can be asked whether they have already performed some behavior, such as homework. They can be rewarded with praise or some small material reward for demonstrating correspondence between what they said and what they did. In other words, a reward is given only if the child's statement is verified. This has the advantage of placing the focus on increasing deficit behaviors rather punishing undesirable behavior.

Homework

Research clearly demonstrates that homework improves academic achievement (Miller & Kelley, 1991). Furthermore, it is one of the few variables with an impact on achievement that can be manipulated and controlled by teachers and parents (Olympia et al ., 1992). The question that many parents ask is how to improve homework completion. Chapter 10 presented a behavior management program based on school-home notes, designed to improve homework completion. Olympia et al. (1992) describe a five-week program designed to help parents improve homework performance. The program was developed at the University of Utah by Olympia, Jenson, and Neville (1990). According to the authors, parents are encouraged to develop an individualized program for their child based on the key components emphasized during the training program for parents. Interaction among the parents is encouraged, so that they often learn more from each other than from the school psychologist who leads the sessions.

The program emphasizes practical skills such as establishing communication with the classroom teacher, establishing a good environment for completing homework, organizing a schedule for homework completion, managing homework behavior, teaching the child self-management skills, setting up tutoring if needed, and troubleshooting typical problems. At this writing, the manual is being field-tested, but the authors cite no published empirical support for its efficacy. On the other hand, the principles on which the program is based are sound and have had empirical support. For example, Fish and Mendola (1986) demonstrated that self-instruction training improved homework completion rates. Through modeling, practice, and instructions to use the self-instructions at home, elementary students were taught to remind themselves what needed to be done, how to do it, and to remain on task using cognitive-behavioral procedures (see Chapter 8). The primary advantage of combining empirically validated strategies into a parent training program is that parents are given the professional and peer support they need to adjust the program to meet the unique needs of their own family. Other programs, such as Canter (1988), may also be helpful.

Academic Skills

Reading skills are essential to successful academic performance and progress. If remedial training is not provided to the reader who has fallen behind, that child's difficulties in reading will be compounded and failure in other academic areas is likely as well. Learning to read fluently is such an important skill that remediation techniques would seem to merit separate discussion.

Ryback and Staats (1970) reported on a home-based

program for remediation of reading deficits. In this program, the child's parents were trained to reward correct reading responses with tokens that could be exchanged for cash. The training procedure consisted of five steps. In the individual word learning phase, the child was presented with a series of new words to be learned, each printed on a card. Each word remained in the series until it was pronounced correctly without prompting. When all the words in the series had been read without prompting, the child went to the next step, reading the paragraph from which the words had been taken. When the paragraph had been read with no errors, the procedure was repeated until all the paragraphs of the story had been completed. Then the child read the story silently and answered questions about it. If a question was missed, the child reread the relevant paragraph and responded to the question again. A vocabulary review was presented at the end of each 20 lessons. Over a six-month period, the children who were trained with this method showed substantial gains in reading performance.

Blanchard (1981) described a similar strategy for training poor readers, which consists of concentrated flashcard drill on new words to be encountered in a story or passage. When all the words in a passage could be pronounced within two seconds of being presented, the pupil read the story and answered multiple-choice questions about it. Any new words not already known by the pupil were given special attention until their meaning was understood. Blanchard reported two successful tests of this method. In each test, sixth-grade disabled readers who were trained in the procedure correctly answered significantly more comprehension questions than did control groups of disabled readers. It was also found that the procedure was most effective for students whose reading performance was two or more grade levels below the level of the target reading material. It was interesting that most of the students in Blanchard's study reported that reading the materials was easier when the words in them were known beforehand.

In general, techniques that focus on whole-word reading and vocabulary preparation prior to exposure to reading passages seem to result in significantly improved reading and comprehension in disabled readers. Of course, before beginning any behavior management program to improve reading performance, academic handicaps should be ruled out.

The remainder of this chapter describes step-by-step programs that parents are likely to find useful. The presentations are designed to be used as parent handouts.

However, most parents will need some contact with school staff in order to adjust programs to their particular needs and solve their own problems. It is particularly important for school personnel to realize that parents are so close to a problem that it may be very difficult for them to attain the level of objectivity needed to manage a behavior successfully. For example, if a parent wishes to develop a program so her child will be ready for school on time, it may be difficult to be objective when one of the consequences is that she may be late for work. Consequently, the parent may be impatient to see the program take effect and may become frustrated and angry when the impact is not immediate.

This situation needs to be approached empathetically by school personnel. They should communicate that behavior change is not likely to occur immediately and that it takes patience to modify behavior. Listening carefully to the parent's concerns and frustrations will also encourage parents to continue the program. Carefully collected baseline data will be very helpful in illustrating small positive changes that may have occurred. In the long run, one outcome of a home-based behavior management program may be to help parents establish a more assertive and favorable relationship with their child as well as develop skills for solving future behavior problems. This will take time, energy, and persistence.

Following are descriptions of how behavior contracts and token programs may be used at home.

BEHAVIOR CONTRACTS AT HOME: A PARENT HANDOUT

A behavior contract is a written agreement that describes a program for behavior change. It provides a detailed description of the rules and consequences that govern a particular situation such as doing homework or using the family car. Behavior contracts can range from one- or two-sentence documents that simply express in writing the rules that parents wish to enforce in a particular situation to complex negotiated documents describing responsibilities of both parents and children. The most complex behavior contracts can function as negotiating tools for reducing family conflict. In complex situations, the assistance of a mediator such as a family therapist may be needed to keep negotiations productive and on track. If a mediator seems necessary, your local school district's psychologist will be able either to assist directly or to refer you to a competent source of help. The goal of this handout is to describe some ways that parents can use behavior contracts in the home.

Like most other complex activities, developing a successful behavior contract can be viewed as a series of steps. Eight steps describe the process of developing a behavior contract:

1. Identify the problem.
2. Develop a concrete, easily understood definition of the problem and desired behavior.
3. Determine how often and when the problem situation occurs.
4. Identify the reward for desired behavior and (if necessary) how to deal with undesirable behavior.
5. Write a contract and have everybody sign it.
6. Observe whether the contract is effective.
7. Modify the contract, if necessary.
8. Fade out the contract and allow natural consequences to take over for the contract.

Each step will be described next.

Step 1: Identify the problem. Behavior contracts can be helpful in a wide variety of situations, ranging from getting dressed on time in the morning to agreeing not to drive while intoxicated or ride with an intoxicated driver. It is up to parents and their children to decide when a contract may be useful. To illustrate the process, one behavior contract designed to encourage the child of a single parent to be dressed on time in the morning and another contract specifying rules for using the family car will be described.

Single parents often find themselves pressured by time because they are working and raising a child. Mornings can be a particularly difficult time because parents often need to get a child ready for school and themselves ready for work. The problem is that single parents, trying to do two things at once, leave children to accomplish tasks on their own, without direct supervision. A common complaint is that these children watch TV when they are supposed to be getting themselves dressed for school or eating breakfast. Reminders and scolding fail to motivate the child to perform the expected task. The result is that the single parent is stressed every morning and is sometimes late for work.

An area of occasional conflict between parents and adolescents is responsible exercise of driving privileges. Undesired behaviors include arriving home late, inconveniencing other family members who need the car,

getting traffic tickets, drinking and driving, finances, and being unwilling to run errands for the family. Rules, expectations, and consequences related to exercise of driving privileges and getting ready in the morning as well as other situations can be clarified with behavior contracts.

Step 2: Develop a concrete, easily understood definition of the problem and desired behavior.
Dealing with dawdling in the morning begins with defining the tasks to be accomplished. For example, the weekday morning routine of most children would include getting up, getting dressed, eating breakfast, brushing teeth, gathering needed supplies (bookbag, coat, homework, etc.), and catching the school bus. The order in which tasks are accomplished and the precise list of tasks will vary from family to family. For example, some parents may wish to add "bed made and room neat" to the list of tasks, whereas this would not concern other parents. Regardless of what morning tasks are desirable, the goal is to accomplish these tasks as independently as possible and in a timely manner.

Responsible use of a car is also likely to be defined differently from family to family. Adolescents with access to their own car will have different restrictions than adolescents who use the family car. In either case, however, rules for using the car might include: (1) arriving home at an acceptable time, (2) expectations about traffic tickets and speeding, (3) setting aside time for errands, (4) expectations regarding use of alcohol, and (5) financial responsibility.

Step 3: Determine how often and when the problem situation occurs. To learn whether a behavior problem has improved, it is helpful to know how often it has occurred in the past. A count of exactly how many times per week the child is ready on time provides a standard against which to judge the effectiveness of the behavior contract. If the number of on-time days increases, the contract remains in force. If the number of on-time days does not improve, the contract needs to be modified to make it more effective.

Responsible use of a car can be approached in the same way. If a household rule states that the adolescent must be home by 7:00 P.M., weekdays and 11:00 P.M. on weekend nights, an exact tabulation of the number of on-time nights should be possible. A more ambiguous situation may arise if the adolescent is not "available" to run an occasional errand because errands need to be run on an irregular schedule. Finally, a contract may seem desirable because of a single incident, such as receiving a speeding ticket. The important thing is to use the available information to determine a reasonable goal for future behavior.

Step 4: Identify the reward for desired behavior and (if necessary) how to deal with undesirable behavior. Rewards are the essential element of any behavior management program, including a behavior contract. Probably the most important aspect of a reward is that it must be attractive to the person receiving it. A good way to decide on effective rewards is to involve the child or adolescent in the decision. Rewards do not need to be material things. They can be privileges or special activities. Here is a sampling of reward ideas:

watching TV	fishing trip
money, extra alowance	new shoes
staying up past normal bedime	sports equipment
curfew extended by one hour	auto accessories
full tank of gas	trip to amusement
sports card	park
clothing	taking family to
toys	dinner
electronic game	concert tickets
movie rental	compact disc
magazine subscription	hosting a party

This list is far from complete, but it should indicate the wide variety of things that can serve as rewards. As long as the reward is something the person finds interesting or attractive, it should be possible to make it part of a successful behavior contract.

It is also possible to include sanctions or punishments for undesired behavior in a contract. Sanctions will not be as effective as rewards because punishments do not teach correct behavior. Here are a few examples:

- loss of driving privileges
- loss of TV time
- getting up earlier in the morning
- earlier bedtime
- earlier curfew
- clean garage

Step 5: Write a contract and have the participants sign it. The final step in getting a behavior contract started is to write the contract and have the participants sign it. The most effective contracts emphasize behaviors to be increased, are concrete and clear with carefully defined target behaviors, and ensure prompt delivery of reinforcement. Model contracts for the two situations described here are presented in the boxes on pages 219 and 220.

Step 6: Observe whether the contract is effective. The purpose of a behavior contract is to change behavior. The only way to learn whether behavior has changed is to compare behavior before and after the contract. Missy's contract provides for a specific record-keeping system, whereas Alex's contract is less precise, but nevertheless specifies just what needs to occur in order to satisfy the contract. Alex's contract actually contains a flaw in that it does not specify any rewards for meeting the conditions of paragraph 4, picking up his brother after football practice. Once an adolescent earns the privilege of driving the family car, it seems reasonable that some of the accompanying responsibilities could be met without a specific consequence. Later, if availability for errands became an area of conflict, the contract could be renegotiated to everyone's satisfaction.

Step 7: Modify the contract, if necessary. Behavior contracts are meant to be a flexible approach to behavior management. However, even the best contract may have flaws that need to be corrected. For example, Alex may have his own after-school activities to attend and may be unavailable to pick up his brother at times. These types of flaws can be handled by simple agreement among the parties signing the contract. A more serious problem occurs when behavior does not change in the expected direction. Perhaps Missy is still not motivated to be ready on time, despite having signed the contract. In this case, two issues need to be examined. First, it is important to ensure that the contract is clear and understood by everyone. Many child–parent conflicts result from lack of agreement on the definition of key behaviors. If Missy misses her school bus because she is unable to find the materials she needs for school, this aspect of the contract needs to be clarified. One solution could be to require that Missy have school materials in the red chair before she goes to bed.

A second possible problem with any behavior contract is that the rewards are not sufficient to motivate behavior change. One way that Missy's contract could be modified is to include a penalty for failure to be ready on time in addition to "losing" the quarter. Each day she is not ready on time, she could be required to go to bed and wake up half an hour earlier. This could be considered a logical consequence because not being ready on time suggests that she needs more time to get ready. On the

Contract for Getting Ready Quickly

1. The reason for this contract is to help *Missy* get ready for school quickly so her mother can get to work on time.
2. Missy's alarm will be set for 6:45 A.M.. When the alarm rings, she must get up and
   —put on the clothes laid out the previous night
   —eat the breakfast prepared by her mother
   —brush teeth and fix hair
   —put bookbag, coat, and lunch on the red chair
   —catch the schoolbus at 8:10 A.M.
3. Missy is not allowed to watch TV, read, or play with toys until she is ready to catch the school bus.
4. Missy's mother will remind her what time it is every fifteen minutes while she is getting ready.
5. Missy receives $0.25 each day she is ready (dressed, finished breakfast, teeth brushed, hair fixed, stuff on red chair) before 8:00 A.M.
6. If Missy is ready by 8:00 A.M., five school days in a row, she gets to choose one of these things as a reward
   a. _____
   b. _____
   c. _____
   d. _____
   e. _____
7. Missy's mother will keep a weekly chart on the refrigerator door showing what time Missy was ready each weekday morning.
8. Signatures:
   _____   _____

other hand, it may be observed that Missy begins watching TV or engaging in other activities before her morning tasks are completed. This behavior could be circumvented by placing a clause in the contract dealing directly with it or by prevention, such as requiring that the TV remain off until tasks are done.

Finally, there remains the possibility that the situation is more complex than it seems and that professional guidance is needed to mediate disputes and help parents and children reach workable compromises.

Step 8: Fade out the contract and allow natural consequences to take over. Behavior contracts have an artificial element to them in that most parents would prefer that children met their responsibilities without needing a contract. This outcome is most likely to occur when natural rewards such as praise and positive attention follow desirable behavior. In Missy's case, we would hope that she receives plenty of attention and

praise when she is ready for school on time. The reduction of stress and tension in the morning should also support the behavior. If Missy was successful in meeting the main contract goal (five on-time days in succession), the contract could be changed to offer a larger reward for ten on-time days in succession, or for eighteen out of twenty on-time days, depending on the needs of the parents and the child. Once on-time behavior had been successfully maintained over a month or two, Missy could "graduate" from the contract, an event that could be accompanied by a major reward such as a clothes shopping trip, movie, or other attractive reinforcer.

Behavior contracts are a very effective way of clarifying expectations and consequences at almost any age. The key to success is to be as concrete and clear as possible about expectations while remaining flexible and open to negotiation. Contracts not only help parents make their expectations clear to their children; they also help teach children to negotiate for their own needs.

Responsible Driving Contract

1. The purpose of this contract is to clarify the rules and responsibilities for <u>Alex's</u> use of the family cars.
2. In order to use a family car, Alex agrees to drive safely and responsibly, be home by 7 P.M. on weekdays and midnight on weekends, receive no traffic tickets, and pay $50 per month from his job to help pay for insurance.
3. Alex must also keep a grade point average of 3.0 or higher, which lowers the cost of insurance. If Alex's grade point average falls below 3.0, he must pay an extra $25 a month toward insurance. If his GPA falls below 2.5, Alex loses driving privileges until his GPA is above 2.5.
4. Alex also needs to be available to pick up his brother from football practice on Monday, Tuesday, and Wednesday of each week.
5. As part of this contract, Alex also agrees never to ride with a driver who has been drinking alcohol and not to drink alcohol himself until he reaches age twenty-one. Alex also agrees that he will call his parents for a ride if any situation involving alcohol and driving develops.
6. If Alex receives a traffic ticket, his driving privileges are lost for two weeks.
7. As long as Alex continues to follow this agreement, he will be able to use a family car at least three nights per week. His parents will also provide gas to meet his needs and will help him save and plan for the purchase of his own car. Alex will also receive $500 toward the purchase of a car if he meets these conditions during the next year:
   —no more than one traffic ticket
   —GPA above 3.0 for the whole year
   —no involvement with alcohol
8. Violations of rules 1 to 7 will be noted on the back of this contract.
9. Signatures:

   _____   _____

   _____   _____

TOKEN PROGRAMS AT HOME: A PARENT HANDOUT

A token reward system works the same way with children that money and salaries work for adults. No reasonable adult would continue working at a regular job without pay because he or she could not purchase the essentials and luxuries that money can buy. A token program rewards behavior with points, marbles, special coupons, stickers, poker chips, or anything else that can be easily delivered and saved. The tokens have no inherent value but can be used to purchase desirable rewards such as toys, CDs, clothing, or privileges. Because tokens can "buy" a variety of rewards, children find them desirable for a long time and in a wide variety of situations. This flexibility makes token programs an effective way of dealing with many behavior problems.

Setting Up a Program

The "Record Form for a Home or Classroom Token System" illustrates how a token program may be structured. Any token program begins by selecting behaviors to be reinforced. Reinforced behavior must be defined in concrete, observable, and relatively unambiguous terms that specify exactly what is desired. If a reinforced behavior called "clean room daily" is included in a program, the behavior should be defined so that both the child and the program administrator can agree that the room is clean. A working definition of "clean room daily" might consist of the following: bed made neatly, all toys put away, snack dishes taken to the kitchen, and all clothes put away before 10:00 A.M. each morning.

A second way to award points is through the use of bonuses. This may include awarding points when the administrator neglects the computations for any particular day or fails to deliver a previously promised reward. It is *very* important that the token program administrator *consistently* perform his or her role. Otherwise, the child is not likely to respond to the program. Another helpful bonus is to award points when the child completes all or most of the tasks under "reinforced behaviors."

Points or tokens may be subtracted from the total earned for two reasons: (1) the child is fined for misbehavior, or (2) the child purchases a reward. Fines for misbehavior should be kept to a minimum because the most effective use of a token program is to *increase* desirable behavior. When desirable behavior increases, undesirable behavior is less likely to occur. Temper tantrums, fighting, or failure to obey commands could result in fines. Like reinforced behaviors, misbehaviors must be defined in concrete, unambiguous terms so that fines are administered consistently.

The main advantage of token programs is that they are flex*i*ble. If attractive rewards are on the "menu," desired behavior will increase and undesirable behavior will decrease within a short period of time. It is particularly important that the reward menu be negotiated with the child. Without his or her input, the token program may fail. Money is a nearly universal reinforcer that almost always works. Other possible reinforcers include special trips, a party, school supplies, taking the family out for pizza, small toys, children's collectible items (baseball cards, marbles, etc.), large toys, special activities (sports camps, camping trips, fishing trips, etc.), or anything else parents find acceptable.

Using the Record Form

To use the Record Form, reinforced behaviors, bonuses, misbehaviors to be fined, and reinforcers available for purchase need to be entered in the left-hand column. Then the menu of reinforcers, prices, and fines needs to be set. Most token reinforcers and fines should be around 10 points, with more important behaviors rewarded or fined 15 or 20 points. This would mean that about 100 to 200 points would be available each day, minus fines for misbehavior. Consequently, prices for purchased rewards might range from about 50 to 1,000 or more points. Lower priced items on the menu will ensure that the child's enthusiasm remains high, while higher prices should be reserved for special rewards. The use of a least a few high-priced rewards encourages saving and budgeting of points, important skills for the hyperactive, impulsive children who often need the structure of a token program.

The bank is used to compute the status of the child's points. The carryover to the next day consists of the previous day's carryover *plus* the total gained (reinforced behaviors plus bonuses) *minus* the total spent (fines plus purchases). On the first day of the program, the carryover from the previous day would be zero. On subsequent days the carryover must be zero or above because the child is never allowed to go into "debt." However, fines may be subtracted from points earned on previous days. The "total carried to next day" represents the current total of earned points and is entered twice: at the bottom of the current day's column and at the top of the next day's column, where it is called "total from previous day."

Variations on the Point System

Children under eight years old may respond best to something more concrete than a point system, such as poker chips or gold stars. A number of variations in the way they are delivered are possible. Poker chips or marbles may be kept in a jar, and the child may spend them in the same way as points. More valuable rewards can be earned by filling a jar with tokens awarded for good behavior. Similarly, a sheet of paper with five or ten squares could be filled with stickers to be traded for a privilege or prize. Younger children are not likely to understand response cost or fines. Instead, timeout may be employed, if needed, to decrease misbehavior. There are numerous variations of token reward programs, but the key to success is to keep the program simple and age-appropriate.

Although it is always preferable to reward appropriate behavior, some situations demand a different approach. A response cost contingency can be used at home or in public places such as a shopping mall, church, or anyplace where it is difficult to administer timeout. In this technique, the child is given tokens ahead of time and *loses* them when he or she does not follow the rules. On a shopping trip, for instance, three rules could be established: (1) Stay right next to me unless you have permission to go somewhere else, (2) do not touch anything without permission, and (3) obey all commands of your parents. Give the child eight coupons or poker chips and tell the child that each time a rule is broken he or she loses a coupon. If five coupons remain when it is time to leave, the child can have a valuable reward; if only one coupon is left, the child can have a much smaller reward. If all the coupons are taken away, the trip is immediately ended and the child spends time in the timeout chair at home.

Parents who use this program need to be fairly strict and prepared to end a couple of shopping trips early. Later, a real improvement in the child's behavior in public should be noticeable. This program can also be adapted to classroom situations and has been very popular with teachers. In the early stages of a coupon program, frequent review of the rules may enhance the child's success.

Ending a Token Reward Program

After some initial adjustments and patience, token programs are usually effective. However, parents often observe that token programs are artificial and appear to bribe the child for doing things that they feel should be done without material rewards. In addition, children who must be "paid" are not learning to be "responsible." These are important concerns; children do need to learn to take a long-term view of some behavior rather than doing only those things that result in immediate reward. We would like to see children do well in school because they recognize the value and future rewards of learning rather than because they receive 10 points for each worksheet they complete. The transition from a full token program to something more natural and less time-consuming can be made gradually and effectively using a few simple guidelines.

Parents must first set reasonable goals for their child, taking into consideration the child's age and the severity of the behavioral problems. Some children showing severe hyperactivity may need a highly structured behavior management program throughout their childhood. Specific goals for each child will depend on the expectations and values of the parents. What is acceptable to some parents may not be acceptable to others. For example, some parents may want their child to keep his or her room clean and to spend time each night on schoolwork. Other parents may not care how clean the bedroom is kept but may expect the child to mow lawns, deliver papers, or do other chores to earn spending money. Parents must decide what is desirable on the basis of their own values and priorities. With respect to a token program, parents must decide how much independence is desirable and age-appropriate for their child.

Assuming that a token program has been in place and effective for a reasonable length of time (four to eight weeks, for example), the program can be reduced or

faded in several ways depending on the goals of the parents or the program administrator. One way to fade or eliminate a token program is to enlist the child's cooperation in slowly dismantling or simplifying the program as desirable behavior increases. For instance, total points could be computed weekly instead of daily, or well-established behaviors could be dropped from the list of reinforced behaviors. If children are encouraged to view this as a sign of maturity or growing up, they may be eager to see the token system eliminated. *The ultimate goal is to eliminate the token system entirely while desired behaviors continue at a high rate.*

Generous verbal praise that mentions the child's specific appropriate behavior should be given immediately following good behavior and again when the tokens or points are awarded. Ideally, verbal praise will eventually take over the functions of the token system, so desired behavior continues at a high rate while the token program is gradually eliminated.

Here are some specific suggestions regarding methods of fading or slowly eliminating a token program:

1. Increase the amount of time between computations of the status of the program. Instead of computing the status every day, perform the computations every other day, every three days, and then once a week.

2. Instead of awarding points every time the behavior is performed, require the child to perform the behavior several times in a row before points are awarded. If the child received 10 points each day for making her or his bed, this could be changed so that the child receives 20 points for making the bed for two days in a row. Next, the child could be rewarded with 50 points for making the bed every day for a week.

3. Another approach is to increase slowly the number of behaviors that are required in order to earn points. At the beginning of a program, 10 points could be awarded for making the bed, 10 points for taking out the garbage, and 10 points for completing homework. Fading out the program could begin by changing the rule so that points are awarded only when all three tasks are performed. That is, the child earns 30 points for making the bed, taking out the garbage, *and* completing homework. The child must now complete all three tasks to receive any points.

4. Finally, these options can be combined. Instead of awarding points for each behavior once a day, it would be reasonable to award points once a week based on successful completion of a high percentage of the assigned tasks. Suppose that there are seven important

"reinforced behaviors" in the token program. Across the week, this would equal a total of 49 tasks ($7 \times 7 = 49$). During the week (Saturday to Friday) the program administrator would place a checkmark on the Record Form, each time the task was performed, remembering to give lots of verbal praise for successes. On Saturday morning, the number of check marks would be counted. A child with more than, for example, 40 checkmarks would receive a predetermined number of points. Alternatively, the child's weekly allowance could depend on earning more than 40 checkmarks, and the use of points could be eliminated. Another variation is that the allowance could depend on the number of checkmarks: 35 checkmarks = 50 percent of normal allowance; 40 checkmarks = 75 percent of normal allowance; 45 or more checkmarks = 100 percent of normal allowance. If the child regularly earns a high number of checkmarks, it should be possible to eliminate the monitoring system entirely and simply give the child his or her weekly allowance. Logical consequences such as not allowing the child to play or leave the house until assigned tasks are completed could be used when the child fails to complete a task.

Problems in Fading or Eliminating a Program

The most common problem in fading or eliminating any management program is that the child's behavior gets worse. If this happens, returning to a previously successful level of the program is the standard remedy. This is a common occurrence, so it should not discourage parents or the program administrator to try again later when behaviors are even more strongly established. Often, a token program can eventually be completely eliminated while the child continues to behave appropriately. Unfortunately, some children may need the structure of a behavior management program over a long period of time because attention problems and distractibility make it difficult for them to complete several tasks independently. In these cases, the child still needs to learn how to cope with those problems that may remain with them even into adulthood. Making lists of things to do, writing down appointments, keeping a list of assignments, and other common organizational tools can be learned. Thus, a token program could evolve into a "list of things to do." Learning such coping skills will improve the child's success in school and on the job.

A Sample Token Program

Figure 12.2 shows a hypothetical example of a completed Record Form based on a combination of actual programs. Initially, this program rewarded these seven behaviors:

1. Clean bedroom daily: defined as bed made, dirty clothes in hamper, snack dishes in kitchen, and toys put away. When the program began, this task was valued at 10 points, but this was increased to 30 points beginning with the third week of the program.
2. Brush teeth in the morning and evening. Points were awarded only for brushing at both times.
3. Ready for school by 8:00 A.M.: defined as being dressed, coat on, and school supplies ready.
4. In bed with the light off by 9:00 A.M.
5. Mow the lawn on Saturday or Sunday. It would have been more convenient to place this behavior under "Bonuses."
6. No phone call from the teacher. By prior arrangement, Cory's teacher agreed to call Cory's parents whenever Cory misbehaved in school (name and two checkmarks on the board). If no phone call was made, Cory received 10 points.
7. Read out loud to parents for ten minutes. This was included at the recommendation of Cory's teacher, who hoped Cory would gain additional practice in oral reading.
8. Correctly spell eight out of ten words on practice spelling test. Every Thursday morning Cory's class had a spelling test of ten words. Cory could earn 30 points by spelling eight out of ten words correctly on Wednesday night. This behavior was added during the eighth week of the program.

Cory received a bonus of 20 points whenever behaviors 1, 2, 3, 4, and 6 were performed on the same day. Also, it was Cory's parents' responsibility to complete the calculations on the Behavior Record each night after he went to bed. If Cory found that points were not calculated in the morning, a bonus of 50 points was awarded. Cory lost points for swearing or using foul language at the rate of 10 points per word. Striking his little sister cost Cory 20 points.

Cory's reward menu was typical for a boy of twelve and included baseball cards, candy, spending money, taking the family for pizza, and fishing trips with his father. Most of the time, Cory spent his points on baseball cards and pizza for the family. Cory's parents no-

Child's name: _____   Program administrator: _____

Starting date: _____

Gains in Tokens   Week: _____

Reinforced Behaviors	Points		S	M	T	W	T	F	S
1									
2									
3									
4									
5									
6									
7									
8									
9									

Bonuses	Points								
1									
2									
3									
4									
5									

Daily total gained

Decreases in tokens

Fines for Misbehavior	Points		S	M	T	W	T	F	S
1									
2									
3									
4									
5									

Purchases	Points		S	M	T	W	T	F	S
1									
2									
3									
4									
5									
6									
7									
8									
9									

Daily total lost

Bank

Previous day's points

+ Total gained

– Total spent

= Total carried over

Week: _____

S	M	T	W	T	F	S

Week: _____

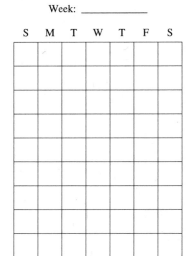

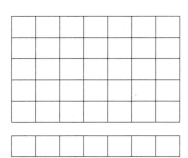

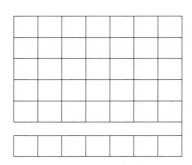

S	M	T	W	T	F	S

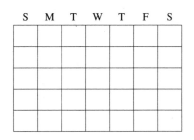

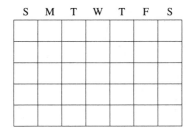

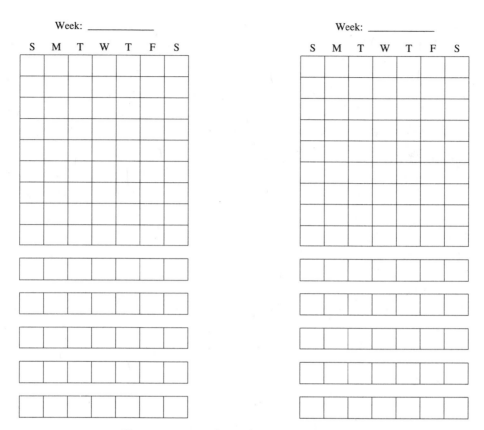

Figure 12.1. Record Form for a Home Token System

Child's name: __Cory S.__   Program Administrator: __Mrs. S.__

Starting date: __4-19__

Gains in tokens

Reinforced Behaviors	Points	Wk1 S	M	T	W	T	F	S	Wk2 S	M	T	W	T	F	S	Wk3 S	M	T	W	T	F	S
1 Clean bedroom daily	10	—	—	—	—	—	—	—	30	—	30	30	—	30	30	30	30	30	—	30	30	30
2 Brush teeth—A.M. and P.M.	10	10	—	10	10	10	10	10	10	10	10	10	10	10	10	10	10	10	10	10	10	10
3 Ready for school by 8	20	—	—	—	20	—	—	—	—	20	—	—	20	20	—	—	20	20	20	20	20	—
4 In bed by 9 P.M.	10	—	10	—	10	10	—	—	—	10	10	10	10	—	—	10	10	—	10	10	10	—
5 Mow lawn on Sat or Sun	30	30						—	30	—	—	—	—	—	—	—	—	—	—	—	—	30
6 No phone call fr teach	10		—	10	—	—	10			10	—	10	10	—			—	10	10	10	—	10
7 Read out loud to parents	10	—	—	—	10	10	—	10	—	10	10	10	—	10	—	20	10	20	—	10	—	10
8 Add: Rev spelling Wed	30																		30			
9																						

Bonuses

Bonuses	Points	Wk1 S	M	T	W	T	F	S	Wk2 S	M	T	W	T	F	S	Wk3 S	M	T	W	T	F	S
1 1, 2, 4, 6 on one day	20	—	—	—	—	—	—	—	—	—	—	—	—	—	—	—	20	—	—	20	20	—
2 Parents don't compute	50	—	—	—	—	—	—	—	50	—	—	—	—	—	—	—	50	—	50	—	—	—
3																						
4																						
5																						

Daily total gained

Wk1							Wk2							Wk3						
40	10	20	50	30	20	20	120	60	60	70	50	70	40	70	160	90	130	100	100	80

Decreases in tokens

Fines for Misbehavior	Points	Wk1 S	M	T	W	T	F	S	Wk2 S	M	T	W	T	F	S	Wk3 S	M	T	W	T	F	S
1 Hitting little sister	−20	20	20	—	—	—	20	—	—	—	—	—	20	—	—	—	—	—	—	—	—	—
2 Swearing—each word	−10	40	50	40	10	—	10	—	—	—	20	—	10	—	—	—	—	—	20	—	—	10
3																						
4																						
5																						

Week: ___1___   Week: ___5___   Week: 11

Purchases	Points	S	M	T	W	T	F	S	S	M	T	W	T	F	S	S	M	T	W	T	F	S
1 Pack of sports cards	50								50	50			50						50			
2 Candy bar	30				30																	
3 $1.00 spending money	150																					
4 Electronic game	2000																					
5 8 quarters + 2 hours play	500																					
6 Take family for pizza	600									600							600					
7 Go fishing with dad	300																					
8																						
9																						

		S	M	T	W	T	F	S	S	M	T	W	T	F	S	S	M	T	W	T	F	S
Daily total lost			75	75	60	35	20	—	50	650	20		80				600					10

Bank

	Points	S	M	T	W	T	F	S	S	M	T	W	T	F	S	S	M	T	W	T	F	S
Previous day's points	0	0	0	0	40	40	30		630	700	110	150	220	190	260	470	540	700	190	250	350	450
+ Total gained	40	10	20	50	30	20	20		120	20	60	70	50	70	40	70	160	90	130	100	100	80
– Total spent	60	70	40	10	30	30	0		50	650	20	0	80	0	0	0	0	600	70	0	0	10
= Total carried over	–20	–60	–20	40	40	30	50		700	110	150	220	190	260	300	540	700	190	250	350	450	520

Figure 12.2. Sample Record for a Home Token System

ticed that he seemed to enjoy the opportunity to be the center of attention when he took the family out for pizza. He was allowed to order for the family and pay the cashier.

As can be seen from the Record Form, the token program did not do very well during the first week. In fact, on Thursday, Cory's parents pretended not to hear Cory swear so he would be able to earn a small reward. Buying a candy bar with his points seemed to improve Cory's motivation. At the beginning of the third week Cory's parents increased the number of points for room cleaning from 10 to 30 points. By the fifth week of the program, Cory was really beginning to enjoy it, as shown by the substantial improvement in his behavior. By the eleventh week, things were going so well that Cory's parents forgot to perform their daily computations. At this point it was decided that a major change in the program could be made.

Cory was informed that his progress was so good that his parents wished to change the program substantially. The new rules went like this: Cory was to be on the program only five days per week, Monday through Friday. For each weekday that he performed behaviors 1, 2, 3, 4, and 6, he would receive 150 points. The fines for misbehavior and the reinforcer menu remained in effect. Also, Cory was allowed to use his remaining 520 points to buy a Nintendo game cartridge as recognition of his success. The new rules worked well during week 12, but week 13 was not as good. However, for weeks 14 through 17, Cory's behavior was excellent and he earned enough points for a second Nintendo game cartridge. At this time, Cory was placed on a regular weekly allowance and the token program was discontinued. If Cory hit his sister, swore, or failed to perform his daily tasks, he lost TV privileges for a day.

FINAL WORD

This chapter has completed the cycle by describing programs for improving behavior deficits in the home environment. The chapter was included in a book directed mainly at improvement of school-based behaviors because a home-based program can make an important contribution to the general adjustment of a child and to a child's behavior in school. Any time behavior management programming is consistent across the school and home environments, behavior change will be quicker and more durable.

In conclusion, it is reasonable to ask what element of behavior management makes the greatest contribution to the success of programs. In my experience, the key word is *flexibility*. Each of the programs described throughout this book should be considered an outline or rough draft of a behavior management program, not the final draft. Each situation is unique; each child is unique. The key to success is to identify the unique elements in each new situation and adapt to them.

REVIEW

Terms to Remember and Review

behavior deficit	behavior excess
generalization	token program
biofeedback	family therapy
school–home note	restitution
timeout	correspondence training
behavior contract	cognitive-behavioral therapy
natural consequences	flexibility

Study and Discussion Questions

1. Give some reasons that generalization across time and settings would be better for programs that actively involve parents as opposed to exclusively school-based programs.

2. Examine the sample behavior contract for Missy. Does it have any serious flaws or components that may need to be modified?

3. Examine the sample behavior contract for Alex. Does it have any serious flaws or components that may need to be modified?

4. In a single paragraph, using the simplest language possible, write what you would say to explain to parents how a token program works.

5. Both teachers and parents sometimes argue that behavior management programs amount to nothing more than bribes and that they are bad for children because they teach them to expect rewards for everything they do. What might you say in this situation that could convince a parent to consider a behavior management program?

6. What are some of the problems that might be encountered when school-based professionals attempt to help parents develop effective behavior management programs to be done at home.

Group Projects

1. Homework has been empirically demonstrated to improve academic achievement. Have students divide into small groups and develop a homework policy for a sixth-grade classroom or a high school class. One way to approach this task is to draft a student handout describing homework policies and procedures. The handout should also provide some hints to students, along with a statement from the teacher regarding how quickly assignments will be graded and their weight in grading.

2. Examine the two sample behavior contracts provided in this chapter. Have students assume the roles of parents, child or adolescent, and family therapist; then role-play the situation where the contract has failed and needs to be renegotiated.

3. Have students divide into small groups and role-play development of behavior contracts to deal with the following situations:

    a. An adolescent with high average intellectual ability and outstanding athletic skills is failing three out of six courses in the ninth grade and will end the first semester with a 1.80 GPA.

    b. An elementary-age child is misbehaving in class and not completing work. The teacher has already suggested a school–home note.

GLOSSARY

abuse *See* **child abuse**.

adaptive behavior A wide domain of behavior associated with individuals' effectiveness in meeting the standards for personal independence and social responsibility expected for their age and cultural group. Toileting skills, dressing, cooking, balancing a checkbook, waiting in line, counting, and managing finances are just a few of the many skills associated with adaptive behavior.

ADD *See* Attention-Deficit Hyperactivity Disorder.

ADHD *See* Attention-Deficit Hyperactivity Disorder.

adolescence A developmental period beginning at about age thirteen and continuing to young adulthood.

aggression Behavior toward others in which the rights of others are violated. Aggression may be verbal, physical, or even psychological. When aggression is a target behavior, a starting point for defining the behavior is unwanted physical contact. Careful collection of baseline data is needed to confirm whether a particular definition of aggression is adequate.

alcoholism A condition in which a child, adolescent, or adult abuses alcohol or is dependent on alcohol to the extent that drinking interferes with social, occupational, or academic adjustment. A formal diagnosis requires an extensive assessment by a professional trained in chemical dependency evaluation.

appetitive stimulus A desirable stimulus, such as food or adult attention, that a child will seek and that can serve as a reinforcer.

assertive Standing up for one's personal rights and expressing thoughts, feelings, and beliefs in direct, honest, and appropriate ways that do not violate the rights of others. Assertive behavior is a positive approach to communication that involves respecting oneself and the adult or child with whom one is communicating.

assessment The information-gathering process that leads to decisions about how to approach a problem situation. A reasonably complete assessment requires information from the child, the child's parents, and school personnel. An assessment must also examine the context out of which the problem behavior arises, including the child's developmental status and the systems in which the child functions.

Attention-Deficit Hyperactivity Disorder The recognized DSM-IV term for hyperactivity. It is likely to be seen in medical and psychological reports and other professional sources dealing with this topic.

autism A childhood disorder characterized by severe language impairment, lack of awareness and interest in social interactions; often accompanied by stereotypical, repetitive movements. Children with autism often become extremely upset over trivial changes in their environment or daily routine and become attached to unusual objects.

aversive stimulus A stimulus such as a spanking that a child will tend to avoid and that can serve as a punisher. Timeout can be viewed as an aversive stimulus.

avoidance A contingency in which the child's behavior can postpone an aversive event—for example, when an apology for undesirable behavior allows the child to avoid punishment.

baseline data One of the most crucial components of a behavior management program. It consists of precise data about the occurrence of a target behavior that are collected before and during a behavior management program. Changes in the occurrence of the target behavior signal whether the program is successful.

basic behavioral repertoires Basic skills such as paying attention or listening to a command that need to exist in order for most learning to take place, especially in a classroom setting.

behavior An observable response of a child. Behavior would not include such descriptors as *frustrated,* which, themselves, cannot be observed. Instead, the observable behavior might be a temper tantrum, an indicator of frustration.

behavior chain A series of discrete behaviors learned in a particular sequence. The steps in making a bed or doing a long division problem are examples of behavior chains.

behavior contract A document signed by a child and others stating the rules of a behavior management program.

behavior deficit Failure of the child to perform a desired behavior at an acceptable rate. For example, a child who rarely completes assignments could be said to have a deficit in that behavior. Generally, behavior management programs are best directed at behavior deficits.

behavior excess Doing too much of something undesirable. For example, a child who emits a temper tantrum every day might be regarded as showing a behavior excess.

biofeedback A behavior management technique in which a person is rewarded for producing physiological changes, often changes associated with relaxation. Biofeedback is usually accomplished by electronically monitoring a bodily function such as heart rate or brain waves and giving feedback to individuals indicating that they are progressing toward a more relaxed state.

CABAS Comprehensive Application of Behavior Analysis to Schooling. Each instructional trial is planned, presented, and recorded along with the student's response.

child abuse Any one of several categories of child mistreatment including physical abuse, sexual abuse, emotional abuse or neglect, and physical neglect.

childhood depression A clinical syndrome in which ordinary sadness becomes severe and debilitating. Signs of clinical depression include poor appetite or loss of weight, increased appetite or significant weight gain, loss of energy, difficulty in concentrating or thinking, and sleep irregularities. Other signs of depression include apathy, indecisiveness, excessive crying, apprehension, poor school performance, excessive or inappropriate guilt, low self-esteem, statements about death or suicide, a suicide attempt, and social isolation.

classical conditioning In classical conditioning, an appetitive or aversive stimulus is presented after a neutral *stimulus.* Behavior has no influence on whether the aversive or appetitive stimulus is delivered; instead, stimuli are *paired.* The outcome of classical conditioning is that the stimulus presented first takes on characteristics of the aversive or appetitive stimulus, in terms of its ability to elicit certain responses from the organism. Classical conditioning is believed to play a role in the acquisition and treatment of fear, anxiety, and phobias.

coaching Providing verbal cues regarding correct behavior; a useful component of social skills training.

cognitive-behavioral therapy An emerging behavior management technology in which individuals are taught how to examine and modify the cognitive components of their overt behavior. With children, this often takes the form of teaching them to think about alternatives before acting impulsively.

conduct disorder A diagnosis typically associated with delinquent behavior. Symptoms include threatening others, getting into physical fights, using a weapon, engaging in cruelty, stealing, lying, and destroying others' property.

contingency A rule that relates behavior to its consequences. For example, a rule stating that a child who hits another child must go to timeout could be called a contingency.

contingent observation A form of timeout in which the student who violates a rule is told to leave an activity temporarily and only observe what is happening. It is less restrictive than other forms of timeout because the student is only partially excluded from the instruction.

continuous reinforcement Delivery of a reinforcer following each instance of a particular response.

corporal punishment   Physical punishment of children by hitting them with a hand, paddle, or other object. Research evidence indicates that corporal punishment is an ineffective form of discipline, especially in schools.

correspondence training   A method of rewarding truthfulness and honesty by rewarding children for making what they *say* correspond with what they *do,* hence the name, *correspondence training.* For example, a parent may ask the child whether he or she will perform a particular behavior such as being on time and then reward the child only if he or she follows through with the promise.

coupon program   A response cost program in which a child receives a predetermined number of tokens, which are taken away each time a rule is violated; an example of applying negative punishment.

depression   *See* **childhood depression.**

developmentally appropriate   Means that a behavior management program has been designed so it is compatible with the cognitive ability of the child.

developmentally disabled   Refers to a cognitive or physical impairment that manifests before the age of twenty-two and results in a lifelong need for supportive services.

diffusion parent   Parent characterized by generally poor and inconsistent child management techniques that allow aggression to be rewarded and positive, prosocial behavior to go unrewarded.

disabled   Children who show a problem that prevents or interferes with their ability to benefit from regular classroom instruction. Such children may qualify for special education services.

discipline slip   A note or form used to communicate to the student, administrators, or parents the nature of a rule violation.

discrimination   The process through which an individual learns to respond differently to two stimuli. For example, young children must learn to discriminate the letter *F* from the letter *P.*

discriminative stimulus   A stimulus that signals that a reinforcement (or punishment) is available or not available; for instance, when a teacher leaves the classroom, the children often act up and begin violating classroom rules; this is predictable because the teacher who serves as a discriminative stimulus for the contingencies that enforce the rules is absent.

DSM-IV   A reference book published by the American Psychiatric Association that contains the most generally accepted diagnostic criteria (definitions) of all psychological/psychiatric disorders.

early childhood   A developmental period beginning at approximately one year of age and continuing to six or seven years.

escape   An individual who first experiences an aversive stimulus and then performs a response that causes the stimulus to end has *escaped* that stimulus.

exclusion timeout   In this procedure, a child is excluded from seeing or being seen by others. It is regarded as being at least moderately restrictive because access to instructional activity is eliminated.

externalizing problem   *See* **behavior excess.**

extinction   Ceasing to deliver a consequence for behavior. The predicted result is that the behavior will eventually cease to occur. The most common application of extinction is when adults ignore a child's annoying or undesirable behavior.

fading   In the context of behavior management, *fading* refers to the process of gradually changing the structure of a behavior management program until it is no longer needed.

family therapy   Therapy in which the emphasis is on helping the family system instead of an individual. Family therapy can be an important component in the treatment plan for some childhood problems; see Sayger (1992) for an overview.

flexibility   The capacity to approach problems in a way that is open to change an innovation. Consistent success in behavior management requires flexibility.

generalization   The occurrence of a response in a new environment after it has occurred in the training environment. Ensuring that the results of a behavior management program have generalized to the natural environment after a behavior management program is a crucial step in any behavior management program.

giftedness   The presence of high intellectual ability and exceptional talent; gifted children are likely to master grade-level material much faster than other students.

GOALS Group-Oriented Adapted Levels System. A levels system based on group contingencies in that the entire group earns a particular level rather than individual students.

Golden Rule of Behavior Management Ignore, as much as possible, all minor annoyances and misbehavior and spend as much time as possible giving positive attention to students who are behaving correctly.

group contingency With a group contingency, each individual's behavior contributes or detracts from the rewards given to the entire group. An advantage of group contingencies is that the entire group benefits from the performance of its member, which can create a cooperative climate.

handicapped Children who show a problem that prevents or interferes with their ability to benefit from regular classroom instruction. Such children may qualify for special education services. *See* **disabled**.

hyperactivity A behavior disorder characterized by problems in focusing attention, excessive impulsivity, and a high rate of activity. Other terms for this cluster of behaviors are Attention-Deficit/Hyperactivity Disorder (ADHD), Attention-Deficit Disorder with Hyperactivity, Attention-Deficit Disorder without Hyperactivity, minimal brain dysfunction (an older term infrequently seen nowadays), ADD, and ADD-H. *See also* **Attention-Deficit/Hyperactivity Disorder**.

IDEA The Individuals with Disabilities Education Act. It specifies parental rights, definitions of handicapping conditions, and rules to ensure that fair and valid decisions are made about children who may be disabled or handicapped.

IEP Individualized Educational Plan. An IEP is the document that specifies a handicapped child's current level of functioning and the goals and objectives that the team would like to see the child accomplish in the future.

ignoring A behavior management technique in which all attention (i.e., requests to stop the behavior) directed toward an undesirable behavior are eliminated.

in-school suspension A consequence for misbehavior in which a student is assigned to a special classroom where freedom is severely restricted and the focus is on completing academic work.

incompatible response A response that cannot occur at the same time as another response. For instance, a child cannot have a temper tantrum and clean his room at the same time. Increasing a desirable behavior is one method of decreasing an undesirable behavior.

indiscriminable contingencies A technique for enhancing generalization of learned behavior to another environment or situation. In this technique, to some extent, contingencies (i.e., the rules for delivery of rewards) are made unpredictable.

intermittent reinforcement The process of following a behavior by a contingent event only a fraction of the times that the behavior occurs. Behavior that has been intermittently reinforced is much more resistant to change (extinction) than behavior that has been reinforced each time it occurred.

internalizing problem *See* **behavior deficit**.

Law of Effect Edward L. Thorndike's observations that responses followed by "satisfaction" (i.e., food) tended to be more likely to recur in the same situation and that responses followed by "discomfort" were less likely to recur in that situation.

learning disability When a child's academic achievement is unexpectedly lower than what would be predicted from an assessment of intellectual ability, a learning disability is presumed to exist.

least restrictive alternative/environment The concept of least restrictiveness encourages meeting a child's needs with behavior management techniques and in environments that are as similar to the child's normal environment as possible. Within school settings, the least restrictive environment is a regular education classroom.

levels program or system An approach to managing behavior in a group setting in which there are several different levels of supervision and structure available that enable individualizing of programs within an overall organizational framework. At the lowest level, students are restricted and closely supervised, and at higher levels the student has less supervision and more privileges.

logical consequences Use of logical consequences means to allow a child's behavior to result in natural consequences that are directly related to the behavior. For instance, a child who refuses to pick up dirty clothes could experience a logical consequence when his or her parents also refuse to pick them up, so the clothes remain dirty.

mandatory reporting   Refers to state policies that require reporting suspicions of child abuse to police or social service agencies.

mental retardation   *See* **developmental disability**.

middle childhood   A developmental period beginning at approximately age six or seven years and continuing to about twelve years.

multiple-baseline design   A method of assessing the effectiveness of an intervention in which baseline data are obtained in more than one environment or setting while the intervention is performed in only one environment. Generalization and the causal relationship between the intervention and the target behavior can be assessed by observing the impact of the intervention in other environments.

natural consequences   *See* **logical consequences**.

natural contingencies   The contingencies that exist in the environment in the absence of formal behavior management programs. Consequences associated with school rules and the parental praise that results from bringing a school paper home are examples of natural contingencies.

negative attention   Social attention directed at undesired behavior having the potential to reward that behavior, and therefore increase its frequency, rather than decreasing it. May consist of adult responses such as scolding or telling a child to cease a behavior, or laughter from peers.

negative contingency   A contingency in which an appetitive or aversive stimulus is removed as a consequence of a behavior.

negative punishment   The contingency of removing a pleasant stimulus (food, attention) contingent on a behavior causing it to decrease in frequency. For example, losing dessert for acting out during dinner could be called negative punishment.

negative reinforcement   The process of removing an unpleasant stimulus (pain, boredom) contingent on a behavior, causing it to increase in frequency; negative reinforcement may be occurring when a child's behavior (e.g., a temper tantrum) allows him or her to avoid an unpleasant task.

nonassertive   Failing to express honest feelings, thoughts, and beliefs; or expressing one's thoughts and feelings in such a timid, apologetic, diffident, or self-effacing manner that they can easily be disregarded or ignored.

operant conditioning   A generic term for behavior management techniques involving reward or punishment delivered as a consequence of a predefined response; contrasted with classical conditioning.

partial reinforcement   *See* **intermittent reinforcement**.

physical abuse   A category of child maltreatment consisting of the use of excessive force, beating, burning, hitting with objects, or other violence that may result in injuries to the child.

positive contingency   A contingency in which an appetitive or aversive stimulus is presented as a consequence of a behavior.

(positive) punishment   Presentation of an aversive (undesirable) stimulus (e.g., spanking, timeout) contingent on a behavior with the intention of reducing the frequency of that behavior.

positive reinforcement   The process of following a behavior by an appetitive stimulus (food, attention) causing the behavior to increase in frequency.

Premack principle   A general law of behavior that states that a low-probability behavior (e.g., cleaning one's room) can be reinforced by allowing access to a high-probability behavior (e.g., playing). The Premack principle merely reminds the person who wishes to change a child's behavior to observe the child to see what he or she likes to do and use access to those activities as reinforcers.

primary issue   Any one of four basic issues that need to be addressed each time a behavior management program is implemented: (1) What is the goal to be accomplished? (2) In what environment is the goal to be accomplished? (3) What is the developmental status of the child? (4) What is the least restrictive behavior management program?

primary reinforcer   Reinforcers such as candy or other food that directly satisfy a biological need.

program common stimuli   A technique of promoting generalization in which elements from environments targeted for generalization are included in the original training.

prompting A stimulus presented to an individual that makes a particular response more likely, such as verbal directions, physical guidance, gestures, or modeling (demonstrating).

Public Law 94-142 The Education for All Handicapped Children Act. The law provides money to states for education of handicapped children and specifies parental rights, definitions of handicapping conditions, assessment procedures, and various rules to ensure that impartial, fair, and valid decisions about children are made. Essentially, P.L. 94-142 states that handicapped children are entitled to a "free and appropriate" public education in the "least restrictive environment." The principles set forth in P.L. 94-142 have a history of court decisions behind them and therefore provide a solid base against which to judge the validity of procedures used to place or not place a handicapped child.

punishment The application of an unpleasant stimulus such as a spanking contingent on a behavior causing it to decrease in frequency.

pupil support assistant A staff person hired to support a student in a regular or special education classroom. A pupil support assistance may be available to provide behavior management programming to some students.

regular education Regular public or private school education for nonhandicapped or nondisabled children.

reinforcement Presentation of a desirable or appetitive stimulus contingent on a behavior. The predicted result is that the frequency of the target behavior will increase.

relaxation training A therapeutic technique in which an individual is given explicit training in how to relax. May involve biofeedback or tensing and relaxing of muscle groups. The goal is to teach a relaxation response that can be invoked when the individual is experiencing anxiety.

resistance to extinction Refers to the time it takes for a response to cease after all sources of reinforcement have been eliminated. When a response is reinforced irregularly (i.e., sometimes reinforced and sometimes ignored), its resistance to extinction may be very high.

response cost A contingency in which a child may lose something (usually a token) for misbehavior; could also be described as negative punishment.

response cost lottery A group application of response cost contingencies in which a rule violation results in loss of a coupon. Coupons that are not lost are placed in a container with the child's name on them, and one coupon is drawn randomly to determine who receives the backup reward. The fewer coupons the child loses, the greater his or her chances of winning the lottery and receiving the back-up reward.

restitution Restoring the environment to the conditions that existed prior to a misbehavior; may involve apologizing, cleaning up a mess, or other actions.

reward A stimulus presented with the intention of increasing the frequency of the behavior it follows.

Ritalin Brand name for the most commonly used medication for hyperactivity. The generic name of this medication is methylphenidate.

satiation The situation where a child loses interest in a previously attractive reward after receiving it regularly. Food reward is particularly subject to satiation, but a child may lose interest in any reward after a period of time.

schedules of reinforcement Specific patterns of rewarding responses; the two major classes are *continuous* (each response is reinforced) and *intermittent* reinforcement (only some responses are reinforced). Intermittently reinforced responses are more resistant to extinction than continuously reinforced responses.

school climate The degree to which a school environment supports student learning in a positive way.

school phobia A childhood disorder characterized by school avoidance and absence.

school–home note Any note from a teacher to home that provides information about a child's behavior or academic performance in school. Can be used in behavior management programs in which parents provide rewards for behavior in school.

seclusion timeout A form of timeout in which a child is taken to a safe and secured room away from instructional activities; the most restrictive level of timeout. Use of seclusion timeout should be approached cautiously and is likely to be regulated by state rule or law.

secondary issues Important questions that need to be answered in the process of planning some behavior management programs; these issues are crucial to designing good programs and may indicate a need for additional services. The three secondary issues are: (1) What is the status of the child's family system? (2) What are the child's cultural roots and how should they influence school programming? (3) What diagnostic issues are raised by the child's behavior?

secondary reinforcer   Reinforcers that gain their reinforcing power through *association* with primary reinforcers and do not directly satisfy a biological need. Examples are money, attention, good grades in school, being first in line, points, gift certificates, verbal praise, smile faces, and sports cards.

self-graphing   When students graph their own behavioral performance.

self-monitoring   A behavior management technique in which students monitor their own behavior.

self-stimulating behavior   Stereotypical, repeated patterns of behavior, often associated with autism.

separation anxiety   An anxiety disorder in which the fear-evoking situation is separation of a child from his or her parents.

seriously emotionally disturbed   The most likely special education category of handicap for a child with behavioral problems. Associated conditions include an inability to learn not explainable by other factors, an inability to establish or maintain satisfactory interpersonal relationships with peers and teachers, inappropriate behavior or feelings, unhappiness or depression, and physical symptoms or fears associated with personal or school problems; also called serious emotional/behavioral disturbance, emotional/behavioral disorder.

sexual abuse   Unlawful sexual contact between a child under age eighteen and an older individual who may or may not be a relative.

shaping   Rewarding successive approximations of a target behavior; beginning by rewarding less accurate or expert responses than are acceptable later. The criterion for reward is raised in small steps until only a polished performance is rewarded.

Sit and Watch   An example of a contingent observation procedure in which the child ceases to participate in an activity while sitting and watching other children behaving appropriately; an effective form of mild punishment.

social skills   Behaviors that enhance social relationships and social interactions with peers and adults.

special education   Education for a child who has been labeled as handicapped. A child's special education can take place in environments ranging from a regular education classroom with no special considerations to a special residential school for the most severely handicapped children.

stimulus   Any perceivable event in a child's environment.

suicide policy   A school district policy that informs school staff with signs that precede suicide and a concrete set of guidelines regarding how to react to a student who is or may be threatening suicide.

suspension   Temporary exclusion of a child from school as a consequence for misbehavior.

target behavior   A behavior at which a behavior management program is directed; may consist of a behavior to be increased or decreased.

test anxiety   Anxiety or nervousness accompanying a testing situation that interferes with the individual's ability to perform at his or her best.

three-chance plan   A method for handling rule violations in which, the first time a rule is broken, a warning is given; the second time a rule is broken, the warning is repeated and the consequence (such as extra work, a logical consequence, or detention) is stated; the third time a rule is broken, the stated consequence is administered.

timeout   Similar to negative punishment; the process of removing a child to a boring place where reinforcement is unavailable, contingent on a behavior, causing it to decrease in frequency.

token   A reinforcer that has value because it can be exchanged for something desirable.

token economy   A system in which the behavior of individuals is managed with token reward; in a token economy, tokens are used to reward a variety of behaviors, and the tokens can be exchanged for a wide variety of privileges, activities, and tangible rewards.

token reinforcement   Rewarding a behavior with a token (gold star, points, poker chip) that has value because it can be exchanged for other, more desirable rewards.

"train and hope"   A method for promoting generalization in which a behavior change program is designed without any explicit attention to promoting generalization and then noting any generalization that happens.

train loosely   A technique for promoting generalization of behavior in which the trainers are somewhat irregular in the conditions of training and in the definition of acceptable responses. The more liberal are the training conditions, the less likely is behavior change to be restricted to the exact training conditions.

train sufficient examples   A technique of promoting generalization that involves training under several stimulus conditions or examples to obtain generalization across a number of untrained conditions.

REFERENCES

Abikoff, H. (1985). Efficacy of cognitive training interventions in hyperactive children: A critical review. *Clinical Psychology Review, 5,* 479–512.

Abramowitz, A. J., & O'Leary, S. G. (1991). Behavioral interventions for the classroom: Implications for students with ADHD. *School Psychology Review, 20,* 220–234.

Ackerman, R. J. (1983). *Children of alcoholics: A guidebook for educators, therapists, and parents* (2nd ed.). Holmes Beach, FL: Learning Publications.

Adams, C. D., & Kelley, M. L. (1992). Managing sibling aggression: Overcorrection as an alternative to time-out. *Behavior Therapy, 23,* 707–717.

Ager, C. L., & Cole, C. L. (1991). A review of cognitive-behavioral interventions for children and adolescents with behavioral disorders. *Behavioral Disorders, 16,* 276–287.

Alberti, R. E., & Emmons, M. L. (1978). *Your perfect right: A guide to assertive behavior.* (3rd ed.). San Luis Obispo, CA: Impact Publishers.

Alberto, P. A., & Troutman, A. C. (1986). *Applied behavior analysis for teachers* (2nd ed.). Columbus, OH: Merrill Publishing.

Alibrandi, T. (1978). *Young alcoholics.* Minneapolis, MN: Compcare Publications.

Alladin, W. J. (1993). Transcultural counselling: Theory, research and practice. *British Journal of Clinical Psychology, 32,* 255–256.

Allen, L. J., Howard, V. F., Sweeney, W. J., & McLaughlin, T. F. (1993). Use of contingency contracting to increase on-task behavior with primary students. *Psychological Reports, 72,* 905–906.

Allison, T. S., & Allison, S. L. (1971). Time-out from reinforcement: Effect on sibling aggression. *The Psychological Record, 21,* 81–86.

Alvord, J. R. (1973). *Home token economy: An incentive program for children and their parents.* Champaign, IL: Research Press.

American Psychiatric Association. (1980). *Diagnostic and statistical manual of mental disorders* (3rd ed.). Washington, DC: Author.

American Psychiatric Association. (1987). *Diagnostic and statistical manual of mental disorders* (3rd ed., revised). Washington, DC: Author.

American Psychiatric Association. (1994). *Diagnostic and statistical manual of mental disorders* (4th ed.). Washington, DC: Author.

Argulewicz, E. N., Elliott, S. N., & Spencer, D. (1982). Application of a cognitive-behavioral intervention for improving classroom attention. *School Psychology Review, 11,* 90–95.

Asarnow, J. R., & Callan, J. W. (1985). Boys with peer adjustment problems: Social cognitive processes. *Journal of Consulting and Clinical Psychology, 53,* 80–87.

Asarnow, J. R., & Carlson, G. A. (1985). Depression Self-Rating Scale: Utility with child psychiatric inpatients. *Journal of Consulting and Clinical Psychology, 53,* 491–499.

Asarnow, J. R., & Carlson, G. A. (1988). Childhood depression: Five-year outcome following combined cognitive-behavior therapy and pharmacotherapy. *American Journal of Psychotherapy, 42,* 456–464.

Asarnow, J. R., & Guthrie, D. (1989). Suicidal behavior, depression, and hopelessness in child psychiatric inpatients: A replication and extension. *Journal of Clinical Child Psychology, 18,* 129–136.

Atkeson, B. M., & Forehand, R. (1979). Homebased reinforcement programs designed to modify classroom behavior: A review and methodological evaluation. *Psychological Bulletin, 86,* 1298–1308.

Ayllon, T., & Azrin, N. (1968). *The token economy: A motivational system for therapy and rehabilitation.* New York: Appleton-Century Crofts.

Ayllon, T., & Azrin, N. H. (1965). The measurement and reinforcement of behavior of psychotics. *Journal of the Experimental Analysis of Behavior, 8,* 357–383.

Axelrod, S. (1992). Applied behavior analysis and the mainstreaming movement. *Journal of Behavioral Education, 2,* 219–224.

Azrin, N. H., & Foxx, R. M. (1974). *Toilet training in less than a day.* New York: Pocket Books.

Azrin, N. H., & Holz, W. C. (1966). Punishment. In W. K.

Honig (Ed.), *Operant behavior: Areas of application and research*. New York: Appleton-Century-Crofts.

Bandura, A. (1969). *Principles of behavior modification*. New York: Holt, Rinehart, & Winston.

Bandura, A. (1977). *Social learning theory*. Englewood Cliffs, NJ: Prentice-Hall.

Bane, M. J. (1979). Marital disruption and the lives of children. In G. Loevingen & O. C. Moles (Eds.), *Divorce and separation: Context, causes and consequences*. New York: Basic Books.

Barahal, R. M., Waterman, J., & Martin, H. P. (1981). The social cognitive development of abused children. *Journal of Consulting and Clinical Psychology, 49,* 508–516.

Barbetta, P. M. (1990). GOALS: Group-oriented adapted levels system for children with behavior disorders. *Academic therapy, 25,* 645–656.

Barkley, R. A. (1981). *Hyperactive children: A handbook for diagnosis and treatment*. New York: Guilford Press.

Barkley, R. A. (1987b). *Defiant children: A clinician's manual for parent training*. New York: Guilford Press.

Barkley, R. A. (1987a). *Defiant children: Parent–teacher assignments*. New York: Guilford Press.

Barkley, R. A. (1990). *Attention deficit hyperactivity disorder: A handbook for diagnosis and treatment*. New York: Guilford Press.

Barkley, R. A. (1991). *Attention-deficit hyperactivity disorder: A clinical workbook*. New York: Guilford Press.

Barkley, R. A. (1993a). Eight principles to guide ADHD children. *The ADHD Report, 1*(2), 1–4.

Barkley, R. A. (1993b). An update on draft of DSM-IV criteria for ADHD. *The ADHD Report, 1*(3), 7–8.

Barrish, H. H., Saunders, M., & Wolf, M. M. (1969). Good behavior game: Effects of individual contingencies for group consequences on disruptive behavior in a classroom. *Journal of Applied Behavior Analysis, 2,* 119–124.

Bauer, A. M., Shea, T. M., & Keppler, R. (1986). Levels systems: A framework for the individualization of behavior management. *Behavioral Disorders, 12,* 28–35.

Bauer, W. D., & Twentyman, C. T. (1985). Abusing, neglectful and comparison mothers' responses to child-related and non-child-related stressors. *Journal of Consulting and Clinical Psychology, 53,* 335–343.

Beattie, J. R., & Maniscalo, G. O. (1985). Special education and divorce: Is there a link? *Techniques: A Journal for Remedial Education and Counseling, 1,* 342–345.

Becker, W. C., Madsen, C. H., Arnold, R., & Thomas, D. R. (1967). The contingent use of teacher attention and praise in reducing classroom behavior problems. *Journal of Special Education, 1,* 287–307.

Bellack, A. S., & Hersen, M. (Eds.). (1985). *Dictionary of behavior therapy techniques*. New York: Pergamon Press.

Belsky, J. (1980). Child maltreatment: An ecological integration. *American Psychologist, 35,* 320–335.

Bennett, J. C. (1990). Nonintervention into siblings' fighting as

a catalyst for learned helplessness. *Psychological Reports, 66,* 139–145.

Benson, H. B. (1979). *Behavior modification and the child*. Westport, CT: Greenwood Press.

Berger, K. S. (1994). *The developing person through the life span* (3rd ed.). New York: Worth Publishers.

Berger, M. (1981). Remediating hyperkinetic behavior with inpulse [sic] control procedures. *School Psychology Review, 10,* 405–407.

Bernstein, L. (1994, January). Thumbs away! *Parents, 69*(1), 73–74.

Bersoff, D. N. (1982). The legal regulation of school psychology. In C. R. Reynolds & T. B. Gutkin (Eds.), *The handbook of school psychology* (pp. 1043–1074). New York: Wiley.

Bersoff, D. N., & Hofer, P. T. (1990). The legal regulation of school psychology. In C. R. Reynolds & T. B. Gutkin (Eds.), *The handbook of school psychology* (2nd ed.) (pp. 937–961). New York: Wiley.

Bickel, W. E. (1990). The effective schools literature: Implications for research and practice. In C. R. Reynolds & T. B. Gutkin (Eds.), *The handbook of school psychology* (2nd ed.) (pp. 847–867). New York: Wiley.

Biran, M., & Wilson, G. T. (1981). Treatment of phobic disorders using cognitive and exposure methods: A self-efficacy analysis. *Journal of Consulting and Clinical Psychology, 49,* 886–889.

Blagg, N. R., & Yule, W. (1984). The behavioral treatment of school refusal—A comparative study. *Behavior Research and Therapy, 22,* 119–127.

Blanchard, J. S. (1981). A comprehension strategy for disabled readers in the middle school. *Journal of Reading, 24,* 331–336.

Blechman, E. A., Taylor, C. J., & Schrader, S. M. (1981). Family problem solving versus home notes as early intervention with high-risk children. *Journal of Consulting and Clinical Psychology, 49,* 919–926.

Bolles, R. C. (1975). *Learning theory*. New York: Holt, Rinehart and Winston.

Bongiovanni, A. F., & Hyman, I. (1978). Leviton is wrong on the use of corporal punishment in the schools. *Psychology in the Schools, 15,* 290–291.

Bonner, B. L., Kaufman, K. L., Harbeck, C., & Brassard, M. R. (1992). Child maltreatment. In C. E. Walker & M. C. Roberts (Eds.), *Handbook of clinical child psychology* (2nd ed.) (pp. 967–1008). New York: Wiley.

Bower, G. H., & Hilgard, E. R. (1981). *Theories of learning*. Englewood Cliffs, NJ: Prentice-Hall.

Bowman, P., & Goldberg, M. (1983). "Reframing": A tool for the school psychologist. *Psychology in the Schools, 20,* 210–214.

Brantley, D. C., & Webster, R. E. (1993). Use of an independent group contingency management system in a regular classroom setting. *Psychology in the Schools, 30,* 60–66.

Brassard, M. R., Hyman, I., & Dimmitt, C. (1991). What can

children expect? Protecting and nurturing children in a school and community context. *School Psychology Review, 20,* 369–381.

Braswell, L., & Bloomquist, M. L. (1991). *Cognitive-behavioral therapy with ADHD children.* New York: Guilford Press.

Brown, L. J., Black, D. D., & Downs, J. C. (1984). *School Social Skills (S-3) manual.* East Aurora, NY: Slosson Educational Publications.

Brown, C. M., Meyers, A. W., & Cohen, R. (1984). Self-instruction training with preschoolers: Generalization to proximal and distal problem-solving tasks. *Cognitive Therapy and Research, 8,* 427–438.

Brown, R. T., & Conrad, K. J. (1982). Impulse control or selective attention: Remedial programs for hyperactivity. *Psychology in the Schools, 19,* 92–97.

Brown, P., & Elliot, R. (1965). Control of aggression in a nursery school class. *Journal of Experimental Child Psychology, 2,* 103–107.

Brunk, M., Henggeler, S. W., & Whelan, J. P. (1987). Comparison of multisystemic therapy and parent training in the brief treatment of child abuse and neglect. *Journal of Consulting and Clinical Psychology, 55,* 171–178.

Bushell, D., Wrobel, P. A., & Michaelis, M. L. (1968). Applying "group" contingencies to the classroom study behavior of preschool children. *Journal of Applied Behavior Analysis, 1,* 55–61.

Butler, L., Miezitis, S., Friedman, R., & Cole, E. (1980). The effect of two school-based intervention programs on depressive symptoms in preadolescents. *American Educational Research Journal, 17,* 111–119.

Camara, K. A., & Resnick, G. (1989). Styles of conflict resolution and cooperation between divorced parents: Effects on child behavior and adjustment. *Journal of Orthopsychiatry, 59,* 560–575.

Canter, L. (1988). *Homework without tears for parents.* Santa Monica, CA: Lee Canter & Associates.

Canter, L., & Canter, M. (1992). *Assertive discipline: Positive behavior management for today's classroom* (new & revised ed.). Santa Monica, CA: Lee Canter & Associates.

Cantor, P. (1983). Depression and suicide in children. In C. E. Walker & M. C. Roberts (Eds.), *Handbook of clinical child psychology* (pp. 453–474). New York: Wiley.

Cantrell, R. P., & Cantrell, M. L. (1993). Countering gang violence in American schools. *Principal, 73*(2), 6–9.

Cantwell, D. P. (1986). Attention deficit disorder in adolescents. *Clinical Psychology Review, 6,* 237–247.

Carlson, J. G., & Wielkiewicz, R. M. (1976). Mediators of the effects of magnitude of reinforcement. *Learning and Motivation, 7,* 184–196.

Cartledge, G., & Milburn, J. F. (Eds.). (1986). *Teaching social skills to children* (2nd ed.). New York: Pergamon Press.

Cautela, J. R. (1982). Covert conditioning with children. *Journal of Behavior Therapy and Experimental Psychiatry, 13,* 209–214.

Chadwick, B. A., & Day, R. C. (1971). Systematic reinforcement: Academic performance of under-achieving students. *Journal of Applied Behavior Analysis, 4,* 211–219.

Christenson, S., Abery, B., & Weinberg, R. A. (1986). An alternative model for the delivery of psychology in the school community. In S. N. Elliott & J. C. Witt (Eds.), *The delivery of psychological services in the schools: Concepts, processes, and results* (pp. 349–392). Hillsdale, NJ: Lawrence Erlbaum.

Christenson, S. L., & Conoley, J. C. (1992). *Home school collaboration: Enhancing children's academic and social competence.* Silver Spring, MD: National Association of School Psychologists.

Christian, B. (1983). A practical reinforcement hierarchy for classroom behavior modification. *Psychology in the Schools, 20,* 83–84.

Christie, D. J., Hiss, M., & Lozanoff, B. (1984). Modification of inattentive classroom behavior: Hyperactive children's use of self-recording with teacher guidance. *Behavior Modification, 8,* 391–406.

Christopherson, E. R., & Rapoff, M. A. (1992). Toileting problems in children. In C. E. Walker & M. C. Roberts (Eds.), *Handbook of clinical child psychology* (2nd ed.) (pp. 399–411). New York: Wiley.

Clark, E., Kehle, T. J., Jenson, W. R., & Beck, D. E. (1992). Evaluation of the parameters of self-modeling interventions. *School Psychology Review, 21,* 246–254.

Clark, L. (1985). *SOS! Help for parents.* Bowling Green, KY: Parents Press.

Cole, C. (Ed.). (1992). Self-management interventions in the schools [Mini-series]. *School Psychology Review, 21*(2).

Conger, J. C., & Keane, S. P. (1981). Social skills intervention in the treatment of isolated or withdrawn children. *Psychological Bulletin, 90,* 478–495.

Conning, A. M., & Head, D. M. (1990). Friends—Who needs them? Two case studies illustrating the assessment and treatment of boys with peer relationship difficulties. *Behavioural Psychotherapy, 18,* 221–233.

Conoley, J. C., & Bahns, T. (1992). Nurturing children of divorce: A shared responsibility. In S. L. Christenson, & J. C. Conoley (pp. 455–466). *Home school collaboration: Enhancing children's academic and social competence.* Silver Spring, MD: National Association of School Psychologists.

Cosentino, C. E. (1989). Child sexual abuse prevention: Guidelines for the school psychologist. *School Psychology Review, 18,* 371–385.

The Council for Children with Behavioral Disorders. (1990). Position paper on use of behavior reduction strategies with children with behavioral disorders. *Behavioral Disorders, 15,* 243–260.

Coyne, J. C., & Biglan, A. (1984). Paradoxical techniques in strategic family therapy: A behavioral analysis. *Journal of Behavior Therapy and Experimental Psychiatry, 15,* 221–227.

Dardig, J. C., & Heward, W. L. (1981). *Sign here: A contracting book for children and their parents* (2nd ed.). Bridgewater, NJ: F. Fournies and Associates.

Darley, J. M., Glucksberg, S., Kamin, L., & Kinchla, R. A. (1981). *Psychology*. Englewood Cliffs, NJ: Prentice-Hall.

Darveaux, D. X. (1984). The Good Behavior Game plus Merit: Controlling disruptive behavior and improving student motivation. *School Psychology Review, 13,* 510–514.

Davis, J. M. (1985). Suicidal crises in schools. *School Psychology Review, 14,* 313–324.

Deutsch, M. (1993). Educating for a peaceful world. *American Psychologist, 48,* 510–517.

DiGangi, S. A., Maag, J. W., & Rutherford, R. B., Jr. (1991). Self-graphing of on-task behavior: Enhancing the reactive effects of self-monitoring on on-task and academic performance. *Learning Disabilities Quarterly, 14,* 221–230.

Dobson, J. (1970). *Dare to discipline*. Wheaton, IL: Tyndale House Publishers.

Dodge, K. A., McClaskey, C. L., & Feldman, E. (1985). Situational approach to the assessment of social competence in children. *Journal of Consulting and Clinical Psychology, 53,* 344–353.

Doll, B. (1987). *A protocol for the assessment and treatment of school phobia*. Paper presented at the Annual Convention of the National Association of School Psychologists, New Orleans, LA.

Dollard, J., & Miller, N. E. (1950). *Personality and psychotherapy*. New York: McGraw-Hill.

Drabman, R. S., Spitalnick, R., & O'Leary, K. D. (1973). Teaching self-control to disruptive children. *Journal of Abnormal Psychology, 82,* 10–16.

Drake, E. A. (1981). Helping children cope with divorce: The role of the school. In I. R. Stuart & L. E. Abt (Eds.), *Children of separation and divorce: Management and treatment*. New York: Van Nostrand Reinhold.

Dreikurs, R., & Grey, L. (1970). *A parent's guide to child discipline*. New York: Hawthorn/Dutton.

Ducharme, J. M., & Popynick, M. (1993). Errorless compliance to parental requests: Treatment effects and generalization. *Behavior Therapy, 24,* 209–226.

Dunst, C. J., & Trivette, C. M. (1987). Enabling and empowering families: Conceptual and intervention issues. *School Psychology Review, 16,* 443–456.

Dunst, C. J., Johanson, C., Rounds, T., Trivette, C. M., & Hamby, D. (1992). Characteristics of parent-professional partnerships. In S. L. Christenson & J. C. Conoley (Eds.), *Home–school collaboration: Enhancing children's academic and social competence* (pp. 157–174). Silver Spring, MD: National Association of School Psychologists.

Dura, J. R. (1991). Controlling extremely dangerous aggressive outbursts when functional analysis fails. *Psychological Reports, 69,* 459–459.

Durand, V. M., Crimmins, D. B., Caulfield, M., & Taylor, J. (1989). Reinforcer assessment. I: Using problem behavior to select reinforcers. *Journal of the Association for Persons with Severe Handicaps, 14,* 113–126.

Durlak, J. A. (1992). School problems of children. In C. E. Walker & M. C. Roberts (Eds.), *Handbook of clinical child psychology* (2nd ed.) (pp. 497–510). New York: Wiley.

Dush, D. M., Hirt, M. L., & Schroeder, H. E. (1989). Self-statement modification in the treatment of child behavior disorders: A meta-analysis. *Psychological Bulletin, 106,* 97–106.

Ehrlich, V. Z. (1982). *Gifted children: A guide for parents and teachers*. Englewood Cliffs, NJ: Prentice-Hall.

Eimers, R., & Aitchison, R. (1978). *Effective parents/Responsible children*. New York: McGraw-Hill.

Elliott, C., & Ozolins, M. (1983). Use of imagery and imagination in treatment of children. In C. E. Walker & M. C. Roberts (Eds.), *Handbook of clinical child psychology* (pp. 1026–1049). New York: Wiley.

Elliott, S. N., & Ershler, J. (1990). Best practices in preschool social skills training. In A. Thomas & J. Grimes (Eds.), *Best practices in school psychology—II* (pp. 591–606). Washington, DC: National Association of School Psychologists.

Emery, R. E. (1982). Interparental conflict and the children of discord and divorce. *Psychological Bulletin, 92,* 310–330.

Epstein, J. (1988). *Teacher attitudes and practices of parent involvement in inner-city elementary and middle schools*. Paper presented at the annual meeting of the American Sociological Association. Atlanta, GA; Session 79.

Erickson, H. L. (1988, May). The boy who couldn't be disciplined. *Principal, 67*(5), pp. 36–37.

Eron, L. D. (1980). Prescription for the reduction of aggression. *American Psychologist, 35,* 244–252.

Eron, L. D. (1986). The development of aggressive behavior from the perspective of a developing behaviorism. *American Psychologist, 42,* 435–442.

Essex, N. L., & Schifani, J. (1992, March). Attention deficit disorder and the principal. *Principal,* pp. 30, 32.

Fabry, B. D., & Cone, J. D. (1980). Auto-graphing: A one-step approach to collecting and graphing data. *Education and Treatment of Children, 3,* 361–368.

Farmer, E. (1985). Current issues in pupil transportation. *Education Digest, 50*(1), 34–35.

Feindler, E. L. (1991). Cognitive strategies in anger control interventions for children and adolescents. In P. C. Kendall (Ed.), *Child and adolescent therapy: Cognitive-behavioral procedures*. New York: Guilford Press.

Feindler, E. L., & Guttman, J. (1994). Cognitive-behavioral anger control training. In C. W. LeCroy (Ed.), *Handbook of child and adolescent treatment manuals* (pp. 170–199). New York: Lexington Books.

Ferritor, D. E., Buckholdt, D., Hamblin, R. L., & Smith, L. (1972). The non-effects of contingent reinforcement for attending behavior upon work accomplishment. *Journal of Applied Behavior Analysis, 5,* 7–17.

Finch, A. J., Saylor, C. F., & Edwards, G. L. (1985). Children's depression inventory: Sex and grade norms for normal children. *Journal of Consulting and Clinical Psychology, 53,* 424–425.

Finch, M., & Hopps, H. (1982). Remediation of social withdrawal in young children: Considerations for the practitioner. *Child and Youth Services, 5*(3/4), 29–42.

Fine, M. J., & Holt, P. (1983a). Corporal punishment in the family: A systems perspective. *Psychology in the Schools, 20,* 85–92.

Fine, M. J., & Holt, P. (1983b). Intervening with school problems: A family systems perspective. *Psychology in the Schools, 20,* 59–66.

Fish, M. C., & Mendola, L. R. (1986). The effect of self-instruction training on homework completion in an elementary special education class. *School Psychology Review, 15,* 268–276.

Forehand, R., & McMahon, R. (1981). *Helping the noncompliant child: A clinician's guide to parent training.* New York: Guilford Press.

Forman, S. G., & O'Malley, P. L. (1984). School stress and anxiety interventions. *School Psychology Review, 13,* 162–170.

Foster, S. L., & Robin, A. L. (1992). Family conflict and communication in adolescence. In E. J. Mash & L. G. Terdal (Eds.), *Behavioral assessment of childhood disorders* (2nd ed.) (pp. 717–775). New York: Guilford Press.

Foxx, R. M. (1982). *Decreasing behaviors of severely retarded and autistic persons.* Champaign, IL: Research Press.

Foxx, R. M., & Shapiro, S. T. (1978). The timeout ribbon: A nonexclusionary timeout procedure. *Journal of Applied Behavior Analysis, 11,* 125–136.

Frisby, C. L. (1992). Issues and problems in the influence of culture on the psychoeducational needs of African-American children. *School Psychology Review, 21,* 532–551.

Garland, A. F., & Zigler, E. (1993). Adolescent suicide prevention: Current research and social policy implications. *American Psychologist, 48,* 169–182.

Garman, G. C. (1983). *Taking a look at discipline.* Elizabethtown, PA: Continental Press.

Garvey, W. P., & Hegrenes, J. R. (1966). Desensitization techniques in the treatment of school phobia. *American Journal of Orthopsychiatry, 36,* 147–152.

Gazda, G. M. (Ed.). (1976). *Theories and methods of group counseling in the schools* (2nd ed.). Springfield, IL: Charles C Thomas.

Gleason, M. M., Colvin, G., & Archer, A. L. (1991). Interventions for improving study skills. In G. Stoner, M. R. Shinn, & H. M. Walker (Eds.), *Interventions for achievement and behavior problems* (pp. 137–160). Silver Spring, MD: National Association of School Psychologists.

Goldstein, S., & Goldstein, M. (1990). *Managing attention disorders in children: A guide for practitioners.* New York: Wiley.

Goldstein, S., & Goldstein, M. (1992). *Hyperactivity: Why won't my child pay attention?* New York: Wiley.

Gresham, F. M. (1985). Utility of cognitive-behavioral procedures for social skills training with children: A critical review. *Journal of Abnormal Child Psychology, 13,* 411–423.

Gresham, F. M., & Nagle, R. J. (1980). Social skills training with children: Responsiveness to modeling and coaching as a function of peer orientation. *Journal of Consulting and Clinical Psychology, 48,* 718–729.

Gridley, B. E. (1990). Best practices in working with gifted children. In A. Thomas & J. Grimes (Eds.), *Best practices in school psychology—II* (pp. 811–821). Washington, DC: National Association of School Psychologists.

Grossman, P. B., & Hughes, J. N. (1992). Self-control interventions with internalizing disorders: A review and analysis. *School Psychology Review, 21,* 229–245.

Guetzloe, E. C. (1989). *Youth Suicide: What the educator should know.* Reston, VA: Council for Exceptional Children.

Guidubaldi, J., Cleminshaw, H. K., Perry, J. D., & Mcloughlin, C. S. (1983). The impact of parental divorce on children: Report of the nationwide NASP study. *School Psychology Review, 12,* 300–323.

Guidubaldi, J., & Perry, J. D. (1984). Divorce, socioeconomic status, and children's cognitive-social competence at school entry. *American Journal of Orthopsychiatry, 54,* 459–468.

Gutkin, T. B., & Reynolds, C. R. (Eds.). (1990). *The handbook of school psychology* (2nd ed.). New York: Wiley.

Guyer, M. J. (1982). Child abuse and neglect statutes: Legal and clinical implications. *American Journal of Orthopsychiatry, 52,* 73–81.

Hall, R. V., Lund, D., & Jackson, D. (1968). Effects of teacher attention on study behavior. *Journal of Applied Behavior Analysis, 1,* 1–12.

Hammill, D. D. (1990). On defining learning disabilities: An emerging consensus. *Journal of Learning Disabilities, 23,* 74–83.

Hamilton, J. E. (1993, December). Smart ways to use timeout. *Parents, 68*(12), pp. 110–112.

Harris, K. R. (1985). Definitional, parametric, and procedural considerations in timeout interventions and research. *Exceptional Children, 51,* 279–288.

Harris, K. R., Wong, B. Y. L., & Keogh, B. K. (1985). Cognitive-behavior modification with children: A critical review of the state-of-the-art. *Journal of Abnormal Child Psychology, 13,* 327–476.

Harris, V. W., & Sherman, J. A. (1973). Use and analysis of the "good behavior game" to reduce disruptive classroom behavior. *Journal of Applied Behavior Analysis, 6,* 405–417.

Harvey, J. H., & Weary, G. (1984). Current issues in attribution theory and research. *Annual Review of Psychology, 35,* 427–459.

Hatzenbuehler, L. C., & Schroeder, H. E. (1978). Desensitization procedures in the treatment of childhood disorders. *Psychological Bulletin, 85,* 831–844.

Hearst, E. (Ed.). (1979). *The first century of experimental psychology.* Hillsdale, NJ: Lawrence Erlbaum Associates.

Hersen, M., & Ammerman, R. T. (1989). Overview of new developments in child behavior therapy. In M. Hersen (Ed.), *Innovations in child behavior therapy.* New York: Springer.

Hetherington, E. M. (1979). Divorce: A child's perspective. *American Psychologist, 34,* 851–858.

Hewett, F. (1968). *The emotionally disturbed student in the classroom.* Boston: Allyn and Bacon.

Hightower, A. D., Johnson, D., & Haffey, W. G. (1990). Best practices in adopting a prevention program. In A. Thomas & J. Grimes (Eds.), *Best practices in school psychology—II* (pp. 63–79). Washington, DC: National Association of School Psychologists.

Hinshaw, S. P., & Erhardt, D. (1991). Attention-deficit hyperactivity disorder. In P. C. Kendall (Ed.), *Child and adolescent therapy: Cognitive-behavioral procedures.* New York: Guilford Press.

Hodges, W. F. (1991). *Interventions for children of divorce: Custody, access, and psychotherapy.* (2nd ed.). New York: Wiley.

Hollon, S. D. (1984, October 11). *Cognitive therapy: An advanced workshop.* Workshop presented at the Annual Convention of the North Dakota Psychological Association.

Homme, L. E., DeBacca, P. C., Devine, J. V., Steinhorst, R., & Rickert, E. J. (1963). Use of the Premack principle in controlling the behavior of nursery school children. *Journal of the Experimental Analysis of Behavior, 6,* 544.

Hops, H. (1983). Children's social competence and skill: Current research practices and future directions. *Behavior Therapy, 14,* 3–18.

Hops, H., & Greenwood, C. R. (1988). Social skill deficits. In E. J. Mash & L. G. Terdal (Eds.), *Behavioral assessment of childhood disorders* (2nd ed.) (pp. 263–314). New York: Guilford Press.

Horan, J. J., & Williams, J. M. (1982). Longitudinal study of assertion training as a drug abuse prevention strategy. *American Educational Research Journal, 19,* 341–351.

Houlihan, D. D., & Jones, R. N. (1989). Treatment of a boy's school phobia with in vivo systematic desensitization. *Professional School Psychology, 4,* 285–293.

Houts, A. C. (1991). Nocturnal enuresis as a biobehavioral problem. *Behavior Therapy, 22,* 133–151.

Huffman, K., Vernoy, M., & Vernoy, J. (1994). *Psychology in action* (3rd ed.). New York: Wiley.

Hughes, J. N., & Hall, R. J. (1987). Proposed model for the assessment of children's social competence. *Professional School Psychology, 2,* 247–260.

Hyman, I. A., & Wise, J. H. (Eds.). (1979). *Corporal punishment in American education.* Philadelphia: Temple University Press.

Ingersoll, B. (1988). *Your hyperactive child: A parent's guide to coping with attention deficit disorder.* New York: Doubleday.

Iwata, B. A., & Bailey, J. S. (1974). Reward versus cost token systems: An analysis of the effects on students and teacher. *Journal of Applied Behavior Analysis, 7,* 567–576.

Iwata, B. A., Pace, G. M., Kalsher, M. J., Cowdery, G. E., & Cataldo, M. F. (1990). Experimental analysis and extinction of self-injurious escape behavior. *Journal of Applied Behavior Analysis, 23,* 11–27.

Jacob-Timm, S., & Hartshorne, T. S. (1994). Section 504 and school psychology. *Psychology in Schools, 31,* 26–39.

Jensen, M. (1988). An unexpected effect: Restitution maintains object throwing. *Education and Treatment of Children, 11,* 252–256.

Jones, R. R., & Herndon, C. (1992). The status of Black children and adolescents in the academic setting: Assessment and treatment issues. In C. E. Walker & M. C. Roberts (Eds.), *Handbook of clinical child psychology* (2nd ed.) (pp. 901–917). New York: Wiley.

Jones, R. T., & Kazdin, A. E. (1981). Childhood behavior problems in the school. In S. M. Turner, K. S. Calhoun, & H. E. Adams (Eds.), *Handbook of clinical behavior therapy.* New York: Wiley.

Kalter, N., Pickar, J., & Lesowitz, M. (1984). School-based developmental facilitation groups for children of divorce: A preventive intervention. *American Journal of Orthopsychiatry, 54,* 613–623.

Kane, M. T., & Kendall, P. C. (1989). Anxiety disorders in children: A multiple-baseline evaluation of a cognitive-behavioral treatment. *Behavioral Therapy, 20,* 499–508.

Kanfer, F. H., & Phillips, J. S. (1970). *Learning foundations of behavior therapy.* New York: Wiley.

Kanfer, F. H., & Schefft, B. K. (1988). *Guiding the process of therapeutic change.* Champaign, IL: Research Press.

Kazdin, A. E. (1977). *The token economy: A review and evaluation.* New York: Plenum Press.

Kazdin, A. E. (1978). *History of behavior modification.* Baltimore: University Park Press.

Kazdin, A. E. (1982). Applying behavioral principles in the schools. In Reynolds, C. R., & Gutkin, T. B., (Eds.). (1982). *The handbook of school psychology* (pp. 501–529). New York: Wiley.

Kazdin, A. E. (1983). The token economy: A decade later. *Journal of Applied Behavior Analysis, 15,* 431–445.

Kazdin, A. E. (1988). Childhood depression. In E. J. Mash & L. G. Terdal (Eds.), *Behavioral assessment of childhood disorders* (2nd ed.) (pp. 157–195). New York: Guilford Press.

Kazdin, A. E., Esveldt-Dawson, K., French, N. H., & Unis, A. S. (1987). Problem-solving skills training and relationship therapy in the treatment of antisocial child behavior. *Journal of Consulting and Clinical Psychology, 55,* 76–85.

Kazdin, A. E., Moser, J., Colbus, D., & Bell, R. (1985). Depressive symptoms among physically abused and psychiatrically disturbed children. *Journal of Abnormal Psychology, 94,* 298–307.

Kazdin, A. E., Siegel, T. C., & Bass, D. (1992). Cognitive problem-solving skills training and parent management training in the treatment of antisocial behavior in children. *Journal of Consulting and Clinical Psychology, 60,* 733–747.

Kehle, T. J., Clark, E., Jenson, W. R., & Wampold, B. E. (1986). Effectiveness of self-observation with behavior disordered elementary school children. *School Psychology Review, 15,* 289–295.

Kelley, M. L. (1990). *School-home notes: Promoting children's classroom success.* New York: Guilford Press.

Kelly, M. B., & Bushell, D. B., Jr. (1987). Student achievement and differential reinforcement of incompatible behavior: Hand raising. *Psychology in the Schools, 24,* 273–281.

Kendall, P. C. (1987). Ahead to basics: Assessments with children and families. *Behavioral Assessment, 9,* 321–332.

Kendall, P. C. (Ed.). (1991). *Child and adolescent therapy: Cognitive-behavioral procedures.* New York: Guilford Press.

Kendall, P. C. (1993). Cognitive-behavioral therapies with youth: Guiding theory, current status, and emerging developments. *Journal of Consulting and Clinical Psychology, 61,* 235–247.

Kendall, P. C. (1994). Treating anxiety disorders in children: Results of a randomized clinical trial. *Journal of Consulting and Clinical Psychology, 62,* 100–110.

Kendall, P. C., & Braswell, L. (1982a). Assessment for cognitive-behavioral interventions in the schools. *School Psychology Review, 11,* 21–31.

Kendall, P. C., & Braswell, L. (1982b). Cognitive-behavioral self-control therapy for children: A components analysis. *Journal of Consulting and Clinical Psychology, 50,* 672–689.

Kendall, P. C., & Braswell, L. (1985). *Cognitive-behavioral therapy for impulsive children.* New York: Guilford Press.

Kendall, P. C., & Braswell, L. (1993). *Cognitive-behavioral therapy for impulsive children* (2nd ed.). New York: Guilford Press.

Kendall, P. C., Chansky, T. E., Friedman, M., Kim, R., Kortlander, E., Sessa, F. M., & Siqueland, L. (1991). Treating anxiety disorders in children and adolescents. In P. C. Kendall (Ed.), *Child and adolescent therapy: Cognitive-behavioral procedures* (pp. 131–164). New York: Guilford Press.

Kendall, P. C., & Wilcox, L. C. (1979). Self-control in children: Development of a rating scale. *Journal of Consulting and Clinical Psychology, 47,* 1020–1029.

Kerr, M. M., & Nelson, C. M. (1989). *Strategies for managing behavior problems in the classroom* (2nd ed.). Columbus, OH: Merrill.

King, H. E. (1992). The reactions of children to divorce. In C. E. Walker & M. C. Roberts (Eds.), *Handbook of clinical child psychology* (2nd ed.) (pp. 1009–1023). New York: Wiley.

King, H. E., & Kleemeier, C. P. (1983). The effect of divorce on parents and children. In C. E. Walker & M. C. Roberts (Eds.), *Handbook of clinical child psychology* (pp. 1249–1272). New York: Wiley.

King, R. P., Marcattilio, A. J. M., & Hanson, R. H. (1981). Some functions of videotape equipment in training social skills to institutionalized mentally retarded adults. *Behavioral Engineering, 6,* 159–167.

Kirk, S. A., & Chalfant, J. C. (1984). *Academic and developmental learning disabilities.* Denver, CO: Love.

Kirschenbaum, D. S., & Flanery, R. C. (1984). Toward a psychology of behavioral contracting. *Clinical Psychology Review, 4,* 597–618.

Kovacs, M. (1980/1981). Rating scales to assess depression in school-aged children. *Acta Paedopsychiatrica, 46,* 305–315.

Kratochwill, T. R., Elliott, S. N., & Rotto, P. C. (1990). Best practices in behavioral consultation. In A. Thomas & J. Grimes (Eds.), *Best practices in school psychology—II* (pp. 147–170). Washington, DC: National Association of School Psychologists.

Kratochwill, T. R., & French, D. C. (1984). Social skills training for withdrawn children. *School Psychology Review, 13,* 331–338.

Kuepper, J. E. (1990). Best practices in study skills. In A. Thomas & J. Grimes (Eds.), *Best practices in school psychology—II* (pp. 711–721).

Ladd, G. W., & Mize, J. (1982). Social skills training and assessment with children: A cognitive-social learning approach. *Child and Youth Services, 5,* 61–74.

Ladd, G. W., & Oden, S. (1979). The relationship between peer acceptance and children's ideas about helpfulness. *Child Development, 50,* 402–408.

La Greca, A. M., & Mesibov, G. B. (1979). Social skills intervention with learning disabled children: Selecting skills and implementing training. *Journal of Clinical Child Psychology, 8,* 234–241.

LaClave, L. J., & Brack, G. (1989). Reframing to deal with patient resistance: Practical application. *American Journal of Psychotherapy, 43,* 68–76.

Lam, A. L., Cole, C. L., Shapiro, E. S., & Bambara, L. M. (1994). Relative effects of self-monitoring on-task behavior, academic accuracy, and disruptive behavior in students with behavior disorders. *School Psychology Review, 23,* 44–58.

Lange, A. J., & Jakubowski, P. (1976). *Responsible assertive behavior.* Champaign, IL: Research Press.

Last, C. G. (1992). Anxiety disorders in childhood and adolescence. In W. M. Reynolds (Ed.), *Internalizing disorders in children and adolescents.* New York: Wiley.

Lawson, G. W., & Lawson, A. W. (1992). *Adolescent substance abuse: Etiology, treatment, and prevention.* Gaithersburg, MD: Aspen Publishers.

Lazarus, B. D. (1993). Self-management and achievement of students with behavior disorders. *Psychology in the Schools, 30,* 67–74.

LeCroy, C. W. (Ed.). (1982). Social skills training for children and youth. *Child and Youth Services, 5,* 1–152.

LeCroy, C. W. (Ed.). (1994a). *Handbook of child and adolescent treatment manuals.* New York: Lexington Books.

LeCroy, C. W. (1994b). Social skills training. In C. W. LeCroy (Ed.), *Handbook of child and adolescent treatment manuals* (pp. 126–169). New York: Lexington Books.

Leff, L. (1992, August 21). Fake cameras on buses to aid P.G. school discipline. *Washington Post,* p. D6.

Lewis, R. O., & Blampied, N. M. (1985). Self-management in a special class. *Techniques: A Journal for Remedial Education and Counseling, 1,* 346–354.

Lipsey, M. W., & Wilson, D. B. (1993). The efficacy of psychological, educational, and behavioral treatment: Confirmation from meta-analysis. *American Psychologist, 48,* 1181–1209.

Little, L. M., & Kelley, M. L. (1989). The efficacy of response cost procedures for reducing children's noncompliance to parental instructions. *Behavior Therapy, 20,* 525–534.

Lloyd, J. W., Landrum, T. J., & Hallahan, D. P. (1991). Self-monitoring applications for classroom intervention. In G. Stoner, M. R. Shinn, & H. M. Walker (Eds.), *Interventions for achievement and behavior problems* (pp. 201–213). Silver Spring, MD: National Association of School Psychologists.

Lochman, J. E., Dunn, S. E., & Klimes-Dougan, B. (1993). An intervention and consultation model from a social cognitive perspective: A description of the anger coping program. *School Psychology Review, 22,* 458–471.

Loschen, E. L., & Osman, O. T. (1992). Self-injurious behavior in the developmentally disabled: Assessment techniques. *Psychopharmacology Bulletin, 28,* 433–438.

Lucco, A. A. (1991). Assessment of the school-age child. *Families in Society: The Journal of Contemporary Human Services, 72,* 394–408.

Madsen, C. H., Becker, W. C., & Thomas, D. R. (1968). Rules, praise, and ignoring: Elements of elementary classroom control. *Journal of Applied Behavior Analysis, 1,* 139–150.

Marsella, A. J. (1993). Counseling and psychotherapy with Japanese Americans: Cross-cultural considerations. *American Journal of Orthopsychiatry, 63,* 200–208.

Martin, G., & Pear, J. (1988). *Behavior modification: What it is and how to do it* (3rd ed.). Englewood Cliffs, NJ: Prentice-Hall.

Maser, J. D., & Seligman, M. E. P. (Eds.). (1977). *Psychopathology: Experimental models.* San Francisco: W. H. Freeman.

Mash, E. J., & Barkley, R. A. (Eds.). (1989). *Treatment of childhood disorders.* New York: Guilford Press.

Mash, E. J., & Terdal, L. G. (1988). Behavioral assessment of child and family disturbance. In E. J. Mash & L. G. Terdal (Eds.), *Behavioral assessment of childhood disorders* (2nd ed.) (pp. 3–65). New York: Guilford Press.

Mastropieri, M. A., Jenne, T., & Scruggs, T. E. (1988). A level system for managing problem behaviors in a high school resource program. *Behavioral Disorders, 13,* 202–208.

Mathews, B., McLaughlin, T. F., & Hunsaker, D. (1980). Effects of teacher attention and activity reinforcers on on-task behavior. *Education and Treatment of Children, 3,* 13–19.

Matthews, L. H., Leibowitz, J. M., & Matthews, J. R. (1992). Tics, habits, and mannerisms. In C. E. Walker & M. C. Roberts (Eds.), *Handbook of clinical child psychology* (2nd ed.) (pp. 283–302). New York: Wiley.

McCarney, S. B., Leigh, J. E., & Cornbleet, J. A. (1983). *Behavior Evaluation Scale.* Columbia, MO: Educational Services.

McClannahan, L. E., & Krantz, P. J. (1985). Some next steps in rights protection for developmentally disabled children. *School Psychology Review, 14,* 143–149.

McEvoy, A. (1990, October). Combating gang activities in schools. *Education Digest, 56*(2), 31–34.

McGinnis, E., Goldstein, A. P., Sprafkin, R. P., & Gershaw, N. J. (1984). *Skill-streaming the elementary school child.* Champaign, IL: Research Press.

McGuffin, P. W. (1991). The effect of timeout duration on frequency of aggression in hospitalized children with conduct disorders. *Behavioral Residential Treatment, 6,* 279–288.

McMahon, R. J., Forehand, R., & Griest, D. L. (1981). Effects of knowledge of social learning principles on enhancing treatment outcome and generalization in a parent training program. *Journal of Consulting and Clinical Psychology, 49,* 526–532.

Medland, M. B., & Stacknick, T. J. (1972). Good behavior game: A replication and systematic analysis. *Journal of Applied Behavior Analysis, 5,* 45–51.

Meharg, S., & Woltersdorf, M. (1990). Therapeutic use of videotape self-modeling: A review. *Advances in Behaviour Research and Therapy, 12,* 85–99.

Meichenbaum, D. H., & Goodman, J. (1971). Training impulsive children to talk to themselves: A means of developing self-control. *Journal of Abnormal Psychology, 77,* 115–126.

Melton, G. B., & Ehrenreich, N. S. (1992). Ethical and legal issues in mental health services for children. In C. E. Walker & M. C. Roberts (Eds.), *Handbook of clinical child psychology* (2nd ed.) (pp. 1035–1055). New York: Wiley.

Merrell, K. W. (1993a). *School social behavior scales.* Brandon, VT: Clinical Psychology Publishing Company.

Merrell, K. W. (1993b). Using behavior rating scales to assess social skills and antisocial behavior in school settings: Development of the school social behavior scales. *School Psychology Review, 22,* 115–133.

Meyerhoff, M. K., & White, B. L. (1986, September). Making the grade as parents. *Psychology Today,* pp. 38, 42–45.

Miller, D. L. & Kelley, M. L. (1991). Interventions for improving homework performance: A critical review. *School Psychology Quarterly, 6,* 174–185.

Miller, L. C. (1983). Fears and anxiety in children. In C. E. Walker & M. C. Roberts (Eds.), *Handbook of clinical child psychology* (pp. 337–308). New York: Wiley.

Miller, P. M. (1983). *Theories of developmental psychology.* San Francisco: W. H. Freeman.

Milling, L., & Martin, B. (1992). Depression and suicide in preadolescent children. In C. E. Walker & M. C. Roberts (Eds.), *Handbook of clinical child psychology* (2nd ed.) (pp. 319–339). New York: Wiley.

Millman, H. L., Schaefer, C. E., & Cohen, J. J. (1980). *Therapies for school behavior problems.* San Francisco: Jossey-Bass.

Miranda, A. H. (1993). Consultation with culturally diverse families. *Journal of Educational and Psychological Consultation, 4,* 89–93.

Morris, C. G. (1988). *Psychology: An introduction* (6th ed.). Englewood Cliffs, NJ: Prentice-Hall.

Morris, R. J., & Kratochwill, T. R. (Eds.) (1983a). *The practice of child therapy.* New York: Pergamon Press.

Morris, R. J., & Kratochwill, T. R. (1983b). *Treating children's fears and phobias.* New York: Pergamon Press.

Morris, R. J., & Kratochwill, T. R. (1985). Behavioral treatment of children's fears and phobias. *School Psychology Review, 14,* 84–93.

Mulvey, E. P., Arthur, M. W., & Reppucci, N. D. (1993). The prevention and treatment of juvenile delinquency: A review of the research. *Clinical Psychology Review, 13,* 133–167.

Murray L., & Sefchik, G. (1992). Regulating behavior management practices in residential treatment facilities. *Children and Youth Services Review, 14,* 519–539.

National Association of School Psychologists. (1992). Helping children grow up in the '90s: A resource book for parents and teachers. Silver Spring, MD: Author.

Nelson, C. M., & Rutherford, R. B. (1983). Timeout revisited: Guidelines for its use in special education. *Exceptional Education Quarterly, 3,* 56–67.

Nelson, J. R., Smith, D. J., Young, R. K., & Dodd, J. M. (1991). A review of self-management outcome research conducted with students who exhibit behavioral disorders. *Behavioral Disorders, 16,* 169–179.

Newby, R. F., Fischer, M., & Roman, M. A. (1991). Parent training for families of children with ADHD. *School Psychology Review, 20,* 252–265.

Newman, B. M., & Newman, P. R. (1979). *Development through life: A psychosocial perspective.* Homewood, IL: Dorsey Press.

Ninness, H. A. C., Fuerst, J., & Rutherford, R. D. (1991). Effects of self-management training and reinforcement on the transfer of improved conduct in the absence of supervision. *Journal of Applied Behavior Analysis, 24,* 499–508.

Northup, J., Wacker, D., Sasso, G., Steege, M., Cicrand, K., Cook, J., & DeRaad, A. (1991). A brief functional analysis of aggressive and alternative behavior in an outclinic setting. *Journal of Applied Behavior Analysis, 24,* 509–522.

Nuttall, E. V., De Leon, B., & Valle, M. (1990). Best practices in considering cultural factors. In A. Thomas & J. Grimes (Eds.), *Best practices in school psychology—II* (pp. 219–233). Washington, DC: National Association of School Psychologists.

Oden, S., & Asher, S. R. (1977). Coaching children in skills for friendship making. *Child Development, 48,* 495–506.

O'Leary, K. D., & Drabman, R. (1971). Token reinforcement programs in the classroom: A review. *Psychological Bulletin, 75,* 379–398.

Ollendick, T. H., & Cerny, J. A. (1981). *Clinical behavior therapy with children.* New York: Pergamon Press.

Ollendick, T. H., Matson, J. L., & Helsel, W. J. (1985). Fears in children and adolescents: Normative data. *Behavior Research and Therapy, 23,* 465–467.

Olympia, D., Jenson, W. R., Clark, E., & Sheridan, S. (1992). Training parents to facilitate homework completion: A model for home-school collaboration. In S. L. Christenson & J. C. Conoley (Eds.), *Home-school collaboration: Enhancing children's academic and social competence* (pp. 309–331). Silver Spring, MD: National Association of School Psychologists.

Olympia, D. E., Jenson, W. R., & Neville, M. R. (1990). *Do it yourself homework manual: A sanity saver for parents.* Manuscript submitted for publication.

Overcast, T. D., Sales, B., & Sacken, D. M. (1990). Students' rights in public schools. In T. B. Gutkin & C. R. Reynolds (Eds.), *The handbook of school psychology* (2nd ed.) (pp. 962–990). New York: Wiley.

Overmier, J. B. (1988). *Expectations: From animal laboratory to the clinic.* Paper presented and the Annual Convention of the Midwestern Psychological Association.

Palkes, H., Stewart, M., & Freedman, J. (1972). Improvement in maze performance of hyperactive boys as a function of verbal training procedures. *Journal of Special Education, 5,* 337–342.

Paniagua, F. A. (1989). Lying by children: Why children say one thing, do another? *Psychological Reports, 64,* 971–984.

Paniagua, F. A., & Black, S. A. (1990). Management and prevention of hyperactivity and conduct disorders in 8–10 year old boys through correspondence training procedures. *Child & Family Behavior Therapy, 12,* 23–56.

Parker, H. C. (1988). *The ADD hyperactivity workbook for parents, teachers, and kids.* Plantation, FL: Impact Publications.

Parker, H. C. (1991). *The goal card program.* Plantation, FL: Impact Publications.

Patterson, G. R. (1986). Performance models for antisocial boys. *American Psychologist, 41,* 432–444.

Patterson, G. R., Chamberlain, P., & Reid, J. B. (1982). A comparative evaluation of a parent-training program. *Behavior Therapy, 13,* 638–650.

Patterson, G. R., Cobb, J. A., & Ray, R. S. (1973). A social engineering technology for retraining the families of aggressive boys. In H. E. Adams & I. P. Unikel (Eds.), *Issues and trends in behavior therapy.* Springfield, IL: Charles C Thomas.

Patterson, G. R., & Stouthamer-Loeber, M. (1984). The correlation of family management practices and delinquency. *Child Development, 55,* 1299–1307.

Patton, J. R., Payne, J. S., & Beirne-Smith, M. (1986). *Mental retardation* (2nd ed.). Columbus, OH: Charles E. Merrill.

Pavchinski, P., Evans, J. H., & Bostow D. E. (1989). Increasing word recognition and math ability in a severely learning-disabled student with token reinforcers. *Psychology in the Schools, 26,* 397–411.

Peterson, L., Zink, M., & Farmer, J. (1992). Prevention of disorders in children. In C. E. Walker & M. C. Roberts (Eds.), *Handbook of clinical child psychology* (2nd ed.) (pp. 951–965). New York: Wiley.

Peterson, N. J., & Moe, G. L. (1984). A multimethod assessment and intervention with a socially rejected child. *School Psychology Review, 13,* 391–396.

Pfeffer, C. R. (1981). Developmental issues among children of separation and divorce. In I. R. Stuart & L. E. Abt (Eds.), *Children of separation and divorce: Management and treatment.* New York: Van Nostrand Reinhold.

Phares, V., Compas, B. E., & Howell, D. C. (1989). Perspectives on child behavior problems: Comparisons of children's self-reports with parent and teacher reports. *Psychological Assessment, 1,* 68–71.

Phelps, L., Cox, D., & Bajorek, E. (1992). School phobia and separation anxiety: Diagnostic and treatment comparisons. *Psychology in the Schools, 29,* 384–394.

Piers, E. V. (1984). *The Piers-Harris Children's Self-Concept Scale: Revised manual.* Los Angeles: Western Psychological Services.

Pisterman, S., McGrath, P., Firestone, P., Goodman, J. T., Webster, I., & Mallory, R. (1989). Outcome of parent-mediated treatment of preschoolers with attention deficit disorder with hyperactivity. *Journal of Consulting and Clinical Psychology, 57,* 628–635.

Poland, S., & Pitcher, G. (1990). Best practices in crisis intervention. In A. Thomas & J. Grimes (Eds.), *Best practices in school psychology-II* (pp. 259–274). Washington, DC: National Association of School Psychologists.

Porterfield, J. K., Herbert-Jackson, E., & Risley, T. R. (1976). Contingent observation: An effective and acceptable procedure for reducing disruptive behavior of young children. *Journal of Applied Behavior Analysis, 9,* 55–64.

Premack, D. (1959). Toward empirical behavior laws: I. Positive reinforcement. *Psychological Review, 66,* 219–233.

Proctor, M. A., & Morgan, D. (1991). Effectiveness of a response cost raffle procedure on the disruptive classroom behavior of adolescents with behavior problems. *School Psychology Review, 20,* 97–109.

Prout, H. T. (1984). A comparative review of child behavior therapy books. *School Psychology Review, 13,* 533–534.

Rafferty, Y., & Shinn, M. (1991). The impact of homelessness on children. *American Psychologist, 46,* 1170–1179.

Ramsey, E., Walker, H. M., Shinn, M., O'Neill, R. E., & Stieber, S. (1989). Parent management practices and school adjustment. *School Psychology Review, 18,* 513–525.

Rapport, M. D., Murphy, H. A., & Bailey, J. S. (1982). Ritalin vs. response cost in the control of hyperactive children: A within-subject comparison. *Journal of Applied Behavior Analysis, 15,* 205–216.

Reed, L. J., Carter, B. D., & Miller, L. C. (1992). Fear and anxiety in children. In C. E. Walker & M. C. Roberts (Eds.), *Handbook of clinical child psychology* (2nd ed.) (pp. 237–260). New York: Wiley.

Reschly, D. J. (1990). Best practices in adaptive behavior. In A. Thomas & J. Grimes (Eds.), *Best practices in school psychology—II.* Washington, DC: National Association of School Psychologists.

Reynolds, C. J., Salend, S. J., & Beahan, C. L. (1989). Motivating secondary students: Bringing in the reinforcements. *Academic Therapy, 25,* 81–90.

Reynolds, C. J., Salend, S. J., & Beahan, C. L. (1992). Reinforcer preferences of secondary students with disabilities. *International Journal of Disability, Development and Education, 39,* 77–86.

Reynolds, C. R., & Gutkin, T. B., (Eds.). (1982). *The handbook of school psychology.* New York: Wiley.

Reynolds, C. R., & Kamphaus, R. W. (1992). *Behavior Assessment System for Children (BASC) Manual.* Circle Pines, MN: American Guidance Service.

Reynolds, W. M. (1992) (Ed.). *Internalizing disorders of children and adolescents.* New York: Wiley.

Reynolds, W. M., & Coats, K. I. (1986). A comparison of cognitive-behavioral therapy and relaxation training for the treatment of depression in adolescents. *Journal of Consulting and Clinical Psychology, 54,* 653–660.

Rhode, G., Morgan, D. P., & Young, K. R. (1983). Generalization and maintenance of treatment gains of behaviorally handicapped students from resource rooms to regular classrooms using self-evaluation procedures. *Journal of Applied Behavior Analysis, 16,* 171–188.

Richard, B. A., & Dodge, K. A. (1982). Social maladjustment and problem solving in school-aged children. *Journal of Consulting and Clinical Psychology, 50,* 226–233.

Richter, N. C. (1984). The efficacy of relaxation training with children. *Journal of Abnormal Child Psychology, 12,* 319–344.

Roberts, M. W., & Powers, S. W. (1990). Adjusting chair timeout enforcement procedures for oppositional children. *Behavior Therapy, 21,* 257–271.

Rogers-Wiese, M. R. (1990, August). *The implementation of a suicide prevention team: A case study.* Paper presented at the Ninety-eighth Annual Convention of the American Psychological Association, Boston.

Rooney, K. J., & Hallahan, D. P. (1988). The effects of self-monitoring on adult behavior and student performance. *Learning Disabilities Research, 3,* 88–93.

Rosenberg, M. S. (1986). Maximizing the effectiveness of structured classroom management programs: Implementing rule-review procedures with disruptive and distractible students. *Behavioral Disorders, 11,* 239–248.

Rosenthal, P. A., & Rosenthal, S. (1984). Suicidal behavior by preschool children. *American Journal of Psychiatry, 141,* 520–525.

Ross, A. O. (1981). *Child behavior therapy.* New York: Wiley.

Rubin, K. H., & Mills, R. S. L. (1988). The many faces of social isolation in childhood. *Journal of Consulting and Clinical Psychology, 56,* 916–924.

Rutherford, R. B., Jr., & Nelson, C. M. (1988). Generalization of treatment effects. In J. C. Witt, S. N. Elliott, & F. M. Gresham (Eds.), *Handbook of behavior therapy in education.* New York: Plenum Press.

Ryback, D., & Staats, A. W. (1970). Parents as behavior therapy technicians in treating reading deficits (dyslexia). *Journal of Behavior Therapy Research and Experimental Psychiatry, 1,* 109–119.

Saigh, P. S., & Antoun, F. T. (1984). Endemic images and the desensitization process. *Journal of School Psychology, 22,* 177–183.

Salend, S., & Maragulia, D. (1983). The timeout ribbon: A procedure for the least restrictive environment. *Journal for Special Educators, 20,* 9–115.

Salend, S. J., & Allen, E. M. (1985). Comparative effects of externally managed and self-managed response-cost systems on inappropriate classroom behavior. *Journal of School Psychology, 23,* 59–67.

Salend, S. J., Reynolds, C. J., & Coyle, E. M. (1989). Individualizing the Good Behavior Game across type and frequency of behavior with emotionally disturbed adolescents. *Behavior Modification, 13,* 108–126.

Salzberg, B. H., Wheeler, A. J., Devar, L. T., & Hopkins, B. L. (1971). The effect of intermittent feedback and intermittent contingent access to play on printing of kindergarten children. *Journal of Applied Behavior Analysis, 4,* 163–171.

Sattler, J. M. (1988). *Assessment of children.* San Diego: CA: Author.

Sayger, T. V. (1992). Family psychology and therapy. In C. E. Walker & M. C. Roberts (Eds.), *Handbook of clinical child psychology* (2nd ed.) (pp. 783–807). New York: Wiley.

Schaefer, C. E., & Briesmeister, J. M. (Eds.). (1989). *Handbook of parent training: Parents as co-therapists for children's behavior problems.* New York: Wiley.

Schaefer, C. E., & Millman, H. L. (1981). *How to help children with common problems.* New York: Litton Educational Publishing. (Paperback edition published by Plume Books, New American Library.)

Schumaker, J. B., Hovell, M. F., & Sherman, J. A. (1977). An analysis of daily report cards and parent-managed privileges

in the improvement of adolescents' classroom performance. *Journal of Applied Behavior Analysis, 10,* 449–464.

Schwartz, S., & Johnson, J. H. (1985). *Psychopathology of childhood* (2nd ed.). New York: Pergamon Press.

Seligman, M. E. P., Abramson, L. Y., Semmel, A., & Von Baeyer, C. (1979). Depressive attribution style. *Journal of Abnormal Psychology, 88,* 242–247.

Selinske, J. E., Greer, R. D., & Lodhi, S. (1991). A functional analysis of the comprehensive application of behavior analysis to schooling. *Journal of Applied Behavior Analysis, 24,* 107–117.

Schantl, W. (1991). *A bus behavioral modification plan for grades K–5: A practicum report.* Center for the Advancement of Nova University. (ERIC Document Reproduction Service No. ED 335 787)

Shapiro, E. S. (1987). Academic problems. In M. Hersen & V. S. Van Hasselt (Eds.), *Behavior therapy with children and adolescents: A clinical approach.* New York: Wiley.

Shapiro, E. S., & Goldberg, R. (1986). A comparison of group contingencies for increasing spelling performance among sixth-grade students. *School Psychology Review, 15,* 546–557.

Shapiro, E. S., & Lentz, F. E., Jr. (1985). Assessing academic behavior: A behavioral approach. *School Psychology Review, 14,* 325–338.

Shelton, J. L., & Levy, R. L. (1981). *Behavioral assignments and treatment compliance: A handbook of clinical strategies.* Champaign, IL: Research Press.

Sheras, P. L. (1992). Depression and suicide in adolescence. In C. E. Walker & M. C. Roberts (Eds.), *Handbook of clinical child psychology* (2nd ed.) (pp. 587–606). New York: Wiley.

Sheridan, S. M., Kratochwill, T. R., & Elliott, S. N. (1990). Behavioral consultation with parents and teachers: Delivering treatment for socially withdrawn children at home and school. *School Psychology Review, 19,* 33–52.

Silberman, M. L., & Wheelan, S. A. (1980). *How to discipline without feeling guilty.* Champaign, IL: Research Press.

Simeonsson, R. J., & Rosenthal, S. L. (1992). Developmental models and clinical practice. In C. E. Walker & M. C. Roberts (Eds.), *Handbook of clinical child psychology* (2nd ed.) (pp. 19–31). New York: Wiley.

Skinner, B. F. (1938). *The behavior of organisms: An experimental analysis.* New York: Appleton.

Skinner, B. F. (1953). *Science and human behavior.* New York: Macmillan.

Slater, E. J., & Haber, J. D. (1984). Adolescent adjustment following divorce as a function of family conflict. *Journal of Consulting and Clinical Psychology, 52,* 920–921.

Sloane, H. N. (1979). *The good kid book.* Champaign, IL: Research Press (reprinted in 1988).

Sloane, H. N., Endo, G. T., Hawkes, T. W., & Jenson, W. R. (1991). Improving child compliance through self-instructional materials. *Child and Family Behavior Therapy, 12,* 39–64.

Smith, D. J., Young, R., West, R. P., Morgan, D. P., & Rhode, G. (1983). Reducing the disruptive behavior of junior high school students: A classroom self-management procedure. *Behavioral Disorders, 13,* 231–239.

Solnick, J. V., Rincover, A., & Peterson, C. R. (1977). Some determinants of the reinforcing and punishing effects of timeout. *Journal of Applied Behavior Analysis, 10,* 415–424.

Sparrow, S. S., Balla, D. A., & Cicchetti, D. V. (1984). *Vineland Adaptive Behavior Scales, interview edition, survey form manual.* Circle Pines, MN: American Guidance Service.

Staats, A. W. (1963). *Complex human behavior.* New York: Holt, Rinehart and Winston.

Staats, A. W. (1971). *Child learning, intelligence, and personality.* New York: Harper & Row.

Staats, A. W. (1975). *Social behaviorism.* Homewood, IL: Dorsey Press.

Stark, K. D., Brookman, C. S., & Frazier, R. (1990). A comprehensive school-based treatment program for depressed children. *School Psychology Quarterly, 5,* 111–140.

Stark, K. D., Rouse, L. W., & Livingston, R. (1991). Treatment of depression during childhood and adolescence: Cognitive-behavioral procedures for the individual and family. In P. C. Kendall (Ed.), *Child and adolescent therapy: Cognitive-behavioral procedures* (pp. 165–206). New York: Guilford Press.

Stokes, T. F., & Baer, D. M. (1977). An implicit technology of generalization. *Journal of Applied Behavior Analysis, 10,* 349–368.

Stokes, T. F., & Osnes, P. G. (1990). Honesty, lying, and cheating: Their elaboration and management. In G. Stoner, M. R. Shinn, & H. M. Walker (Eds.), *Interventions for achievement and behavior problems* (pp. 617–631). Silver Spring, MD: National Association of School Psychologists.

Stoner, G., Shinn, M. R., & Walker, H. M. (Eds.). (1991). *Interventions for achievement and behavior problems.* Silver Spring, MD: National Association of School Psychologists.

Strauss, M. A. (1991). Discipline and deviance: Physical punishment of children and violence and other crime in adulthood. *Social Problems, 38,* 133–156.

Sue, D. W., & Sue, D. (1990). *Counseling the culturally different* (2nd ed.). New York: Wiley-Interscience.

Sullivan, J. S. (1989, April). Elements of a successful inschool suspension program. *NASSP Bulletin, 73*(516), 32–38.

Sullivan, M. A., & O'Leary, S. G. (1990). Maintenance following reward and cost token programs. *Behavior Therapy, 21,* 139–149.

Sulzbacher, S. I., & Houser, J. E. (1968). A tactic to eliminate disruptive behaviors in the classroom: Group contingent consequences. *American Journal of Mental Deficiency, 73,* 88–90.

Sulzer-Azaroff, B., & Mayer, C. R. (1991). *Behavior analysis for lasting change.* Fort Worth, TX: Holt, Rinehart and Winston.

Swanson, H. L. (1985). Effects of cognitive-behavior training on emotionally disturbed children's academic performance. *Cognitive Therapy and Research, 9,* 201–216.

Swap, S. M. (1992). Parent involvement and success for all children: What we know now. In S. L. Christenson & J. C. Conoley (Eds.), *Home-school collaboration: Enhancing children's academic and social competence.* Silver Spring, MD: National Association of School Psychologists.

Swift, M. S., & Spivack, G. (1975). *Alternative teaching strategies.* Champaign, IL: Research Press.

Thackwray, D., Meyers, A., Schleser, R., Cohen, R. (1985). Achieving generalization with general versus specific instructions: Effects on academically deficient children. *Cognitive Therapy and Research, 9,* 297–308.

Tharinger, D. J., & Koranek, M. E. (1988). Children of alcoholics—at risk and unserved: A review of research and service roles for school psychologists. *School Psychology Review, 17,* 166–191.

The most innocent victims. (1990, August 13). *Newsweek.* p. 39.

Thomas, A., & Grimes, J. (Eds.). (1990). *Best practices in school psychology—II.* Washington, DC: National Association of School Psychologists.

Thomas, J. (1991, September). "You're the greatest." *Principal, 71,* 32–33.

Thomas, R. M. (1979). *Comparing theories of child development.* Belmont, CA: Wadsworth.

Thorndike, E. L. (1898). Animal intelligence: An experimental study of the associative processes in animals. *Psychological Review Monograph Supplement, 2*(Whole No. 8).

Townsend, R. B. (1984). *School corporal punishment, home discipline, and violence: Some unhealthy relationships.* Paper presented at the Annual Convention of the National Association of School Psychologists, Philadelphia.

Turecki, S., & Tonner, L. (1985). *The difficult child.* New York: Bantam Books.

Turkington, C. (1993, January). New definition of retardation includes the need for support. *APA Monitor.* p. 26.

Turner, J. S., & Helms, D. B. (1990). *Lifespan development* (4th ed.). New York: Holt, Rinehart and Winston.

Turner, S. M., Calhoun, K. S., & Adams, H. E. (1981). *Handbook of clinical behavior therapy.* New York: Wiley.

Ullman, L. P., & Krasner, L. (1975). *A psychological approach to abnormal behavior* (2nd ed.). Englewood Cliffs, NJ: Prentice-Hall.

U.N. Convention on the rights of the child: Unofficial summary of articles. (1991) *School Psychology Review, 20,* 339–343.

U.S. Department of Education (1987). *What works.* Washington, DC: Author.

Van Londen, A., Van Londen-Barentsen, M. W. M., Van Son, M. J. M., Mulder, G. A. L. A. (1993). Arousal training for children suffering from nocturnal enuresis: A two-and-a-half-year follow-up. *Behaviour Research and Therapy, 31,* 613–615.

Vernon, A. (1989). *Thinking, feeling, behavior: An emotional education curriculum for children.* Champaign, IL: Research Press.

Vogrin, D., & Kassinove, H. (1979). Effects of behavior rehearsal, audiotaped observation, and intelligence on assertiveness and adjustment in third-grade children. *Psychology in the Schools, 16,* 422–429.

Wahler, R. G. (1980). The insular mother: Her problem in parent–child treatment. *Journal of Applied Behavior Analysis, 13,* 207–219.

Wanlass, R. L., & Prinz, R. J. (1982). Methodological issues in conceptualizing and treating childhood social isolation. *Psychological Bulletin, 92,* 39–55.

Walker, C. E., & Roberts, M. C. (Eds.). (1983). *Handbook of clinical child psychology.* New York: Wiley.

Walker, C. E., & Roberts, M. C. (Eds.). (1992). *Handbook of clinical child psychology* (2nd ed.). New York: Wiley.

Waterman, J. (1982). Assessment of the family system. In G. Ulrey & S. J. Rogers (Eds.), *Psychological assessment of handicapped infants and young children.* New York: Thiene-Stratton.

Webber, J., Scheuermann, B., McCall, C., & Coleman, M. (1993). Research on self-monitoring as a behavior management technique in special education classrooms: A descriptive review. *Remedial and Special Education, 14,* 38–56.

Webster-Stratton, C., Hollinsworth, T., & Kolpacoff, M. (1989). The long-term effectiveness and clinical significance of three cost-effective training programs for families with conduct-problem children. *Journal of Consulting and Clinical Psychology, 57,* 550–553.

Webster-Stratton, C., Kolpacoff, M., & Hollinsworth, T. (1988). Self-administered videotape therapy for families with conduct-problem children: Comparison with two cost-effective treatments and a control group. *Journal of Consulting and Clinical Psychology, 56,* 558–566.

Weiss, G., & Hechtman, L. T. (1993). *Hyperactive children grown up* (2nd ed.). New York: Guilford Press.

Weist, M. D., Ollendick, T. H., & Finney, J. W. (1991). Toward the empirical validation of treatment targets in children. *Clinical Psychology Review, 11,* 515–538.

Weiten, W. (1992). *Psychology: Themes and variations.* Pacific Grove, CA: Brooks/Cole.

Weiten, W. (1994). *Psychology: Themes and variations, briefer edition* (2nd ed.). Pacific Grove, CA: Brooks/Cole.

Wells, K. C., & Forehand, R. (1981). Child behavior problems in the home. In S. M. Turner, K. S. Calhoun, & H. E. Adams (Eds.), *Handbook of clinical behavior therapy* (pp. 527–567). New York: Wiley.

Wells, A. S. (1991, February 6). School bus offers a bonus with the ride: Videos. *New York Times,* p. B5.

Welsh, R. S. (1976). Severe parental punishment and delinquency: A developmental theory. *Journal of Clinical Child Psychology, 5,* 17–23.

Wherry, J. N. (1983). Some legal considerations and implications for the use of behavior modification in the schools. *Psychology in the Schools, 20,* 46–51.

Whitaker, L. C., & Slimak, R. E. (Eds.). (1990). *College student suicide.* New York: Haworth Press.

White, A. G., & Bailey, J. S. (1990). Reducing disruptive behaviors of elementary physical education students with sit and watch. *Journal of Applied Behavior Analysis, 23,* 353–359.

Whitmore, J. R. (1980). *Giftedness, conflict, and underachievement.* Boston, MA: Allyn and Bacon.

Wielkiewicz, R. M. (1986). *Behavior management in the school: Principles and procedures.* New York: Pergamon Press.

Wielkiewicz, R. M. (1992). Behavioral intervention: A home and school approach. In S. L. Christenson & J. C. Conoley (Eds.), *Home–school collaboration: Enhancing children's academic and social competence* (pp. 333–356). Silver Spring, MD: National Association of School Psychologists.

Wielkiewicz, R. M. (1993, Fall). Pay attention *Saint Benedict's Today,* pp. 14–17, 30.

Wielkiewicz, R. M., & Calvert, C. R. X. (1989). *Training and habilitating developmentally disabled people: An introduction.* New York: Sage Publications.

Williams, B. F., Williams, R. L., & McLaughlin, T. F. (1991a). Classroom procedures for remediating behavior disorders. *Journal of Developmental and Physical Disabilities, 3,* 349–384.

Williams, B. F., Williams, R. L., & McLaughlin, T. F. (1991b). Treatment of behavior disorders by parents in the home. *Journal of Developmental and Physical Disabilities, 3,* 385–407.

Williams, G. J. R. (1983). Child abuse. In C. E. Walker & M. C. Roberts (Eds.), *Handbook of clinical child psychology* (pp. 1219–1248). New York: Wiley.

Williams, J. (1989, Winter). Reducing the disproportionately high frequency of disciplinary actions against minority students. *Equity & Excellence, 24*(2), 31–37.

Wimbarti, S., & Self, P. A. (1992). Developmental psychology for the clinical child psychologist. In C. E. Walker & M. C. Roberts (Eds.), *Handbook of clinical child psychology* (2nd ed.) (pp. 33–45). New York: Wiley.

Witt, J. C., & Elliott, S. N. (1982). The response cost lottery: A time efficient and effective classroom intervention. *Journal of School Psychology, 20,* 155–161.

Witt, J. C., & Martens, B. K. (1984). Adaptive behavior: Tests and assessment issues. *School Psychology Review, 13,* 478–484.

Wolfe, D. A. (1985). Child-abusive parents: An empirical review and analysis. *Psychological Bulletin, 97,* 462–482.

Woltersdorf, M. A. (1992). Videotape self-modeling in the treatment of Attention-deficit Hyperactivity Disorder. *Child & Family Behavior Therapy, 14,* 53–73.

Workman, E. A. (1982). *Teaching behavioral self-control to students.* Austin, TX: Pro-Ed.

Yoshikawa, H. (1994). Prevention as cumulative protection: Effects of early family support and education on chronic delinquency and its risks. *Psychological Bulletin, 115,* 28–54.

Youngstrom, N. (1992, January). Inner-city youth tell of life in "a war zone." *APA Monitor,* p. 36.

Zarb, J. M. (1992). *Cognitive-behavioral assessment and therapy with adolescents.* New York: Brunner/Mazel.

Zimmerman, E. H., & Zimmerman, J. (1962). The alteration of behavior in a special classroom situation. *Journal of the Experimental Analysis of Behavior, 5,* 59–60.

Zimmerman, J., & Sims, D. (1983). Family therapy. In C. E. Walker & M. C. Roberts (Eds.), *Handbook of clinical child psychology* (pp. 995–1025). New York: Wiley.

Index

Abuse, child, 67–69, 78, 98
  prevention, 77–78
Academic behavior
  assessment, 32
  remediation by parents, 215–216
Academic performance
  and behavior problems, 32
  and expected level of achievement, 32–33
  and homework, 215
  improvement of, 134, 156–185, 188–203, 215–216
  and sensory capacity, 35–36
Adaptive behavior, 63, 232
ADD Hyperactivity Workbook, 140
ADHD, 8, 11, 57–58, 59, 78, 139, 190, 232
  behavior management for, 58
  and training parents, 140
Adolescence, 232
Aggression, 3, 232
  and behavior management, 6
  management of, 113–115, 126–133, 134, 213 (table)
  among siblings, 214
Alcohol
  abuse, 57
Alcoholism, 232
  parental, 67, 78
  teenage and preteenage, 65, 78, 89
Alphabet, teaching the, 188–193
American Association on Mental Deficiency, 63
Adaptive Behavior Scale, School Edition, 63
Analysis of self-control, 34–35
Analysis of social relationships, 35
Analysis of sensory capacity, 35–36
Analysis of home environment, 36–38
Analysis of interpersonal relationships, 38
Anger, management of, 134

Anxiety, 60, 134
  remediation of, 168–169
Appetitive stimulus, defined, 17, 232
Assertive, defined, 232
Assertive behavior, 5–7
  and behavior management, 6, 84
  definition, 6
Assertive, Nonassertive, and Aggressive Characteristics (Table), 7
Assessment,
  appropriate level of, 98
  defined, 30, 232
  of family systems, 36–38, 55–56
  informal vs. formal, 31
  need for flexibility in, 38
  steps in, 31–39
  summary of steps (table), 40–41
Attention-Deficit/Hyperactivity Disorder, 232 (see also ADHD, Hyperactivity)
Attributions, parent, 142
Autism, defined, 232
Aversive stimulus, defined, 17, 232
Avoidance, 19, 165, 167, 215, 232

Baseline data, 232–233
Baseline observations
  definition, 43
  forms for, 79, 105, 122, 128, 149, 150, 158, 170, 171, 173, 176, 198, 224–226
  methods of collecting, 43–45
Basic behavioral repertoires, 189, 233
Basic facts, 189
Basic regular classroom behavior management program, 156–160

Basketball, in a behavior management program, 135–137
Begin the program, 48
Behavior
    deficit, 53, 98–99
    defined, 233
    excess, 32, 53, 98–99
    at home, 36
Behavior chain, 233
Behavioral Indicators of Hearing Difficulty (table), 36
Behavioral Indicators of Visual Difficulty (table), 36
Behavior Assessment System for Children (BASC), 205
Behavior chains, 22, 23–24, 233
Behavior contract, 48, 54–55, 89, 178–185, 233
    applications, 178–179
    for getting ready on time, 217–220
    guidelines for writing, 179
    parent handout for developing, 216–220
    for responsible driving, 217–220
    sample, 180, 181, 182
Behavior deficit, 98–99, 233
Behavior excess, 98–99, 233
Behaviorism, 2
Behavior management, 2, 3, 53
    additional information about, 70
    in adolescents, 54
    of basic skills, 188–193
    books, for parents, 93, 141, 212–213
    and child development, 54–55
    and children of divorce, 66–67
    and child's culture, 56–57
    of chronic discipline problems, 78
    as continuous process, 41, 51
    of daily school behavior, 174–178
    diagnostic issues in, 57
    in early childhood, 54
    empirical nature, 16, 31
    and the family system, 55–56
    as feedback process, 39
    goals of, 53
    of homework completion, 181–185
    journals
        with behavior contracts, 178–185
        via extinction, 103–107
        scientific basis, 16
    and least restrictive environment, 12
    in middle childhood, 54
    need for flexibility in, 31, 97, 99, 100, 178, 230

    of observational learning, 25
    of on-task behavior, 195–203
    and parent training, 139
    program
        components of, 45
        defined, 45
    and parental alcoholism, 67
    and reading skill, 25
    of school bus behavior, 80–81
    and school climate, 72, 73
    of school phobia, 160–168
    schoolwide policies for, 73–77
    and selecting programs, 97–100
    of social skills, 203–211
    systematic approach, 1–2, 30
    and token rewards, 25–26
    as team effort, 52
Behavior modification, 2
Behavior shaping (see Shaping)
"Belt theory" of delinquency, 68, 76
Best interests, child's, 8
Biofeedback, 233
Bipolar disorder, 60
Books for Parents (table), 141
Building a behavior management library, 70
Buses, school, 80–81

CABAS, 233
Case study: Jack, 185–186
Chair timeout, 114
Characteristics of Hyperactive Children (table), 59
Child abuse, 2, 67–69
    and attributional style, 69
    defined, 233
Childhood depression, 233
Child rights (see Rights)
Child's best interests, 8
Child's strengths, 34, 89
Chronic discipline problems, 78–80
Clarifying problem behavior, 33
Classical conditioning, 24, 233
Classroom organization essay, 94
Classroom rules, 82–83
    and coupon program, 107
    and Good Behavior Game, 116
    and response cost lottery, 121
Coaching, defined, 233
Cognitive-behavioral techniques, 133–137
Cognitive-behavioral therapy, 233

Common Childhood Behavior Problems (table), 213
Competence, of treatment, 8
Comprehensive Application of Behavior Analysis to
        Schooling, 90, 233
Conduct disorder, 60, 233
Consequences, hazardous, 24
Constitutional principles and child rights, 6–7
Contingencies for Changing Behavior (Table), 17
Contingency
    defined, 17, 233
    natural, 49
    negative, 17
    positive, 17
    stating the, 47
Contingent observation, 112–115, 233
Continuous reinforcement, 22, 49, 103, 233
Corporal punishment, 76, 234
Correspondence training, 215, 234
Counting behavior, as baseline observation, 43
Coupon program, 53, 54, 107–111, 234
    at home, 145–153
    parent handout, 152–153 (table)
Cultural issues in behavior management, 56–57

Daily/Weekly Report Card (figures)
    long form, 171
    short form, 170
Daily Performance Record, 175 (figure), 176
Data Chart, Sample (figure), 105
    explanation, 104
Data collection forms, 79, 105, 122, 128, 149, 150,
        158, 170, 171, 173, 176, 198, 224–226
Depression, 58–60, 78, 134, 185–186
    and attributions, 142
    and behavior in school, 60
    defined, 233
    and environmental events, 60
    measures of, 60
Designing behavioral contingencies, 45
Developmental analysis, 34, 54
Developmental disabilities, 63–64
Developmentally appropriate, 234
Developmentally disabled, 234
Diagnostic issues, 57–69
Discipline, classroom, 81–89
Discipline techniques, handout for parents, 146–148
Difficult children, 156–157
Diffusion parent, 4

Disability,
    defined, 9
Disabled, 234
Discipline
    file, 78
    policy, 73
    regular classroom, 82
    slip, 75, 234
Discrimination, stimulus 21–22, 28, 234
Discriminative stimulus, 21
Divorce, parental, 65–66, 78
DSM-IV, 58, 234
Dysthymia, 60

Early childhood, 54, 234
Effectiveness,
    of learning environments, 73
    of treatment, 8
Emotional abuse, 69
Emotional neglect, 69
Empirical approach to selecting target behaviors,
        42–43
Empowering parents, 38
Environment, as context for behavior, 2, 53
Equal protection, right to, 6–7
Escape, 19, 167, 215, 234
Ethical issues, 6–14
Examples of Assertive, Nonassertive . . . (table), 20
Examples of Four Basic Techniques (table), 20
Examples of Positive Feedback and Approval
        (table), 84
Exclusion timeout, 125, 234
Expulsion, 80
Externalizing problem, 53, 234
Extinction, 26
    defined, 5, 22, 234
    programs, as behavior management tool, 103–107,
        140, 142–146
    resistance to, 22
    sample program, 104–106

Fading, 234
    a behavior management program, 50
Fading, stimulus, 167
Family system
    assessment, 37, 55–56
    disturbances, 65–69
    impact on child, 55–56
Family therapy, 234

Fighting among siblings, 214
Fines for misbehavior, 198–199
Flexibility, 234
    in behavior assessment, 38
    in behavior management, 31, 39, 51, 57, 97, 99,
        100, 160, 203
    in designing parent training programs, 139
    in reinforcer selection, 33, 46–47, 177, 194
Formal assessment, 31
Formal behavior management program, 31, 41
Free and appropriate public education, 9, 11, 12

Generalization, 48
    definition, 48, 234
General impact level of an intervention, 204
Giftedness, 64, 234
GOALS (see also Group-Oriented Adapted Levels
        System), 235
Golden Rule of Behavior Management, 5, 22, 53, 81,
        85, 103, 106, 140, 152 (table), 160, 235
    parent version, 140–142
Good Behavior Game plus Merit, 115–118
Group contingencies, 116, 235
Group-Oriented Adapted Levels System (GOALS), 90
Guidelines for Classroom Management (Table), 86–87

Handicapped (see also Disability), 11, 235
Hearing, 35
    signs of problems in, 36
Helplessness, in parents, 142, 143
Home environment, 2
    assessment of, 36–38
    behavior management in, 54
Home note programs, 54, 88, 93, 169–174
    forms for, 170, 171, 173
Home Situations Questionnaire, 143, 147
Homework, 88
    behavior management of, 181–185
Hyperactive children, characteristics of (table), 59
Hyperactivity (see also ADHD), 110, 134, 235

IDEA, 10, 11, 195, 235
Identify the problem, 41, 98
IEP (see Individualized Education Program)
Ignoring behavior, 26, 102, 235
    at home, 140–146
Impulsive behavior, 133, 204
    remediation of, 135–137
Inattention, 133

Incompatible response, 235
Independent group contingency, 157
Indiscriminable contingencies, 49, 235
Individualized Education Program (IEP), 11, 12, 47,
        90, 195, 235
Individuals with Disabilities Education Act, 10
Informal assessment, 31
Informed consent for evaluation, 13
Initial identification of the problem behavior, 38
In-school suspension, 75–76, 235
Integrating assessment information, 38–39
Intermittent reinforcement, 22, 49, 103, 235
Internal and stable attributions, 142
Internalizing problem, 53, 235
Interview
    forms, 37
    questions, 37
IQ score, 63

Key Issues in Planning a Behavior Management Pro-
        gram (table), 97

Law of Effect, 3, 235
Learning disabilities, 64, 139, 235
Learning problems
    and behavior management, 32–33
Least restrictive
    alternative, 100, 235
    behavior management program, 55, 100
    environment, 11, 12, 235
Levels systems, 90–92, 235
    example, 91–92
Logical consequences, 28, 74, 103, 218, 235–236
Lying, 215

Mandatory reporting, 77–78, 236
Major depression, 59
Marital relationship, 37
Mental retardation, 63
Middle childhood, 54, 236
Minority cultures, 56–57
Modeling (see Observational learning)
Modifying a behavior management program, 49–50
Monitoring a program's effectiveness, importance
        of, 9
Monitoring daily school performance, 174–178
Motivational analysis, 33–34
Multiple baseline, 206, 236

Natural contingency, 48, 236
Negative attention, 3, 4, 103, 236
Negative contingency, 17, 236
Negative punishment, 16, 17, 18, 19, 28, 102, 120
  examples of, 20, 28
  at home, 145–153, 236
Negative reinforcement, 16, 17, 19, 156, 188, 236
  examples of, 20, 62, 75, 80, 165
Nonassertion, 5, 6, 236

Obedience, of parent commands, 213–214
Observational learning, 24–25
  and attention, 24
Observation methods, 43–45
Observe the effects of the program, 48
Office referrals, 74–75
  and consequences, 75
Operant conditioning, 24, 236
Operational definition, 41–42
Organizational skills, improving, 174–178
Organizing a special classroom, 89–92

Parental alcoholism, 67
Parental conflict, 66
Parental divorce, 65–67
Parent Handout for an Extinction/Ignoring Program
  (table), 144
Parent Handout for Timeout and Other Discipline
  Techniques (table), 146–148
Parenting skills, 36
Parent rights, 6, 11–13
Parent training programs, 139–153
Partial reinforcement (see also Intermittent reinforce-
  ment), 22
Participation in behavior management programs,
  child, 9
Pavlov, I. P., 16
Percentages, as baseline observations, 43
Phobia, school, 62
Physical abuse, 236
Physical aggression, and timeout, 126
Physical neglect, 69
Positive contingency, 17, 236
Positive punishment (see also Punishment), 16, 17,
  18, 19, 120, 236
  examples of, 20
Positive reinforcement (see also Reinforcement), 16,
  17, 18, 19, 156, 188, 236
  examples of, 20

Premack principle, 26, 47, 194, 236
Prevention of behavior problems, 72–93
  in elementary classes, 87
  in high school, 89
  and home-school relationships, 92–93
  in middle school classes, 88–89
  in regular classrooms, 81–87
    guidelines for, 82–87
  on school buses, 80–81
  and school rules, 73–74
  schoolwide, 73–80
  in special classes, 89–92
Primary issues
  defined, 52, 236
  list of, 52–53
Primary reinforcer, 25
Programming common stimuli, 49, 236
Prompting, 202, 237
Public Law 94-142, 10, 11, 12, 13, 64, 65, 237
Public Law 99-457, 10
Public Law 101-476, 10
Public Law 923-112, 10
Punishment
  corporal, 76
  definition, 4, 237
  explanation of, 18
  problems associated with, 5, 76
Pupil support assistant, 237

Reading readiness skills, 189–190
Record of Timeouts (figure), 149, 150
Refining the definition of the problem, 41
Reframing, 37–38, 166
Regular classrooms, 53
Regular education, 237
Rehabilitation Act of 1973, 10, 11
Reinforcement, 5
  analysis, 33
  continuous, 22
  definition, 4, 237
  intermittent, 22
  of other behavior, 103
  primary, 25
  secondary, 25
  survey, 34
Reinforcers
  identifying, 34
  menu, example, 108
  selecting, 46, 50

Relaxation training, 168, 237
Reliability of observations, 42
Remediation Plan for School Phobia, 161–168
Removing privileges, 28, 102
Resistance to extinction, 22, 103, 237
Response cost contingency, 107, 237
    at home, 146–150
Response cost lottery, 120–124, 237
Restitution, 43
Reward (see also Reinforcement), 3
    of successive approximations, 23
    token, 25–26
Rights,
    child, 6–11
    to free and appropriate public education, 12
    guidelines for upholding, 13
    parent, 6,
    teacher, 6, 13–14
Restitution, 237
Reward, 237
Ritalin, 237
Rules (see also Classroom rules), 73–74, 82
    violations, 107
Running log or behavior record, 33, 206

Sample Behavior Change Contract (tables), 180, 181,
    182
Sample Data Chart (figure), 105, 122
Sample Data Collection Form (figure), 158
Sample Parent Handout for an Extinction/Ignoring
    Program, 144
Sample Parent Handout for Timeout and Other Disci-
    pline Techniques (table), 146–148
Sample Written Program Description for a School–
    Home Note Program (table), 173
Satiation, 237
Saying no, 28
Schedule of reinforcement, 22
    definition, 237
    fixed interval, 22
    fixed ratio, 22
    variable interval, 22
    variable ratio, 22
School bus behavior, 80–81
School climate, 72, 73, 237
School discipline policy, 73
School environment, 2
School-home notes, 88, 93, 169–174, 237

School phobia, 62, 160–161, 237
    remediation plan for, 161–168
School readiness, 189
School rules and policies, 73–74, 139
School Social Behavior Scales, 205
School Social Skills Rating Scale, 205, 206
Seclusion timeout, 100, 129, 237
Secondary issues, 55–69, 237–238
    defined, 52
Secondary reinforcement, 25–26
Secondary reinforcer, 238
Section 504, 10, 11
Selecting behavior management programs, 97
Selecting reinforcers, 46
Self-control 34–35
    characteristics of, 35
    deficit in, 34–35
    defined, 34
    excessive, 35
Self-graphing, 238
Self-modeling, 203
Self-monitoring, 49, 109–110, 200–202, 238
Self-observation, 203
Self-stimulating behavior, 238
Sensory capacity, 35–36
Separation anxiety, 238
Sequential modification, 49
Serious emotional/behavioral disturbance, 64–65
Seriously emotionally disturbed, 12, 238
Sexual abuse, 69, 238
Shaping, behavior, 22–24, 202, 238
Sit and Watch, 114, 238
Skill deficit
    defined, 32
Skinner, B. F., 3, 16
Social attention, 3
Social isolation, remediating, 205–209
Social learning theory, 2
Social relationships, assessment of, 35
Social skills, 203–205, 238
    behavioral component, 203
    cognitive component, 204
    and problem solving, 204
SOS! Help for Parents (book) 140
Special classrooms, 53–54
Special education, 9, 10, 238
Specific learning disabilities, 64
Stating the contingency, 47
Steps in behavioral assessment, 31–39

summary table, 40–41
Steps in a behavior management program, 1, 39–50
Stimulus, 24
    defined, 17, 238
    hierarchy, and school phobia 164, 165
Strengthening generalization, 48
Student Handout for a Classroom Token System
        (table), 196
Student Performance Checklist, 79
Student Record Form (figure), 198
Study skills training, 168
Successful schools, five traits of, 73
Suicidal behavior, 60–62, 98
    signs of, 61
    policy, 77, 238
    prevention, 77
Summary of General Assessment Procedure (table),
        40–41
Suspension, 75, 80, 238
Systematic approach
    and behavior management, 1–2, 30, 36, 57, 155
    defined, 1
Systematic desensitization, 168

Target behavior
    defined, 238
    identifying, 38, 41–43, 98–99, 143
Teacher rights, 6, 13–14
Template matching, 43
Test anxiety, 62–63, 238
"Thinking chair," 87
Thorndike, E. L., 3, 4, 16
Three-chance plan, 83, 238
Timeout, 26–28, 47, 50, 53, 54, 55, 100
    and child rights, 27, 112, 125–126
    chair, 114
    considered as punishment, 111
    definition, 238
    exclusion, 125, 234

and physical aggression, 126
    in regular classrooms, 111–115
    regulation, 7, 55
    in special classrooms, 124–133
Timeout Record (figure), 128
Timeout Record, home (figure), 154
Timeout ribbon, 27–28, 132
Time-sampling, 44, 206–207
Token, definition, 238
Token economy
    definition, 238
    description of, 90–91, 193–203
Token Programs at Home (parent handout), 220–230
Token reinforcement, 25–26, 54, 159, 165
Token reward, 25–26, 107, 175–178
    advantages, 26
    in behavior management programs, 25–26
    in elementary classes, 87
    in junior and senior high school, 174–178
    in middle school classes, 88
    in special classes, 188–203
"Train and hope," 48, 238–239
Train loosely, 49, 239
Train sufficient examples, 49, 239

Undesirable behavior, decreasing, 102–103
United Nations Convention on the Rights of the
        Child, 7
U.S. Constitution and behavior management, 6–7

Verbal praise, 84, 87
Verbal reprimands, 26, 83, 84
Verbal threats, from pupil, 127
Vineland Adaptive Behavior Scales, 63, 204
Vision, signs of problems with, 36
Vocational goals, 89

Writing the program description, 47–48